Nāgārjuna
on
Mindfulness of the Buddha

To refrain from doing any manner of evil,
to respectfully perform all varieties of good,
and to purify one's own mind—
This is the teaching of all buddhas.

The Ekottara Āgama Sūtra
(T02 n.125 p.551a 13–14)

A Note on the Proper Care of Dharma Materials

Traditional Buddhist cultures treat books on Dharma as sacred. Hence it is considered disrespectful to place them in a low position, to read them when lying down, or to place them where they might be damaged by food or drink.

Kalavinka Press books are printed on acid-free paper.
Cover and interior designed by Bhikshu Dharmamitra.
Printed in the United States of America

NĀGĀRJUNA
ON
MINDFULNESS OF THE BUDDHA

The Easy Practice
Nāgārjuna's *Treatise on the Ten Grounds,* Chapter 9

The Pratuyutpanna Samādhi
Nāgārjuna's *Treatise on the Ten Grounds,* Chapters 20–25

Recollection of the Buddha
Nāgārjuna's *Exegesis on the Mahāprajnāpāramitā Sūtra*
Chapter 1, Part 36-1

As Translated into Chinese by Tripiṭaka Master Kumārajīva
Annotated English Translation by Bhikshu Dharmamitra

KALAVINKA PRESS
SEATTLE, WASHINGTON
WWW.KALAVINKAPRESS.ORG

Kalavinka Press
8603 39th Ave SW / Seattle, WA 98136 USA
(www.kalavinkapress.org)

Kalavinka Press is associated with the Kalavinka Dharma Association, a non-profit organized exclusively for religious educational purposes as allowed within the meaning of section 501(c)3 of the Internal RevenueCode. Kalavinka Dharma Association was founded in 1990 and gained formal approval in 2004 by the United States Internal Revenue Service as a 501(c)3 non-profit organization to which all donations are tax deductible.

Edition: NMOB-SA-1019-1.0 / Kalavinka Buddhist Classics Book 14a

ISBN: 978-1-935413-15-8 / Library of Congress Control #: 2019032382

Library of Congress Cataloging-in-Publication Data

Names: Nāgārjuna, active 2nd century, author. | Dharmamitra, Bhikshu, translator. | Kumārajīva, -412? translator. | Nāgārjuna, active 2nd century. Daśabhūmivibhāṣāśāstra. Selections. Chinese. | Nāgārjuna, active 2nd century. Daśabhūmivibhāṣāśāstra. Selections. English.

Title: Nāgārjuna on mindfulness of the Buddha / as translated into Chinese by Tripiṭaka Master Kumārajīva ; annotated English translation by Bhikshu Dharmamitra.

Other titles: Shi zhu pi po sha lun.

Description: Nmob-sa-1019-1.0-chinese/english. | Seattle, Washington : Kalavinka Press, 2019. | Series: Kalavinka Buddhist classics ; book 14a | Includes bibliographical references. | English and Chinese. | Summary: ""Nāgārjuna on Mindfulness of the Buddha" consists of three extended passages from Bhikshu Dharmamitra's original annotated translations from Sino-Buddhist Classical Chinese of works written by Ārya Nāgārjuna (circa 150 ce). All three of these passages have been selected from Tripitaka Master Kumārajīva's early Fifth Century Sanskrit-to-Chinese translations of works by Nāgārjuna, as follows: 1) "The Easy Practice" -- Nāgārjuna's Treatise on the Ten Grounds, Chapter 9; 2) "The Pratuyutpanna Samādhi" -- Nāgārjuna's Treatise on the Ten Grounds, Chapters 20-25; and 3) "Recollection of the Buddha" -- Nāgārjuna's Exegesis on the Mahāprajnāpāramitā Sūtra, Chapter 1, Part 36-1 This special bilingual edition (English / Chinese) includes the facing-page simplified and traditional Chinese scripts to facilitate close study by academic buddhologists, students in Buddhist universities, and Buddhists in Taiwan, Hong Kong, Mainland China, and the West.""-- Provided by publisher.

Identifiers: LCCN 2019032382 | ISBN 9781935413158 (paperback)

Subjects: LCSH: Nāgārjuna, active 2nd century. Daśabhūmivibhāṣāśāstra--Criticism, interpretation, etc. | Tripiṭaka. Sūtrapiṭaka. Daśabhūmīśvara--Commentaries--Early works to 1800. | Bodhisattva stages (Mahayana Buddhism)--Early works to 1800. | Pure Land Buddhism--Doctrines--Early works to 1800.

Classification: LCC BQ1632.A1 D425 2019b | DDC 294.3/85--dc23

LC record available at https://lccn.loc.gov/2019032382

Dedication

Dedicated to the memory of the selfless and marvelous life of the Venerable Dhyāna Master Hsuan Hua, the Guiyang Ch'an Patriarch and the very personification of the bodhisattva's six perfections.

Dhyāna Master Hsuan Hua

宣化禪師

1918–1995

About the Chinese Text

This translation is supplemented by inclusion of Chinese source text on verso pages in both traditional (above) and simplified (below) scripts. For the traditional character version variant readings from other canonical editions are found as an appendix in the back of the book and, where I have incorporated those variants into the translation, they are usually signaled with an endnote along with my rationale for making the emendation. The traditional-character Chinese text and its variant readings are from the April, 2004 version of the Chinese Buddhist Electronic Text Association's digital edition of the Taisho Buddhist canon. The simplified-character Chinese text is as downloaded from the online Qianlong Chinese Buddhist Canon on July 23, 2018 (http://www.qldzj.com/).

Those following the translation in the traditional Chinese version should be aware that the original Taisho scripture punctuation contained in this 2004 edition is not traceable to original editions, is not reliable, and is probably best ignored altogether. (In any case, accurate reading of Classical Chinese should never depend on a previous editor's punctuation.)

Outlining in This Work

The chapter titles in this work are from the Taisho Chinese text. All other outline headings originate with the translator. Buddhist canonical texts are often so structurally dense that they are best navigated with the aid of at least a simple outline structure such as I have supplied here.

Acknowledgments

The accuracy and readability of this translation have been greatly improved by many corrections, preview comments, and editorial suggestions generously contributed by Bhikkhu Bodhi (Parts 1 and 2), Feng Ling, and Nicholas Weeks.

Expenses incurred in bringing forth this publication were underwritten by generous donations from Craig and Karen Neyman, Madalena Lew, Shuyu Yang, Jiajing Li, Kam Chung Wong, Loritta Chan, David Fox, Nicholas Weeks, Yuen-Lin Tan, and the BDK English Tripiṭaka Project. Assistance with aspects of Adobe Indesign book layout was provided by Anagarika Mahendra.

Were it not for the ongoing material support provided by my late guru's Dharma Realm Buddhist Association and the serene translation studio provided by Seattle's Bodhi Dhamma Center, creation of this translation would have been much more difficult.

Additionally, it would have been impossible for me to produce this translation without the Dharma teachings and personal inspiration provided to me by my late guru, the awesomely wise and compassionate Dhyāna Master Hsuan Hua, the Guiyang Ch'an Patriarch, Dharma teacher, and exegete.

Finally, I owe an immense debt of gratitude to the members of the liver care and transplant teams at Seattle's University of Washington Medical Center who cured me of liver cancer in 2010, gave me a liver transplant several months later, and finally cured me of hepatitis C in the winter of 2014–15. Without their wonderfully attentive and compassionate care along with the marvelous generosity of an anonymous liver donor, I would have died a half dozen years ago and thus never could have completed the scriptural translations I have produced in the last eight years.

List of Abbreviations

AN	Aṅguttara Nikāya
BCSD	Hirakawa's *Buddhist Chinese-Sanskrit Dictionary*
BHSD	Edgerton's *Buddhist Hybrid Sanskrit Dictionary*
CBETA	Chinese Buddhist Electronic Text Association's edition of the Taisho edition of the Chinese Buddhist canon.
CDB	*The Connected Discourses of the Buddha*
DN	*Dīgha Nikāya*
EA	*Ekottara Āgama*
KB	Kumārajīva and Buddhayaśas (T286)
KJ	Kumārajīva
MDPL	*Materials for a Dictionary of the Prajñāpāramitā Literature*
MLDB	*The Middle Length Discourses of the Buddha*
MN	*Majjhima nikāya*
Mppu	*Mahāprajñāpāramitā upadeśa*
MW	Monier Williams' *A Sanskrit-English Dictionary*
N	Ārya Nāgārjuna
NDB	*Numerical Discourses of the Buddha*
PDB	Princeton Dictionary of Buddhism
PTS	Pali Text Society
SN	Saṃyutta Nikāya
SYMG	The Song, Yuan, Ming, Gong editions of the Chinese Buddhist canon.
SZPPS	*Shizhu piposha lun*
T	Taisho Chinese Buddhist Canon via CBETA (Version 2004. ed.) Taibei)
VB	Venerable Bhikkhu Bodhi

General Table of Contents

Directory to Chapter Subsections

Part One: The Easy Practice

Part Two: The Pratyutpanna Samādhi

Part Three: Recollection of the Buddha

Translator's Introduction

In this volume I present Ārya Nāgārjuna's explanations of three closely related but rather different "mindfulness-of-the-Buddha" practices that are sometimes mistaken for each other:

"Mindfulness of the Buddha" as Pure land practice;
"Mindfulness of the Buddhas" as cultivation of the "seeing-the-Buddhas" (*pratyutpanna*) samādhi;[1] and
"Recollection of the Buddha" as a protective practice.

In order to facilitate the clear understanding of the first two of these three topics, I present exemplary chapters from Nāgārjuna's *Treatise on the Ten Grounds,*[2] and, to distinguish and clarify the final topic, I present a long passage from Nāgārjuna's *Exegesis on the Great Perfection of Wisdom Sutra.*[3]

In his *Treatise on the Ten Grounds,* a third of the way through his discussion of the first bodhisattva ground, Nāgārjuna explains the "pure land" practice that involves reverential devotion to and invocation of the name of a particular buddha with the aim of achieving irreversibility on the bodhisattva path with the option of gaining rebirth in that buddha's purified buddha world. It is my translation of that single-chapter discussion, "The Easy Practice" (Chapter 9) that constitutes the first section of this book.

Later in that same text, in the final third of his discussion of the first bodhisattva ground, Nāgārjuna explains in great detail how to engage in "mindfulness of the Buddhas" practice in such a way that one may then enter the *pratyutpanna* samādhi,[4] the samādhi in which one is able to see the buddhas of the ten directions and listen to them teach the Dharma. It is my translation of that marvelously detailed six-chapter discussion of "mindfulness of the Buddhas" that forms the second section of this book.

Two thirds of the way through the immense (34-fascicle) "Introduction" to his 100-fascicle *Exegesis on the Great Perfection of Wisdom Sutra,* Nāgārjuna presents a very detailed description of "the eight recollections" of which the initial subsection is his discussion of "recollection of the Buddha." It is my translation of that discussion that forms the third section of this book.

The Rationale for Issuing This Volume

My primary reason for bringing forth this volume is to introduce to the English-speaking Buddhist audience selections from two classic Indian Mahāyāna texts that serve to distinguish and clarify the meaning and practice of these three important Mahāyāna practices that may otherwise be so closely associated with each other as to be thought of as somewhat synonymous.

The first of these three practices, "mindfulness of the Buddha" as "pure land" practice, is seldom recognized in Western Buddhism as a very early and important classic Indian Mahāyāna practice used as a means of progressing on the bodhisattva path to buddhahood. Rather it is most often associated with the later pure land schools of, first, China, and then, much later, Japan, where pure land practice has often been most focused on mere recitation of Amitābha Buddha's name with the aim of being reborn in his pure land. I feel it is very important for students of the Dharma to understand this practice in accordance with its early Mahāyāna character and meaning wherein it was regarded as a practice to be integrated into one's practice of the bodhisattva path.

The second of these three practices, "mindfulness of the Buddhas" aimed at acquisition of the *pratyutpanna* samādhi, is not much known in Western Buddhism. Where it is known, it may be easily confused with the "mindfulness of the Buddha samādhi" that one may enter through recitation of Amitābha Buddha's name. But these are two somewhat different samādhis and it is important to distinguish them and understand them as such. Nāgārjuna's extensive explanation of the practice leading to acquisition of this "seeing-the-Buddhas" samādhi eliminates any such confusion.

The third and last of these three practices, "recollection of the Buddha," is also easily confused with pure land practice. In fact, it is an entirely different practice with very different purposes that is found in both Southern Tradition Buddhism[5] and classic Indian Mahāyāna Buddhism. It has as its principal aims the allaying of fear and the provision of protection for practitioners attempting to pursue practice of the path in frightening, dangerous, or discouraging circumstances. The initial section of Nāgārjuna's discussion of the "eight recollections" focuses exclusively on "recollection of the Buddha" and serves quite well to distinguish this practice from others while also clarifying precisely how to employ this practice as an aid to cultivation.

Part One: The Easy Practice

In Nāgārjuna's discussion of the first bodhisattva ground, in response to a discouraged interlocutor fearful of the difficulty of achieving "irreversibility" on the seemingly interminably long bodhisattva path, he offers an alternative means for the bodhisattva practitioner to very quickly and easily achieve irreversibility on this path to buddhahood. This alternative means which he refers to as "the easy practice" involves earnest invocation of the name of particular buddhas who have vowed to come to the aid of anyone who sincerely calls upon them. The practitioner who takes up this "easy practice" is then said to be able to achieve irreversibility on the path to buddhahood by this means.

In this chapter entitled "The Easy Practice," Nāgārjuna first lists the names of ten buddhas, one from each of the ten directions, stating that, through the practice of invoking these buddhas' names, one can swiftly reach the ground of irreversibility. He then quotes a long passage in the *Questions of Precious Moon Sutra*[6] that describes the purified buddha world of Meritorious Qualities Buddha off in the East and describes how, through faith in this buddha, one may achieve irreversibility on the bodhisattva path.

After quoting this sutra, Nāgārjuna then notes the identical circumstances and practices associated with the nine other exemplary buddhas that dwell off in the other nine directions. Having done so, he then names and describes each of these other nine buddhas and their buddha lands.

Next, in response to a questioner wondering if there are other such buddhas, Nāgārjuna lists the names of Amitābha Buddha and 108 other such buddhas, after which he presents a 32-stanza verse praising and describing Amitābha Buddha, his vows, his pure land, his audience, and the advantages of achieving rebirth in his land. This praise verse concludes with Nāgārjuna's declaration of his own personal aspiration to always be borne in mind by this buddha and to succeed in achieving eternal purification of mind in Amitābha Buddha's presence.

Having so extensively described and praised Amitābha Buddha, Nāgārjuna then instructs us to praise and revere the seven historical buddhas of this era (including Śākyamuni Buddha) as well as Maitreya, the next buddha to appear in this world, after which he sets forth verses in praise of each of them. Then he lists ten[7] more buddhas followed by corresponding praise verses after which he lists "all buddhas of the past, the future, and the present" and also sets forth corresponding praise verses to them.

"The Easy Practice" chapter then concludes with Nāgārjuna's instruction to also bear in mind all of the great bodhisattvas, after which he lists 143 great bodhisattvas and states: "One should bear in mind all such bodhisattvas and bow down to them in reverence as one seeks to attain the *avaivartika*'s "ground of irreversibility."[8]

Part Two: The *Pratyutpanna* Samādhi

Toward the end of his discussion of the first bodhisattva ground, the Ground of Joyfulness, Nāgārjuna sets forth a verse indicating that, once the bodhisattva path practitioner has already come to dwell on the first ground, "he will naturally be able to see several hundred buddhas," whereupon he is immediately asked by an interlocutor who is clearly worried about the immense difficulty of even reaching the first bodhisattva ground: "Is it solely through the power of roots of goodness and merit [resulting from completely fulfilling the first-ground practices] that one becomes able to see buddhas, or is there instead some other method by which one can do so?"

In answer to this question, quoting from the *Pratyutpanna Samādhi Sūtra*,[9] Nāgārjuna sets forth a very detailed explanation of the means by which, without first reaching the first bodhisattva ground, acquiring the heavenly eye, or acquiring the heavenly ear, one may nonetheless be able to see the buddhas of the ten directions and listen to them speak the Dharma.

In the extremely detailed and precisely organized subsequent discussion, Nāgārjuna describes how to envision the Buddhas as seated on a lion throne in the midst of a great assembly and tells how to recollect the qualities of the Buddhas, including their vows, their four immeasurable minds, their four bases of meritorious qualities, their six perfections, and their thirty-two major marks and eighty minor characteristics along with the causes for acquiring each of those physical signs. After describing many more qualities and skills of the Buddhas, this "Mindfulness of the Buddhas" chapter ends with a long reiterative verse.

This initial chapter on "Mindfulness of the Buddhas" is then followed by three chapters devoted to close explanation of "forty dharmas exclusive to the Buddhas," a single chapter consisting entirely of praise verses, and a final very detailed chapter on exactly which practices to cultivate and how to cultivate them in order to acquire this *pratyutpanna* samādhi wherein one can see and hear the buddhas of the present. This final chapter is entitled "Teachings to Assist the Mindfulness of the Buddhas Samādhi."

Part Three: Recollection of the Buddha

In subchapter 36 of the 52-part introductory chapter to his *Exegesis on the Great Perfection of Wisdom Sutra,* Nāgārjuna discusses the "eight recollections" of which "recollection of the Buddha" is the first part. It is preceded by a short prefatory introduction to this practice wherein its fear-allaying, protective, and practice-inspiring functions are described.

After noting the role of the eight recollections in allaying fear, depression, discouragement, or disgust to which an isolated practitioner may have become subject, particularly in the wake of cultivating the nine reflections on the deterioration of a corpse, the introductory part of this "eight recollections" discussion then turns to an explanation of the first of these eight recollections, "recollection of the Buddha." This discussion involves a detailed topic-by-topic treatment of a series of bases for carrying out an orderly reflection on the Buddha as an object of contemplation that inspires fearlessness, determination, and happiness. The main subsections of that reflection are as follows:

a) The listing and explanation of the underlying meanings of the ten names of the Buddha;
b) A description of the illustrious lineage and marvelous birth of the Buddha;
c) A description of the physical characteristics, strength, and extraordinary physical marks of the Buddha's body;
d) A long and detailed description of the Buddha's perfection of the five "accumulations," namely moral precepts, meditative absorptions, wisdom, liberations, and the knowledge and vision associated with the liberations;
e) A summarizing list of other qualities of the Buddha upon which one should reflect which includes: the Buddha's omniscience; his manifold types of knowledge and vision; his great kindness and great compassion; his ten powers; his four fearlessnesses, his four types of unimpeded knowledge, and his eighteen special dharmas.

Nāgārjuna's discussion of "recollection of the Buddha" then concludes with a summary of various *abhidharma*-related factors regarding the stations of existence in which it can be practiced, the presence or absence of the contaminants in the practitioner, its association with bliss, joy, and equanimity, and the potential for achieving facility in "recollection of the Buddha" either through practice or as a result of prior karmic actions. In the case of those who acquire it through practice, this refers to those who practice the "mindfulness of the Buddha" samādhi. As for those who acquire it as a karmic result, this refers to such beings as those that inhabit the purified buddha world of Amitābha Buddha.

On the Authorship of the Texts

The author of both these texts, the *Treatise on the Ten Grounds* and the *Exegesis on the Great Perfection of Wisdom Sutra,* is considered by the Sino-Mahāyāna tradition to be Ārya Nāgārjuna, the same 2nd century CE Indian monk who produced such works as the *Mūlamadhyamaka-kārikā,* the *Bodhisaṃbhāra-śāstra,* the *Ratnāvalī,* and the *Suhṛllekha.* Although there have been a number of scholars who have doubted the Nāgārjunian authorship of this *Exegesis on the Great Perfection of Wisdom Sutra,* there arguments tend to boil down to an abundance of opinionation, for there is nothing but very thin circumstantial evidence for their doubts. I have found the internal evidence of doctrinal consistency with other Nāgārjunian texts to be quite strong and I think that the testimony of Kumārajīva (the translator who produced the Chinese edition) is far more trustworthy on the issue of this text's authorship, not least because he lived within 200 years of the life of Nāgārjuna and was the foremost authority on these matters at the time.

In Summation

I hope that this volume of Nāgārjunian texts focused on "mindfulness of the Buddha" practices will be both useful and inspiring to students of Dharma who wish to study, understand, and correctly cultivate these closely related modes of contemplation and practice common in classic Indian Mahāyāna Buddhism.

Bhikshu Dharmamitra
Seattle
May 14, 2019

Introduction Endnotes

1 *"Pratyutpanna samādhi"* is an abbreviation for *pratyutpanna-buddha-saṃmukha-avasthita-samādhi*, "the samādhi in which one encounters the buddhas of the present face-to-face."

2 *Daśabhūmika-vibhāṣā* (十住毘婆沙論 / T26, no. 1521). This is Nāgārjuna's 17-fascicle, 35-chapter discussion on the meaning of the *Ten Grounds Sutra* (*Daśabhūmika-sūtra* [十住經 / T10, no. 286]).

3 *Mahāprājnāpāramitopedeśa* (大智度論 / T25, no. 1509).

4 The complete name of this samādhi is "the *pratyutpanna-buddha-saṃmukha-avasthita samādhi*," lit., "the samādhi in which the Buddhas of the present stand directly before one."

5 "Recollection of the Buddha" constitutes the first of the "four protective meditations" in Southern Tradition Buddhism. (The other three protective meditations are loving-kindness, the unloveliness of the body, and death.)

6 See *The Sutra on the Youth Precious Moon's Questions on Dharma* (大乘寶月童子問法經 – T14n0437_p108c01-110a07).

7 Actually, the text lists eleven buddha names, but it is probable that one of those names is included only as a scribal error involving unintentional redundancy. This conclusion is corroborated by the absence of any mention of this "eleventh" buddha in the ensuing verses that individually praise each of these buddhas.

8 An *"avaivartika"* is one who has achieved irreversibility on the bodhisattva path to buddhahood.

9 "The Pratyutpanna Samādhi Sūtra" (*Pratyutpanna-buddha-saṃmukha-avasthita-samādhi-sūtra*) is preserved in the *Taisho* Canon as the *Banzhou Sanmei Jing* (般舟三昧經 / T13.no. 0418.902c23-919c05) of which Paul Harrison has produced a translation for the BDK English Tripitaka.

Nāgārjuna
on
Mindfulness of the Buddha

Part 1: The Easy Practice

Nāgārjuna's *Treatise on the Ten Grounds,* Chapter 9

As Translated into Chinese by Tripiṭaka Master Kumārajīva
Annotated English Translation by Bhikshu Dharmamitra

Introductory Note on "The Easy Practice

This chapter on "The Easy Practice" is preceded by Nāgārjuna's very detailed description in earlier chapters of his "Treatise on the Ten Grounds" of the difficulties, hazardousness, and lengthiness of the bodhisattva path to buddhahood in contrast to the relative ease of the much swifter paths of śrāvaka disciples and *pratyekabuddhas*.[1] In the immediately preceding chapter on the *avaivartika*,[2] he describes the qualities of the bodhisattva who, while cultivating the ten grounds, finally achieves "irreversibility" on the bodhisattva path, qualities that are very rare, very hard won, and only acquired after a very long time on the bodhisattva path.[3]

In Chapter One, with regard to the length of time required to perfect the cultivation of the ten bodhisattva grounds and become a fully enlightened buddha, Nāgārjuna says:

> In the case of those who cultivate the Great Vehicle, some may require a number of great kalpas as numerous as the sands of a single Ganges River, and some may require a number of great kalpas as numerous as the sands in two, three, or four Ganges Rivers, and so forth until we come to kalpas as numerous as the sands contained in ten, one hundred, one thousand, ten thousand, or a *koṭi* of Ganges Rivers. They may require an even longer period of time than that.

With this background in mind, it should become much easier then for us to understand the rationale of the interlocutor in this chapter when, at the bottom of the first page, he asks Nāgārjuna for an easier alternative path, "an easily-practiced path by which one might rapidly succeed in arriving at the ground of the *avaivartika*."

Then again, given how much effort Nāgārjuna has just devoted in the first seven chapters of his treatise to describing the incredible heroism of the bodhisattva who so fearlessly conquers all obstacles on the ten grounds, it is perhaps understandable, too, why, at the top of the second page, he responds so harshly to a question that searches instead for an "easy" way to reach the "irreversibility" by which one avoids the possibility of falling down onto the śrāvaka or *pratyekabuddha* grounds.

Endnotes

1 In Chapter one, Nāgārjuna notes that it may require only as few as one or two lifetimes for someone to become an arhat and only as few as seven lifetimes for someone to become a *pratyekabuddha.*

2 An *avaivartika* is someone who has become irreversible on either the individual liberation path of the arhats or on the universal-liberation path of the bodhisattvas and buddhas.

3 In the immediately preceding chapter on the *avaivartika* (irreversible) bodhisattva, we have a verse describing such a bodhisattva's qualities:

> The bodhisattva does not apprehend the existence of any self,
> and also does not apprehend the existence of any being.
> He does not engage in discriminations as he discourses on Dharma,
> nor does he apprehend the existence of bodhi.
>
> He does not perceive a buddha by his [physical] signs.
> It is on account of these five meritorious qualities
> that he is referred to as a great bodhisattva
> and becomes an *avaivartika.*

正體字

040c24 ‖ 十住毘婆沙論卷第五 040c25 ‖
040c26 ‖ 聖者龍樹造
040c27 ‖ 後秦龜茲國三藏鳩摩羅什譯
040c28 ‖ [12]易行品第九
040c29 ‖ 問曰。是阿惟越致菩薩初事如先說。至阿惟
041a01 ‖ 越致地者。行諸難行久乃可得。或墮聲聞
041a02 ‖ 辟支佛地。若爾者是大衰患。如助道法中說。
041a03 ‖ 若墮聲聞地 及辟支佛地
041a04 ‖ 是名菩薩死 則失一切利
041a05 ‖ 若墮於地獄 不生如是畏
041a06 ‖ 若墮二乘地 則為大怖畏
041a07 ‖ 墮於地獄中 畢竟得至佛
041a08 ‖ 若墮二乘地 畢竟遮佛道
041a09 ‖ 佛自於經中 解說如是事
041a10 ‖ 如人貪壽者 斬首則大畏
041a11 ‖ 菩薩亦如是 若於聲聞地
041a12 ‖ 及辟支佛地 應生大怖畏
041a13 ‖ 是故若諸佛所說有易行道疾得至阿惟越
041a14 ‖ 致地方便者。願為說之。

简体字

易行品第九

问曰。是阿惟越致菩萨初事如先说。至阿惟越致地者。行诸难行久乃可得。或堕声闻辟支佛地。若尔者是大衰患。如助道法中说。

若堕声闻地 及辟支佛地
是名菩萨死 则失一切利
若堕于地狱 不生如是畏
若堕二乘地 则为大怖畏
堕于地狱中 毕竟得至佛
若堕二乘地 毕竟遮佛道
佛自于经中 解说如是事
如人贪寿者 斩首则大畏
菩萨亦如是 若于声闻地
及辟支佛地 应生大怖畏

是故若诸佛所说有易行道疾得至阿惟越致地方便者。愿为说之。

Part One
The Easy Practice

Ch. 9: On the Easy Practice

I. Chapter Nine: On the Easy Practice

A. Q: How Difficult! Is There an Easier Path to the Avaivartika Ground?

Question: Given that this *avaivartika* bodhisattva's initial endeavors are such as previously discussed, one aspiring to reach the ground of the *avaivartika* would have to practice all manner of difficult practices for a long time and only then be able to reach it. [This being the case], he might become prone then to fall down onto the grounds of the *śrāvaka* disciples or *pratyekabuddhas*. If that were the case, this would be for him an immensely ruinous calamity. As stated in the Dharma of *The Provisions Essential for Bodhi* (*Bodhisambhāra Śāstra*):[1]

> If one were to fall onto the ground of the *śrāvaka* disciples
> or onto the ground of the *pratyekabuddha*s,
> this amounts to "death" for a bodhisattva,
> for he then loses all beneficial effects [of his bodhisattva practice].
>
> If one faced the prospect of falling into the hells,
> he would not become filled with such fear as this.
> If one were to [contemplate] falling onto the Two Vehicles' ground,
> then this would bring about great terror.
>
> If one were to fall into the hells,
> he could still ultimately succeed in reaching buddhahood.
> If one were to fall onto the grounds of the Two Vehicles, however,
> this would ultimately block the realization of buddhahood.
>
> In the scriptures, the Buddha himself
> explained matters such as these, stating that
> this is just as with a person who covets a long lifespan:
> If he is faced with decapitation, he is then filled with great fear.
>
> The bodhisattva is also just like this.
> If [confronted with the prospect of] the *śrāvaka* disciples' ground
> or the *pratyekabuddha*s' ground,
> he should react with great terror.

Therefore, if, as a skillful means, the Buddhas have mentioned the existence of an easily-practiced path by which one might rapidly succeed in arriving at the ground of the *avaivartika*, then please explain it for me.

正體字

答曰。如汝所說是
041a15 ‖ 儜弱怯劣無有大心。非是丈夫志幹之言
041a16 ‖ 也。何以故。若人發願欲求阿耨多羅三藐三
041a17 ‖ 菩提。未得阿惟越致。於其中間應不惜
041a18 ‖ 身命。晝夜精進如救頭燃。如助道中說。
041a19 ‖ 菩薩未得至　阿惟越致地
041a20 ‖ 應常勤精進　猶如救頭燃
041a21 ‖ 荷負於重擔　為求菩提故
041a22 ‖ 常應勤精進　不生懈怠心
041a23 ‖ 若求聲聞乘　辟支佛乘者
041a24 ‖ 但為成己利　常應勤精進
041a25 ‖ 何況於菩薩　自度亦度彼
041a26 ‖ 於此二乘人　億倍應精進
041a27 ‖ 行大乘者佛如是說。發願求佛道。重於
041a28 ‖ 舉三千大千世界。汝言阿惟越致地是法甚
041a29 ‖ 難久乃可得。若有易行道疾得至阿惟越
041b01 ‖ 致地者。是乃怯弱下劣之言。非是大人志幹
041b02 ‖ 之說。汝若必欲聞此方便今當說之。佛法
041b03 ‖ 有無量門。如世間道

简体字

答曰。如汝所说是儜弱怯劣无有大心。非是丈夫志干之言也。何以故。若人发愿欲求阿耨多罗三藐三菩提。未得阿惟越致。于其中间应不惜身命。昼夜精进如救头燃。如助道中说。

菩萨未得至　阿惟越致地
应常勤精进　犹如救头燃
荷负于重担　为求菩提故
常应勤精进　不生懈怠心
若求声闻乘　辟支佛乘者
但为成己利　常应勤精进
何况于菩萨　自度亦度彼
于此二乘人　亿倍应精进

行大乘者佛如是说。发愿求佛道。重于举三千大千世界。汝言阿惟越致地是法甚难久乃可得。若有易行道疾得至阿惟越致地者。是乃怯弱下劣之言。非是大人志干之说。汝若必欲闻此方便今当说之。佛法有无量门。如世间道

B. A: How Weak & Inferior! But, If You Want That, I Will Explain

Response: Statements such as you have just made are symptomatic of a weak, pusillanimous, and inferior mind devoid of the great resolve. These are not the words of a heroic man possessed of determination and ability.

How is this so? If a person has brought forth the vow to strive for the realization of *anuttarasamyaksaṃbodhi,* during that interim period in which he has not yet gained the *avaivartika* stage, he must not be sparing of even his own body or life. Rather he should strive with vigor both day and night, acting with the same urgency to save himself as someone whose turban has just caught fire. This is as stated in the *Bodhisambhara Śāstra*:

So long as the bodhisattva has not yet succeeded in reaching
the ground of the *avaivartika,*
he should always diligently practice vigor,
acting with the urgency of one whose turban has caught fire.

Taking up the heavy burden
for the sake of striving to attain bodhi,
he should always act with diligent vigor,
refraining from developing an indolent mind.[2]

Even were one to seek the *śrāvaka* disciples' vehicle
or the *pratyekabuddha*'s vehicle,
thus seeking only to perfect one's own benefit,
even then, one should always diligently practice vigor.

How much the more should this be so in the case of the bodhisattva,
one who strives to liberate both himself and others.
Compared to these men of the Two Vehicles,
he should be a *koṭi's* number of times more vigorous than they are.[3]

In speaking of the practice of the Great Vehicle, the Buddha described it thus: "As for generating the vow to attain buddhahood, it is a challenge heavier than lifting all of the worlds in a great trichiliocosm."

As for your saying, "This dharma of the *avaivartika* ground is so extremely difficult to accomplish that one can only reach it after a long time" and "If there were only some easily-traveled path by which one could swiftly reach the *avaivartika* ground," these are the words of those who are weak and inferior. These are not statements of a great man possessed of determination and ability. Still, if you definitely do wish to hear of this skillful means, then I shall now explain it for you.

1. The Practice of Calling on Ten Buddhas, One in Each Direction

The Dharma of the Buddha has measurelessly many gateways. This is just as with the world's various routes among which there are those

正體字

有難有易。陸道步行
041b04 ‖ 則苦。水道乘船則樂。菩薩道亦如是。或有
041b05 ‖ 勤行精進。或有以信方便易行疾至阿惟
041b06 ‖ 越致者。如偈說。
041b07 ‖ 　東方善德佛　　南栴檀德佛
041b08 ‖ 　西無量明佛　　北方相德佛
041b09 ‖ 　東南無憂德　　西南寶施佛
041b10 ‖ 　西北華德佛　　東北三[1]行佛
041b11 ‖ 　下方明德佛　　上方廣眾德
041b12 ‖ 　如是諸世尊　　今現在十方
041b13 ‖ 　若人疾欲至　　不退轉地者
041b14 ‖ 　應以恭敬心　　執持稱名號
041b15 ‖ 若菩薩欲於此身得至阿惟越致地成
041b16 ‖ [2]就阿耨多羅三藐三菩提者。應當念是十
041b17 ‖ 方諸佛稱其名號。如寶月童子所問經阿惟
041b18 ‖ 越致品中說。佛告寶月。東方去此過無量
041b19 ‖ 無邊不可思議恒河沙等佛土有世界名無
041b20 ‖ 憂。其地平坦七寶合成。紫磨金縷交絡[3]其
041b21 ‖ 界。寶樹羅列以為莊嚴。無有地獄畜生餓
041b22 ‖ 鬼阿修羅道及諸難處。清淨無穢無有沙礫
041b23 ‖ 瓦石山陵[4]埠阜深坑幽壑。天常雨華以布 041b24 ‖ 其地。

简体字

有难有易。陆道步行则苦。水道乘船则乐。菩萨道亦如是。或有勤行精进。或有以信方便易行疾至阿惟越致者。如偈说。

　东方善德佛　　南栴檀德佛
　西无量明佛　　北方相德佛
　东南无忧德　　西南宝施佛
　西北华德佛　　东北三行佛
　下方明德佛　　上方广众德
　如是诸世尊　　今现在十方
　若人疾欲至　　不退转地者
　应以恭敬心　　执持称名号

若菩萨欲于此身得至阿惟越致地成就阿耨多罗三藐三菩提者。应当念是十方诸佛称其名号。如宝月童子所问经阿惟越致品中说。佛告宝月。东方去此过无量无边不可思议恒河沙等佛土有世界名无忧。其地平坦七宝合成。紫磨金缕交络其界。宝树罗列以为庄严。无有地狱畜生饿鬼阿修罗道及诸难处。清净无秽无有沙砾瓦石山陵堆阜深坑幽壑。天常雨华以布其地。

that are difficult and those that are easy. When taking overland routes, the traveling may involve suffering, whereas in the case of water routes where one boards a boat, it may instead be pleasurable.

So too it is in the case of the bodhisattva path. In some instances, one is diligently devoted to the practice of vigor, whereas in others that involve faith and skillful means, one adopts an easy practice by which one swiftly arrives at the station of the *avaivartika*. This is as described in the following verse:

> In the East, there is Meritorious Qualities Buddha.
> In the South, there is Candana Qualities Buddha.
> In the West, there is Measureless Light Buddha.
> In the North, there is Emblematic Qualities Buddha.
>
> In the Southeast, there is Sorrowless Qualities Buddha.
> In the Southwest, there is Giver of Jewels Buddha.
> In the Northwest, there is Floral Qualities Buddha.
> In the Northeast, there is Three Vehicles' Practices Buddha.[4]
>
> Toward the Nadir, there is Brilliant Qualities Buddha.
> Toward the Zenith, there is Vast Multitude of Qualities Buddha.
> *Bhagavats* such as these
> now abide throughout the ten directions.
>
> If a person wishes to swiftly reach
> the ground of irreversibility,
> he should, with a reverential mind,
> take up and maintain the practice of invoking these buddhas' names.

If a bodhisattva wishes in this very body to succeed in reaching the ground of the *avaivartika* and then attain *anuttarasamyaksaṃbodhi,* then he should bear in mind these buddhas of the ten directions and invoke their names. This is just as explained in the "Avaivartika Chapter" of the *Sutra Spoken in Response to the Questions of the Youth Precious Moon,*[5] in which the Buddha told Precious Moon:

> Off in the East, going beyond a number of buddha lands equal to the sands in a measureless, boundless, and inconceivable number of Ganges Rivers, there is a world system named Sorrowless. Its ground is level and composed of the seven precious things. Strands of purple powdered gold are woven throughout that realm and rows of jeweled trees serve as adornments there.
>
> There are no destinies of the hells, animals, hungry ghosts, or *asuras,* nor are there any places beset by difficulties. It is pure, free of any filth, and also free of gravel, ceramic shards, stones, mountains, hillocks, deep pits, and dark ravines. The devas' always rain down flowers that cover its ground.

正體字

時世有佛號曰善德如來應[5]供正遍
041b25 ‖ 知明行足善逝世間解無上士調御丈夫天人
041b26 ‖ 師佛世尊。大菩薩眾恭敬圍繞。身相光色如
041b27 ‖ 燃大金山如大珍寶聚。為諸大眾[6]廣說
041b28 ‖ 正法。初中後善有辭有義。所說不雜具足
041b29 ‖ 清淨如實不失。何謂不失不失地水火風。
041c01 ‖ 不失欲界色界無色界。不失色受想行識。
041c02 ‖ 寶月。是佛成道已來過六十億劫。又其佛國
041c03 ‖ 晝夜無異。但以此間閻浮提日月歲數說
041c04 ‖ 彼劫壽。其佛光明常照世界。於一說法令
041c05 ‖ 無量無邊千萬億阿僧祇眾生住無生法忍。
041c06 ‖ 倍此人數得住初忍第二第三忍。寶月。其
041c07 ‖ 佛本願力故。若有他方眾生。於先佛所種
041c08 ‖ 諸善根。是佛但以光明觸身。即得無生法
041c09 ‖ 忍。寶月。若善男子善女人聞是佛名能信受
041c10 ‖ 者。即不退阿耨多羅三藐三菩提。餘九佛事
041c11 ‖ 皆亦如是。今當解說諸佛名號及國土名 041c12 ‖號。

简体字

时世有佛号曰善德如来应供正遍知明行足善逝世间解无上士调御丈夫天人师佛世尊。大菩萨众恭敬围绕。身相光色如燃大金山如大珍宝聚。为诸大众广说正法。初中后善有辞有义。所说不杂具足清净如实不失。何谓不失不失地水火风。不失欲界色界无色界。不失色受想行识。宝月。是佛成道已来过六十亿劫。又其佛国昼夜无异。但以此间阎浮提日月岁数说彼劫寿。其佛光明常照世界。于一说法令无量无边千万亿阿僧祇众生住无生法忍。倍此人数得住初忍第二第三忍。宝月。其佛本愿力故。若有他方众生。于先佛所种诸善根。是佛但以光明触身。即得无生法忍。宝月。若善男子善女人闻是佛名能信受者。即不退阿耨多罗三藐三菩提。余九佛事皆亦如是。今当解说诸佛名号及国土名号。

That world now has a buddha named Meritorious Qualities Tathāgata, Worthy of Offerings, of Right and Universal Enlightenment, Perfect in Knowledge and Conduct, Well-Gone One, Knower of the Worlds, Unsurpassable One, Tamer of Those to Be Tamed, Teacher of Devas and Humans, Buddha, Bhagavat. He is respectfully surrounded by an assembly of great bodhisattvas. His body's characteristic radiance and appearance are like a great flaming gold mountain and like a great aggregation of precious jewels.

For the sake of everyone in that great assembly, he extensively proclaims the right Dharma that is good in the beginning, middle, and end, that is eloquently presented and meaningful. Whatever he proclaims is free of admixture, perfect in its purity, accordant with reality, and free of error.

What is meant by "free of error"? It is free of any error with respect to the [four great elements of] earth, water, fire, and wind, is free of any error with respect to the desire realm, the form realm, and the formless realm and is free of error with respect to [the five aggregates of] form, feelings, perceptions, formative factors, and consciousness.

Precious Moon, from the time this buddha achieved buddhahood until the present, sixty *koṭis* of kalpas have passed. Moreover, in that buddha's country, there is no difference between the day and the night. It is only by reference to the enumeration of days, months and years of Jambudvīpa that one describes his lifetime in terms of a particular number of kalpas.

The light from that buddha always illuminates that world. In the course of a single discourse on Dharma, he causes a measureless and boundless number of thousands of myriads of *koṭis* of *asaṃkhyeyas* of beings to abide in the unproduced-dharmas patience. Twice this number of people are thereby caused to abide in the first, second, and third type of patience.

Precious Moon, the power of that buddha's original vows is such that, if there are any beings in other regions who have planted roots of goodness under a previous buddha, he need only be touched by this buddha's light in order to immediately attain the unproduced-dharmas patience.

Precious Moon, if there is a son or daughter of good family who but hears this buddha's name and is then able to have faith and accept him, such a person will immediately achieve irreversibility with respect to the attainment of *anuttarasamyaksaṃbodhi*.

The circumstances related to the other nine buddhas are just like this. Now we shall explain the names of those Buddhas as well as the names of their lands.

正體字

善德者。其德淳善但有安樂。非如諸天
041c13 ‖ 龍神福德[7]惑惱眾生。栴檀德者。南方去此
041c14 ‖ 無量無邊恒河沙等佛土有世界名歡喜。
041c15 ‖ 佛號栴檀德。今現在說法。譬如栴檀香而
041c16 ‖ 清涼。彼佛名稱遠聞如香流布。滅除眾生三
041c17 ‖ 毒火熱令得清涼。無量明佛者。西方去此
041c18 ‖ 無量無邊恒河沙等佛土有世界名[8]善。佛
041c19 ‖ 號無量明。今現在說法。其佛身光及智慧明
041c20 ‖ 炤無量無邊。相德佛者。北方去此無量無邊
041c21 ‖ 恒河沙等佛土有世界名不可動。佛名相
041c22 ‖ 德。今現在說法。其佛福德高顯猶如幢相。
041c23 ‖ 無憂德者。東南方去此無量無邊恒河沙等
041c24 ‖ 佛土有世界名月明。佛號無憂德。今現在
041c25 ‖ 說法。其佛神德令諸天人無有憂愁。寶施
041c26 ‖ 佛者。西南方去此無量無邊恒河沙等佛土
041c27 ‖ 有世界名眾相。佛號寶施。今現在說法。其
041c28 ‖ 佛以諸無漏根力覺道等寶常施眾生。華德
041c29 ‖ 佛者。西北方去此無量無邊恒河沙等佛土

简体字

善德者。其德淳善但有安乐。非如诸天龙神福德惑恼众生。栴檀德者。南方去此无量无边恒河沙等佛土有世界名欢喜。佛号栴檀德。今现在说法。譬如栴檀香而清凉。彼佛名称远闻如香流布。灭除众生三毒火热令得清凉。无量明佛者。西方去此无量无边恒河沙等佛土有世界名善。佛号无量明。今现在说法。其佛身光及智慧明昭无量无边。相德佛者。北方去此无量无边恒河沙等佛土有世界名不可动。佛名相德。今现在说法。其佛福德高显犹如幢相。无忧德者。东南方去此无量无边恒河沙等佛土有世界名月明。佛号无忧德。今现在说法。其佛神德令诸天人无有忧愁。宝施佛者。西南方去此无量无边恒河沙等佛土有世界名众相。佛号宝施。今现在说法。其佛以诸无漏根力觉道等宝常施众生。华德佛者。西北方去此无量无边恒河沙等佛土

As for "Meritorious Qualities Buddha," his qualities are associated with pure goodness and the possession of peace and happiness. They are unlike the meritorious qualities of devas, dragons, and spirits which delude and trouble beings.

As for "Candana Qualities Buddha," in the South, off at a distance from here of buddha lands as numerous as the sands in incalculably and boundlessly many Ganges Rivers, there is a world named Delightful. The name of the buddha there is Candana Qualities. He is right now proclaiming the Dharma that is as fragrant and cooling as *candana*.[6] The fame of that buddha's name is heard afar, circulating and spreading about like the fragrance of incense. It extinguishes the heat from the fire of beings' three poisons and thereby causes them to experience refreshing coolness.

As for "Measureless Light Buddha," off in the West, at a distance from here of buddha lands as numerous as the sands in incalculably and boundlessly many Ganges Rivers, there is a world named "Excellence." That buddha is named Measureless Light. He is at this very time proclaiming the Dharma. The light from that buddha's body and the brilliant illumination from his wisdom reach an incalculable and boundless distance.

As for "Emblematic Qualities Buddha," off in the North, at a distance from here of buddha lands as numerous as the sands in incalculably and boundlessly many Ganges Rivers, there is a world known as "Immovable." Its buddha is known as Emblematic Qualities. He is right now proclaiming the Dharma. That buddha's meritorious qualities are lofty and prominently displayed, appearing like a banner.

As for "Sorrowless Qualities Buddha," in the Southeast, off at a distance from here of buddha lands as numerous as the sands in incalculably and boundlessly many Ganges Rivers, there is a world named "Lunar Brilliance." The buddha who abides there is named Sorrowless Qualities. He is even now proclaiming the Dharma. That buddha's spiritual qualities are such that they cause all of the devas and men there to be free of any sort of sorrow.

As for "Giver of Jewels Buddha," in the Southwest, off at a distance from here of buddha lands as numerous as the sands in incalculably and boundlessly many Ganges Rivers, there is a world named "Multitude of Signs." The buddha who abides there is known as Giver of Jewels. Even now he is proclaiming the Dharma. That buddha always bestows on beings the jewels of the uncontaminated root-faculties, powers, limbs of enlightenment, the path, and so forth.

As for "Floral Qualities Buddha," in the Northwest, off at a distance from here of buddha lands as numerous as the sands in incalculably

正體字

042a01 ‖ 有世界名眾音。佛號華德。今現在說法。其
042a02 ‖ 佛色身猶如妙華其德無量。三乘行佛者。東
042a03 ‖ 北方去此無量無邊恒河沙等佛土有世界
042a04 ‖ 名安隱。佛號三乘行。今現在說法。其佛常
042a05 ‖ 說聲聞行辟支佛行諸菩薩行。有人言。說上
042a06 ‖ 中下精進故。號為三乘行。明德佛者。下方
042a07 ‖ 去此無量無邊恒河沙等佛土有世界名
042a08 ‖ 廣大。佛號明德。今現在說法。明名身明智
042a09 ‖ 慧明寶樹光明。是三種明常照世間。廣眾德
042a10 ‖ 者。上方去此無量無邊恒河沙等佛土有世
042a11 ‖ 界名眾月。佛號廣眾德。[1]今現在說法。其
042a12 ‖ 佛[2]弟子福德廣大故號廣眾德。[3]今是十方
042a13 ‖ 佛善德為初。廣眾德為後。若人一心稱其
042a14 ‖ 名號。即得不退於阿耨多羅三藐三菩提。
042a15 ‖ 如[4]偈說。
042a16 ‖ 若有人得聞　說是諸佛名
042a17 ‖ 即得無量德　如為寶月說

简体字

有世界名众音。佛号华德。今现在说法。其佛色身犹如妙华其德无量。三乘行佛者。东北方去此无量无边恒河沙等佛土有世界名安隐。佛号三乘行。今现在说法。其佛常说声闻行辟支佛行诸菩萨行。有人言。说上中下精进故。号为三乘行。明德佛者。下方去此无量无边恒河沙等佛土有世界名广大。佛号明德。今现在说法。明名身明智慧明宝树光明。是三种明常照世间。广众德者。上方去此无量无边恒河沙等佛土有世界名众月。佛号广众德。今现在说法。其佛弟子福德广大故号广众德。今是十方佛善德为初。广众德为后。若人一心称其名号。即得不退于阿耨多罗三藐三菩提。如偈说。

若有人得闻　说是诸佛名
即得无量德　如为宝月说

and boundlessly many Ganges Rivers, there is a world known as "Multitude of Sounds." The Buddha who abides there is known as Floral Qualities. Even now, he is proclaiming the Dharma. That buddha's physical body is like a marvelous flower and his meritorious qualities are incalculably numerous.

As for "Three Vehicles' Practices Buddha," in the Northeast, off at a distance from here of buddha lands as numerous as the sands in incalculably and boundlessly many Ganges Rivers, there is a world known as "Peaceful and Secure." The buddha who abides there is known as Three Vehicles' Practices Buddha. Even now, he is proclaiming the Dharma. That buddha always explains the practices of the *śrāvaka* disciples, the practices of the *pratyekabuddhas,* and the practices of the bodhisattvas. There are those who state that it is because he explains the superior, the middling, and the lesser levels of vigor that he is named Three Vehicles' Practices.

As for "Brilliant Qualities Buddha," in the Nadir, off at a distance from here of buddha lands as numerous as the sands in incalculably and boundlessly many Ganges Rivers, there is a world known as "Expansive." The buddha who abides there is known as Brilliant Qualities. Even now he is proclaiming the Dharma. "Brilliant" refers to the light that shines from his body, the light of his wisdom, and the light that shines from his jeweled tree. These three kinds of brilliance always illuminate that world.

As for "Vast Multitude of Qualities Buddha," in the Zenith, off at a distance from here of buddha lands as numerous as the sands in incalculably and boundlessly many Ganges Rivers, there is a world known as "Many Moons." The buddha who abides there is known as Vast Multitude of Qualities. Even now he is proclaiming the Dharma. It is because the meritorious qualities of that buddha's disciples are vast that he is known as Vast Multitude of Qualities.

Now, as for these buddhas of the ten directions, beginning with Meritorious Qualities Buddha and concluding with Vast Multitude of Qualities Buddha, if a person single-mindedly invokes their names, he will thereby immediately succeed in gaining irreversibility with respect to the attainment of *anuttarasamyaksaṃbodhi.* This is as described in a verse:

> If there is a person who is able to hear
> the utterance of all these buddhas' names,
> he will immediately acquire countless meritorious qualities,
> just as was explained for Precious Moon.

正體字

042a18 ‖	我禮是諸佛	今現在十方
042a19 ‖	其有稱名者	即得不退轉
042a20 ‖	東方無憂界	其佛號善德
042a21 ‖	色相如金山	名聞無邊際
042a22 ‖	若人聞名者	即得不退轉
042a23 ‖	我今合掌禮	願悉除憂惱
042a24 ‖	南方歡喜界	佛號栴檀德
042a25 ‖	面淨如滿月	光明無有量
042a26 ‖	能滅諸眾生	三毒之熱惱
042a27 ‖	聞名得不退	是故稽首禮
042a28 ‖	西方善世界	佛號無量明
042a29 ‖	身光智慧明	所照無邊際
042b01 ‖	其有聞名者	即得不退轉
042b02 ‖	我今稽首禮	願盡生死際
042b03 ‖	北方無動界	佛號為相德
042b04 ‖	身具眾相好	而以自莊嚴
042b05 ‖	摧破魔怨眾	善化諸[5]人天
042b06 ‖	聞名得不退	是故稽首禮
042b07 ‖	東南月明界	有佛號無憂
042b08 ‖	光明踰日月	遇者滅[6]煩惱

简体字

我礼是诸佛	今现在十方
其有称名者	即得不退转
东方无忧界	其佛号善德
色相如金山	名闻无边际
若人闻名者	即得不退转
我今合掌礼	愿悉除忧恼
南方欢喜界	佛号栴檀德
面净如满月	光明无有量
能灭诸众生	三毒之热恼
闻名得不退	是故稽首礼
西方善世界	佛号无量明
身光智慧明	所照无边际
其有闻名者	即得不退转
我今稽首礼	愿尽生死际
北方无动界	佛号为相德
身具众相好	而以自庄严
摧破魔怨众	善化诸人天
闻名得不退	是故稽首礼
东南月明界	有佛号无忧
光明踰日月	遇者灭烦恼

I bow in reverence to these buddhas
presently abiding throughout the ten directions.
Whosoever invokes their names
immediately attains irreversibility.

Off in the East, in the realm known as Sorrowless,
that buddha named Meritorious Qualities
has a form resembling a mountain of gold.
The reach of his fame is boundless.

If a person so much as hears his name,
he immediately attains irreversibility.
With palms pressed together, I now bow in reverence to him
and pray that worries and afflictions may be entirely dispelled.

Off in the South, in the realm known as Delightful,
there is a buddha named Candana Qualities.
His countenance is as pristine as the full moon
and the radiance of his light is measureless.

He is able to bring about the extinguishing of beings'
fiery afflictions produced by the three poisons.
If one but hears his name, he then attains irreversibility.
I therefore bow down in reverence to him.

Off in the West, in a realm known as Excellence,
there is a buddha known as Limitless Light.
The light from his body and the brilliance of his wisdom
are boundless in the range of their illumination.

If there be anyone who but hears his name
he will immediately attain irreversibility.
I now bow down in reverence to him,
praying that I may put an end to the limits imposed by *saṃsāra.*

Off in the North, in a realm known as Immovable,
there is a buddha named Emblematic Qualities.
His body is replete with the many signs and minor characteristics
with which he is personally adorned.

He utterly defeats the hordes of Māra, the enemy,
and skillfully teaches both humans and devas.
Those who hear his name attain irreversibility.
I therefore bow down in reverence to him.

Off in the Southeast, in a world known as Lunar Brilliance,
there is a buddha named Sorrowless.
His illumination surpasses that of the sun and moon.
Those who encounter it are thus able to extinguish their afflictions.

正體字

042b09 ║ 常為眾說法　除諸內外苦
042b10 ║ 十方佛稱讚　是故稽首禮
042b11 ║ 西南眾相界　佛號為寶施
042b12 ║ 常以諸法寶　廣施於一切
042b13 ║ 諸天頭面禮　寶冠在足下
042b14 ║ 我今以五體　歸命寶施尊
042b15 ║ 西北眾音界　佛號為華德
042b16 ║ 世界眾寶樹　演出妙法音
042b17 ║ 常以七覺華　莊嚴於眾生
042b18 ║ 白毫相如月　我今頭面禮
042b19 ║ 東北安隱界　諸寶所合成
042b20 ║ 佛號[7]三乘行　無量相嚴身
042b21 ║ 智慧光無量　能破無明闇
042b22 ║ 眾生無憂惱　是故稽首禮
042b23 ║ 上方眾月界　眾寶所莊嚴
042b24 ║ 大德聲聞眾　菩薩無有量
042b25 ║ 諸聖中師子　號曰廣眾德
042b26 ║ 諸魔所怖畏　是故稽首禮
042b27 ║ 下方廣世界　佛號為明德
042b28 ║ 身相妙超絕　閻浮檀金山

简体字

常为众说法　除诸内外苦
十方佛称赞　是故稽首礼
西南众相界　佛号为宝施
常以诸法宝　广施于一切
诸天头面礼　宝冠在足下
我今以五体　归命宝施尊
西北众音界　佛号为华德
世界众宝树　演出妙法音
常以七觉华　庄严于众生
白毫相如月　我今头面礼
东北安隐界　诸宝所合成
佛号三乘行　无量相严身
智慧光无量　能破无明闇
众生无忧恼　是故稽首礼
上方众月界　众宝所庄严
大德声闻众　菩萨无有量
诸圣中师子　号曰广众德
诸魔所怖畏　是故稽首礼
下方广世界　佛号为明德
身相妙超绝　阎浮檀金山

He always explains the Dharma for the sake of the multitude,
thus ridding them of all inward and outward sufferings.
The buddhas of the ten directions praise him.
I therefore bow down in reverence to him.

Off in the Southwest, in a realm known as Multitude of Signs,
there is a buddha named Giver of Jewels.
He always uses all manner of Dharma jewels
to engage in extensive universal giving.

All the devas bow down in reverence to him
so that their jeweled crowns are brought low at his feet.
I now, bowing in reverence with all five extremities,
take refuge in the Bhagavat, Giver of Jewels.

Off in the Northwest, in a realm known as Multitude of Sounds,
there is a buddha named Floral Qualities.
That world is graced with an abundance of jeweled trees
that send forth sounds expounding the sublime Dharma.

He always uses the flowers of the seven limbs of enlightenment
to bestow adornments on those beings.
His mid-brow white hair tuft mark is like the moon.
I now bow down in reverence to him.

Off in the Northeast, in a world known as Peaceful and Secure,
one that is composed of all manner of jewels,
there is a buddha named Three Vehicles Practices
whose body is adorned with the measureless marks.

The light from his wisdom is measureless.
It is able to dispel the darkness of ignorance
and cause beings to become free of worry and afflictions.
I therefore bow down in reverence to him.

Off toward the Zenith, in a world known as Many Moons,
adorned with the many types of jewels,
attended by a congregation of greatly virtuous *śrāvaka* disciples
and bodhisattvas who are incalculable in number,

there is a lion among the Āryas
named Vast Multitude of Qualities.
He is feared by all the *māras*.
I therefore bow down in reverence to him.

Off toward the Nadir, there is world known as Expansive
in which there is a buddha named Brilliant Qualities.
His physical marks are far more marvelous
even than a mountain of *jambūnada* gold.

正體字

042b29 ‖ 常以智慧日　開諸善根華
042c01 ‖ 寶土甚廣大　我遙稽首禮
042c02 ‖ 過去無數劫　有佛號海德
042c03 ‖ 是諸現在佛　皆從彼發願
042c04 ‖ 壽命無有量　光明照無極
042c05 ‖ 國土甚清淨　聞名定作佛
042c06 ‖ 今現在十方　具足成十力
042c07 ‖ 是故稽首禮　人天中最尊
042c08 ‖ 問曰。但聞是十佛名號執持在心。便得不
042c09 ‖ 退阿耨多羅三藐三菩提。為更有餘佛餘
042c10 ‖ 菩薩名得至阿惟越致耶。答曰。
042c11 ‖ [8]阿彌陀等佛　及諸大菩薩
042c12 ‖ 稱名一心念　亦得不退轉
042c13 ‖ 更有阿彌陀等諸佛。亦應恭敬禮拜稱其名
042c14 ‖ 號。今當具說。無量壽佛。世自在王佛。師子
042c15 ‖ [9]意佛。法意佛。梵相佛。世相佛。世妙佛。慈悲
042c16 ‖ 佛。世王佛。人王佛。月德佛。寶德佛。相德佛。
042c17 ‖ 大相佛。[10]珠蓋佛。師子[11]鬘佛。破無明佛。智華
042c18 ‖ 佛。多摩羅跋栴檀香佛。持大功德佛。

简体字

常以智慧日　开诸善根华
宝土甚广大　我遥稽首礼
过去无数劫　有佛号海德
是诸现在佛　皆从彼发愿
寿命无有量　光明照无极
国土甚清净　闻名定作佛
今现在十方　具足成十力
是故稽首礼　人天中最尊

问曰。但闻是十佛名号执持在心。便得不退阿耨多罗三藐三菩提。为更有余佛余菩萨名得至阿惟越致耶。答曰。

阿弥陀等佛　及诸大菩萨
称名一心念　亦得不退转

更有阿弥陀等诸佛。亦应恭敬礼拜称其名号。今当具说。无量寿佛。世自在王佛。师子意佛。法意佛。梵相佛。世相佛。世妙佛。慈悲佛。世王佛。人王佛。月德佛。宝德佛。相德佛。大相佛。珠盖佛。师子鬘佛。破无明佛。智华佛。多摩罗跋栴檀香佛。持大功德佛。

He always uses the sun of his wisdom
to open the blossoms of beings' roots of goodness.
His land of jewels is extremely vast.
From afar, I bow down in reverence to him.

In the past, countless kalpas ago,
there was a buddha named Oceanic Meritorious Qualities.
These buddhas of the present era
all made their vows under him.

His lifespan was incalculably long
and the reach of his light's illumination was endless.
His country was extremely pure.
Those hearing his name became definitely bound for buddhahood.

These [buddhas] who now abide in the ten directions
are completely equipped with the ten powers.
I therefore bow down in reverence to them,
these most venerable ones among all humans and devas.

2. Q: Can One Instead Call on Other Buddhas and Bodhisattvas?

Question: Is it the case that one may only be able to reach irreversibility with respect to *anuttarasamyaksaṃbodhi* through hearing these ten buddhas' names and bearing them in mind? Or is it the case that there are yet other buddhas' and other bodhisattvas' names through which one may succeed in reaching the station of the *avaivartika*?

3. A: Yes, There is Amitābha as Well as Other Such Buddhas

Response:

There is Amitābha and also other such buddhas
as well as the great bodhisattvas.
If one invokes their names and single-mindedly bears them in mind,
one will also thereby attain irreversibility.

In addition, there is Amitābha as well as other buddhas to whom one should also respectfully bow down in reverence and utter their names. I shall now set forth their names in full:

Limitless Life Buddha, King of Sovereign Mastery in the World Buddha, Lion Mind Buddha, Dharma Mind Buddha, Brahman Signs Buddha, World Signs Buddha, Sublimity of the World Buddha, Kindness and Compassion Buddha, World King Buddha, King Among Men Buddha, Moon-like Virtues Buddha, Precious Virtues Buddha, Qualities of the Marks Buddha, Great Marks Buddha, Jeweled Canopy Buddha, Lion Mane Buddha, Destroyer of Ignorance Buddha, Flower of Wisdom Buddha, Tamālapattra Candana Fragrance Buddha, and Upholder of Great Meritorious Qualities Buddha.

正體字

雨七寶 042c19 ‖ 佛。超勇佛。離瞋恨佛。大莊嚴佛。無相佛。寶
042c20 ‖ 藏佛。德頂佛。多伽羅香佛。栴檀香佛。蓮華香
042c21 ‖ 佛。莊嚴道路佛。龍蓋佛。雨華佛。散華佛。華
042c22 ‖ 光明佛。日音聲佛。蔽日月佛。琉璃藏佛。梵音
042c23 ‖ 佛。淨明佛。金藏佛。須彌頂佛。山王佛。音聲
042c24 ‖ 自在佛。淨眼佛。月明佛。如須彌山佛。日月
042c25 ‖ 佛。得眾佛。華[12]生佛。梵音說佛。世主佛。師子
042c26 ‖ 行佛。妙法意師子吼佛。珠寶蓋珊瑚色佛。破
042c27 ‖ 癡愛闇佛。水月佛。眾華佛。開智慧佛。持雜寶
042c28 ‖ 佛。菩提佛。華超出佛。真琉璃明佛。蔽日明
042c29 ‖ 佛。持大功德佛。得正慧佛。勇健佛。離諂曲
043a01 ‖ 佛。除惡根栽佛。大香佛。道[1]映佛。水光佛。海
043a02 ‖ 雲慧遊佛。德頂華佛。華莊嚴佛。日音聲佛。月
043a03 ‖ 勝佛。琉璃佛。梵聲佛。光明佛。金藏佛。山頂
043a04 ‖ 佛。山王佛。音王佛。龍勝佛。無染佛。淨面佛。
043a05 ‖ 月面佛。如須彌佛。栴檀香佛。威勢佛。燃燈
043a06 ‖ 佛。難勝佛。寶德佛。喜音佛。光明佛。龍勝佛。
043a07 ‖ 離垢明佛。師子佛。王王佛。力勝佛。華[2]齒佛。
043a08 ‖ 無畏明佛。香頂佛。普賢佛。普華佛。寶相佛。

简体字

雨七宝佛。超勇佛。离嗔恨佛。大庄严佛。无相佛。宝藏佛。德顶佛。多伽罗香佛。栴檀香佛。莲华香佛。庄严道路佛。龙盖佛。雨华佛。散华佛。华光明佛。日音声佛。蔽日月佛。琉璃藏佛。梵音佛。净明佛。金藏佛。须弥顶佛。山王佛。音声自在佛。净眼佛。月明佛。如须弥山佛。日月佛。得众佛。华生佛。梵音说佛。世主佛。师子行佛。妙法意师子吼佛。珠宝盖珊瑚色佛。破痴爱闇佛。水月佛。众华佛。开智慧佛。持杂宝佛。菩提佛。华超出佛。真琉璃明佛。蔽日明佛。持大功德佛。得正慧佛。勇健佛。离谄曲佛。除恶根栽佛。大香佛。道映佛。水光佛。海云慧游佛。德顶华佛。华庄严佛。日音声佛。月胜佛。琉璃佛。梵声佛。光明佛。金藏佛。山顶佛。山王佛。音王佛。龙胜佛。无染佛。净面佛。月面佛。如须弥佛。栴檀香佛。威势佛。燃灯佛。难胜佛。宝德佛。喜音佛。光明佛。龙胜佛。离垢明佛。师子佛。王王佛。力胜佛。华齿佛。无畏明佛。香顶佛。普贤佛。普华佛。宝相佛。

There are also: Rain of the Seven Precious Things Buddha, Excellent Bravery Buddha, Enmity Transcendence Buddha, Great Adornment Buddha, Signlessness Buddha, Jewel Treasury Buddha, Summit of Virtue Buddha, Tagara Fragrance Buddha, Candana Incense Buddha, Lotus Fragrance Buddha, Adorned Path Buddha, Dragon Canopy Buddha, Rain of Flowers Buddha, Scatterer of Flowers Buddha, Floral Radiance Buddha, Solar Voice Buddha, Eclipsing the Sun and Moon Buddha, Lapis Lazuli Treasury Buddha, Brahman Sound Buddha, and Pure Radiance Buddha.

There are also: Treasury of Gold Buddha, Sumeru Summit Buddha, King of the Mountains Buddha, Masterful Voice Buddha, Pure Eyes Buddha, Lunar Radiance Buddha, Mount Sumeru Likeness Buddha, Sun and Moon Buddha, Acquirer of Multitudes Buddha, Flower-born Buddha, Proclaimer of the Brahman Sounds Buddha, Lord of the Worlds Buddha, Lion-like Practice Buddha, Sublime Dharma Mind Lion's Roar Buddha, Pearl Canopy Coral Appearance Buddha, Dispeller of the Darkness of Delusion and Desire Buddha, Water Moon Buddha, Multitude of Flowers Buddha, Opener of Wisdom Buddha, and Retainer of Various Jewels Buddha.

There are also: Bodhi Buddha, Flower Transcendence Buddha, Radiance of True Lapis Lazuli Buddha, Outshining Sunlight Buddha, Retainer of Great Qualities Buddha, Realizer of Right Wisdom Buddha, Heroic Strength Buddha, Beyond Flattery and Deception Buddha, Dispensing with Planting Roots of Evil Buddha, Great Fragrance Buddha, Path Splendor Buddha, Water Light Buddha, Roamer in Oceanic Clouds of Wisdom Buddha, Virtue Summit Flower Buddha, Floral Adornment Buddha, Solar Voice Buddha, Lunar Supremacy Buddha, Lapis Lazuli Buddha, Brahmā-like Voice Buddha, and Light Buddha.[7]

There are also: Treasury of Gold Buddha, Mountain Summit Buddha, Mountain King Buddha, Sound King Buddha, Dragon Vigor Buddha, Stainless Buddha, Pure Countenance Buddha, Lunar Countenance Buddha, Sumeru Semblance Buddha, Candana Fragrance Buddha, Awesome Strength Buddha, Blazing Lamp Buddha, Difficult to Overcome Buddha, Precious Virtue Buddha, Joyous Sound Buddha, Radiance Buddha,[8] Dragon Supremacy Buddha, Defilement Transcendence Light Buddha, Lion Buddha, and King Among Kings Buddha.

And there are also Supremacy of Powers Buddha, Floral Garden Buddha,[9] Fearless Brilliance Buddha, Fragrant Summit Buddha, Universally Worthy Buddha, Universal Flower Buddha, and Precious Signs Buddha.

正體字

043a09 ‖ 是諸佛世尊現在十方清淨世界。皆稱名憶
043a10 ‖ 念。阿彌陀佛本願如是。若人念我稱名自
043a11 ‖ 歸。即入必定得阿耨多羅三藐三菩提。是
043a12 ‖ 故常應憶念以偈稱讚。
043a13 ‖ 無量光明慧 身如真金山
043a14 ‖ 我今身口意 合掌稽首禮
043a15 ‖ 金色妙光明 普流諸世界
043a16 ‖ 隨物[3]增其色 是故稽首禮
043a17 ‖ 若人命終時 得生彼國者
043a18 ‖ 即具無量德 是故我歸命
043a19 ‖ 人能念是佛 無量力[4]威德
043a20 ‖ 即時入必定 是故我常念
043a21 ‖ 彼國人命終 設應受諸苦
043a22 ‖ 不墮惡地獄 是故歸命禮
043a23 ‖ 若人生彼國 終不墮三趣
043a24 ‖ 及與阿修羅 我今歸命禮
043a25 ‖ 人天身相同 猶如金山頂
043a26 ‖ 諸勝所歸處 是故頭面禮
043a27 ‖ 其有生彼國 具天眼耳通
043a28 ‖ 十方普無礙 稽首聖中尊

简体字

是诸佛世尊现在十方清净世界。皆称名忆念。阿弥陀佛本愿如是。若人念我称名自归。即入必定得阿耨多罗三藐三菩提。是故常应忆念以偈称赞。

无量光明慧 身如真金山
我今身口意 合掌稽首礼
金色妙光明 普流诸世界
随物增其色 是故稽首礼
若人命终时 得生彼国者
即具无量德 是故我归命
人能念是佛 无量力威德
即时入必定 是故我常念
彼国人命终 设应受诸苦
不堕恶地狱 是故归命礼
若人生彼国 终不堕三趣
及与阿修罗 我今归命礼
人天身相同 犹如金山顶
诸胜所归处 是故头面礼
其有生彼国 具天眼耳通
十方普无碍 稽首圣中尊

These buddhas, *bhagavats,* abide now in pure worlds throughout the ten directions. One should invoke the names of all of them and bear them in mind.

a. Amitābha's Original Vows and a Praise Verse

The original vows of Amitābha are of this sort: "If any person bears me in mind, invokes my name, and takes refuge in me, he will immediately enter the stage of certainty with respect to attaining *anuttarasamyaksaṃbodhi."*

One should therefore always remain mindful of him. I set forth his praises here with a verse:

He possesses boundless illumination and wisdom
and his body is like a mountain of gold.
Paying homage to him with body, speech, and mind, I now
place my palms together and bow down in reverence to him.

His marvelous golden-colored light
everywhere streams into all worlds,
increasing in its brilliance in response to each being.
I therefore bow down in reverence to him.

If, when life's end comes, a person
succeeds in being reborn in that land,
he immediately acquires countless meritorious qualities.
I do therefore take refuge in him.

Whoever is able to bear in mind this buddha
possessed of measureless powers and awe-inspiring qualities
will immediately enter the stage of certainty.
I do therefore always bear him in mind.

That land is such that if, at the end of one's life,
one should otherwise undergo all manner of suffering,
even so, one will not then fall into those terrible hells.
Therefore, taking refuge in him, I now bow down in reverence.

If a person gains rebirth in his land,
he will never again fall into the three wretched destinies
or into the realms of the *asuras.*
Taking refuge in him, I now bow down in reverence.

Though his body is similar to that of humans and devas,
it resembles the summit of a mountain of gold.
This is the place to which all supreme [qualities] return.
I therefore bow down in reverence to him.

Those who have been reborn in his land,
gain the powers of the heavenly eye and ear
that reach unimpededly throughout the ten directions.
I bow down in reverence to the one honored among the Āryas.

正體字

043a29 ‖	其國諸眾生	神變及心通
043b01 ‖	亦具宿命智	是故歸命禮
043b02 ‖	生彼國土者	無我無我所
043b03 ‖	不生彼此心	是故稽首禮
043b04 ‖	超出三界獄	目如蓮華葉
043b05 ‖	聲聞眾無量	是故稽首禮
043b06 ‖	彼國諸眾生	其性皆柔和
043b07 ‖	自然行十善	稽首眾聖[5]王
043b08 ‖	從善生淨明	無量無邊數
043b09 ‖	二足中第一	是故我歸命
043b10 ‖	若人願作佛	心念阿彌陀
043b11 ‖	應時為現身	是故我歸命
043b12 ‖	彼佛本願力	十方諸菩薩
043b13 ‖	來供養聽法	是故我稽首
043b14 ‖	彼土諸菩薩	具足諸相好
043b15 ‖	以自莊嚴身	我今歸命禮
043b16 ‖	彼諸大菩薩	日日於三時
043b17 ‖	供養十方佛	是故稽首禮
043b18 ‖	若人種善根	疑則華不開
043b19 ‖	信心清淨者	華開則見佛

简体字

其国诸众生	神变及心通
亦具宿命智	是故归命礼
生彼国土者	无我无我所
不生彼此心	是故稽首礼
超出三界狱	目如莲华叶
声闻众无量	是故稽首礼
彼国诸众生	其性皆柔和
自然行十善	稽首众圣王
从善生净明	无量无边数
二足中第一	是故我归命
若人愿作佛	心念阿弥陀
应时为现身	是故我归命
彼佛本愿力	十方诸菩萨
来供养听法	是故我稽首
彼土诸菩萨	具足诸相好
以自庄严身	我今归命礼
彼诸大菩萨	日日于三时
供养十方佛	是故稽首礼
若人种善根	疑则华不开
信心清净者	华开则见佛

All the beings in his land
perform supernatural transformations, know others' thoughts,
and are endowed with the knowledge of past lives as well.
Therefore, taking refuge in him, I bow down in reverence.

Those who are reborn in his land
have no conception of either "I" or "mine."
They do not have thoughts conceiving of "others" or "self."
I therefore bow down in reverence to him.

He has stepped beyond the prison of the three realms.
His eyes are like the petals of a lotus.
The assembly of *śrāvaka* disciples there is measurelessly vast.
I therefore bow down in reverence to him.

All the beings in his land
are in nature gentle and harmonious
and they naturally practice the ten good deeds.
I bow down in reverence to this king of the many *āryas*.

It is from such goodness that his pure light is produced
that, in the number of its rays, is measureless and boundless.
He is foremost among those who stand on two feet.
I do therefore take refuge in him.

If a person vows to become a buddha
and then bears in mind Amitābha,
when the time is right, he will appear for his sake.
I do therefore take refuge in him.

Through the power of that buddha's vows
the bodhisattvas of the ten directions
come to make offerings and listen to the Dharma.
I therefore bow down in reverence to him.

All the bodhisattvas in his land
are endowed with all the major marks and secondary characteristics
by which they thereby adorn their own bodies.
Taking refuge in him, I now bow down in reverence.

Three times every day,
all those great bodhisattvas
make offerings to the buddhas of the ten directions.
I therefore bow down in reverence.

If a person who has planted roots of goodness
retains doubts, then the flower will not open.
If one's mind of faith is pure,
the flower will open and one will then see the Buddha.

正體字

043b20 ‖	十方現在佛	以種種因緣
043b21 ‖	歎彼佛功德	我今歸命禮
043b22 ‖	其土[6]甚嚴飾	殊彼[7]諸天宮
043b23 ‖	功德甚深厚	是故禮佛足
043b24 ‖	佛足千輻輪	柔軟蓮華色
043b25 ‖	見者皆歡喜	頭面禮佛足
043b26 ‖	眉間白毫光	猶如清淨月
043b27 ‖	增益面光色	頭面禮佛足
043b28 ‖	本求佛道時	行諸奇妙事
043b29 ‖	如諸經所說	頭面稽首禮
043c01 ‖	彼佛所言說	破除諸罪根
043c02 ‖	美言多所益	我今稽首禮
043c03 ‖	以此美言說	救諸著樂病
043c04 ‖	已度今猶度	是故稽首禮
043c05 ‖	人天中最尊	諸天頭面禮
043c06 ‖	七寶冠摩[8]足	是故我歸命
043c07 ‖	一切賢聖眾	及諸人天眾
043c08 ‖	咸皆共歸命	是故我亦禮
043c09 ‖	乘彼八道船	能度難度海
043c10 ‖	自度亦度彼	我禮自在者

简体字

十方现在佛	以种种因缘
叹彼佛功德	我今归命礼
其土甚严饰	殊彼诸天宫
功德甚深厚	是故礼佛足
佛足千辐轮	柔软莲华色
见者皆欢喜	头面礼佛足
眉间白毫光	犹如清净月
增益面光色	头面礼佛足
本求佛道时	行诸奇妙事
如诸经所说	头面稽首礼
彼佛所言说	破除诸罪根
美言多所益	我今稽首礼
以此美言说	救诸着乐病
已度今犹度	是故稽首礼
人天中最尊	诸天头面礼
七宝冠摩足	是故我归命
一切贤圣众	及诸人天众
咸皆共归命	是故我亦礼
乘彼八道船	能度难度海
自度亦度彼	我礼自在者

For many different reasons,
the buddhas of the present throughout the ten directions
praise the qualities of that buddha.
Taking refuge in him, I now bow down in reverence.

His land is especially majestic in its adornment,
surpassing in its excellence the palaces of all the devas.
Its qualities are especially profound and abundant.
I therefore bow down in reverence at the feet of the Buddha.

The Buddha's feet carry the sign of the thousand-spoked wheel.
They are soft and, in appearance, resemble the blossoms of a lotus.
Those who see them are all filled with delight
and bow down their heads in reverence at the feet of the Buddha.

The light from the white hair tuft between his brows
appears like a pristinely shining moon,
enhancing the radiance displayed by his countenance.
I bow down in reverence at the feet of the Buddha.

When he originally sought out the path to buddhahood,
he performed all manner of distinctive and marvelous works.
These are just as described in the sutras.
I bow down in reverence to him.

That which is proclaimed by that buddha
eliminates the roots of karmic offenses.
His eloquent discourse brings benefit to many.
I now bow down in reverence to him.

By resorting to such eloquent discourse,
he rescues beings from all maladies arising by clinging to pleasures.
He has already liberated such beings and now liberates yet more.
I therefore bow down in reverence to him.

The devas bow down in reverence
to he who is the most honored of all humans and devas.
Their seven-jeweled crowns are brought low and touch his feet.
I do therefore take refuge in him.

The Sangha of all the Worthies and the Āryas
as well as the multitudes of humans and devas
all join in taking refuge in him.
Therefore I too bow down in reverence to him.

One who boards his ship of the eight-fold path,
will be able to cross beyond that sea so difficult to cross,
delivering himself to liberation while liberating others as well.
I bow in reverence to he who has achieved sovereign mastery in this.

正體字

043c11 ‖ 諸佛無量劫　讚揚其功德
043c12 ‖ 猶尚不能盡　歸命清淨人
043c13 ‖ 我今亦如是　稱讚無量德
043c14 ‖ 以是福因緣　願佛常念我
043c15 ‖ 我於今先世　福德若大小
043c16 ‖ 願我於佛所　心常得清淨
043c17 ‖ 以此福因緣　所獲上妙德
043c18 ‖ 願諸眾生類　皆亦悉當得
043c19 ‖ 又亦應念毘婆尸佛。尸棄佛。毘首婆[9]伏佛。
043c20 ‖ 拘樓珊提佛。迦那迦牟尼佛。迦葉佛。釋迦牟
043c21 ‖ 尼佛。及未來世彌勒佛。皆應憶念禮拜以043c22 ‖偈稱讚。
043c23 ‖ 毘婆尸世尊　無憂道樹下
043c24 ‖ 成就一切智　微妙諸功德
043c25 ‖ 正觀於世間　其心得解脫
043c26 ‖ 我今以五體　歸命無上尊
043c27 ‖ 尸棄佛世尊　在於邠[10]他利
043c28 ‖ 道場樹下坐　成就於菩提
043c29 ‖ 身色無有比　如然紫金山
044a01 ‖ 我今自歸命　三界無上尊
044a02 ‖ 毘首婆世尊　坐娑羅樹下
044a03 ‖ 自然得通達　一切妙智慧

简体字

诸佛无量劫　赞扬其功德
犹尚不能尽　归命清净人
我今亦如是　称赞无量德
以是福因缘　愿佛常念我
我于今先世　福德若大小
愿我于佛所　心常得清净
以此福因缘　所获上妙德
愿诸众生类　皆亦悉当得

又亦应念毗婆尸佛。尸弃佛。毗首婆伏佛。拘楼珊提佛。迦那迦牟尼佛。迦葉佛。释迦牟尼佛。及未来世弥勒佛。皆应忆念礼拜以偈称赞。

毗婆尸世尊　无忧道树下
成就一切智　微妙诸功德
正观于世间　其心得解脱
我今以五体　归命无上尊
尸弃佛世尊　在于邠他利
道场树下坐　成就于菩提
身色无有比　如然紫金山
我今自归命　三界无上尊
毗首婆世尊　坐娑罗树下
自然得通达　一切妙智慧

If, for countless kalpas, the Buddhas
proclaimed their praises of his meritorious qualities,
they would still be unable to come to the end of them.
I take refuge in he who has become such a purified person.

In this same manner, I now proclaim
the praises of his boundless qualities.
I pray that, due to the causes and conditions of this merit,
the Buddha may therefore always bear me in mind.

By whatever merit I have created in the present or previous lives,
whether it be but little or much,
I pray that my mind will become forever purified
in the very presence of the Buddha.

As for the supremely marvelous qualities that may be acquired
through the causes and conditions of such merit as this,
I pray that all of the many varieties of beings
shall all become able to acquire them as well.

4. Also, the Seven Buddhas of the Past as Well as Maitreya

One should also bear in mind Vipaśyin Buddha, Śikhin Buddha, Viśvabhū Buddha, Krakucchanda Buddha, Kanakamuni Buddha, Kāśyapa Buddha, and Śākyamuni Buddha, as well as Maitreya, the future Buddha. One should bear them all in mind and bow down in reverence to them. I set forth their praises here in verse:

The Bhagavat Vipaśyin
abides beneath an *aśoka* bodhi tree,[10]
having perfected all-knowledge
and all of the subtle and marvelous meritorious qualities.

Having rightly contemplated the world,
his mind has succeeded in gaining liberation.
I now, with all five extremities, bow down in reverence,
taking refuge in that unsurpassable Honored One.

The Bhagavat, Śikhin Buddha,
sat in the *bodhimaṇḍa*
beneath a *puṇḍarīka* bodhi tree
where he then achieved the complete realization of bodhi.[11]

His physical appearance is incomparable.
It resembles a mountain of flaming purple gold.
I now take refuge in the Honored One
who is unsurpassed by anyone in the three realms of existence.

Viśvabhū Bhagavat
sits beneath the *śāla* tree
where he naturally acquired the penetrating comprehension
of all forms of sublime wisdom.

正體字

044a04 ║ 於諸人天中　第一無有[1]比
044a05 ║ 是故我歸命　一切最勝尊
044a06 ║ 迦求村大佛　得阿耨多羅
044a07 ║ 三藐三菩提　尸利沙樹下
044a08 ║ 成就大智慧　永脫於生死
044a09 ║ 我今歸命禮　第一無比尊
044a10 ║ 迦那含牟尼　大聖無上尊
044a11 ║ 優曇鉢樹下　成就得佛道
044a12 ║ 通達一切法　無量無有邊
044a13 ║ 是故我歸命　第一無上尊
044a14 ║ 迦葉佛世尊　眼如雙蓮華
044a15 ║ [2]弱拘樓陀樹　於下成佛道
044a16 ║ 三界無所畏　行步如象王
044a17 ║ 我今自歸命　稽首無極尊
044a18 ║ 釋迦牟尼佛　阿輸陀樹下
044a19 ║ 降伏魔怨敵　成就無上道
044a20 ║ 面貌如滿月　清淨無瑕塵
044a21 ║ 我今稽首禮　勇猛第一尊
044a22 ║ 當來彌勒佛　那伽樹下坐
044a23 ║ 成就[3]廣大心　自然得佛道

简体字

于诸人天中　第一无有比
是故我归命　一切最胜尊
迦求村大佛　得阿耨多罗
三藐三菩提　尸利沙树下
成就大智慧　永脱于生死
我今归命礼　第一无比尊
迦那含牟尼　大圣无上尊
优昙钵树下　成就得佛道
通达一切法　无量无有边
是故我归命　第一无上尊
迦葉佛世尊　眼如双莲华
弱拘楼陀树　于下成佛道
三界无所畏　行步如象王
我今自归命　稽首无极尊
释迦牟尼佛　阿输陀树下
降伏魔怨敌　成就无上道
面貌如满月　清净无瑕尘
我今稽首礼　勇猛第一尊
当来弥勒佛　那伽树下坐
成就广大心　自然得佛道

Among all humans and devas,
he is the foremost and without peer.
I do therefore take refuge in the Honored One
who is the most supreme among them all.

Krakucchanda Buddha
succeeded in attaining
anuttarasamyaksaṃbodhi
beneath the *śirīṣa* tree.[12]

He perfected the great wisdom,
and became forever liberated from *saṃsāra.*
I now take refuge and bow in reverence
to that supreme and incomparable Honored One.

Kanakamuni,
the great Ārya and unsurpassable Honored One,
attained the perfect realization of buddhahood
beneath the *udumbara* tree

and reached the penetrating comprehension
of all the measurelessly and boundlessly many dharmas.
I do therefore take refuge in him,
that foremost and unsurpassable Honored One.

Kāśyapa Buddha, the Bhagavat,
with eyes like a pair of lotus blossoms,
achieved the perfect realization of buddhahood
beneath the *nyagrodha* tree.

Throughout the three realms, there is nothing he fears.
His gait is like that of the king of the elephants.
I now take refuge in him, bowing down in reverence
to that insuperable Honored One.

Śākyamuni Buddha,
beneath the *aśvattha* tree,[13]
conquered Māra, the enemy,
and perfected the unsurpassed enlightenment.

His countenance is like the full moon,
pure and free of any blemish.
I now bow down in reverence
To that heroically brave and supreme Honored One.

Maitreya, the buddha of the future,
sitting beneath the *nāga* tree,
shall attain the perfect realization of the vast resolve
and then naturally realize buddhahood.

正體字

044a24 ‖ 功德甚堅牢　莫能有勝者
044a25 ‖ 是故我自歸　無比妙法王
044a26 ‖ 復有德勝佛。普明佛。勝敵佛。王相佛。相王
044a27 ‖ 佛。無量功德明自在王佛。藥王無[4]閦佛。寶
044a28 ‖ 遊行佛。寶華佛。安住佛。山王佛。亦應憶念
044a29 ‖ 恭敬禮拜以偈稱讚。
044b01 ‖ 無勝世界中　有佛號德勝
044b02 ‖ 我今稽首禮　及法寶僧寶
044b03 ‖ 隨意喜世界　有佛號普明
044b04 ‖ 我今自歸命　及法寶僧寶
044b05 ‖ 普賢世界中　有佛號勝敵
044b06 ‖ 我今歸命禮　及法寶僧寶
044b07 ‖ 善淨集世界　佛號王幢相
044b08 ‖ 我今稽首禮　及法寶僧寶
044b09 ‖ 離垢集世界　無量功德明
044b10 ‖ 自在於十方　是故稽首禮
044b11 ‖ 不誑世界中　無礙藥王佛
044b12 ‖ 我今頭面禮　及法寶僧寶
044b13 ‖ [5]今集世界中　佛號寶遊行
044b14 ‖ 我今頭面禮　及法寶僧寶

简体字

功德甚坚牢　莫能有胜者
是故我自归　无比妙法王

复有德胜佛。普明佛。胜敌佛。王相佛。相王佛。无量功德明自在王佛。药王无閦佛。宝游行佛。宝华佛。安住佛。山王佛。亦应忆念恭敬礼拜以偈称赞。

无胜世界中　有佛号德胜
我今稽首礼　及法宝僧宝
随意喜世界　有佛号普明
我今自归命　及法宝僧宝
普贤世界中　有佛号胜敌
我今归命礼　及法宝僧宝
善净集世界　佛号王幢相
我今稽首礼　及法宝僧宝
离垢集世界　无量功德明
自在于十方　是故稽首礼
不诳世界中　无碍药王佛
我今头面礼　及法宝僧宝
今集世界中　佛号宝游行
我今头面礼　及法宝僧宝

His meritorious qualities are so extremely solid and durable
that no one is able to surpass them.
I do therefore take refuge in him,
that incomparable king of the sublime Dharma.

5. Also, by Calling on Ten Other Buddhas

Additionally, there are: Supreme in Meritorious Qualities Buddha, Universal Illumination Buddha, Victorious over Adversaries Buddha, Marks of the Sovereign[14] Buddha, King of the Marks Buddha,[15] King of Measureless Qualities' Brilliance and Sovereign Mastery Buddha, Unimpeded Medicine King Buddha, Jeweled Traveler Buddha, Precious Flower Buddha, Peacefully Abiding Buddha,[16] and Mountain King Buddha. One should remain mindful of them as well, respectfully bowing in reverence to them. I set forth their praises here in verse:

In the world known as Invincible,
there is a buddha named Supreme in Meritorious Qualities.
I now bow down in reverence to him
as well as to his Dharma Jewel and his Sangha Jewel.

In a world known as Joy in Whatever One Wishes,
there is a buddha named Universal Illumination.
I now take refuge in him
as well as in his Dharma Jewel and his Sangha Jewel.

In the world known as Universal Excellence,
there is a buddha named Victorious over Adversaries.
I now take refuge in him and bow down in reverence to him
as well as to his Dharma Jewel and his Sangha Jewel.

In the world known as Accumulation of Goodness and Purity,
there is a buddha named Marks of the Sovereign's Banner.
I now bow down in reverence to him
as well as to his Dharma Jewel and his Sangha Jewel.

In the world known as Accumulation of Stainlessness,
there is a buddha named Measureless Qualities' Brilliance
whose sovereign mastery extends throughout the ten directions.
I therefore bow down in reverence to him.

In the world known as Undeceptive,
there is a buddha named Unimpeded Medicine King.
I now bow down in reverence to him
as well as to his Dharma Jewel and his Sangha Jewel.

In the world known as Present Accumulation,
there is a buddha named Jeweled Traveler.
I now bow down in reverence to him
as well as to his Dharma Jewel and his Sangha Jewel.

正體字

044b15 ‖ 美音界寶花 安立山王佛
044b16 ‖ 我今頭面禮 及法寶僧寶
044b17 ‖ 今是諸如來 住在東方界
044b18 ‖ 我以恭敬心 稱揚歸命禮
044b19 ‖ 唯願諸如來 深加以慈愍
044b20 ‖ 現身在我前 皆令[6]目得見
044b21 ‖ 復次過去未來現在諸佛。盡應總[7]念恭敬禮
044b22 ‖ 拜以偈稱讚。
044b23 ‖ 過去世諸佛 降伏眾魔怨
044b24 ‖ 以大智慧力 廣利於眾生
044b25 ‖ 彼時諸眾生 盡心皆供養
044b26 ‖ 恭敬而稱揚 是故頭面禮
044b27 ‖ 現在十方界 不可計諸佛
044b28 ‖ 其數過恒沙 無量無有邊
044b29 ‖ 慈愍諸眾生 常轉妙法輪
044c01 ‖ 是故我恭敬 歸命稽首禮
044c02 ‖ 未來世諸佛 身色如金山
044c03 ‖ 光明無有量 眾相自莊嚴
044c04 ‖ 出世度眾生 當入於涅槃
044c05 ‖ 如是諸世尊 我今頭面禮

简体字

美音界宝花 安立山王佛
我今头面礼 及法宝僧宝
今是诸如来 住在东方界
我以恭敬心 称扬归命礼
唯愿诸如来 深加以慈愍
现身在我前 皆令目得见
复次过去未来现在诸佛。尽应总念恭敬礼拜以偈称赞。
过去世诸佛 降伏众魔怨
以大智慧力 广利于众生
彼时诸众生 尽心皆供养
恭敬而称扬 是故头面礼
现在十方界 不可计诸佛
其数过恒沙 无量无有边
慈愍诸众生 常转妙法轮
是故我恭敬 归命稽首礼
未来世诸佛 身色如金山
光明无有量 众相自庄严
出世度众生 当入于涅槃
如是诸世尊 我今头面礼

In the Beautiful Sound World, there is Precious Flower Buddha.
[So too,] Peacefully Established and Mountain King Buddhas.
I now bow down in reverence to them
as well as to their Dharma jewels and sangha jewels.

All of these *tathāgatas* now abide
off in the regions to the East.
With a respectful mind, I spread their praises and,
taking refuge in them, bow down in reverence to them.

I only pray that the Tathāgatas
will bestow their deep kindness and sympathy
and thus manifest their bodies before me
so that I might be allowed to personally[17] see them all.

6. Also, by Calling on All Buddhas of the Three Times

Additionally, one should exhaustively and comprehensively bear in mind and respectfully bow in reverence to all buddhas of the past, the future, and the present. I set forth their praises here in verse:

All buddhas of the past
conquered the many *māras*, their adversaries
and, using the power of great wisdom,
provided vast benefit to beings.

The beings who existed in those eras
were entirely devoted to making offerings to them all,
showed them reverence, and proclaimed their praises.
I therefore bow down in reverence to them.

The incalculably many buddhas of the present
throughout the worlds of the ten directions
are so measurelessly and boundlessly many
as to surpass the number of sands in the Ganges River.

Out of kindness and pity for beings,
they always turn the wheel of the sublime Dharma.
I do therefore accord them respect,
take refuge in them, and bow down my head to them in reverence.

The buddhas of the future
shall appear with bodies resembling mountains of gold
that emanate measureless illumination
and display the self-adornment of their many characteristic signs.

They shall appear in the world and liberate beings,
after which they shall then enter nirvāṇa.
To all such *bhagavats* as these,
I do now bow down in reverence.

正體字

044c06 ‖ 復應憶念諸大菩薩。善意菩薩。善眼菩薩。聞
044c07 ‖ 月菩薩。尸毘王菩薩。一切勝菩薩。知大地菩
044c08 ‖ 薩。大藥菩薩。鳩舍菩薩。阿離念彌菩薩。頂生
044c09 ‖ 王菩薩。喜見菩薩。欝多羅菩薩。[8]薩和檀菩薩。
044c10 ‖ 長壽王菩薩。羼提菩薩。韋藍菩薩。睒菩薩。月
044c11 ‖ 蓋菩薩。明首菩薩。法首菩薩。[9]成利菩薩。彌
044c12 ‖ 勒菩薩。復有金剛藏菩薩。金剛首菩薩。無垢
044c13 ‖ 藏菩薩。無垢稱菩薩。除疑菩薩。無垢德菩薩。
044c14 ‖ 網明菩薩。無量明菩薩。大明菩薩。無盡意菩
044c15 ‖ 薩。意王菩薩。無邊意菩薩。日音菩薩。月音菩
044c16 ‖ 薩。美音菩薩。美音聲菩薩。大音聲菩薩。堅精
044c17 ‖ 進菩薩。常堅菩薩。堅發菩薩。[10]莊嚴王菩薩。
044c18 ‖ 常悲菩薩。常不輕菩薩。法上菩薩。法意菩薩。
044c19 ‖ 法喜菩薩。法首菩薩。法積菩薩。發精進菩薩。
044c20 ‖ 智慧菩薩。淨威德菩薩。那羅延菩薩。善思惟
044c21 ‖ 菩薩。法思惟菩薩。跋陀婆羅菩薩。法益菩薩。
044c22 ‖ 高德菩薩。師子遊行菩薩。喜根菩薩。上寶月
044c23 ‖ 菩薩。不虛德菩薩。龍德菩薩。文殊師利菩薩。
044c24 ‖ 妙音菩薩。雲音菩薩。勝意菩薩。照明菩薩。勇
044c25 ‖ 眾菩薩。勝眾菩薩。威儀菩薩。師子意菩薩。上
044c26 ‖ 意菩薩。益意菩薩。增[11]意菩薩。寶明菩薩。慧
044c27 ‖ 頂菩薩。樂說頂菩薩。有德菩薩。觀世自在王
044c28 ‖ 菩薩。陀羅尼自在王菩薩。

简体字

复应忆念诸大菩萨。善意菩萨。善眼菩萨。闻月菩萨。尸毗王菩萨。一切胜菩萨。知大地菩萨。大药菩萨。鸠舍菩萨。阿离念弥菩萨。顶生王菩萨。喜见菩萨。郁多罗菩萨。萨和檀菩萨。长寿王菩萨。羼提菩萨。韦蓝菩萨。睒菩萨。月盖菩萨。明首菩萨。法首菩萨。成利菩萨。弥勒菩萨。复有金刚藏菩萨。金刚首菩萨。无垢藏菩萨。无垢称菩萨。除疑菩萨。无垢德菩萨。网明菩萨。无量明菩萨。大明菩萨。无尽意菩萨。意王菩萨。无边意菩萨。日音菩萨。月音菩萨。美音菩萨。美音声菩萨。大音声菩萨。坚精进菩萨。常坚菩萨。坚发菩萨。庄严王菩萨。常悲菩萨。常不轻菩萨。法上菩萨。法意菩萨。法喜菩萨。法首菩萨。法积菩萨。发精进菩萨。智慧菩萨。净威德菩萨。那罗延菩萨。善思惟菩萨。法思惟菩萨。跋陀婆罗菩萨。法益菩萨。高德菩萨。师子游行菩萨。喜根菩萨。上宝月菩萨。不虚德菩萨。龙德菩萨。文殊师利菩萨。妙音菩萨。云音菩萨。胜意菩萨。照明菩萨。勇众菩萨。胜众菩萨。威仪菩萨。师子意菩萨。上意菩萨。益意菩萨。增意菩萨。宝明菩萨。慧顶菩萨。乐说顶菩萨。有德菩萨。观世自在王菩萨。陀罗尼自在王菩萨。

7. Also, by Calling on the Great Bodhisattvas

Additionally, one should bear in mind the great bodhisattvas, namely: Good Intentions Bodhisattva, Good Eyes Bodhisattva, Moon Hearer Bodhisattva, King Śibi Bodhisattva, Universally Supreme Bodhisattva, Knower of the Great Earth Bodhisattva, Great Medicine Bodhisattva, Kapotagṛha Bodhisattva, Arenemin Bodhisattva, Summit Born King Bodhisattva, Delightful View Bodhisattva, Uttara Bodhisattva, Sarvadāna Bodhisattva, Long Life King Bodhisattva, Kṣānti Bodhisattva, Velāma Bodhisattva, Flashing Light Bodhisattva, Moon Covering Bodhisattva, Brilliant Leader Bodhisattva, Dharma Leader Bodhisattva, Perfecting Benefit Bodhisattva, and Maitreya Bodhisattva.

In addition, there are: Vajragarbha Bodhisattva, Vajra Leader Bodhisattva, Treasury of Non-defilement Bodhisattva, Vimalakīrti Bodhisattva, Dispeller of Doubts Bodhisattva, Undefiled Virtue Bodhisattva, Net-like Brilliance Bodhisattva, Immeasurable Brilliance Bodhisattva, Great Brilliance Bodhisattva, Akṣayamati Bodhisattva, Mind King Bodhisattva, Boundless Mind Bodhisattva, Sun Sound Bodhisattva, Moon Sound Bodhisattva, Beautiful Sound Bodhisattva, Beautiful Voice Bodhisattva, Great Voice Bodhisattva, Solid Vigor Bodhisattva, Ever Solid Bodhisattva, and Solidly Generated Bodhisattva.

There are also: Adornment King Bodhisattva, Ever Compassionate Bodhisattva, Never slighting Bodhisattva, Dharma Superior Bodhisattva, Dharma Mind Bodhisattva, Dharma Joy Bodhisattva, Dharma Leader Bodhisattva, Dharma Accumulation Bodhisattva, Generator of Vigor Bodhisattva, Wisdom Bodhisattva, Pure Awesome Virtue Bodhisattva, Nārāyaṇa Bodhisattva, Good Meditation Bodhisattva, Dharma Meditation Bodhisattva, Bhadrapāla Bodhisattva, Dharma Benefit Bodhisattva, Lofty Virtue Bodhisattva, Lion Traveler Bodhisattva, Joyous Faculties Bodhisattva, and Supreme Jewel Moon Bodhisattva.

There are also: Virtue Free of Falseness Bodhisattva, Dragon Virtue Bodhisattva, Mañjuśrī Bodhisattva, Wonderful Sound Bodhisattva, Cloud Sound Bodhisattva, Supreme Mind Bodhisattva, Illuminating Brilliance Bodhisattva, Brave Assembly Bodhisattva, Supreme Assembly Bodhisattva, Awesome Deportment Bodhisattva, Lion Mind Bodhisattva, Superior Mind Bodhisattva, Beneficial Intentions Bodhisattva, Augmented Mind Bodhisattva, Precious Brilliance Bodhisattva, Wisdom Summit Bodhisattva, Peak of Eloquence Bodhisattva, Possessed of Virtue Bodhisattva, Avalokiteśvara King Bodhisattva, and Dhāraṇī Mastery King Bodhisattva.

正體字

大自在王菩薩。無
044c29 ‖ 憂德菩薩。不虛見菩薩。離惡道菩薩。一切勇健
045a01 ‖ 菩薩。破闇菩薩。功德寶菩薩。花威德菩薩。金
045a02 ‖ 瓔珞明德菩薩。離諸陰蓋菩薩。心無閡菩薩。
045a03 ‖ 一切行淨菩薩。等見菩薩。不等見菩薩。三昧
045a04 ‖ 遊戲菩薩。法自在菩薩。法相菩薩。明莊嚴菩
045a05 ‖ 薩。大莊嚴菩薩。寶頂菩薩。寶印手菩薩。常舉
045a06 ‖ 手菩薩。常下手菩薩。常慘菩薩。常喜菩薩。喜
045a07 ‖ 王菩薩。得辯才音聲菩薩。虛空雷音菩薩。持
045a08 ‖ 寶炬菩薩。勇施菩薩。帝網菩薩。馬光菩薩。空
045a09 ‖ 無閡菩薩。寶勝菩薩。天王菩薩。破魔菩薩。電
045a10 ‖ 德菩薩。自在菩薩。頂相菩薩。出過菩薩。師子
045a11 ‖ 吼菩薩。雲蔭菩薩。能勝菩薩。山相[1]幢王菩
045a12 ‖ 薩。香象菩薩。大香象菩薩。白香象菩薩。常精
045a13 ‖ 進菩薩。不休息菩薩。妙生菩薩。華莊嚴菩薩。
045a14 ‖ 觀世音菩薩。得大勢菩薩。水王菩薩。山王菩
045a15 ‖ 薩。帝網菩薩。寶施菩薩。破魔菩薩。莊嚴國土
045a16 ‖ 菩薩。金髻菩薩。珠髻菩薩。如是等諸大菩
045a17 ‖ 薩。皆應憶念恭敬禮拜求阿惟越致[2]地。[3]

简体字

大自在王菩萨。无忧德菩萨。不虚见菩萨。离恶道菩萨。一切勇健菩萨。破闇菩萨。功德宝菩萨。花威德菩萨。金璎珞明德菩萨。离诸阴盖菩萨。心无阂菩萨。一切行净菩萨。等见菩萨。不等见菩萨。三昧游戏菩萨。法自在菩萨。法相菩萨。明庄严菩萨。大庄严菩萨。宝顶菩萨。宝印手菩萨。常举手菩萨。常下手菩萨。常惨菩萨。常喜菩萨。喜王菩萨。得辩才音声菩萨。虚空雷音菩萨。持宝炬菩萨。勇施菩萨。帝网菩萨。马光菩萨。空无阂菩萨。宝胜菩萨。天王菩萨。破魔菩萨。电德菩萨。自在菩萨。顶相菩萨。出过菩萨。师子吼菩萨。云荫菩萨。能胜菩萨。山相幢王菩萨。香象菩萨。大香象菩萨。白香象菩萨。常精进菩萨。不休息菩萨。妙生菩萨。华庄严菩萨。观世音菩萨。得大势菩萨。水王菩萨。山王菩萨。帝网菩萨。宝施菩萨。破魔菩萨。庄严国土菩萨。金髻菩萨。珠髻菩萨。如是等诸大菩萨。皆应忆念恭敬礼拜求阿惟越致地。

There are also: Great Sovereign Mastery King Bodhisattva, Sorrowless Virtue Bodhisattva, Not Seen in Vain Bodhisattva, Beyond the Wretched Destinies Bodhisattva, Universally Brave and Strong Bodhisattva, Dispeller of Darkness Bodhisattva, Merit Jewel Bodhisattva, Floral Awesome Virtue Bodhisattva, Gold Necklace Brilliant Virtue Bodhisattva, Beyond the Aggregates and Hindrances Bodhisattva, Unimpeded Mind Bodhisattva, Pure in All Actions Bodhisattva, Equal Vision Bodhisattva, Unequaled Vision Bodhisattva, Wandering Joyfully in Samādhi Bodhisattva, Sovereign Mastery in Dharma Bodhisattva, Dharma Marks Bodhisattva, Brilliant Adornment Bodhisattva, Great Adornment Bodhisattva, and Jeweled Summit Bodhisattva.

There are also: Jeweled Mudrā Hand Bodhisattva, Ever Raised Hand Bodhisattva, Ever Lowered Hand Bodhisattva, Ever Piteous Bodhisattva, Ever Joyful Bodhisattva, Joy King Bodhisattva, Possessed of Eloquent Voice Bodhisattva, Sound of Thunder in Space Bodhisattva, Upholder of the Jeweled Torch Bodhisattva, Valiant Giving Bodhisattva, Imperial Net Bodhisattva, Horse Light Bodhisattva, Empty and Unimpeded Bodhisattva, Jeweled Supremacy Bodhisattva, Celestial King Bodhisattva, Demon Crusher Bodhisattva, Lightning Virtue Bodhisattva, Sovereign Mastery Bodhisattva, Summit Sign Bodhisattva, and Beyond Transgressions Bodhisattva.

And there are also: Lion's Roar Bodhisattva, Cloud Shade Bodhisattva, Able to Conquer Bodhisattva, Mountainous Marks Banner Bodhisattva, Fragrant Elephant Bodhisattva, Great Fragrant Elephant Bodhisattva, White Fragrant Elephant Bodhisattva, Ever Vigorous Bodhisattva, Never Resting Bodhisattva, Sublime Birth Bodhisattva, Floral Adornment Bodhisattva, Avalokiteśvara Bodhisattva, Mahāsthāmaprāpta Bodhisattva, Water King Bodhisattva, Mountain King Bodhisattva, Indra's Net Bodhisattva, Jewel Giving Bodhisattva, Crusher of Demons Bodhisattva, Adorner of Lands Bodhisattva, Golden Topknot Bodhisattva, and Pearl Topknot Bodhisattva.

One should bear in mind all such bodhisattvas and bow down to them in reverence as one seeks to attain the ground of the *avaivartika.*

The End of Chapter Nine

Part One Endnotes

1. These *ślokas* correspond to *ślokas* 24–28 of Nāgārjuna's *Bodhisambhāra Śāstra.* In my English translation of that entire text with its Indian commentary, they read as follows:

    So long as he has not generated great compassion or the patiences,
    even though he may have gained an irreversibility,
    the bodhisattva is still subject to a form of "dying"
    which occurs through allowing negligence to arise.

    The grounds of the *śrāvaka* disciples or the *pratyekabuddhas*,
    if entered, become for him the same as dying
    because he would thereby sever the bodhisattva's
    roots of understanding and awareness.

    Even at the prospect of falling into the hell-realms,
    the bodhisattva would not be struck with fright.
    The grounds of the *śrāvaka* disciples and the *pratyekabuddhas*, however,
    do provoke a great terror in him.

    It is not the case that falling into the hell realms
    would bring about an ultimate obstacle to his bodhi.
    The grounds of the *śrāvaka* disciples and the *pratyekabuddhas*, however,
    do create just such an ultimate obstacle.

    Just as is said of he who loves long life,
    that he becomes fearful at the prospect of his own beheading,
    so too, the grounds of the *śrāvaka* disciples and *pratyekabuddhas*
    should bring about a fearfulness of just this sort.

2. The first two quatrains correspond to the *Bodhisambhāra Śāstra*'s *śloka* numbers 22 and 23 which read as follows:

    In the bodhisattva's striving for bodhi,
    so long as he has not yet gained irreversibility,
    he acts as urgently as the person whose turban has caught fire.
    Thus one should take up just such intensely diligent practice.

    Thus it is that those bodhisattvas,
    when striving for the realization of bodhi,
    should not rest in their practice of vigor,
    for they have shouldered such a heavy burden.

3. These last two quatrains correspond to the *Bodhisambhāra Śāstra*'s *śloka* numbers 91 and 92 which read as follows:

    Even if one were to take up the vehicle of the *śrāvaka* disciples
    or the vehicle of the *pratyekabuddhas*,
    and hence practiced solely for one's own self benefit,

still, one would not relinquish the enduring practice of vigor.

How much the less could it be that a great man,
one committed to liberate himself and liberate others,
might somehow not generate
a measure of vigor a thousand *koṭis* times greater?

4. I emend here the verse-abbreviated "Three Practices Buddha" reading to "Three *Vehicles* Practices Buddha" to accord with the explanatory text which follows at 42a02–06.

5. See *The Sutra on the Youth Precious Moon's Questions on Dharma* (大乘寶月童子問法經 / T14n0437_p108c01–110a07). The names vary, but the ideas are the same, i.e. sincere mindfulness of ten buddhas in the ten directions can bring irreversibility with respect to one's future attainment of buddhahood.

6. "*Candana*" usually refers to sandalwood, but as noted in MW, it may also be used as a term to refer to anything that is the most excellent of its kind. MW: "mn. sandal (*Sirium myrtifolium*, either the tree, wood, or the unctuous preparation of the wood held in high estimation as perfumes; hence; a term for anything which is the most excellent of its kind."

7. The Chinese translation for this eightieth buddha's name, *guangming fo* (光明佛), "Light Buddha," is duplicated in the name of the ninety-sixth buddha (see next paragraph). Since we do not know the Sanskrit antecedents for these two buddhas' names, I have distinguished them here with slightly variant English translations ("Light Buddha," "Radiance Buddha").

8. The Chinese translation for this ninety-sixth buddha's name, *guangming fo* (光明佛), "Radiance Buddha," is duplicated in the name of the eightieth buddha (see previous paragraph). Since we do not know the Sanskrit antecedents for these two buddhas' names, I have distinguished them here with slightly variant English translations ("Light Buddha," "Radiance Buddha").

9. On sensibility grounds, I adopt here the SYMG editions' variant, *hua yuan fo* (華園佛), "Floral Garden Buddha," to correct what seems to be a graphic-similarity scribal error in the *Taisho* edition, *hua chi fo* (華齒佛), "Floral Teeth Buddha."

10. I reconstruct "*aśoka*," lit. "sorrowless" as the name of this bodhi tree as it is a tree that grows throughout India (*Saraca asoca*) and is in fact said to also be the same kind of tree under which the historical Buddha's mother gave birth to him.

11. VB provides the following citation: "See DN II 4: *Sikhī, bhikkhave, bhagavā arahaṃ sammāsambuddho puṇḍarīkassa mūle abhisambuddho.*"

12. The *śirīṣa* tree is identified by MW as *acacia sirissa.*
13. An *"aśvattha"* tree is an ancient name for what is more commonly known in Buddhist texts as the "bodhi" tree (*ficus religiosa*).
14. In the verses below (at 44b07), this Buddha's name is enhanced with an additional character to "Marks of the Sovereign's Canopy" (王幢相).
15. I suspect that there should only be ten buddhas in this list and that this buddha's name may appear here only as a result of an accidental scribal redundancy, this for two reasons:
    a) The Chinese name is identical to that of the previously listed buddha except that the characters are in reverse order (*wangxiang* [王相] versus *xiangwang* [相王]); and
    b) Although the other ten buddhas' names are mentioned in the following praise verses, this buddha's name is not mentioned there at all.
16. This buddha's name is only slightly different in the verses that follow, occurring there (at 44b15) as "Peacefully Established" (安立).
17. I emend the reading of the reading here by preferring the *zi* (自), "personally," of the SYMG editions to the *mu* (目), "eyes" of the *Taisho* text, this to correct an apparent graphic-similarity scribal error.

Part One Variant Readings in Other Chinese Editions

Fascicle Five Variant Readings

[0040012] 不分卷【宋】【元】【明】【宮】
[0041001] 行佛＝乘行【明】，＝乘行佛【宮】
[0041002] 〔就〕－【宋】【元】【明】【宮】
[0041003] 其＝道【宋】【元】【明】【宮】
[0041004] 垍＝埠【宋】【元】【宮】，＝塠【明】
[0041005] 〔供〕－【宋】【元】【明】【宮】
[0041006] 廣＝演【宋】【元】【明】【宮】
[0041007] 惑＝或【宋】【元】【明】【宮】
[0041008] 善＋（解）【宋】【元】【明】
[0042001] 〔今現在說法其佛〕－【宮】
[0042002] 弟子福＝福弟子【宋】【元】
[0042003] 〔今〕－【宋】【元】【明】，今＋（現在說法）【宮】
[0042004] （此）＋偈【宋】【元】【明】【宮】
[0042005] 人天＝天人【宋】【元】【明】【宮】
[0042006] 煩＝憂【宋】【元】【明】【宮】
[0042007] 明註曰三乘行南藏作三行佛
[0042008] 阿彌乃至薩十字宋元明三本俱作長行
[0042009] 意＝音【宮】
[0042010] 珠＝殊【宋】【元】【明】【宮】
[0042011] 鬘＝鬚【宮】
[0042012] 生＝王【宋】【元】【明】【宮】
[0043001] 映＝歎【宋】【元】【明】【宮】
[0043002] 齒＝園【宋】【元】【明】【宮】
[0043003] 增＝示【宋】【元】【明】【宮】
[0043004] 威＝功【宋】【元】【明】【宮】
[0043005] 王＝主【宋】【元】【明】【宮】
[0043006] 甚＝具【宋】【元】【明】【宮】
[0043007] 諸＝之【宮】
[0043008] 足＝尼【宋】【元】【明】【宮】
[0043009] 〔伏〕－【宋】【元】【明】【宮】
[0043010] 他＝陀【宋】【元】【明】，＝地【宮】
[0044001] 比＝上【宋】【元】【明】【宮】
[0044002] 弱＝尼【宋】【元】【明】【宮】
[0044003] 廣＝曠【宋】【元】【明】【宮】
[0044004] 閡＝礙【宋】【元】【明】【宮】下同
[0044005] 今＝金【宋】【元】【明】【宮】
[0044006] 目＝自【宋】【元】【明】【宮】

[0044007] 念＝令【明】
[0044008] 薩＝和【宋】【元】【明】【宮】
[0044009] 成＝法【宋】【元】【明】【宮】
[0044010] 莊嚴王＝堅莊【宋】【元】【明】【宮】
[0044011] 意＝益【宋】【元】【明】【宮】
[0045001] 幢＝博【宋】【元】【宮】
[0045002] 地＝也【宋】【元】【明】，地＋（也）【宮】
[0045003] 卷第四終【宋】【元】【明】【宮】

Nāgārjuna
on
Mindfulness of the Buddha

Part 2: The Pratuyutpanna Samādhi

Nāgārjuna's *Treatise on the Ten Grounds,* Chs. 20–25

As Translated into Chinese by Tripiṭaka Master Kumārajīva
English Translation by Bhikshu Dharmamitra

正體字

068c07 ‖ 念佛品第二十
068c08 ‖ 菩薩於初地。究[9]竟所行處。自以善根力能
068c09 ‖ 見數百佛菩薩。如是[10]降伏其心深愛佛
068c10 ‖ 道。如所聞初地行具足究竟。自以善根福德
068c11 ‖ 力故能見十方現在諸佛皆在目前。問曰。
068c12 ‖ 但以善根福德力故得見諸佛。為更有餘
068c13 ‖ 法耶。答曰。
068c14 ‖ 佛為跋陀婆　所說深三昧
068c15 ‖ 得是三昧寶　能得見諸佛
068c16 ‖ 跋陀婆羅是在家菩薩。能行頭陀。佛為是菩
068c17 ‖ 薩說般舟[11]三昧經。般舟三昧名見諸佛現
068c18 ‖ 前菩薩。得是大寶三昧。雖未得天眼天耳
068c19 ‖ 而能得見十方諸佛。亦聞諸佛所說經法。
068c20 ‖ 問曰。是三昧者當以何道可得。

简体字

念佛品第二十

菩萨于初地。究竟所行处。自以善根力能见数百佛菩萨。如是降伏其心深爱佛道。如所闻初地行具足究竟。自以善根福德力故能见十方现在诸佛皆在目前。问曰。但以善根福德力故得见诸佛。为更有余法耶。答曰。

佛为跋陀婆　所说深三昧
得是三昧宝　能得见诸佛

跋陀婆罗是在家菩萨。能行头陀。佛为是菩萨说般舟三昧经。般舟三昧名见诸佛现前菩萨。得是大宝三昧。虽未得天眼天耳而能得见十方诸佛。亦闻诸佛所说经法。问曰。是三昧者当以何道可得。

Part Two
The Pratyutpanna Samādhi

Ch. 20: Mindfulness of the Buddhas

I. Chapter 20: Mindfulness of the Buddhas

A. On Finishing 1st Ground Practices, the Bodhisattva Sees Buddhas

When the bodhisattva dwelling on the first ground
has completed what is to be practiced,
due to the power of his roots of goodness, he will naturally
be able to see several hundred buddhas.[1]

When, in this [above-discussed] manner, the bodhisattva subdues his own mind, he develops a deep love for the path to buddhahood. He then completely fulfills the first-ground practices in accordance with the way he learned them. Then, due to the power of his roots of goodness and merit, he is naturally able to see the present-era buddhas of the ten directions right before his very eyes.

1. Q: Is There Any Other Way to Be Able to See the Buddhas?

Question: Is it solely through the power of roots of goodness and merit that one is then able to see buddhas or is there some other method by which one can do so?

2. A: On Entering the Pratyutpanna Samādhi, One Sees the Buddhas

Response:

There is a deep samādhi that the Buddha
explained for the sake of Bhadrapāla.
If one acquires this samādhi treasure,
one becomes able to see the Buddhas.

Bhadrapāla was a lay bodhisattva well able to practice the *dhūta* austerities. It was for the sake of this bodhisattva that the Buddha spoke the *Pratyutpanna Samādhi Sūtra*.[2] The *pratyutpanna* samādhi is one in which one sees the Buddhas right before one's very eyes. When the bodhisattva accesses this magnificently precious samādhi, even though he might not yet have gained the heavenly eye and heavenly ear, he is nonetheless able to see the buddhas of the ten directions and he is also able to listen to the Dharma of the sutras being taught by those buddhas.

3. Q: How Can One Acquire This Samadhi?

Question: What means should one use to acquire this samādhi?

正體字

答曰。

068c21 ‖ 當念於諸佛　處在大眾中
068c22 ‖ 三十二相具　八十好嚴身
068c23 ‖ 行者以是三昧念諸佛三十二相八十種好
068c24 ‖ 莊嚴其身。比丘親近諸天供養。為諸大眾
068c25 ‖ 恭敬圍繞。專心憶念取諸佛相。又念諸佛
068c26 ‖ 是大願者。成就大悲而不斷絕。具足大慈
068c27 ‖ 深安眾生。行於大喜滿一切願。行於捨心
068c28 ‖ 捨離憎愛不捨眾生。行於諦處常不欺
068c29 ‖ 誑。行於捨處淨除慳垢。行於善處其心善
069a01 ‖ 寂。行於慧處得大智慧。具行檀波羅蜜為
069a02 ‖ 法施主。具行尸羅波羅蜜戒行清淨。具行
069a03 ‖ 羼提波羅蜜能忍如地。具行毘梨耶波羅
069a04 ‖ 蜜精進超絕。具行禪波羅蜜滅諸定障。具
069a05 ‖ 行般若波羅蜜破智慧障閡。

简体字

答曰。

当念于诸佛　处在大众中
三十二相具　八十好严身

行者以是三昧念诸佛三十二相八十种好庄严其身。比丘亲近诸天供养。为诸大众恭敬围绕。专心忆念取诸佛相。又念诸佛是大愿者。成就大悲而不断绝。具足大慈深安众生。行于大喜满一切愿。行于舍心舍离憎爱不舍众生。行于谛处常不欺诳。行于舍处净除悭垢。行于善处其心善寂。行于慧处得大智慧。具行檀波罗蜜为法施主。具行尸罗波罗蜜戒行清净。具行羼提波罗蜜能忍如地。具行毗梨耶波罗蜜精进超绝。具行禅波罗蜜灭诸定障。具行般若波罗蜜破智慧障阂。

4. A: Envision the Buddhas with the 32 Marks and 80 Characteristics

Response:

One should bring to mind the Buddhas,
envisioning them as residing in a great assembly,
replete with all thirty-two major marks
and eighty secondary characteristics adorning their bodies.

a. Recollection of the Buddhas' Qualities and Accomplishments

In cultivating this samādhi, the practitioner brings to mind the Buddhas with the thirty-two major marks and eighty secondary characteristics gracing their bodies, with bhikshus close by, with devas making offerings, and with a grand and reverential assembly surrounding them. With focused mind, one envisions each of the major marks of those buddhas.

One also recollects the Buddhas as those who are possessed of great vows, recollects their perfection of the great compassion and the fact that it has not been cut off, recollects their perfection of the great kindness through which they bring profound peace to beings, recollects their practice of the great sympathetic joy and their fulfillment of beings' aspirations, and recollects their practice of equanimity through which they have abandoned aversion and craving and do not abandon beings.

One also recollects their practice of the truthfulness basis of meritorious qualities by which they are never deceptive, recollects their practice of the relinquishment basis of meritorious qualities by which they have rid themselves of the miserliness defilement, recollects their practice of the thorough [quiescence][3] basis of meritorious qualities by which their minds maintain a state of thorough-going quiescence, and recollects their practice of the wisdom basis of meritorious qualities through which they have acquired great wisdom.[4]

One recollects too their perfect practice of *dāna pāramitā* by which they have become the lords of Dharma giving, their perfect practice of *śīla pāramitā* by which their observance of the moral precepts is pure, their perfect practice of *kṣānti pāramitā* by which their capacity for patient endurance is analogous to that of the earth, their perfect practice of *vīrya pāramitā* by which their vigor is preeminent, their perfect practice of *dhyāna pāramitā* by which they have destroyed all hindrances to meditative absorption, and their perfect practice of *prajñā pāramitā* by which they have destroyed all obstacles to wisdom.

b. Recollection of the 32 Marks of the Buddhas

One recollects too:

正體字

手足輪相能
069a06 ‖ 轉法輪。足安立相安住諸法。手足網縵相
069a07 ‖ 滅諸煩惱。七處滿相諸功德滿。手足柔軟相
069a08 ‖ 說柔和法。纖長指相長夜修集諸善妙法。
069a09 ‖ 足跟廣相眼廣學廣。大直身相說大直道。足
069a10 ‖ 趺高相一切中[1]高毛上旋相能令眾生住上
069a11 ‖ 妙法。伊[2]泥鹿[[跳-兆+專]>[跳-兆+專]]相[[跳-兆+專]>[跳-兆+專]]傭漸麁。臂長過膝相
069a12 ‖ 臂如金[3]關。陰馬藏相有法寶藏。身金色相
069a13 ‖ 有無量色。皮細薄相說細妙法。一一毛相示
069a14 ‖ 一相法。白毫莊嚴面相樂觀佛面無厭。師
069a15 ‖ 子上身相如師子無畏。肩圓大相善分別五
069a16 ‖ 陰。

简体字

手足轮相能转法轮。足安立相安住诸法。手足网缦相灭诸烦恼。七处满相诸功德满。手足柔软相说柔和法。纤长指相长夜修集诸善妙法。足跟广相眼广学广。大直身相说大直道。足趺高相一切中高毛上旋相能令众生住上妙法。伊泥鹿[跳-兆+專]相[跳-兆+專]佣渐粗。臂长过膝相臂如金关。阴马藏相有法宝藏。身金色相有无量色。皮细薄相说细妙法。一一毛相示一相法。白毫庄严面相乐观佛面无厌。师子上身相如师子无畏。肩圆大相善分别五阴。

Their mark of having the wheel insignia on the hands and feet, emblematic of their ability to turn the wheel of Dharma;
Their mark of securely planted feet, emblematic of their standing securely in every dharma;
Their mark of proximal webbing on fingers and toes, emblematic of the extinguishing of all afflictions;
Their mark of seven places of fullness, emblematic of their complete fulfillment of merit;
Their mark of soft and tender hands and feet, emblematic of their harmonious manner of proclaiming the Dharma;
Their mark of slender and long fingers and toes, emblematic of their cultivation and accumulation of every sort of good and sublime dharma during the long night [of previous lifetimes];
Their mark of having broad heels and wide eyes, emblematic of their vast learning;
Their mark of having a large and erect body, emblematic of their proclamation of the great and upright Dharma;
Their mark of having high arches, emblematic of their being lofty in all things;
Their mark of having upwardly spiraling bodily hairs, emblematic of their ability to cause beings to abide in the supreme and sublime dharma;
Their mark of having legs gradually growing in thickness like those of the *aiṇeya* antelope;
Their mark of long arms reaching past the knees, their arms appearing like golden gate bars;[5]
Their mark of the stallion-like retracted male organ, emblematic of their possession of the treasury of Dharma jewels;
Their mark of the golden-hued body emanating light of countless colors;
Their mark of fine and thin skin, emblematic of their proclamation of subtle and sublime Dharma;
Their mark of one hair per hair pore, emblematic of their revealing of the single-mark Dharma;
Their mark of the [mid-brow] white-down tuft adorning the countenance, due to which beings happily and tirelessly gaze at the Buddha's face;
Their mark of a lion-like upper torso, emblematic of the Buddha, like the lion, being one who is fearless;
Their mark of round and large shoulders, emblematic of their ability to make skillful distinctions regarding the nature of the five aggregates;

正體字

腋下滿相滿大善根。得味味相具足寂滅
069a17 ‖ 味。方身相破生死[4]畏。肉髻相頭未嘗低敬。
069a18 ‖ 舌大相色如真珊瑚能自覆面。梵音相身
069a19 ‖ 相至梵天。師子頰車相肩廣相能破外道。齒
069a20 ‖ 齊相行清白[5]禪。齒平等相平等心於一切眾
069a21 ‖ 生。齒密[6]緻相離諸貪著。四十齒相具足四
069a22 ‖ 十不共法。紺青眼相慈心視眾生。牛王睫相
069a23 ‖ 睫長不亂。得希有色樂見無厭。以此三十
069a24 ‖ 二相莊嚴其身。八十種好間錯映發。福德具
069a25 ‖ 足威力殊絕名聞流布。戒香塗身世法所不
069a26 ‖ 動。諸煩惱所不染。

简体字

腋下满相满大善根。得味味相具足寂灭味。方身相破生死畏。肉髻相头未尝低敬。舌大相色如真珊瑚能自覆面。梵音相身相至梵天。师子颊车相肩广相能破外道。齿齐相行清白禅。齿平等相平等心于一切众生。齿密致相离诸贪着。四十齿相具足四十不共法。绀青眼相慈心视众生。牛王睫相睫长不乱。得希有色乐见无厌。以此三十二相庄严其身。八十种好间错映发。福德具足威力殊绝名闻流布。戒香涂身世法所不动。诸烦恼所不染。

Their mark of fullness in the sub-axillary region, emblematic of their possession of a full measure of good roots;
Their mark of distinguishing every flavor, emblematic of their having perfectly tasted the flavor of quiescence;
Their mark of having a square-set body, emblematic of having crushed the fear of births and deaths;
Their mark of the fleshy prominence atop the crown, emblematic of their heads never having to be lowered in reverence [to someone superior];
Their mark of the large tongue the color of real coral that is even able to cover the face;
Their mark of the Brahmā-like voice and the physical mark that reaches even to the Brahma Heaven;
Their mark of the lion-like jaw;
Their mark of the broad shoulders, these being emblematic of their ability to demolish [the views held by] non-Buddhist traditions;
Their mark of even teeth, emblematic of their practice of pure *dhyāna* meditation;
Their mark of their teeth being of even height, emblematic of their minds' equal regard for all beings;
Their mark of closely set teeth, emblematic of their abandonment of the desires;
Their mark of having forty teeth, emblematic of their perfection of the forty dharmas exclusive to buddhas;
Their mark of blue eyes, emblematic of their looking on beings with minds imbued with kindness;
Their mark of having eyelashes like those of the royal bull, with the lashes long and in no way disarrayed;
Their obtaining of a rare physical form that beings look on without ever tiring of holding it in their gaze;
Their having bodies adorned with these thirty-two marks;

c. Recollection of Other Qualities of the Buddhas

Their having the eighty minor characteristics like inlaid adornments on their bodies, emanating brilliant radiance;
Their complete fulfillment of merit;
Their transcendently supreme and awesome powers;
Their wide-spread illustrious esteem;
Their bodies' incense-like fragrance produced by purity in observing the moral precepts;
Their invulnerability to being moved by worldly dharmas;
Their ability to remain undefiled by any arising of afflictions;

正體字

惡言所不污。遊戲諸
069a27 ‖ 神通。諸佛如是威力猛盛無敢當者。以慧
069a28 ‖ 說法如師子吼如意自在。以精進力破諸
069a29 ‖ 癡闇。以大光明普照天地。諸問答中最無
069b01 ‖ 有上。一切仰瞻無下觀者。常以慈心觀察
069b02 ‖ 眾生。念如大海。定如須彌。忍辱如地。增長
069b03 ‖ 眾[7]主所種福德如水滋潤。能生眾生諸善
069b04 ‖ 根力如風開發。成就眾生如火熟物。智慧
069b05 ‖ 無邊猶如虛空。普雨大法如大密雲。不染
069b06 ‖ 世法猶如蓮華。[8]破外道[9]師如師子搏鹿。
069b07 ‖ 能舉重擔如大象王。能導大眾如大牛王。
069b08 ‖ 眷屬清淨如轉輪王。世間最上如大梵王。

简体字

恶言所不污。游戏诸神通。诸佛如是威力猛盛无敢当者。以慧说法如师子吼如意自在。以精进力破诸痴闇。以大光明普照天地。诸问答中最无有上。一切仰瞻无下观者。常以慈心观察众生。念如大海。定如须弥。忍辱如地。增长众主所种福德如水滋润。能生众生诸善根力如风开发。成就众生如火熟物。智慧无边犹如虚空。普雨大法如大密云。不染世法犹如莲华。破外道师如师子搏鹿。能举重担如大象王。能导大众如大牛王。眷属清净如转轮王。世间最上如大梵王。

Their ability to remain unsullied by others' verbal abuse;
Their ability to roam and sport through use of their spiritual powers;
The ability of the Buddhas to be so intensely magnificent in the manifestation of their awe-inspiring powers that no one would dare obstruct them;
Their freely exercised sovereign mastery in using wisdom to proclaim the Dharma that is like the roaring of a lion;
Their ability to dispel the darkness of delusion by marshaling the power of vigor;
Their use of magnificent brilliance to everywhere illuminate the heavens and the earth;
Their utter invincibility in debate;
Their being such that everyone looks up to them and no one can look down on them;
Their constancy in regarding all beings with kindness;
Their possession of mindfulness as vast as the great oceans;
Their meditative absorption that is like Mount Sumeru [in its unshakability];
Their possession of patience comparable to the earth's [ability to endure anything];
Their ability to bring about growth in the merit planted by beings that is analogous [to the growth-enhancing capacity of] water's moisture;[6]
Their ability to bring forth roots of goodness in beings that, in its power, is like the rising of the wind;
Their ability to ripen beings that is like fire's ability to cook things;
Their possession of wisdom as boundless as empty space;
Their universal raining down of the great Dharma [rain] that is like [the rain that pours done from] immense dense clouds;
Their ability to remain unstained by worldly dharmas that is like lotus blossoms' [ability to rise from mud and yet remain unsullied by it];
Their ability, like lions pouncing on deer, to decisively refute [the doctrines of] non-Buddhist masters;
Their ability to bear a heavy burden that is like that of the great king of the elephants;
Their ability to lead a great congregation of followers that is like that of the great king of bulls;
Their possession of a retinue of pure followers that is like [the retinue of] a wheel-turning king;
Their utter supremacy in the world that is like that of the lord of the Mahābrahma Heaven;

正體字

可
069b09 ‖ 愛[10]可樂如清天明月。普照能然猶如朗
069b10 ‖ 日。與諸眾生安樂因緣。猶如仁父。憐愍眾
069b11 ‖ 生隨宜將護猶如慈母。所行清淨如天真
069b12 ‖ 金。有大勢力如天帝釋。勤利世間如護世
069b13 ‖ 主。治煩惱病猶如醫王。救諸衰患猶如親
069b14 ‖ 族。積諸功德如大庫藏。其戒無量。其定無
069b15 ‖ 邊。其慧無稱。解脫無等解脫知見無等等。
069b16 ‖ 於一切事最無有比。一切世間最無上故
069b17 ‖ 名第一人。成大法故名為[11]大人。如是菩
069b18 ‖ 薩以大人相念觀諸佛。是諸佛者於無量
069b19 ‖ 無邊百千萬億不可思議不可計劫修習功
069b20 ‖ 德。善能守護身口意業。

简体字

可爱可乐如清天明月。普照能然犹如朗日。与诸众生安乐因缘。犹如仁父。怜愍众生随宜将护犹如慈母。所行清净如天真金。有大势力如天帝释。勤利世间如护世主。治烦恼病犹如医王。救诸衰患犹如亲族。积诸功德如大库藏。其戒无量。其定无边。其慧无称。解脱无等解脱知见无等等。于一切事最无有比。一切世间最无上故名第一人。成大法故名为大人。如是菩萨以大人相念观诸佛。是诸佛者于无量无边百千万亿不可思议不可计劫修习功德。善能守护身口意业。

Their ability to inspire fondness and delight that is like that of a bright moon in the clear night sky;
Their universal illumination that is able to burn as brightly as the brilliantly shining sun;
Their bestowal on beings of the causes and conditions for peace and happiness that is like [the generosity of] a humane father;
Their acting out of pity toward beings, protecting them in whatever way is appropriate, that is like the actions of a lovingly kind mother;
Their purity of conduct that is like [the purity of] the real gold in the heavens;
Their possession of the power of great strength that is like that of Indra in the heavens;
Their diligence in benefiting those in the world that is like that of a world-protecting lord;
Their ability to cure the disease of the afflictions that is like [the curative power of] a king of physicians;
Their ability to rescue one from disastrous circumstances that is like that of close relatives;
Their ability to accumulate a store of meritorious qualities that is like an immense treasury;
Their possession of immeasurably vast moral virtue;
Their possession of boundless meditative absorptions;
Their ineffable wisdom;
Their unequaled liberation;
Their knowledge and vision of liberation that is the equal of the unequaled;
Their incomparability in all things;
Their supremacy over everyone in the world due to which they are recognized as foremost among men;
And their perfection of great dharmas by which they are recognized as great men.

It is in this way that the bodhisattva engages in recollective contemplation of all buddhas in accordance with their possession of the qualities characteristic of the great men. [So, too, he recollects]:

d. Recollection of More Special Qualities & Abilities of Buddhas

That these buddhas have cultivated these meritorious qualities for a countless, boundless, inconceivable, and incalculable number of hundreds of thousands of myriads of *koṭis* of kalpas during which they have been well able to guard their physical, verbal, and mental karma;

正體字

於過去未來現在無
069b21 ‖ 為不可說五藏法中悉斷諸疑。定答分別答
069b22 ‖ 反問答置答。於四問答無有錯謬。善說根
069b23 ‖ 力覺道念處正勤如意三十七助道法。善能
069b24 ‖ 分別無明諸行識名色六入觸受愛取有生
069b25 ‖ 老死因果。於眼色耳聲鼻香舌味身觸意法
069b26 ‖ 無所繫著。善說九部經法。[12]所謂修多羅
069b27 ‖ [13]岐夜[14]授記伽陀[15]憂陀那尼陀那[16]如是諸
069b28 ‖ 經[17]斐肥[18]儸未曾有經。不為貪欲瞋恚愚癡
069b29 ‖ 憍慢身見邊見邪見見取戒取疑諸使所使。
069c01 ‖ 不為無信無慚愧諂曲戲調放逸懈怠睡眠
069c02 ‖ 瞋恨慳嫉諸惱所侵。知見苦斷集證滅修
069c03 ‖ 道。可去已去。可見已見。所作已辦。盡破怨
069c04 ‖ 賊。具足諸願。是世間尊是世間父是世間
069c05 ‖ [19]主。是善來善去善意善寂善滅善解脫者。
069c06 ‖ 在無量無邊十方恒河沙等世間中住。

简体字

于过去未来现在无为不可说五藏法中悉断诸疑。定答分别答反问答置答。于四问答无有错谬。善说根力觉道念处正勤如意三十七助道法。善能分别无明诸行识名色六入触受爱取有生老死因果。于眼色耳声鼻香舌味身触意法无所系着。善说九部经法。所谓修多罗岐夜授记伽陀忧陀那尼陀那如是诸经斐肥儸未曾有经。不为贪欲嗔恚愚痴憍慢身见边见邪见见取戒取疑诸使所使。不为无信无惭愧谄曲戏调放逸懈怠睡眠嗔恨悭嫉诸恼所侵。知见苦断集证灭修道。可去已去。可见已见。所作已办。尽破怨贼。具足诸愿。是世间尊是世间父是世间主。是善来善去善意善寂善灭善解脱者。在无量无边十方恒河沙等世间中住。

That they are well able to completely sever all doubts with respect to the five categorical repositories of dharmas: past dharmas, future dharmas, present dharmas, unconditioned dharmas, and ineffable dharmas;

That, without falling into any error, they employ the four modes of reply: the definitive reply, the distinguishing reply, the counter-questioning reply, and the reply that sets aside the question;[7]

That they skillfully explain the dharmas of the thirty-seven enlightenment factors, namely: the faculties, the powers, the limbs of enlightenment, the path, the stations of mindfulness, the right efforts, and the foundations of psychic power;[8]

That they are well able to distinguish [each link comprising the chain of] cause-and-effect, namely: ignorance, actions, consciousness, name-and-form, the six sense faculties, contact, feeling, craving, grasping, becoming, birth, and aging-and-death;

That they are free of any attachment to the eye or visual forms, to the ear or sounds, to the nose or fragrances, to the tongue or flavors, to the body or touch, or to the mind or dharmas [as objects of mind];

That they skillfully expound the nine types of passages contained in the Dharma of the sutras, namely: sutras; *geyas*; prophetic teachings or expositions; *gāthās*; *udānas*; *nidānas*; [short] discourses beginning with "Thus [spoke the Buddha]..."; *vaipulyas*; and unprecedented events;

That they are not influenced by any of the negative influences such as: greed, hatred, delusion, arrogance, the view that conceives of the existence of true personhood, extreme views, wrong views, seizing upon views; seizing on rules and regulations, or doubts;

That they are not assailed by such afflictions as absence of faith, absence of a sense of shame, absence of a dread of blame, flattery, deviousness, frivolousness, neglectfulness, indolence, somnolence, animosity, miserliness, or jealousy;

That they have known and seen the truth of suffering, have cut off its origination, have realized cessation, have cultivated the path, have abandoned what is to be abandoned, have seen what is to be seen, have done what is to be done, have utterly destroyed the foes,[9] and have perfectly fulfilled their vows;

That they are venerated in the world, are as fathers to the world, and are lords of the world, are well come, are well gone, are possessed of the well-cultivated mind, are consummately skilled in meditative stillness, are well-realized in the realization of cessation, and are well liberated;

That, as they abide in countless and boundless worlds throughout the ten directions in worlds as numerous as the sands in the

正體字

如現
069c07 ‖ 在前菩薩。又應以八十種好念觀諸佛。甲
069c08 ‖ 色鮮赤行清白法。甲隆而大生在大家。甲色
069c09 ‖ 潤澤深愛眾生。指圓[20]纖長其行深遠。指肉
069c10 ‖ 充滿善根充滿。指漸次而長次第集諸佛法。
069c11 ‖ 脈覆不見不覆身口意[21]念脈。無麁結破
069c12 ‖ 煩惱結。[22]踝平不現不隱藏法。足不邪曲
069c13 ‖ 度[23]墮邪眾。行如師子是人中師子。行如象
069c14 ‖ 王是人象王。行如鵝王。高飛如鴻。行如
069c15 ‖ 牛王人中最尊。行時右旋善說正道。[24]身不
069c16 ‖ 僂曲心常不曲。身堅而直讚堅牢戒。

简体字

如现在前菩萨。又应以八十种好念观诸佛。甲色鲜赤行清白法。甲隆而大生在大家。甲色润泽深爱众生。指圆纤长其行深远。指肉充满善根充满。指渐次而长次第集诸佛法。脉覆不见不覆身口意念脉。无粗结破烦恼结。踝平不现不隐藏法。足不邪曲度堕邪众。行如师子是人中师子。行如象王是人象王。行如鹅王。高飞如鸿。行如牛王人中最尊。行时右旋善说正道。身不偻曲心常不曲。身坚而直赞坚牢戒。

Ganges, [one envisions them] as if they were appearing directly before one's very eyes.

e. Contemplative Recollection of the 80 Secondary Characteristics

The bodhisattva should also envision in contemplation all of the buddhas as graced with their eighty secondary characteristics,[10] recollecting:

That their nails are copper-colored is emblematic of their practice of pure dharmas;

That their nails are prominent and large is emblematic of birth into the great clan;

That their nails are glossy and smooth is emblematic of a deep affection for beings;

That their fingers are round, tapered, and long is emblematic of the depth and duration of their practice;

That their fingers are fully fleshed is emblematic of fully developed roots of goodness;

That their fingers are tapered and long is emblematic of sequential accumulation of all dharmas of a buddha;

That their veins are hidden and invisible, but they do not hide the lineage of [the quality of their conduct in] body, mouth, and mind;

That there are no thick knots in their veins is emblematic of their having broken up the knots of afflictions;

That their ankle bones are flat and inconspicuous is emblematic of their not hiding away the Dharma;

That their feet are not misaligned in their track is emblematic of their liberation of the multitudes who have fallen into deviant conduct;

That their gait is like that of the lion is emblematic of their being the lions among men;

That their gait is also like that of the king of elephants is emblematic of their being the elephant kings among men;

That their gait is also like the king of geese is emblematic of their flying high, like the wild goose;

That their gait is also like the king of bulls is emblematic of their being the most revered of all men;

That, when walking, they turn around to the right, is emblematic of their skillful proclamation of the right path;

That their posture is not hunched or crooked is emblematic of the fact that their minds are never crooked;

That their bodies stand solid and erect in their posture is emblematic of their praise of solidity and durability in upholding the moral precepts;

正體字

身漸
069c17 ‖ 次大次第說法。普身諸分大而端嚴。善能解
069c18 ‖ 說大妙功德。身相具足具足法者。足步間等
069c19 ‖ 等心眾生。其身淨潔三業清淨。身膚細軟心
069c20 ‖ 性自軟。身離塵垢善見離垢。身不縮沒心
069c21 ‖ 常不沒。身無[25]邊量善根無量。肌肉緊密永
069c22 ‖ 斷後身。支節分明善說十二因緣分別明
069c23 ‖ 了。身色無闇知見無闇。腹圓周滿弟子行具。
069c24 ‖ 腹淨鮮潔善能了知生死過惡。腹不高出
069c25 ‖ 破憍慢[26]山。腹平不現說平等法。臍圓而深
069c26 ‖ 通甚深法。臍晝右旋弟子[27]順教。

简体字

身渐次大次第说法。普身诸分大而端严。善能解说大妙功德。身相具足具足法者。足步间等等心众生。其身净洁三业清净。身肤细软心性自软。身离尘垢善见离垢。身不缩没心常不没。身无边量善根无量。肌肉紧密永断后身。支节分明善说十二因缘分别明了。身色无闇知见无闇。腹圆周满弟子行具。腹净鲜洁善能了知生死过恶。腹不高出破憍慢山。腹平不现说平等法。脐圆而深通甚深法。脐画右旋弟子顺教。

That their bodies gradually grew large is emblematic of their sequential exposition of Dharma;

That all parts of their bodies are large and majestic is emblematic of their ability to skillfully explain the great and sublime meritorious qualities;

That their bodies are perfectly developed is emblematic of their perfection in the Dharma;

That their strides are of equal length is emblematic of their equal-minded regard for all beings;

That their bodies are pristine in their cleanliness is emblematic of the purity of their three types of karma;

That their skin is fine and soft is emblematic of the naturally pliant character of their minds;

That their bodies remain free of all dust and dirt is emblematic of their good views that have abandoned all defilement;

That their bodies do not shrink through wasting [even in old age] is emblematic of their minds' always remaining unsinkable;

That their bodies are boundless and immeasurable is emblematic of the immeasurability of their roots of goodness;

That the flesh of their bodies is taut and finely textured is emblematic of their eternal severance of [karmically-compulsory] later incarnations;

That all of their joints are smooth in their articulations is emblematic of their skillful explication of the twelve causes and conditions and their perfectly clear distinguishing of each of them;

That the hue of their bodies is not dark is emblematic of their knowledge and vision being free of any darkness;

That their waists are full all around is emblematic of their disciples' possession of fully developed conduct;

That their bellies are clear [of blemishes] and of fresh and immaculate appearance is emblematic of their being well able to completely know the serious faults of *saṃsāra;*

That their bellies do not protrude is emblematic of their having crushed the mountain of arrogance;

That their bellies are flat and do not show is emblematic of the fact that their proclamation of Dharma is directed equally toward everyone;

That their umbilici are round and deep is emblematic of their penetrating comprehension of extremely deep dharmas;

That their umbilici have a rightward swirl is emblematic of their disciples' compliance with instruction;

正體字

身遍端嚴
069c27 ‖ 弟子遍淨。威儀[28]鮮潔心淨無比。身無點子
069c28 ‖ 無黑印法。手濡勝兜羅綿。受化者身輕如
069c29 ‖ 毛。手畫[29]文深威儀深重。手畫文長觀受法
070a01 ‖ 者長遠後事。手畫潤澤捨親愛潤得大道
070a02 ‖ 果。面貌不長結戒有開。脣赤如頻婆果。見
070a03 ‖ 一切世間。如鏡中像。舌柔而軟先以軟語
070a04 ‖ [1]度脫眾生。舌薄而廣功德純厚。舌赤如[2]深
070a05 ‖ 紅凡夫心難解佛法令解。聲如雷震不畏
070a06 ‖ 雷聲。其聲和柔說柔軟法。四牙圓直說直道
070a07 ‖ 法。四牙俱利度利根者四牙鮮白清白第一。

简体字

身遍端严弟子遍净。威仪鲜洁心净无比。身无点子无黑印法。手濡胜兜罗绵。受化者身轻如毛。手画文深威仪深重。手画文长观受法者长远后事。手画润泽舍亲爱润得大道果。面貌不长结戒有开。唇赤如频婆果。见一切世间。如镜中像。舌柔而软先以软语度脱众生。舌薄而广功德纯厚。舌赤如深红凡夫心难解佛法令解。声如雷震不畏雷声。其声和柔说柔软法。四牙圆直说直道法。四牙俱利度利根者四牙鲜白清白第一。

That their bodies are in every way graceful in their refinements is emblematic of the thoroughgoing purity of their disciples;

That their awesomeness in deportment is utterly immaculate is emblematic of the incomparable purity of their minds;

That their bodies are free of blemishes is emblematic of their being completely free of any black dharmas;

That the softness of their hands is superior even to that of *tūla*-cotton silk is emblematic of the experience of those receiving their instruction who feel as if their bodies have become as light as a wisp of down;

That the lines on their palms form a deep pattern is emblematic of the profoundly dignified nature of their awesome deportment;

That the lines on their palms are long is emblematic of their contemplative regard for the long-term future of those receiving their Dharma teaching;

That the pattern on their palms is lustrous and smooth is emblematic of their relinquishing of the affection of relatives and of their acquisition of the fruits of the great path;

That their countenances remain free of any long-faced expression is emblematic of the presence of exceptional circumstances in the moral precepts they establish;

That their lips are as red as *bimba* fruit is emblematic of their looking on the entire world as merely like an image reflected in a mirror;

That their tongues are soft and pliant is emblematic of their initial use of gentle speech in liberating beings;

That their tongues are thin and wide is emblematic of the purity and abundance of their meritorious qualities;

That their tongues are crimson red is emblematic of their Dharma's ability to cause common people to understand what they find difficult to understand;

That their voices are like thunder is emblematic of their not fearing the boom of a thunderclap;

That their voices are harmonious and gentle is emblematic of their proclamation of soft and gentle Dharma;

That their four central incisors are rounded [in their visible profile] and straight is emblematic of their proclamation of the Dharma of the straight path;

That their four central incisors are all sharp is emblematic of their liberation of those beings who are possessed of sharp faculties;

That their four central incisors are immaculately white is emblematic of their being foremost in purity;

正體字

070a08 ‖ 四牙齊等住戒平地。牙漸次細漸次說四諦
070a09 ‖ 法。鼻高隆直住智高山。鼻中清淨弟子清白。
070a10 ‖ 眼廣而長智慧廣遠。睫不希踈善擇眾生。
070a11 ‖ 眼白黑[3]鮮淨如青蓮華葉。天人婇女以好
070a12 ‖ 眼敬禮。眉高而長名聞遠流。眉毛潤澤善知
070a13 ‖ 軟法。耳等相似聞法者等。耳根不壞度不壞
070a14 ‖ 心眾生。額平而好善離諸見。額廣無妨廣
070a15 ‖ 破外道。頭分具足善具大願。髮色如黑蜂
070a16 ‖ 轉五欲樂。髮厚而[＊]緻結使[4]已盡。美髮柔
070a17 ‖ [5]軟軟利智[6]者能知法味。

简体字

四牙齐等住戒平地。牙渐次细渐次说四谛法。鼻高隆直住智高山。鼻中清净弟子清白。眼广而长智慧广远。睫不希疏善择众生。眼白黑鲜净如青莲华叶。天人婇女以好眼敬礼。眉高而长名闻远流。眉毛润泽善知软法。耳等相似闻法者等。耳根不坏度不坏心众生。额平而好善离诸见。额广无妨广破外道。头分具足善具大愿。发色如黑蜂转五欲乐。发厚而致结使已尽。美发柔软软利智者能知法味。

That their four central incisors are evenly and equally set is emblematic of their standing on the level ground of the moral precepts;

That the profile of their rows of teeth gradually taper to those that are smaller [in height] is emblematic of the graduated sequence in their explanation of the dharma of the four truths;

That they have noses that are high and straight-ridged is emblematic of their standing atop the high mountain of wisdom;

That their nasal apertures are clear and clean is emblematic of the purity of their disciples;

That their eyes are wide and laterally long is emblematic of their wisdom's qualities of being vast and far-reaching;

That their eyelashes are not sparse or in disarray is emblematic of their skill in their differential assessment of beings;

That the whites and pupils of their eyes are as fresh and pristine as the petals of a blue lotus blossom is emblematic of their being such that even devas and heavenly maidens are moved to gaze upon them fondly and bow down in reverence before them;

That their eyebrows are high and long is emblematic of the far-reaching spread of their fame;

That the hair of their eyebrows is smooth and glossy is emblematic of their thoroughgoing knowledge of the dharmas of mental pliancy;

That their ears are equal in their appearance is emblematic of the equality of all who listen to the Dharma;

That their faculty of hearing is undamaged is emblematic of their ability to liberate any being possessed of an undamaged mind;

That their foreheads are flat and of fine appearance is emblematic of their having skillfully abandoned all views;

That their foreheads are unrestricted in their wide breadth is emblematic of their having broadly refuted [the claims of] non-Buddhist traditions;

That their heads are in all respects perfectly developed is emblematic of their having thoroughly perfected [the goals of] their great vows;

That their hair is the color of the black bee is emblematic of their having transformed the pleasures associated with the five types of desire;

That their hair is dense and fine is emblematic of their having already put an end to the fetters;

That their hair, so pleasing in its appearance, is soft in texture is emblematic of their pliant and sharp wisdom's ability to know well the flavor of dharmas;

正體字

髮不散亂言常不
070a18 ‖ 亂。髮潤而澤常無麁言。髮有美香。以七覺
070a19 ‖ 意香華隨宜化導。髮中有德字安字喜字。
070a20 ‖ 手足中亦有德字安字喜字。菩薩如是應
070a21 ‖ 念諸佛處在大眾[7]講說正法坐師子座。
070a22 ‖ 其座以琉璃雜寶為脚。以真珊瑚妙赤真
070a23 ‖ 珠以為[8]枕。金薄[9]幃帳柔軟滑澤種種天衣
070a24 ‖ 以為敷具。[10]以寶師子赤金為身。[11]虎珀為
070a25 ‖ 眼。[12]車璩為尾。珊瑚為舌。白金剛為四牙。
070a26 ‖ 真白銀為髮。毛髮長廣。具足其床在此四
070a27 ‖ 師子上。大象王牙以為凭机。其承足[*]机眾
070a28 ‖ 寶所成。為諸天龍夜叉乾闥婆阿修羅迦樓
070a29 ‖ 羅緊那羅摩睺羅伽之所敬禮。諸佛如是在
070b01 ‖ 此床上。著竭支泥洹僧。不高不下覆身三
070b02 ‖ 分。周匝齊整著淺色袈裟。條數分明不高不
070b03 ‖ 下亦不參差。處[13]八大聖莊嚴眾中人天大
070b04 ‖ 會。龍金翅鳥俱共聽法心無瞋[14]恨。一切大
070b05 ‖ 眾深心慚愧敬愛於佛。皆共一心聽佛所說。

简体字

发不散乱言常不乱。发润而泽常无粗言。发有美香。以七觉意香华随宜化导。发中有德字安字喜字。手足中亦有德字安字喜字。菩萨如是应念诸佛处在大众讲说正法坐师子座。其座以琉璃杂宝为脚。以真珊瑚妙赤真珠以为枕。金薄帏帐柔软滑泽种种天衣以为敷具。以宝师子赤金为身。虎珀为眼。车磲为尾。珊瑚为舌。白金刚为四牙。真白银为发。毛发长广。具足其床在此四师子上。大象王牙以为凭机。其承足机众宝所成。为诸天龙夜叉乾闼婆阿修罗迦楼罗紧那罗摩睺罗伽之所敬礼。诸佛如是在此床上。着竭支泥洹僧。不高不下覆身三分。周匝齐整着浅色袈裟。条数分明不高不下亦不参差。处八大圣庄严众中人天大会。龙金翅鸟俱共听法心无嗔恨。一切大众深心惭愧敬爱于佛。皆共一心听佛所说。

That their hair is not in disarray is emblematic of their words never being disordered;
That their hair is smooth and glossy is emblematic of their always being free of any sort of coarse speech;
That their hair has a marvelous fragrance is emblematic of their use of the fragrant blossoms of the seven branches of bodhi to teach and guide beings in whatever way is appropriate.
That their mark of virtue, peace, and joy appears in their hair.
And that their mark of virtue, peace, and joy also appears on the palms of their hands and on the soles of their feet.

f. Envisioning the Buddhas in an Assembly, Teaching, on the Lion Seat

1) Envisioning the Buddhas as They Sit on the Lion's Seat

It is in this manner that a bodhisattva should envision the Buddhas residing in the midst of a great assembly, speaking on right Dharma, and sitting on the lion seat. The lion seat has feet made from *vaiḍūrya* inset with various jewels, a headrest made from real coral with marvelous red pearls, and a canopy made of hammered gold. It is draped with all sorts of soft, silky, and lustrous heavenly robes and is supported by bejeweled lions whose bodies are made of purple gold. Their eyes are amber and their tails are mother-of-pearl. They have carnelian tongues, four white-diamond tusk-teeth, hair made of real white silver, and long, full manes. That seat rests upon these four lions. They form [the base of] the throne that has armrests made from royal elephant tusks and a footrest made of the many sorts of jewels.

The Buddhas receive there the reverential obeisance of the devas, dragons, *yakṣas, gandharvas, asuras, garuḍas, kinnaras,* and *mahoragas.* The Buddhas appear in this way on this throne. They wear the *saṃkakṣikā*[11] and the *nivāsana,*[12] neither too high nor too low, so that they cover the three regions of the body and are neatly arranged and straight all around. They wear a light-colored *saṃghāṭī* robe,[13] with the strips composing it clearly visible, neither too high nor too low, and not misaligned.

2) Envisioning the Audience as the Buddhas Teach Dharma

They abide in the midst of an audience adorned by the presence of the eight kinds of great *āryas,*[14] surrounded by a great assembly of humans and devas. When in attendance there, the dragons and golden-winged *garuḍa* birds all listen together to the teaching of Dharma, remaining free of any thoughts of mutual hostility.[15]

Everyone in the entire assembly is imbued with a deeply sincere sense of shame and dread of blame as, with reverential affection for the Buddha, they all listen single-mindedly to the discourse of the

正體字

070b06 ‖ 受持思惟如所說行。專心聽受心清淨故能
070b07 ‖ 障諸蓋。一切大眾瞻仰如來無有厭足。衣
070b08 ‖ 毛皆竪泣淚心熱或有大喜。有如是者。則
070b09 ‖ 知其人心得清淨寂默湛然如入禪定。無
070b10 ‖ 愛無恚心無餘緣。有大悲相慈愍眾生。欲
070b11 ‖ 救一切心不諂曲。寂滅清淨分別好醜。有
070b12 ‖ 大志量不沒不縮不高不下。佛悉瞻見處
070b13 ‖ 在如是。大眾說法易解易了樂聞無厭。音
070b14 ‖ 深不散柔軟悅耳從臍而出。咽喉舌根鼻額
070b15 ‖ 上[15]齗齒脣。氣激變成音句。柔軟悅耳。如大
070b16 ‖ 密雲雷聲隱[16]震。如大海中猛風激浪。如
070b17 ‖ 大梵天音聲引導可度眾生。離眉眼脣可
070b18 ‖ 呵語法。言不闕少又不煩重。所說無疑言
070b19 ‖ 必利益。無有謎語可破語等。離如是過遠
070b20 ‖ 近等聞。四種問難隨意能答。開示四諦令
070b21 ‖ 得

简体字

受持思惟如所说行。专心听受心清净故能障诸盖。一切大众瞻仰如来无有厌足。衣毛皆竖泣泪心热或有大喜。有如是者。则知其人心得清净寂默湛然如入禅定。无爱无恚心无余缘。有大悲相慈愍众生。欲救一切心不谄曲。寂灭清净分别好丑。有大志量不没不缩不高不下。佛悉瞻见处在如是。大众说法易解易了乐闻无厌。音深不散柔软悦耳从脐而出。咽喉舌根鼻额上龂齿唇。气激变成音句。柔软悦耳。如大密云雷声隐震。如大海中猛风激浪。如大梵天音声引导可度众生。离眉眼唇可呵语法。言不阙少又不烦重。所说无疑言必利益。无有谜语可破语等。离如是过远近等闻。四种问难随意能答。开示四谛令得

Buddha, accept and uphold it, reflect upon it, and practice in accordance with what is taught. Because their minds are focused as they listen and because their thoughts are pure, they are able to block any interference by the hindrances. Everyone in the great assembly gazes insatiably up at the Tathāgata, with all the hairs raised on their bodies, with their eyes filled with tears, with their minds afire with intensity, or with hearts filled with great joy.

Wherever people have become like this, one knows that their minds have become purified. They remain there motionless and silent, serenely still, and as if having entered *dhyāna* absorption. Their minds are free of either love or hatred and remain undistracted by any extraneous matters. They have thoughts of great compassion[16] by which they feel kindness and pity for beings, wishing to rescue them all. Their minds do not descend into flattery or deviousness, but rather have become utterly quiescent and pure as they distinguish what is good from what is bad. They have an immensely strong determination from which they neither fall away or shrink back and they do not regard themselves as superior or others as inferior.

3) Envisioning the Manner in Which They Teach Dharma

The Buddhas are all observed abiding in such great assemblies, teaching Dharma that is easy to understand and easy to completely fathom. [Their audiences] listen with insatiable delight. Their voices are deep, are not subject to fading [even at a distance], are gentle, and are pleasing to the ear. Originating in the belly, through the interaction of the throat, tongue, nasopharynx, dental palate, teeth, and lips, the air is caused to become sounds and sentences that may be soft and pleasing to the ear, may be as powerfully strong as the earth-quaking thunder emanating from huge, dense rain clouds, may be like those fierce winds off the great ocean that drive up the surf, or may be like the voice of the devas in the Mahābrahma Heaven. With voices such as these, they lead forth and guide those beings that are capable of being liberated.

They have abandoned any modes of expression associated with scolding that may involve contortion of the brow, the countenance, or the lips. Their speech is neither deficient in any way nor unnecessarily long and redundant. There is no doubt in what they proclaim and their words will certainly be beneficial. Their speech is entirely free of any deceptive statements, any statements vulnerable to refutation, or any other such statements. It is entirely free of these faults and it is heard equally well by those far and near.

The Buddhas are freely able to answer the four types of challenging questions. They explain the four truths, thereby causing beings to gain

正體字

四果。建立義端因緣結句。語言法則皆悉
070b22 ‖ 具足。種種所說事義易了。所宜分明[17]不故
070b23 ‖ 隱曲。言不卒疾又不遲緩。始終相稱無能
070b24 ‖ 難者。以如是語敷演說法。初中後善有義
070b25 ‖ 有利唯法具足。能令眾生得今世報。無有
070b26 ‖ 時節可得嘗試能滿所願。深妙智者以內
070b27 ‖ 可知。能滅眾生三毒猛火。能除一切身口
070b28 ‖ 意罪。善能開示戒定慧品。初以名字後令
070b29 ‖ 知義而生歡喜。從喜生樂從樂生定。從
070c01 ‖ 定生如實[18]智。從[19]如實[＊]智生厭離。從厭
070c02 ‖ 離滅結使。滅結使故得解脫。如是能令
070c03 ‖ 此法次第。善能開示諦捨滅慧四處。能示眾
070c04 ‖ 生令滿布施持戒忍辱精進禪定智慧波羅
070c05 ‖ 蜜。能令眾生次第得至喜地淨地明地炎地
070c06 ‖ 難勝現前深遠

简体字

四果。建立义端因缘结句。语言法则皆悉具足。种种所说事义易了。所宜分明不故隐曲。言不卒疾又不迟缓。始终相称无能难者。以如是语敷演说法。初中后善有义有利唯法具足。能令众生得今世报。无有时节可得尝试能满所愿。深妙智者以内可知。能灭众生三毒猛火。能除一切身口意罪。善能开示戒定慧品。初以名字后令知义而生欢喜。从喜生乐从乐生定。从定生如实智。从如实智生厌离。从厌离灭结使。灭结使故得解脱。如是能令此法次第。善能开示谛舍灭慧四处。能示众生令满布施持戒忍辱精进禅定智慧波罗蜜。能令众生次第得至喜地净地明地炎地难胜现前深远

the four fruits of the path. They establish points of meaning and make statements supported by reasons. They are completely equipped with all of the methods used in speaking. In the many different sorts of matters that they discuss, their meaning is easy to completely comprehend. Whatever they proclaim is entirely clear and never intentionally cryptic or convoluted. Their speech is neither too fast nor too slow. The beginnings and conclusions of each discourse are mutually compatible and invulnerable to anyone's challenges.

4) Envisioning the Effects of the Buddhas' Teaching of Dharma

With speech such as this, they spread forth and proclaim the Dharma which is good in the beginning, middle, and end, imbued with meaning, beneficial, devoted solely to Dharma, and, in all respects, perfect.[17] It is able to cause beings to gain karmic rewards in in this very lifetime. Their discourse is not meaningful only for a time, is such that one can test it for oneself, and is such that will lead to the fulfillment of one's aspirations. Those possessed of profound and sublime wisdom realize it within themselves. It can extinguish in beings the raging fire set ablaze by the three poisons. It is able to rid one of all karmic offenses committed by body, speech, and mind, and it is also well able to open up and reveal the essence of moral virtue, the meditative absorptions, and wisdom.

It begins with mere naming that in turn provokes realization of meaning that then in its own turn causes one to be filled with joy. From this joy, there then arises bliss, and from this bliss, there then arises meditative concentration. From this meditative concentration, there arises a wise knowing in accordance with reality, and from this wise knowing in accordance with reality, one then develops renunciation. Due to having developed this renunciation, one becomes able to destroy the fetters, and due to having destroyed those fetters, one then gains liberation.

In this very manner, this Dharma is caused to unfold in a sequence whereby:

It is well able to open forth and reveal the four bases [of meritorious qualities]: truth, relinquishment, quiescence, and wisdom;

It is able to reveal for beings the means by which they are caused to perfectly fulfill the *pāramitās* of giving, moral virtue, patience, vigor, meditative concentration, and wisdom;

It is able to cause beings to sequentially enter and proceed through the Ground of Joyfulness, the Ground of Stainlessness, the ground of Shining Light, the Ground of Blazing Brilliance, the Difficult-to-Conquer Ground, the Ground of Direct Presence, the Far-Reaching

正體字

不動善慧法雲。能分別聲聞
070c07 ‖ 乘辟支佛乘大乘。能令證須陀洹斯陀含阿
070c08 ‖ 那含阿羅漢果。能令成就人天之中所有富
070c09 ‖ 樂。是為一切第一利益諸功德藏。如是正心
070c10 ‖ 憶念諸佛。在閑靜處除却貪欲瞋[20]恚睡眠
070c11 ‖ 疑悔調戲。一心專念不生障礙失定之心。
070c12 ‖ 以如是心專念諸佛。若心沒當起若散當
070c13 ‖ 攝。并見大眾常如現前。未入定時常應
070c14 ‖ 稱讚相好二事。以偈歎佛令心調習。如此
070c15 ‖ 偈說。
070c16 ‖ 世尊諸相好　何業因緣得
070c17 ‖ 我以相及業　稱讚於大聖
070c18 ‖ 足相千輻輪　清淨眷屬施
070c19 ‖ 以是因緣故　賢聖眾圍繞
070c20 ‖ 足下安立相　受善持不失
070c21 ‖ 是故魔軍眾　不能得毀壞

简体字

不动善慧法云。能分别声闻乘辟支佛乘大乘。能令证须陀洹斯陀含阿那含阿罗汉果。能令成就人天之中所有富乐。是为一切第一利益诸功德藏。如是正心忆念诸佛。在闲静处除却贪欲嗔恚睡眠疑悔调戏。一心专念不生障碍失定之心。以如是心专念诸佛。若心没当起若散当摄。并见大众常如现前。未入定时常应称赞相好二事。以偈叹佛令心调习。如此偈说。

世尊诸相好　何业因缘得
我以相及业　称赞于大圣
足相千辐轮　清净眷属施
以是因缘故　贤圣众围绕
足下安立相　受善持不失
是故魔军众　不能得毁坏

Ground, the Ground of Immovability, the Ground of Excellent Intelligence, and the Ground of the Dharma Cloud;

It is able to make clear distinctions with regard to the Śrāvaka Disciple Vehicle, the Pratyekabuddha Vehicle, and the Great Vehicle;

It is able to provoke realization of the fruits of the path gained by the stream enterer, once returner, non-returner and arhat;[18]

And it is able too to cause complete success in gaining wealth and happiness in the realms of humans and devas.

This is what constitutes the treasury of meritorious qualities that provides all of the foremost forms of benefit.

5) Instruction on This Type of Contemplative Mindfulness

It is in this manner that one uses right thought in the recollective mindfulness of all buddhas. One abides in a peaceful and quiet place, rids oneself of sensual desire, ill will, dullness and drowsiness, doubtfulness, regret and agitation, and single-mindedly carries on focused mindfulness in which one refrains from generating thoughts that obstruct or cause one to lose meditative absorption. One employs this sort of mind in one's focused mindfulness of the Buddhas. If one's mind sinks, one should raise it up again. If one's mind becomes scattered, one should draw it back into a focused state. One then sees the entire great assembly as if it were always right before one's very eyes.

6) The Importance of Praising the Major Marks and Secondary Signs

When one has not yet managed to enter concentrated meditative absorption, one should always praise the two types of phenomena that consist of the Buddha's major marks and secondary characteristics, using verses to celebrate the qualities of the Buddhas and to cause one's mind to become well trained in this.

a) Verses in Praise of the Buddhas' 32 Marks

Accordingly, there are these lines of verse as follows:

Referring to the marks and characteristics of the Bhagavats
and the karmic causes and conditions by which they acquired them,
I shall use these marks and their corresponding karmic actions
to set forth the praises of these great *āryas*:

The thousand-spoked wheel mark on the feet
is associated with a pure retinue and with giving.
It is because of these causes and conditions
that the many worthies and *āryas* surround them.

The mark of the stable stance of the feet
arises from upholding without fail all goodness one has taken on.
It is because of this that the legions of Māra's armies
are unable to succeed in destroying them.

正體字

070c22 ║ 手足指網縵 身相紫金色
070c23 ║ 善行攝法故 大眾自然伏
070c24 ║ 手足極柔軟 身相七處滿
070c25 ║ 隨意食施故 多得自然供
070c26 ║ 長指廣脚跟 身[21]傭大直相
070c27 ║ 離殺因緣故 乃至於劫壽
070c28 ║ 毛上向右旋 足趺隆高相
070c29 ║ 常進諸善事 故得不退法
071a01 ║ 伊[1]泥鹿[蹲-酋+(十/田/ム)]相 常樂讀誦經
071a02 ║ 為人說法故 疾得無上道
071a03 ║ 修臂下過膝 一切所有物
071a04 ║ 求者無悋惜 隨意化導人
071a05 ║ 陰藏功德藏 善[和>知]離散故
071a06 ║ 多得人天眾 淨慧眼為子
071a07 ║ 薄皮耀金光 妙衣堂閣施
071a08 ║ 故多得妙衣 清淨房樓觀
071a09 ║ 一孔一毛生 眉間白毫峙
071a10 ║ 常為最上護 故於三界尊
071a11 ║ 身上如師子 兩肩圓而[2]滿
071a12 ║ 常行[3]人愛語 無有違反者

简体字

手足指网缦 身相紫金色
善行摄法故 大众自然伏
手足极柔软 身相七处满
随意食施故 多得自然供
长指广脚跟 身佣大直相
离杀因缘故 乃至于劫寿
毛上向右旋 足趺隆高相
常进诸善事 故得不退法
伊泥鹿[跳-兆+専]相 常乐读诵经
为人说法故 疾得无上道
修臂下过膝 一切所有物
求者无吝惜 随意化导人
阴藏功德藏 善知离散故
多得人天众 净慧眼为子
薄皮耀金光 妙衣堂阁施
故多得妙衣 清净房楼观
一孔一毛生 眉间白毫峙
常为最上护 故于三界尊
身上如师子 两肩圆而满
常行人爱语 无有违反者

Their fingers and toes join with proximal webs
and their bodies have the mark of purple golden coloration.
Because of their skillful practice of the means of attraction,
the great assembly naturally bows in deferential reverence.

Their hands and feet are extremely soft
and the body has the mark of fullness in the seven places.
It is due to giving food that accords with others' wishes
that they are naturally given many offerings.

They have long fingers, broad heels,
and the body has the mark of being large and upright.
This results from abandoning the causes and conditions of killing
and may lead to a lifespan lasting even up to a kalpa in length.

The hairs of the body grow in an upward and rightward spiral
and the feet have the mark of high arches.
By always advancing in good endeavors,
they thereby acquired the dharma of irreversibility.

They have the gradually tapering legs of the *aiṇeya* antelope
due to always delighting in study and recitation of scriptures.
It is through speaking the Dharma for others
that they rapidly realized the unsurpassable path.

As for having long arms that reach below the knees,
this is due to never being miserly in giving
anything one possesses to whoever seeks to acquire them.
Thus they can teach and guide others in ways suited to their wishes.

Genital ensheathment reflects a treasury of meritorious qualities
associated with skillfully reconciling those who are estranged.[19]
As a result, they acquire a great congregation of humans and devas
and use the pure wisdom eye to create their sons.[20]

Their thin skin that radiates golden light
is associated with giving marvelous apparel and halls.
As a consequence, they acquire an abundance of fine robes
as well as pristine quarters, buildings, and viewing terraces.

The single hair in each pore
and the white hair tuft between the eyes
are associated with serving as a supreme protector.
Hence they are revered throughout the three realms of existence.

They have an upper body like that of a lion
with the two shoulders rounded and full.
These result from always using speech that is pleasing to others.
As a consequence, there is no one who opposes them.

正體字

071a13 ‖ 腋滿知味相　病施醫藥故
071a14 ‖ 人天皆敬愛　身無有疾[4]病
071a15 ‖ 身圓肉髻相　和悅心施福
071a16 ‖ 勸化剛強者　法王中自在
071a17 ‖ 迦陵頻伽音　廣舌聲如梵
071a18 ‖ 所言常軟實　得大聖八音
071a19 ‖ 先加以思慮　後言必有實
071a20 ‖ 故得師子相　見者皆信伏
071a21 ‖ 齒白齊密相　所曾供養者
071a22 ‖ 後常不輕故　眷屬心和同
071a23 ‖ 上下四十齒　密[5]緻不疎漏
071a24 ‖ 無讒不妄語　徒眾不可破
071a25 ‖ 眼黑青白明　睫相如牛王
071a26 ‖ 慈心和視故　觀者無厭足
071a27 ‖ 雖轉輪聖王　典主四天下
071a28 ‖ 有是諸相好　光明不如佛
071a29 ‖ 我所稱歎說　諸相好功德
071b01 ‖ 願令一切人　心淨常安樂
071b02 ‖ 菩薩又應以八十種好念諸佛。如此偈說。

简体字

腋满知味相　病施医药故
人天皆敬爱　身无有疾病
身圆肉髻相　和悦心施福
劝化刚强者　法王中自在
迦陵频伽音　广舌声如梵
所言常软实　得大圣八音
先加以思虑　后言必有实
故得师子相　见者皆信伏
齿白齐密相　所曾供养者
后常不轻故　眷属心和同
上下四十齿　密致不疏漏
无谗不妄语　徒众不可破
眼黑青白明　睫相如牛王
慈心和视故　观者无厌足
虽转轮圣王　典主四天下
有是诸相好　光明不如佛
我所称叹说　诸相好功德
愿令一切人　心净常安乐
菩萨又应以八十种好念诸佛。如此偈说。

The marks of sub-axillary fullness and cognition of all tastes
stem from providing medical care and medicines for the sick.
As a consequence, devas and men all revere and love them
and their bodies remain ever free of disease.

The roundness of the mid-body and the crown's fleshy *uṣṇīṣa* sign
reflect the merit of giving with a harmonious and delighted mind.
As a consequence of exhorting and teaching even the stubborn,
they reign as sovereignly masterful kings of Dharma.

As for the voice like that of a *kalaviṅka* bird,
the broad tongue, and the voice like a Great Brahma Heaven deva,
they are from the speaking of words that are both gentle and true.
They therefore acquire the Great Ārya's eight voice qualities.[21]

Having first brought contemplative thought to bear
and then afterward spoken words of definite truthfulness,
they acquired the lion-like mark.
Hence all who see them trust them and defer to them.

That their teeth are white, straight, and close-set
is because they have always refrained from slighting
those who have previously given offerings.
Hence the minds of those in their retinue are agreeable and unified.

Above and below, they have a total of forty teeth
that, being close-set, have no gaps.
These result from never slandering and not lying.
Hence their disciples' [loyalty] cannot be destroyed.

The pupils and whites of their eyes are clearly delineated
and they have the mark of eyelashes like those of a royal bull.
These are caused by kindly thought and an amicable view of others.
Consequently all observers look on them with a tireless gaze.

Even though a wheel-turning king
who rules over four continents
possesses these major marks and secondary characteristics,
their radiance still cannot compare with that of a buddha.

I pray that the power of the merit from my setting forth praises
of the major marks and the secondary characteristics
may be able to cause everyone
to have purified minds as well as everlasting peace and happiness.

a) Verses in Praise of the Buddhas Secondary Characteristics

The bodhisattva should also engage in contemplative mindfulness of the buddhas by way of their eighty secondary characteristics. Accordingly, there are these lines of verse, as follows:

正體字

071b03 ‖	諸佛有妙好	八十莊嚴身
071b04 ‖	汝等應歡喜	一心聽我說
071b05 ‖	世尊圓纖指	其甲紫紅色
071b06 ‖	隆高有潤澤	所有無有量
071b07 ‖	[6]脈平踝不現	雙足無邪曲
071b08 ‖	行如師子王	威望無等比
071b09 ‖	行時身右旋	安庠有儀雅
071b10 ‖	方身分次第	端嚴可愛樂
071b11 ‖	身堅[7]極柔軟	支節甚分明
071b12 ‖	行時不逶迤	諸根悉充滿
071b13 ‖	肌體極密緻	鮮明甚清淨
071b14 ‖	身形甚端雅	無有可呵處
071b15 ‖	腹圓不高現	臍深而無孔
071b16 ‖	其文右向旋	威儀甚清淨
071b17 ‖	身無有疵點	手足極柔軟
071b18 ‖	其文深且長	修直有潤色
071b19 ‖	舌薄面不長	牙白圓[＊]纖利
071b20 ‖	脣色頻婆果	音深若鴻王
071b21 ‖	鼻隆眼明淨	睫[8]緻而不亂
071b22 ‖	眉高毛柔軟	端直不邪曲

简体字

诸佛有妙好	八十庄严身
汝等应欢喜	一心听我说
世尊圆纤指	其甲紫红色
隆高有润泽	所有无有量
脉平踝不现	双足无邪曲
行如师子王	威望无等比
行时身右旋	安庠有仪雅
方身分次第	端严可爱乐
身坚极柔软	支节甚分明
行时不逶迤	诸根悉充满
肌体极密致	鲜明甚清净
身形甚端雅	无有可呵处
腹圆不高现	脐深而无孔
其文右向旋	威仪甚清净
身无有疵点	手足极柔软
其文深且长	修直有润色
舌薄面不长	牙白圆纤利
唇色频婆果	音深若鸿王
鼻隆眼明净	睫致而不乱
眉高毛柔软	端直不邪曲

All buddhas possess the marvelous secondary characteristics,
eighty in number, with which their bodies are adorned.
You should all delight in them
and listen intently as I describe them.

The Bhagavats have round and slender fingers,
nails that are purplish red in hue,
convex in profile, smooth, and glossy,
characteristics of having everything in measureless abundance.

Their veins lie flat, their ankle bones are invisible,
their feet are not skewed in their track,
their gait is like that of the king of lions,
and they are incomparably awe-inspiring to all observers.

When walking, the entire body turns to the right.
They are serene in manner and refined in their deportment.
The parts of their squarely set bodies are orderly in their posture
and their dignified grace inspires fondness and happiness.

Their bodies are firm in tone, but extremely soft.
The articulations of their joints are quite visibly distinct.
When walking, they do not travel in a meandering manner.
All of their sense faculties are fully and perfectly developed.

The flesh on their bodies is extremely taut, finely textured,
freshly radiant, and especially immaculate.
Their physical posture is especially upright, refined,
and devoid of any feature subject to dispraise.

The belly is round, but does not visibly bulge.
The navel, though deep, does not appear to be an orifice.
Its creases manifest as a rightward spiraling swirl.
Their deportment is extremely pure.

The body is free of any blemishes
and the hands and feet are extremely soft.
The lines in the palms are deep and long,
continuous, straight, and lustrous.

The tongue is slender, the face is not too long.
The central incisors are white, rounded, slender, and sharp.
The hue of the lips is like that of the *bimba* fruit.
Their voice is as deep as the king of the wild geese.

The nose is prominent in profile and the eyes are bright and clear.
The eyelashes are close-set and fine, but not in disarray.
The brow is elevated, has eyebrow hair that is soft,
and it is straight and not crooked.

正體字

071b23 ‖ 眉毛齊而整　善知諸法過
071b24 ‖ 眉毛色潤澤　善度潤眾生
071b25 ‖ 耳滿長而等　不壞甚可愛
071b26 ‖ 額廣而齊[9]正　頭相皆具足
071b27 ‖ 髮[*]緻而不亂　如黑蜂王色
071b28 ‖ 清淨而香潔　中有三種相
071b29 ‖ 是名八十種好。以此八十種好間雜莊嚴
071c01 ‖ 三十二相。若人不念三十二相八十種好
071c02 ‖ 讚歎佛身者。是則永失今世後世利樂因
071c03 ‖ 緣。
071c04 ‖ 十住毘婆沙論卷第[10]九

简体字

眉毛齐而整　善知诸法过
眉毛色润泽　善度润众生
耳满长而等　不坏甚可爱
额广而齐正　头相皆具足
发致而不乱　如黑蜂王色
清净而香洁　中有三种相

是名八十种好。以此八十种好间杂庄严三十二相。若人不念三十二相八十种好赞叹佛身者。是则永失今世后世利乐因缘。
十住毗婆沙论卷第九

The hair of the brows, being even and straight,
is emblematic of being well aware of the faults in any dharma.
The hair of the brows is smooth and glossy,
a feature emblematic of skillfully liberating and aiding beings.

The ears are full, long, even in shape,
undamaged, and especially pleasing to the eye.
The forehead is broad and straight.
All of the head's features are perfectly formed.

The hair is fine, dense, never in disarray,
the color of the king of the black bees,
clean, pleasantly fragrant, immaculate,
and possessed of three of the marks.

b) Summation on Importance of Such Recollective Contemplation

This has been the description of the eighty secondary characteristics. Because these eighty secondary characteristics are interspersed with and serve to adorn the thirty-two major marks, if one fails to take up contemplative mindfulness of both the thirty-two marks and the eighty secondary characteristics in one's praises of the Buddha's body, then one may lose forever the causal factors conducing to well-being and happiness in the present and future lives.

The End of Chapter Twenty

正體字

071c07 ‖ 十住毘婆沙論卷第[11]十 071c08 ‖
071c09 ‖ [*]聖者龍樹造
071c10 ‖ [*]後秦龜茲國三藏鳩摩羅什譯
071c11 ‖ 四十不共法品第二十一
071c12 ‖ 菩薩如是以三十二相八十種好念佛生
071c13 ‖ 身已。今應念佛諸功德法。所謂。
071c14 ‖ 又應以四十　不共法念佛
071c15 ‖ 諸佛是法身　非但肉身故
071c16 ‖ 諸佛雖有無量諸法不與餘人共者有
071c17 ‖ 四十法。若人念者則得歡喜。何以故。諸佛
071c18 ‖ 非是色身。是法身故。如經說。汝不應但以
071c19 ‖ 色身觀佛。當以法觀。四十不共法者一者
071c20 ‖ 飛行自在。二者變化無量。三者聖如意無邊。
071c21 ‖ 四[12]聞聲自在。五無量智力知他心。六心得
071c22 ‖ 自在。七常在安慧處。八常不妄誤。九得金
071c23 ‖ 剛三昧力。十善知不定事。十一善知無色定
071c24 ‖ 事。十二具足通達諸永滅事。

简体字

四十不共法品第二十一

菩萨如是以三十二相八十种好念佛生身已。今应念佛诸功德法。所谓。

又应以四十　不共法念佛
诸佛是法身　非但肉身故

诸佛虽有无量诸法不与余人共者有四十法。若人念者则得欢喜。何以故。诸佛非是色身。是法身故。如经说。汝不应但以色身观佛。当以法观。四十不共法者一者飞行自在。二者变化无量。三者圣如意无边。四闻声自在。五无量智力知他心。六心得自在。七常在安慧处。八常不妄误。九得金刚三昧力。十善知不定事。十一善知无色定事。十二具足通达诸永灭事。

Ch. 21: Forty Dharmas Exclusive to Buddhas (Part 1)

II. Chapter 21: Forty Dharmas Exclusive to Buddhas (Part 1)

A. Introduction to the Forty Dharmas Exclusive to Buddhas

It is in the above-discussed manner that the bodhisattva uses the thirty-two major marks and eighty secondary characteristics in his contemplative mindfulness of the Buddha's physical body. Now one should proceed to mindfulness of the dharmas exemplifying the Buddha's meritorious qualities, namely:

> One should also use the forty exclusive dharmas
> in one's contemplation of the Buddhas,
> for the Buddhas are their Dharma body
> and are not merely associated with their physical bodies.

Although the Buddhas possess countless dharmas not held in common with any other persons, there are forty dharmas that, if borne in mind, will cause one to experience joyful happiness. And why [should one bear them in mind]? It is not the case that the Buddhas are their form bodies, for they are rather to be identified with the Dharma body. This accords with this scriptural testimony: "You should not contemplate the Buddha merely in terms of his form body, for it is on the basis of Dharma that one should carry on such contemplation."

As for the forty dharmas exclusive to the Buddhas, they are as follows:[22]

1) Sovereign mastery of the ability to fly;
2) [The ability to manifest] countless transformations;
3) Boundless psychic powers of the sort possessed by *āryas;*
4) Sovereign mastery of the ability to hear sounds;
5) Immeasurable power of knowledge to know others' thoughts;
6) Sovereign mastery in [training and subduing] the mind;
7) Constant abiding in stable wisdom;
8) Never forgetting;
9) Possession of the powers of the vajra samādhi;
10) Thorough knowing of matters that are unfixed
11) Thorough knowing of matters pertaining to the formless realm's meditative absorptions;
12) The completely penetrating knowledge of all matters associated with eternal cessation;

正體字

十三善知心不
071c25 ‖ 相應無色法。十四大勢波羅蜜。十五無礙波
071c26 ‖ 羅蜜。十六一切問答及[13]記具足答波羅蜜。
071c27 ‖ 十七具足三[14]轉說法。十八所說不空。十九
071c28 ‖ 所說無謬失。二十無能害者。二十一諸賢聖
071c29 ‖ 中大將。二十五四不守護。二十九四無所畏。
072a01 ‖ 三十九佛十種力。四十無礙解脫。是為四十
072a02 ‖ 不共之法。今當廣說。飛行自在者。諸佛飛行
072a03 ‖ 如意自在。如意滿足速疾[1]無量無礙。所以者
072a04 ‖ 何。佛若欲於虛空先舉一足次舉一足。即
072a05 ‖ 能如意。若欲舉足躡虛空[2]而去。若欲住
072a06 ‖ 立不動而去。即能得去。若結跏趺安坐而去
072a07 ‖ 亦能得去。若欲安臥而去亦復能去。若欲
072a08 ‖ 於青琉璃莖真珊瑚葉黃金為鬚如意珠臺
072a09 ‖ 無量圍繞如日初出是寶蓮花遍於空中蹈
072a10 ‖ 上而去。若欲如日月宮殿帝釋勝殿夜摩天
072a11 ‖ 兜率陀天化樂天

简体字

十三善知心不相应无色法。十四大势波罗蜜。十五无碍波罗蜜。十六一切问答及记具足答波罗蜜。十七具足三转说法。十八所说不空。十九所说无谬失。二十无能害者。二十一诸贤圣中大将。二十五四不守护。二十九四无所畏。三十九佛十种力。四十无碍解脱。是为四十不共之法。今当广说。飞行自在者。诸佛飞行如意自在。如意满足速疾无量无碍。所以者何。佛若欲于虚空先举一足次举一足。即能如意。若欲举足蹑虚空而去。若欲住立不动而去。即能得去。若结跏趺安坐而去亦能得去。若欲安卧而去亦复能去。若欲于青琉璃茎真珊瑚叶黄金为须如意珠台无量围绕如日初出是宝莲花遍于空中蹈上而去。若欲如日月宫殿帝释胜殿夜摩天兜率陀天化乐天

13) Thorough knowing of the non-form dharmas unassociated with the mind;[23]
14) The great powers *pāramitā;*
15) The [four] unimpeded [knowledges] *pāramitā;*
16) The *pāramitā* of perfectly complete replies and predictions in response to questions;
17) Invulnerability to harm by anyone;
18) Their words are never spoken without a purpose;[24]
19) Their speech is free of errors and mistakes;
20) Complete implementation of the three turnings [of the Dharma wheel] in speaking Dharma;
21) They are the great generals among all *āryas;*
22–25) They are able to remain unguarded in four ways;[25]
26–29) They possess the four types of fearlessness;
30–39) They possess the ten powers;
40) They have achieved unimpeded liberation.

These are the forty dharmas exclusive to the Buddhas. We shall now discuss them more extensively, as below:

B. 1) Sovereign Mastery of the Ability to Fly

As for "sovereign mastery of the ability to fly" all buddhas fly with sovereign mastery, entirely as they wish, and with a manner and speed that are limitless and unimpeded. How is this so? If the Buddha wishes to raise one foot and then the other, walking through space in just such a fashion, then he is immediately able to do so. If he wishes to simply step into space and depart in this manner or if he wishes to simply stand motionlessly in space and depart in this way, he is immediately able to do so.

If he prefers to just sit there peacefully in the full lotus posture and depart like that, then he is also able to leave that way. If he wishes instead to lie down peacefully and then depart, he is able to leave in that way as well.

If he decides to stand upon a precious lotus blossom extending to the very boundaries of empty space, one with a blue *vaiḍūrya* stem, real coral petals, pistils of yellow gold, wish-fulfilling pearls for its pedestal, and countless sorts of surrounding phenomena, one that appears like the sun on first rising—departing in just such a fashion—then he does just that.

Or if, alternatively, he wishes to create through spontaneous psychic transformation a palace like the palaces of the sun or moon, like the supremely marvelous palace of Indra, or like those of the Yāma Heaven devas, the Tuṣita Heaven devas, the Nirmāṇarati Heaven

正體字

他化自在天諸梵王等宮
072a12 ‖ 殿。隨意化作如彼宮殿坐中而去即能成
072a13 ‖ 辦。若更以餘種種因緣隨意能去。是故說
072a14 ‖ 言。隨諸所願皆能滿足。是故諸佛能以一
072a15 ‖ 步。過恒河沙等三千大千世界。有人言。佛
072a16 ‖ 能一念頃過若干[3]百千國土。有人言。若知
072a17 ‖ 佛一步一念能如是去即可得量。經中說
072a18 ‖ 諸佛力無量。是故當知。諸佛虛空飛行自在
072a19 ‖ 無量無邊。何以故。若大聲聞弟子神通自在
072a20 ‖ 以一念頃。能過百億閻浮提瞿陀尼弗婆提
072a21 ‖ 欝多羅越四大[4]王天忉利天夜摩天兜率陀
072a22 ‖ 天化樂天他化自在天梵天。一瞬中過若干
072a23 ‖ 念。積此諸念以成一日七日一月一歲。乃
072a24 ‖ 至百歲。一日過五十三億二百九十六萬六
072a25 ‖ 千三千大千世界。如是聲聞人百歲所過。佛
072a26 ‖ 一念能過。復次假令恒河中沙一沙為一[5]劫。
072a27 ‖ 有大聲聞神通第一壽命如是諸恒河沙大
072a28 ‖ 劫。於一念中過若干世界。

简体字

他化自在天诸梵王等宫殿。随意化作如彼宫殿坐中而去即能成办。若更以余种种因缘随意能去。是故说言。随诸所愿皆能满足。是故诸佛能以一步。过恒河沙等三千大千世界。有人言。佛能一念顷过若干百千国土。有人言。若知佛一步一念能如是去即可得量。经中说诸佛力无量。是故当知。诸佛虚空飞行自在无量无边。何以故。若大声闻弟子神通自在以一念顷。能过百亿阎浮提瞿陀尼弗婆提郁多罗越四大王天忉利天夜摩天兜率陀天化乐天他化自在天梵天。一瞬中过若干念。积此诸念以成一日七日一月一岁。乃至百岁。一日过五十三亿二百九十六万六千三千大千世界。如是声闻人百岁所过。佛一念能过。复次假令恒河中沙一沙为一劫。有大声闻神通第一寿命如是诸恒河沙大劫。于一念中过若干世界。

devas, the Paranirmita Vaśavartin Heaven devas, the Brahma Heaven kings, or like the palaces of any of the other devas, and if he then wishes to create any such palaces, sit down within them, and then depart in that fashion [in one of those flying palaces], then he is immediately able to do precisely that.

Then again, if he prefers to use any of the many other means [for flying from one place to another], then he is freely able to depart however he chooses. Hence it is said, "He is able to completely fulfill whatever wishes he makes." Consequently, with but a single step, the Buddhas can pass beyond great trichiliocosms as numerous as the sands of the Ganges.

There are those who claim that the Buddha is able to move beyond some particular number of hundreds of thousands of lands in but a single mind-moment, whereas there are yet others who claim that, if anyone [supposed he could] know that the Buddha could depart such a distance with but a single step and in but a single mind-moment, then that would be [to infer that the Buddha's abilities] could be limited. But the sutras declare that the powers of the Buddhas surpass all limits. One should therefore realize that the sovereign power of the Buddhas to freely fly through empty space is limitless and boundless.

So how is this the case? Given that one of the great *śrāvaka* disciples using his sovereign mastery of the psychic powers is able in a single mind-moment to pass beyond a hundred *koṭis* of Jambudvīpas, Avara-godānīyas, Pūrva-videhas, Uttara-kurus, Four Heavenly Kings Heavens, Trāyastriṃśa Heavens, Yāma Heavens, Tuṣita Heavens, Nirmāṇarati Heavens, Paranirmita Vaśavartin Heavens, and Brahma Heavens—and given that there are a particular number of mind-moments in the wink of an eye and given that one might aggregate enough of these mind-moments to comprise a whole day, seven whole days, a whole month, a whole year, and so forth, on up to a full hundred years, and if in only a single day, such a *śrāvaka* disciple might pass through fifty-three *koṭis* plus two million, nine hundred and sixty-six thousand, that large a number of great trichiliosms, any Buddha would still be able in a mere mind-moment to exceed that number of great trichiliocosms passed through by such a *śrāvaka* disciple in the course of a full hundred years.

Then again, if one were to allow the passage of a single kalpa for each and every grain of sand in the Ganges—and if there was a great *śrāvaka* disciple foremost in psychic powers who, across the course of a lifespan of kalpas as numerous as the Ganges' sands, passed through in each successive mind-moment just such a number of world systems [as described above]—and if he were to do this for a number of

正體字

積如是念以為
072a29 ‖ 日月歲數以自在力盡是諸大劫數所過
072b01 ‖ 國土。佛能一念中過。諸佛飛行自在如是速
072b02 ‖ 疾。於一切鐵圍山十寶山四天[6]王處忉利
072b03 ‖ 天處夜摩兜率陀化樂他化自在梵世梵眾大
072b04 ‖ 梵少光無量光光音少淨無量淨遍淨廣果無
072b05 ‖ [7]相不廣不惱喜見妙見阿迦尼吒天如是諸
072b06 ‖ 處。大風大水劫盡火等。及諸天龍夜叉乾闥
072b07 ‖ 婆阿修[8]羅緊那羅摩睺羅伽諸天魔及梵沙
072b08 ‖ 門婆羅門及得諸神通者不能為礙。是故
072b09 ‖ 說飛行無礙。又飛行自在如意所作出沒於
072b10 ‖ 地能過石壁諸山障礙等。佛於此事勝諸
072b11 ‖ 聖人。又佛能以常身立至梵天。聲聞人所
072b12 ‖ 不能及。有如是等差別。變化自在者。變化
072b13 ‖ 事中有無量力。餘聖變化有量有邊。諸佛變
072b14 ‖ 化無量無邊。餘聖於一念中變化一身。佛
072b15 ‖ 以一念隨意變化有無量事。

简体字

积如是念以为日月岁数以自在力尽是诸大劫数所过国土。佛能一念中过。诸佛飞行自在如是速疾。于一切铁围山十宝山四天王处忉利天处夜摩兜率陀化乐他化自在梵世梵众大梵少光无量光光音少净无量净遍净广果无相不广不恼喜见妙见阿迦尼吒天如是诸处。大风大水劫尽火等。及诸天龙夜叉乾闼婆阿修罗紧那罗摩睺罗伽诸天魔及梵沙门婆罗门及得诸神通者不能为碍。是故说飞行无碍。又飞行自在如意所作出没于地能过石壁诸山障碍等。佛于此事胜诸圣人。又佛能以常身立至梵天。声闻人所不能及。有如是等差别。变化自在者。变化事中有无量力。余圣变化有量有边。诸佛变化无量无边。余圣于一念中变化一身。佛以一念随意变化有无量事。

mind-moments equivalent to a day, month, or year, doing so with the free exercise of all of his powers even to the exhaustion of such a number of great kalpas—all of those lands passed through by that great *śrāvaka* disciple during that entire time could still be passed through by a buddha in but a single mind-moment. The Buddhas may freely fly from one place to another with just such a speed as this.

In this, they cannot be obstructed by the iron-ring mountains, the ten jeweled mountains, the stations of the Four Heavenly Kings, the stations of the Trāyastriṃśa Heavens, the stations of the Yāma Heavens, Tuṣita Heavens, Nirmāṇarati Heavens, Paranirmita Vaśavartin Heavens, Brahma World Heavens, Brahma Assembly Heavens, Great Brahma Heavens, Lesser Light Heavens, Limitless Light Heavens, Light-and-Sound Heavens, Lesser Purity Heavens, Measureless Purity Heavens, Universal Purity Heavens, Vast Fruition Heavens, Non-Perception Heavens, Not Vast Heavens, No Heat Heavens, Delightful Vision Heavens, Sublime Vision Heavens, or the Akaniṣṭha Heaven.

[Nor can their flight be obstructed by] the great winds, by the great floods, or by the fires that occur at the end of the kalpa. Nor can it be obstructed by any heavenly dragon, *yakṣa, gandharva, asura, kinnara, mahoraga,* deva, Māra, Brahmā, *śramaṇa,* brahmin, or anyone possessed of all the psychic powers. It is therefore said of the Buddhas that they are unimpeded in their ability to fly.

Additionally, by virtue of the sovereign mastery of their flight, they are able to exercise that ability in any manner they wish, by sinking into or emerging from the earth, or by passing through the obstructions presented by stone cliffs, mountains, and such. The Buddha is superior in this ability to any of the other *āryas.* Also, the Buddha is able to make his normal standing body reach in its height on up to the Brahma Heavens. *Śravaka* disciples are unable to match this. There are all manner of differences of this sort.

C. 2) [The Ability to Manifest] Countless Transformations

As for the Buddhas' sovereign mastery in "the ability to manifest transformations," in the matter of manifesting phenomena, they have immeasurable power to do this. The capacity to manifest transformations as possessed by the other classes of *āryas* is both measurable and bounded whereas the Buddhas' capacity to manifest transformations is measureless and unbounded.

The other *āryas* are able, in but a single mind-moment, to manifest a single transformation body whereas the Buddhas are able, in but a single mind-moment, to manifest countless phenomena in whatever way they wish.

正體字

如大神通經
072b16 ‖ 中說。佛從臍中出蓮花。上有化佛次第遍
072b17 ‖ 滿上至阿迦尼吒天。諸佛變化所作眾事。種
072b18 ‖ 種色種種形皆以一念。又聲聞人能於千國
072b19 ‖ 土內變化。諸佛能於無量無邊國土變化自
072b20 ‖ 在。又能倍是諸佛得堅固變化三昧。又諸佛
072b21 ‖ 變化。能過恒沙世界。皆從一身出。復次佛
072b22 ‖ 能普於十方無量無邊世界現生受身墮地
072b23 ‖ 行七步。出家學道破魔軍眾。得道轉法輪。
072b24 ‖ 如是等事皆以一念作之。是諸化佛皆亦復
072b25 ‖ 能施作佛事。如是等諸佛所變化事無量無
072b26 ‖ 邊。又於聖如意中有無量力。聖如意者。所
072b27 ‖ 謂從身放光[9]猶如猛火又出諸雨。變化壽
072b28 ‖ 命隨意長短。於一念頃能至梵天能變諸
072b29 ‖ 物。隨意自在能動大地。光明能照無量世
072c01 ‖ 界而不斷絕。聖如意者。不與凡夫等故。
072c02 ‖ 無有量故。過諸量故。諸凡夫等雖變化諸
072c03 ‖ 物少不足言。聲聞人能裂千國土。還使令
072c04 ‖ 合。

简体字

如大神通经中说。佛从脐中出莲花。上有化佛次第遍满上至阿迦尼吒天。诸佛变化所作众事。种种色种种形皆以一念。又声闻人能于千国土内变化。诸佛能于无量无边国土变化自在。又能倍是诸佛得坚固变化三昧。又诸佛变化。能过恒沙世界。皆从一身出。复次佛能普于十方无量无边世界现生受身堕地行七步。出家学道破魔军众。得道转法轮。如是等事皆以一念作之。是诸化佛皆亦复能施作佛事。如是等诸佛所变化事无量无边。又于圣如意中有无量力。圣如意者。所谓从身放光犹如猛火又出诸雨。变化寿命随意长短。于一念顷能至梵天能变诸物。随意自在能动大地。光明能照无量世界而不断绝。圣如意者。不与凡夫等故。无有量故。过诸量故。诸凡夫等虽变化诸物少不足言。声闻人能裂千国土。还使令合。

This is as described in the *Sutra on the Great Spiritual Powers*: "The Buddha may send forth from his navel a lotus blossom with transformation buddhas sitting atop it that then, in an orderly fashion, fill up all of space on up to the Akaniṣṭha Heaven. The many sorts of transformations created by the Buddhas take all sorts of different forms and all sorts of different shapes and are all created in but a single mind-moment."

Also, *śrāvaka* disciples are able to perform transformations within a thousand lands whereas the Buddhas are able to freely perform transformations within a countless and boundless number of lands and are additionally able to do much more than this, for the Buddhas have gained the solid transformation samādhi. Also, the transformations performed by but one of the Buddhas' bodies are able to occur in worlds as numerous as the sands of the Ganges.

Additionally, a buddha is able in a countless and boundless number of worlds of the ten directions to manifest a buddha being born, taking on a body, dropping to the earth, taking seven steps, leaving the home life, studying the path, defeating Māra's armies, achieving enlightenment, and turning the Dharma wheel. All of these phenomena are created in but a single mind-moment. All of these transformation buddhas are themselves also able to carry out the work of the Buddhas. And the transformation-generated phenomena created by all of those buddhas are themselves countless and boundless.

D. 3) Boundless Psychic Powers of the Sort Possessed by Āryas

Also, the Buddhas have "boundless psychic powers of the sort possessed by *āryas*." As for "the psychic powers possessed by *āryas*," this refers to phenomena such as: radiating light from their bodies that may manifest as raging fire and also pouring forth rains; transforming their length of life however they wish, either lengthening it or shortening it; being able in a single thought to go to the Brahma Heaven; being able to perform transformations of various phenomena, being able to shake the great earth whenever they wish; or being able to ceaselessly radiate light capable of illuminating countless worlds.

Also, "psychic powers possessed by *āryas*," are referred to as such because they are incomparably different from those possessed by common people, because of their being boundless, and because of their going beyond all limits. Although common people may possess some ability to perform transformations of various phenomena, their power to do so is so minor as to be beneath mention here.

A *śrāvaka* disciple may be able to split a thousand lands and then cause them to join back together again, may be able to lengthen his

正體字

能令壽命若至一劫若減一劫。還能令
072c05 ‖ 短。短已[10]不能令長。於一念中能至千國
072c06 ‖ 土梵世界。能於千國土隨意變化。能動千
072c07 ‖ 國土。能身出光明相續不絕照千國土。設
072c08 ‖ 使身滅能留神力變化如本於千國土。小
072c09 ‖ 辟支佛能於萬國土萬種變化。中辟支佛能
072c10 ‖ 於百萬國土百萬種變化。大辟支佛能於三
072c11 ‖ 千大千國土變化如上。諸佛世尊能過諸恒
072c12 ‖ 河沙世界算數變化身出水火能[11]末恒河
072c13 ‖ 沙等世界令如微塵。又能還合能住。壽命無
072c14 ‖ 量劫數還能令少。少已還能令長。能於無量
072c15 ‖ 時住。變化隨意。能以一念至無量無邊恒
072c16 ‖ 河沙等世界。能以常身立至梵世。又能變
072c17 ‖ 化無量無邊阿僧祇世界皆令作金。或令
072c18 ‖ 作銀瑠璃珊瑚[12]車璩馬瑙。取要言之。能令
072c19 ‖ 作無量寶物。隨意所作。又復能變恒河沙
072c20 ‖ 等世界大海水。皆使為乳酥油酪蜜隨意
072c21 ‖ 而成。又能以一念變[13]化諸山皆是真金。
072c22 ‖ 過諸算數不可稱計。又能震動無量無邊
072c23 ‖ 世界一切欲界色界諸天宮殿。又以一念能
072c24 ‖ 令若干金色光明遍照如是無量世界。

简体字

能令寿命若至一劫若减一劫。还能令短。短已不能令长。于一念中能至千国土梵世界。能于千国土随意变化。能动千国土。能身出光明相续不绝照千国土。设使身灭能留神力变化如本于千国土。小辟支佛能于万国土万种变化。中辟支佛能于百万国土百万种变化。大辟支佛能于三千大千国土变化如上。诸佛世尊能过诸恒河沙世界算数变化身出水火能末恒河沙等世界令如微尘。又能还合能住。寿命无量劫数还能令少。少已还能令长。能于无量时住。变化随意。能以一念至无量无边恒河沙等世界。能以常身立至梵世。又能变化无量无边阿僧祇世界皆令作金。或令作银琉璃珊瑚车磲马瑙。取要言之。能令作无量宝物。随意所作。又复能变恒河沙等世界大海水。皆使为乳酥油酪蜜随意而成。又能以一念变化诸山皆是真金。过诸算数不可称计。又能震动无量无边世界一切欲界色界诸天宫殿。又以一念能令若干金色光明遍照如是无量世界。

lifespan to a kalpa or somewhat less than a kalpa in duration and then be able to shorten it, but after having shortened it, he will be unable to make it long again. He may be able in a single mind-moment to go to the brahma worlds associated with a thousand lands, may be able to freely perform transformations in a thousand lands, may be able to shake the earth in a thousand lands, may be able to ceaselessly radiate light from his body that can illuminate a thousand lands, and, even if his body is destroyed, he may retain the presence of his spiritual powers and their ability to perform transformations just as before, doing so in a thousand lands.

The lesser *pratyekabuddha* is able to perform a myriad transformations in a myriad lands. The middling *pratyekabuddha* is able to perform a million transformations in a million lands. A great *pratyekabuddha* is able to perform the sorts of transformations cited above, doing so throughout all lands in a great trichiliocosm.

The Buddhas, the Bhagavats, are able to perform transformations in worlds more numerous than the Ganges' sands wherein they send forth fire and water from their bodies. They are even able to grind to fine dust worlds as numerous as the Ganges' sands and then cause them to be restored. They are able to abide for a lifespan of countless kalpas, are able to shorten that lifespan, and having shortened it, they are then able to lengthen it again. They are able to abide for an immeasurably long period of time. They are able to freely perform transformations such that, in the space of but a single mind-moment, they are able to go to countless and boundless worlds as numerous as the sands in the River Ganges.

They are able to cause their usual body, when standing, to reach all the way up to the Brahma Worlds. They are also able to perform a transformation whereby countless and boundless *asaṃkhyeyas* of worlds are all caused to be transformed into gold, or into silver, or into *vaiḍūrya*, coral, mother-of-pearl, or carnelian. To sum up the essential point, they are freely able in accordance with their wishes to cause them to be transformed into a countless number of precious things.

They are also able in accordance with their wishes to transform the waters of the great oceans in worlds as numerous as the Ganges' sands into milk, ghee, yogurt, or honey. They are also able in but a single mind-moment to transform incalculably many mountains into real gold.

They are also able to shake the heavenly palaces of the desire realm and form realm heavens of countless and boundless worlds. They are also able in but a single mind-moment to cause gold-colored radiance to so universally illuminate an immeasurably great number of worlds

正體字

日月 072c25 ‖光明及欲色界諸天宮殿光明皆令不現。雖
072c26 ‖ 滅度後能於如是諸世界中隨意久近。流
072c27 ‖ 布神力常不斷絕。聞聲自在者。諸佛所聞聲
072c28 ‖ 中隨意自在。若無量百千萬億[14]技樂同時俱
072c29 ‖ 作。若無量百千萬億眾生一時發言。若遠若
073a01 ‖ 近隨意[1]所聞。假令恒河沙等三千大千世界
073a02 ‖ 所有眾生。同時俱作若干百千萬種伎樂遍
073a03 ‖ 滿世界。復有恒河沙等世界眾生。同時以梵
073a04 ‖ 音。遍滿一切世界。諸佛若欲於中聞一音
073a05 ‖ 聲隨意得聞。餘者不聞。聲聞所應聞者。
073a06 ‖ 若有大神力障者不能得聞。諸佛所聞音
073a07 ‖ 聲雖有大神力障亦能得聞。聲聞能聞千
073a08 ‖ 國土內音聲。諸佛世尊所聞音聲過無量無
073a09 ‖ 邊世界最細音聲皆亦得聞。大神力聲聞住
073a10 ‖ 梵世界。發大音聲能滿千國土內。諸佛世
073a11 ‖ 尊若住於此若住梵世若住餘處。音聲能
073a12 ‖ 滿無量無邊世界。若欲令眾生聞過無量
073a13 ‖ 無邊世界最細音聲能令得聞。欲令不聞
073a14 ‖ 即便不聞。

简体字

日月光明及欲色界诸天宫殿光明皆令不现。虽灭度后能于如是诸世界中随意久近。流布神力常不断绝。闻声自在者。诸佛所闻声中随意自在。若无量百千万亿技乐同时俱作。若无量百千万亿众生一时发言。若远若近随意所闻。假令恒河沙等三千大千世界所有众生。同时俱作若干百千万种伎乐遍满世界。复有恒河沙等世界众生。同时以梵音。遍满一切世界。诸佛若欲于中闻一音声随意得闻。余者不闻。声闻所应闻者。若有大神力障者不能得闻。诸佛所闻音声虽有大神力障亦能得闻。声闻能闻千国土内音声。诸佛世尊所闻音声过无量无边世界最细音声皆亦得闻。大神力声闻住梵世界。发大音声能满千国土内。诸佛世尊若住于此若住梵世若住余处。音声能满无量无边世界。若欲令众生闻过无量无边世界最细音声能令得闻。欲令不闻即便不闻。

that the light from all those suns and moons and heavenly palaces of the desire-realm and the form-realm no longer appear at all.

Although a buddha may have already passed into nirvāṇa, afterward, he is still freely ever able in all those worlds to remain for however long he wishes, ceaselessly implementing his spiritual powers.

E. 4) Sovereign Mastery of the Ability to Hear Sounds

As for "sovereign mastery in the ability to hear sounds," the Buddhas have sovereign mastery in their ability to hear sounds however they please. Even if there were countless hundreds of thousands of myriads of *koṭis* of musical sounds being simultaneously played and hundreds of thousands of myriads of *koṭis* of beings simultaneously speaking—whether those sounds are far or near, the Buddhas are freely able to hear whichever sounds they please.[26]

If one were to cause all beings in great trichiliocosms as numerous as a Ganges' sands to simultaneously create any given number of hundreds of thousands of myriads of *koṭis* of kinds of music that filled up all those worlds, and if at the same time all beings in worlds as numerous as a Ganges' sands were to fill up all those worlds with the voice of Brahmā, if any buddha wished to hear only one single sound from among all those sounds, then that buddha would be freely able to hear that single sound while not hearing any other sound.

In the case of the sounds heard by *śrāvaka* disciples, if someone possessed of great spiritual powers were to block any given sound, then they would not be able to hear it. In the case of sounds heard by buddhas, even though there might be someone possessed of great spiritual powers seeking to block their hearing some sound, the Buddhas are nonetheless able to hear it.

A *śrāvaka* disciple may be able to hear any sound within a thousand lands. The Buddhas, the Bhagavats, are able to hear even the most subtle sounds even from a distance spanning countlessly and boundlessly many world systems.

A *śrāvaka* disciple possessed of great spiritual powers and abiding in the Brahma World Heavens is able to issue such a great sound that it is capable of pervasively filling a thousand lands. As for the Buddhas, the Bhagavats, it matters not whether they are abiding here or in the Brahma World Heaven, or are instead in yet some other place—their voices are still able to fill up countlessly and boundlessly many world systems. If they wish to cause a particular being to hear the most subtle sound across a distance of countlessly and boundlessly many worlds, they can cause him to hear it and if they wish to prevent someone from hearing a sound, then that person will indeed be unable to hear it at

正體字

是故但有諸佛於[2]聞聲中得
073a15 ‖ 自在力。知他心無量自在力者。諸佛世尊
073a16 ‖ 於無量無邊世界現在眾生悉知其心。餘人
073a17 ‖ 但隨名相故知。諸佛以名相義故知。又餘
073a18 ‖ 人不能知無色界眾生諸心。諸佛能知。餘
073a19 ‖ 人雖有知他心智。大[3]力者障則不能知。假
073a20 ‖ 使一切眾生成就心通。皆如舍利弗目[4]犍
073a21 ‖ 連辟支佛等。以其神力障一人心。不令他
073a22 ‖ 知。而佛能壞彼神力得知其心。復次佛以
073a23 ‖ 神力悉知眾生上中下心垢心淨心。又知諸
073a24 ‖ 心各有所緣從是緣至是緣次第。遍知一
073a25 ‖ 切諸緣。又以實相知眾生心。是故諸佛以
073a26 ‖ 無[5]量力悉知他心。第一調伏心波羅蜜者。
073a27 ‖ 善知諸禪定三昧解脫住入起時。諸佛若入
073a28 ‖ 定若不入定。欲繫心一緣中。隨意久近
073a29 ‖ 如意能住。

简体字

是故但有诸佛于闻声中得自在力。知他心无量自在力者。诸佛世尊于无量无边世界现在众生悉知其心。余人但随名相故知。诸佛以名相义故知。又余人不能知无色界众生诸心。诸佛能知。余人虽有知他心智。大力者障则不能知。假使一切众生成就心通。皆如舍利弗目犍连辟支佛等。以其神力障一人心。不令他知。而佛能坏彼神力得知其心。复次佛以神力悉知众生上中下心垢心净心。又知诸心各有所缘从是缘至是缘次第。遍知一切诸缘。又以实相知众生心。是故诸佛以无量力悉知他心。第一调伏心波罗蜜者。善知诸禅定三昧解脱住入起时。诸佛若入定若不入定。欲系心一缘中。随意久近如意能住。

all. Consequently, it is only the Buddhas who have gained sovereign mastery with regard to the hearing of sounds.

F. 5) Immeasurable Power of Knowledge to Know Others' Thoughts

As for "measureless power of sovereign mastery in the ability to know others' thoughts," the Buddhas, the Bhagavats, are completely aware of all the thoughts of all beings of the present existing throughout countlessly and boundlessly many worlds. Others may develop the ability to know someone else's thoughts, but only as represented by the words [contained in others' thoughts]. The Buddhas, however, know others' thoughts in terms of the associated meanings of the words [contained in others' thoughts].

Moreover, others remain unable to know the thoughts of beings in the formless realm, but the Buddhas are able to know them. Although others may possess the ability to know someone else's thoughts, if anyone possessed of great powers wishes to block that ability, then they will no longer be able to know others' thoughts.

Supposing that all beings had developed psychic powers to the same degree as Śāriputra, Maudgalyāyana, or a *pratyekabuddha*. Now suppose that they used all of their collective spiritual powers to block anyone from knowing someone's thoughts. In such a case, a buddha would still be able to break their spiritual powers and would still succeed in knowing that person's thoughts.

Additionally, a buddha is able to use his spiritual powers to completely know any being's superior, middling, and inferior thoughts, his defiled thoughts, and his pure thoughts. Moreover, he is able to know with regard to each thought, the condition taken as the object of that thought, is able to know also the sequential progression of each thought as it moves from one objective condition to another, and is able to comprehensively know all of the conditions associated with any given thought. Also, he is able to know any being's thoughts in accordance with their true character.

It is on these bases that the Buddhas are acknowledged to have immeasurable powers to completely know the thoughts of others.

G. 6) Sovereign Mastery in [Training and Subduing] the Mind

As for the Buddhas' "*pāramitā* of being foremost in training and subduing the mind," they well know all of the *dhyānas*, samādhis, and liberations and well understand entry into them, abiding in them, and emerging from them. Whether a buddha is immersed in meditative absorption or not, should he wish to focus his mind on a single object, then he is freely able to focus upon it for however long he wishes and

正體字

從此緣中更住餘緣隨意能住。
073b01 ‖ 若佛住常心欲令人不知則不能知。假使
073b02 ‖ 一切眾生。知他心智如大梵王如大聲聞
073b03 ‖ 辟支佛。成就智慧知他人心。以此[6]諸智
073b04 ‖ 令一人得。是人欲知佛常心。若佛不聽則
073b05 ‖ 不能知。如七方便經中說。行者善知定相。
073b06 ‖ 善知住定相。善知起定相。善知安隱定相。
073b07 ‖ 善知定行處相。善知定生相。善知宜諸
073b08 ‖ 定法不宜諸定法。是名諸佛第一調伏心
073b09 ‖ 波羅蜜。諸佛常安慧者。諸佛安慧常不動
073b10 ‖ 念常在心。何以故。先知而後[7]行。隨意所緣
073b11 ‖ 中住無疑行故。斷一切煩惱故。出過動
073b12 ‖ 性故。如佛告阿難。佛於此夜得阿耨多羅
073b13 ‖ 三藐三菩提。一切世間若天魔梵沙門婆羅
073b14 ‖ 門。以盡苦道教化周畢入無餘涅槃。於其
073b15 ‖ 中間佛於諸受知起知住

简体字

从此缘中更住余缘随意能住。若佛住常心欲令人不知则不能知。假使一切众生。知他心智如大梵王如大声闻辟支佛。成就智慧知他人心。以此诸智令一人得。是人欲知佛常心。若佛不听则不能知。如七方便经中说。行者善知定相。善知住定相。善知起定相。善知安隐定相。善知定行处相。善知定生相。善知宜诸定法不宜诸定法。是名诸佛第一调伏心波罗蜜。诸佛常安慧者。诸佛安慧常不动念常在心。何以故。先知而后行。随意所缘中住无疑行故。断一切烦恼故。出过动性故。如佛告阿难。佛于此夜得阿耨多罗三藐三菩提。一切世间若天魔梵沙门婆罗门。以尽苦道教化周毕入无余涅槃。于其中间佛于诸受知起知住

then is able to change from this object to focusing on some other condition, freely abiding in that focus for however long he wishes.

If the Buddha, abiding in his normal thoughts, wishes to cause others to remain unaware of his thoughts, then they would be unable to know them. Even if all beings had perfected the ability to know others' minds to a degree comparable to the ability to know others' thoughts as possessed by a king of the Great Brahma Heaven, a great *śrāvaka* disciple, or a *pratyekabuddha,* and they all then caused a single person to acquire their collective abilities in this, and this person then wished to know the normal thought of a buddha, so long as that buddha did not permit it, that person would still be unable to acquire that knowledge.

This is as described in the *Sutra on the Seven Expedients*: "The practitioner:

Well knows the signs of meditative absorption;
Well knows the signs of abiding in meditative absorption;
Well knows the signs of emerging from meditative absorption;
Well knows the signs of stable and secure meditative absorption;
Well knows the signs of the stations of practice in meditative absorption;
Well knows the signs of the development of meditative absorption;
And well knows what is and is not appropriate to the dharmas of meditative absorption."[27]

This is what is meant by the Buddhas' "*pāramitā* of being foremost in training and subduing the mind."

H. 7) Constant Abiding in Stable Wisdom

As for the Buddhas' "constant abiding in stable wisdom," the Buddhas' stable wisdom is constant and unshakeable and their mindfulness is always maintained in their minds. And why is this the case? It is because they first know and then act, because they freely dwell on whichever object they choose while having no doubt in their actions, because they have cut off all afflictions, and because they have gone utterly beyond the realm[28] of movement itself.

This is as the Buddha told Ānanda:

The Buddha, in this one evening, gains *anuttarasamyaksaṃbodhi* and proceeds then to teach the path to the ending of suffering to everyone in the world, whether they be a deva, Māra, Brahmā, a *śramaṇa,* or a brahmin, and then, in the end, finally enters the nirvāṇa without residue.

During the interim, the Buddha, with respect to every feeling, is aware of its arising, is aware of its abiding, is aware of its birth and

正體字

知生知滅。諸相
073b16 ‖ 諸觸諸覺諸念亦知起知住知生知滅。惡
073b17 ‖ 魔七年晝夜不息常隨逐佛不得佛短。不
073b18 ‖ 見佛念不在念安慧。是名諸佛常住安慧
073b19 ‖ 行中。不忘失法者。諸佛得不退法故。通達
073b20 ‖ 五藏法故。得無上法故。諸佛常不忘失。諸
073b21 ‖ 佛菩提樹下所得。乃至入無餘涅槃。若天魔
073b22 ‖ 梵沙門婆羅門。及餘聖人。無能令佛有所
073b23 ‖ 忘失。如法印經中說。道場所得是名實得
073b24 ‖ 更無勝法。如衣毛竪經說。舍利弗。若人實
073b25 ‖ 語。有能於法不忘失者。應說我是。何以
073b26 ‖ 故。唯我一人無所忘失。是名諸佛於法無
073b27 ‖ 忘失。金剛三昧者。諸佛世尊金剛三昧。是不
073b28 ‖ 共法。無能壞故。於一切處無有障礙故。
073b29 ‖ 得正遍知故。壞一切法障礙故。等貫穿故。
073c01 ‖ 得諸功德利益力故。諸禪定中最上故。

简体字

知生知灭。诸相诸触诸觉诸念亦知起知住知生知灭。恶魔七年昼夜不息常随逐佛不得佛短。不见佛念不在念安慧。是名诸佛常住安慧行中。不忘失法者。诸佛得不退法故。通达五藏法故。得无上法故。诸佛常不忘失。诸佛菩提树下所得。乃至入无余涅槃。若天魔梵沙门婆罗门。及余圣人。无能令佛有所忘失。如法印经中说。道场所得是名实得更无胜法。如衣毛竖经说。舍利弗。若人实语。有能于法不忘失者。应说我是。何以故。唯我一人无所忘失。是名诸佛于法无忘失。金刚三昧者。诸佛世尊金刚三昧。是不共法。无能坏故。于一切处无有障碍故。得正遍知故。坏一切法障碍故。等贯穿故。得诸功德利益力故。诸禅定中最上故。

is aware of its cessation. With respect to all perceptions,[29] all tactile contact, all ideation, and all mental discursion, he is aware of their arising, aware of their abiding, aware of their birth, and aware of their cessation.

Māra the Evil One,[30] constantly and without resting, followed along after the Buddha both day and night for seven years yet was never in all that time able to come upon any shortcomings of the Buddha and was never able to observe an instance of the Buddha's mindfulness not abiding in a state of stable wisdom. This is what is meant by the Buddha's constant abiding in the practice of stable wisdom.

I. 8) Never Forgetting

As for the dharma of "never forgetting," because the Buddhas have gained the dharma of irreversibility, have reached a penetrating understanding of the five categorical repositories of dharmas,[31] and have acquired the unsurpassable Dharma, the Buddhas never forget.

With respect to all that the Buddhas have realized beneath the bodhi tree and have then subsequently acquired up to the time when they enter the nirvāṇa without residue, no matter whether it be a deva, Māra, Brahmā, a *śramaṇa,* a brahmin, or some other *ārya,* there is no one who is able to cause the Buddhas to forget anything at all.

This is as described in the *Sutra on the Seal of Dharma*: "As for that which is realized at the *bodhimaṇḍa,* this is known as the genuine realization and there is no dharma superior to it."

This is also as described in the *Horripilation Sutra*: "Śāriputra. If anyone could claim truthfully that they do not have any aspect of Dharma that they forget, I would be the one who could make that claim. How is this so? I alone do not forget anything whatsoever."

This is what is intended when it is said that the Buddhas never forget Dharma.

J. 9) Possession of the Powers of the Vajra Samādhi

As for "the vajra samādhi," the vajra samādhi of all the Buddhas, the Bhagavats, is one of the exclusive dharmas, [so named]:

Because it cannot be destroyed by anything;
Because there is no place where it can be obstructed;
Because it is associated with right and universal knowledge;
Because it destroys all hindrances to Dharma;
Because it is able to equally penetrate [all dharmas];
Because it brings about the power to acquire the benefit of all meritorious qualities;
And because it is the most supreme of all *dhyāna* samādhis.

正體字

無能 073c02 ‖壞者。是故名為金剛三昧。如金剛寶無物
073c03 ‖ 能破者。是三昧亦如是。無[8]有法可以壞
073c04 ‖ 者。是故名金剛三昧。問曰。何故不可壞。答
073c05 ‖ 曰。一切處無有[9]閡故。如帝釋金剛無有
073c06 ‖ 閡處。是三昧亦如是。問曰。是三昧。何故
073c07 ‖ 名一切處不閡。答曰。正通達一切法故。諸
073c08 ‖ 佛住是三昧。悉能通達過去現在未來。過
073c09 ‖ [10]出三世不可說五藏所攝法。是故名一切
073c10 ‖ 處不閡。若諸佛住是三昧。諸所有法若不通
073c11 ‖ 達名為有礙。而實不爾。是故名無礙。問曰。
073c12 ‖ 何以故。是三昧通達一切法。答曰。是三昧能
073c13 ‖ 開一切障礙法故。所謂煩惱障閡定障閡智
073c14 ‖ 障閡能開故。是名能通達一切法。問曰。是
073c15 ‖ 三昧。何故能開一切障。餘三昧不能。答曰。
073c16 ‖ 是三昧善等貫穿[11]二法。能壞諸煩惱山令
073c17 ‖ 無餘故。正遍通達一切法故。善得不壞心
073c18 ‖ 解脫故。是故此三昧能開一切障閡。

简体字

无能坏者。是故名为金刚三昧。如金刚宝无物能破者。是三昧亦如是。无有法可以坏者。是故名金刚三昧。问曰。何故不可坏。答曰。一切处无有阂故。如帝释金刚无有阂处。是三昧亦如是。问曰。是三昧。何故名一切处不阂。答曰。正通达一切法故。诸佛住是三昧。悉能通达过去现在未来。过出三世不可说五藏所摄法。是故名一切处不阂。若诸佛住是三昧。诸所有法若不通达名为有碍。而实不尔。是故名无碍。问曰。何以故。是三昧通达一切法。答曰。是三昧能开一切障碍法故。所谓烦恼障阂定障阂智障阂能开故。是名能通达一切法。问曰。是三昧。何故能开一切障。余三昧不能。答曰。是三昧善等贯穿二法。能坏诸烦恼山令无余故。正遍通达一切法故。善得不坏心解脱故。是故此三昧能开一切障阂。

As for its being called "the vajra samādhi" because there is nothing that can destroy it, it is like the precious vajra gem that cannot be crushed by anything at all. This samādhi is just like this. There is no dharma capable of destroying it. It is therefore known as "the vajra samādhi."

Question: Why is it that it cannot be destroyed?

Response: This is because there is nothing anywhere that obstructs it. It is just as with Indra's vajra that meets no obstruction anywhere. This samādhi is just like that.

Question: Why is this samādhi said to have nothing anywhere that obstructs it?

Response: Because it possesses a right and utterly penetrating comprehension of all dharmas. All buddhas, abiding in this samādhi, are able to utterly penetrate all of the dharmas subsumed within the five categorical repositories of dharmas: all dharmas of the past, of the present, of the future, those that transcend the three periods of time, and those that are ineffable dharmas. It is for this reason that it is said to meet with no obstruction anywhere.

If it were the case that, while abiding in this samādhi, all buddhas still did not have an utterly penetrating comprehension of all dharmas, then that would be a case of still having obstructions. But, in truth, this is not the case. It is therefore said to not be obstructed by anything whatsoever.

Question: How is it that this samādhi brings about a penetrating comprehension of all dharmas?

Response: It is because this samādhi is able to open up all obstructive dharmas, namely the obstacle of the afflictions, the obstacles to meditative absorption, and the obstacles to knowledge. Because it is able to open up all obstructions, it is therefore said to bring about an utterly penetrating comprehension of all dharmas.

Question: How is it that this samādhi is able to open up all obstructions whereas other samādhis remain unable to do so?

Response: This samādhi is well able to penetrate three[32] dharmas:

Because it is able to destroy the mountain of afflictions so that nothing remains of them;

Because it brings about the right and universal comprehension of all dharmas;

And because it brings about the thorough-going attainment of the liberation of the indestructible resolve.

It is for these reasons that this samādhi is said to be able to open up all obstructions.

正體字

問曰。
073c19 ‖ 是三昧何故等貫穿[*]二法。答曰。住是三昧
073c20 ‖ 得力故。能得一切諸功德。餘三昧無如是
073c21 ‖ 力。是故是三昧能等貫穿。問曰。何故住是
073c22 ‖ 三昧得力故能得一切諸功德。答曰。是三
073c23 ‖ 昧於諸定中最為第一。是故住是三昧能
073c24 ‖ 得諸功德。問曰。何故是三昧於諸定中最
073c25 ‖ 為第一。答曰。是三昧無量無邊善根所成
073c26 ‖ 故。於諸定中最為第一。問曰。是三昧何故
073c27 ‖ 無量無邊善根所成。答曰。是三昧唯一切智
073c28 ‖ 人有餘人所無。是故名為金剛三昧。

简体字

问曰。是三昧何故等贯穿二法。答曰。住是三昧得力故。能得一切诸功德。余三昧无如是力。是故是三昧能等贯穿。问曰。何故住是三昧得力故能得一切诸功德。答曰。是三昧于诸定中最为第一。是故住是三昧能得诸功德。问曰。何故是三昧于诸定中最为第一。答曰。是三昧无量无边善根所成故。于诸定中最为第一。问曰。是三昧何故无量无边善根所成。答曰。是三昧唯一切智人有余人所无。是故名为金刚三昧。

Question: How is it that this samādhi is able to equally penetrate these three dharmas?[33]

Response: This is because, when one abides in this samādhi, one gains the power by which one is then able to acquire every sort of meritorious quality. None of the other samādhis possess this sort of power. It is for this reason that this samādhi is able to "equally penetrate" [all dharmas].

Question: How is it that, abiding in this samādhi, one gains the power by which one is then able to acquire every sort of meritorious quality?

Response: This samādhi is the foremost among all meditative absorptions. It is because of this that, abiding in this samādhi, one is able to gain every sort of meritorious quality.

Question: How is it that this samādhi is foremost among all samādhis?

Response: This samādhi is foremost among all meditative absorptions because it is produced through the possession of measurelessly and boundlessly many roots of goodness.

Question: How is it that this samādhi is produced through the possession of measurelessly and boundlessly many roots of goodness?

Response: This samādhi is possessed only by those who are equipped with all-knowledge. It has not been acquired by anyone else. Hence it is known as "the vajra samādhi."

The End of Chapter Twenty-One

正體字

073c29 ‖ 四十不共法中難一切智人品第二十二
074a01 ‖ 問曰。汝說金剛三昧。唯一切智人有。餘人所
074a02 ‖ 無。若是三昧但一切智人有。餘人無者。即
074a03 ‖ 無是三昧。何以故。無一切智人故。何以故。
074a04 ‖ 所知法無量無邊。而智慧有量有邊。以此有
074a05 ‖ 量有邊智慧。不應知無量事。如今現閻浮
074a06 ‖ 提水陸眾生過諸算數。是眾生三品。若男若
074a07 ‖ 女非男非女在胎孩童少壯衰老苦樂等法。
074a08 ‖ 過去未來現在諸心心數法。及諸善惡業。已
074a09 ‖ 集今集當集。已受報今受報未受報。萬物
074a10 ‖ 生滅及閻浮提中山河泉池草木叢林根莖枝
074a11 ‖ 葉花果。所可知者無有邊際。餘三天下亦
074a12 ‖ 如是[1]如四天下三千大千世界物亦如是。
074a13 ‖ [*]如三千大千世界物一切世界所可知物亦
074a14 ‖ 如是。但世間數尚無量無邊難可得知。何
074a15 ‖ 況諸閻浮提諸世間中。眾生非眾生諸物[2]分。

简体字

四十不共法中难一切智人品第二十二

问曰。汝说金刚三昧。唯一切智人有。余人所无。若是三昧但一切智人有。余人无者。即无是三昧。何以故。无一切智人故。何以故。所知法无量无边。而智慧有量有边。以此有量有边智慧。不应知无量事。如今现阎浮提水陆众生过诸算数。是众生三品。若男若女非男非女在胎孩童少壮衰老苦乐等法。过去未来现在诸心心数法。及诸善恶业。已集今集当集。已受报今受报未受报。万物生灭及阎浮提中山河泉池草木丛林根茎枝叶花果。所可知者无有边际。余三天下亦如是如四天下三千大千世界物亦如是。如三千大千世界物一切世界所可知物亦如是。但世间数尚无量无边难可得知。何况诸阎浮提诸世间中。众生非众生诸物分。

Ch. 22: Forty Dharmas Exclusive to Buddhas (Part 2)

Challenges to the Reality of Omniscience

III. Chapter 22: Forty Dharmas Exclusive to Buddhas (Part 2)

A. Q: Your Claim That Omniscience Exists Is False for these Reasons

Question: You claim that only those possessed of all-knowledge possess the vajra samādhi and no one else has it. If this samādhi was only possessed by someone who has all-knowledge and no one else possessed it, then this samādhi does not even exist. Why? Because there is no one who possesses all-knowledge.

And why is this? It is because the dharmas that might be known are measureless and boundless whereas the knowledge that might know them is measurable and bounded. It should not be the case that this measurable and bounded knowledge could know measurelessly many phenomena.

For instance, on the present-day continent of Jambudvīpa, the number of beings dwelling in its waters and on its lands are beyond count. Also, consider the three categories of beings, whether male, female, or neither male nor female, those still in the womb, the children, the young and strong, the frail and old, and also the dharmas associated with their suffering, happiness, and so forth. Also, consider all of the mind and mental dharmas of the past, future, and present, as well as all good and bad karmic actions accumulated in the past, present, and future, all the karmic retributions undergone in the past, present, and future, all the births and deaths of the myriad creatures, and also all of Jambudvīpa's mountains, rivers, springs, ponds, grasses, trees, dense forests, roots, stems, branches, leaves, blossoms, and fruit. The things that can be known are limitlessly many.

The same is true for the other three continents. And just as this is the case with these four continents, it is also the case throughout all of the worlds of the great trichiliocosm. And just as this is the case with all of the worlds of the great trichiliocosm, so too is it also the case for all things that can be known in all other worlds.

As for the number of the worlds, that matter alone is measureless, boundless, and difficult to know. How much the more so is this the case for all of the sentient and insentient beings and all other categories of things on the Jambudvīpa continents in all those worlds.

正體字

074a16 ‖ 以是因緣當知。所可知物無量無邊故。無
074a17 ‖ 一切智者。若謂智慧有大力於所知法中
074a18 ‖ 無障閡故遍知一切可知。法如虛空遍
074a19 ‖ 在一切法中。是故應有一切智人者。是事
074a20 ‖ 不然。智大力可爾。[3]大智不能自知。如指
074a21 ‖ 端不自觸。是故無一切智。若謂更有智能
074a22 ‖ 知是智。是亦不然。何以故。有無窮過故。[4]智
074a23 ‖ 若自知若以他知。二俱不然。若是[*]智有
074a24 ‖ 無量力。以不自知故。不得言有無量力。
074a25 ‖ 是故無有能知一切法[5]智。無知一切法
074a26 ‖ 智故。則無一切智者。何以故。一切智者。以
074a27 ‖ 智知一切法[6]故。復次所知法無量無邊。若
074a28 ‖ 和合百千萬億智人尚不能盡知。何況一
074a29 ‖ 人。是故無有一人能知一切法。無有一切
074b01 ‖ 智。若謂不以遍知一切山河眾生非眾生
074b02 ‖ 故名一切智人。但以盡知一切經書故名

简体字

以是因缘当知。所可知物无量无边故。无一切智者。若谓智慧有大力于所知法中无障阂故遍知一切可知。法如虚空遍在一切法中。是故应有一切智人者。是事不然。智大力可尔。大智不能自知。如指端不自触。是故无一切智。若谓更有智能知是智。是亦不然。何以故。有无穷过故。智若自知若以他知。二俱不然。若是智有无量力。以不自知故。不得言有无量力。是故无有能知一切法智。无知一切法智故。则无一切智者。何以故。一切智者。以智知一切法故。复次所知法无量无边。若和合百千万亿智人尚不能尽知。何况一人。是故无有一人能知一切法。无有一切智。若谓不以遍知一切山河众生非众生故名一切智人。但以尽知一切经书故名

For these reasons, one should realize that the things that can be known are countless and limitless and, because of that, it cannot be that there is anyone at all who is possessed of all-knowledge.

Suppose that one were to claim that the knowledge [of someone who is omniscient] is possessed of such great power that, because it is unimpeded with respect to those dharmas it cognizes, it is able to pervasively know all those dharmas in just the same manner as empty space is able to reach everywhere in its universal pervasion of all things. Suppose too that one were to claim that, because of this, it ought to be the case that there truly is such a thing as an omniscient person. If one were to make such a claim, this still could not be so, for even if knowledge could possess such a great power as this, even such great knowledge as this would still remain unable to know itself in just the same way that one's fingertip remains unable to touch itself. Therefore, there is no such thing as all-knowledge.

If, [in response to this], one were to claim that there is yet some other knowledge possessed of the capacity to know this knowledge, this could not be the case, either. And why not? That is because this proposition would then fall into the fallacy of infinite regression. Knowledge either knows itself or is known by something other. They cannot both be true.

If, as you say, this knowledge is somehow possessed of measureless power, because of the fact that it still remains unable to know itself, one really cannot claim that it is possessed of measureless power. Therefore there is no such thing as some knowledge possessed of the ability to know all dharmas.

If there is no such thing as some knowledge possessed of the ability to know all dharmas, then there could not be anyone possessed of all-knowledge. And why is this the case? It is because anyone possessed of all-knowledge [could only be so by] availing himself of just such a [non-existent] knowledge that knows all dharmas.

Furthermore, the dharmas that can be known are measureless and boundless. Even if one were to employ the combined knowing capacity of a hundred thousand myriads of *koṭis* of wise men, they would still be unable to exhaustively know them all. How much the less could a single person do so. Therefore there is no such thing as any single person who is able to know all dharmas and there is no such thing as "all-knowledge."

If one were to claim that it is not on the basis of comprehensively knowing every mountain, river, being, or non-being that we speak of someone possessed of all-knowledge, but rather it is simply on the basis of exhaustively knowing all scriptures that one speaks of

正體字

074b03 ‖ 一切智人者。是亦不然。何以故。佛法中不
074b04 ‖ 說韋陀等經書義。若佛是一切智[7]人者。應
074b05 ‖ 用韋陀等經書而實不用是故。佛非一切
074b06 ‖ 智人。又四韋陀羅經有量有限。今世尚無盡
074b07 ‖ 能知者。況有盡知一切經書。是故無有一
074b08 ‖ 切智人。復次有經書能增長貪欲。歌舞音樂
074b09 ‖ 等。若一切智人知是事者即有貪欲。是經
074b10 ‖ 書[8]者是貪欲因緣。若有因必有果。若一切
074b11 ‖ 智人不知此事則不名一切智人。復次有
074b12 ‖ 諸經書能助瞋恚喜誑於人。所謂治世經書
074b13 ‖ 等。若知是事則有瞋恚。何以故。有因必有
074b14 ‖ 果故。若不知則不名一切智人。是故知無
074b15 ‖ 一切智人。復次佛不必盡知未來世事。譬
074b16 ‖ 如我今難一切智人。佛無經書[9]豫記是人
074b17 ‖ 如是姓如是家在某處以如是事難一切
074b18 ‖ 智人。若謂佛盡知何以故不說是事。

简体字

一切智人者。是亦不然。何以故。佛法中不说韦陀等经书义。若佛是一切智人者。应用韦陀等经书而实不用是故。佛非一切智人。又四韦陀罗经有量有限。今世尚无尽能知者。况有尽知一切经书。是故无有一切智人。复次有经书能增长贪欲。歌舞音乐等。若一切智人知是事者即有贪欲。是经书者是贪欲因缘。若有因必有果。若一切智人不知此事则不名一切智人。复次有诸经书能助嗔恚喜诳于人。所谓治世经书等。若知是事则有嗔恚。何以故。有因必有果故。若不知则不名一切智人。是故知无一切智人。复次佛不必尽知未来世事。譬如我今难一切智人。佛无经书豫记是人如是姓如是家在某处以如是事难一切智人。若谓佛尽知何以故不说是事。

someone possessed of all-knowledge, this is also wrong. How so? It is because, within the sphere of the Buddha's Dharma, one does not speak of the concepts treated in the Vedas and other such scriptures. If the Buddha really were, [in this sense of the term], a man possessed of all-knowledge, then he should make use of the Vedas and other such scriptures, but in truth, he does not use these, and so, because of this, the Buddha is not an all-knowing man.

Moreover, the scriptures comprising the four Vedas are themselves measurable and limited in their scope and, even so, there is not even anyone capable of exhaustively knowing those scriptures, how much the less could there be anyone who exhaustively knows all the scriptures in existence. Therefore there is no such thing as a person possessed of "all-knowledge" [even in this limited sense of the term].

Moreover, there are scriptures that are able to cause the proliferation of desire and that devote themselves to such things as dance and music and such. If a person possessed of all-knowledge were to become knowledgeable with respect to these matters, then he would be subjected to the arising of desire. Scriptures of these sorts constitute the causes and conditions for the arising of desire. Where there is a given cause, there must necessarily be the corresponding result [ensuing from it]. If a person possessed of all-knowledge does not know these matters, then he could not be validly referred to as someone possessed of all-knowledge.

Furthermore, there are scriptures that are able to influence a person to become full of hate and to take delight in deceiving others, specifically such works as those classics concerned with ruling the world. Were one to become knowledgeable about such matters, then one would come to be possessed of hatred. How is the case? It is because, where there is such a given cause, then there must necessarily be the corresponding result ensuing from it. And were one to not know such matters, then one could not be validly referred to as possessed of all-knowledge. One should therefore realize that there really is no such thing as a person who is possessed of all-knowledge.

Additionally, it is not necessarily the case that a buddha could exhaustively know matters pertaining to the future. Take for instance my present challenge to the plausibility of there being anyone who is omniscient. The Buddha has no scriptural record of having predicted that in the future there would be this particular man of this particular caste from this particular clan in this particular place who would on these particular grounds challenge the plausibility of there being anyone who might be omniscient. If one were to claim that the Buddha exhaustively knows such things, why did he not speak of this matter? If

正體字

若說
074b19 ‖ 經者經中應有不說是事。是故知非一切
074b20 ‖ 智人。復次佛若盡知未來世事。應當[*]豫知
074b21 ‖ 調達出家已破僧。若知者不應聽出家。復
074b22 ‖ 次佛不知木機激石。佛若[*]豫知者則不應
074b23 ‖ 於中經行。復次佛不知旃遮婆羅門女以
074b24 ‖ 婬欲謗。若佛先知。應告諸比丘未來當
074b25 ‖ 有是事。復次有梵志嫉佛故於餘處殺
074b26 ‖ 梵志女孫陀羅於祇洹塹中埋。佛不知是
074b27 ‖ 事。若知是者。應於諸梵志所救此女命。
074b28 ‖ 至調達所推石下。不說婆羅門女梵志女
074b29 ‖ 事。以不知故。當知佛不盡知未來世。是故
074c01 ‖ 非一切智人。復次佛入婆羅門聚落乞食
074c02 ‖ 空鉢而出。不能豫知魔時轉諸人心。乃至
074c03 ‖ 不得一食。佛若知者則不應入婆羅門聚
074c04 ‖ 落。是[10]故知佛不盡知未來事。復次阿闍世
074c05 ‖ 王欲害佛故放守財醉象。佛不知故入王
074c06 ‖ 舍城乞食。若[*]豫知者則不應入[11]城。是[12]故

简体字

若说经者经中应有不说是事。是故知非一切智人。复次佛若尽知未来世事。应当豫知调达出家已破僧。若知者不应听出家。复次佛不知木机激石。佛若豫知者则不应于中经行。复次佛不知旃遮婆罗门女以淫欲谤。若佛先知。应告诸比丘未来当有是事。复次有梵志嫉佛故于余处杀梵志女孙陀罗于祇洹堑中埋。佛不知是事。若知是者。应于诸梵志所救此女命。至调达所推石下。不说婆罗门女梵志女事。以不知故。当知佛不尽知未来世。是故非一切智人。复次佛入婆罗门聚落乞食空钵而出。不能豫知魔时转诸人心。乃至不得一食。佛若知者则不应入婆罗门聚落。是故知佛不尽知未来事。复次阿阇世王欲害佛故放守财醉象。佛不知故入王舍城乞食。若豫知者则不应入城。是故

he is the one who spoke these scriptures, then those scriptures should have a record of such matters, but he did not speak of these matters. Therefore one knows that he was not omniscient.

Moreover, if the Buddha exhaustively knew future matters, then he should have known in advance that, after Devadatta left home to become a monk, he would then create a schism in the Sangha. If he had knowledge of that, then he should not have allowed Devadatta to become a monk. Also, the Buddha did not know that Devadatta would use a stick to pry loose a boulder [that would roll down and draw blood from the Buddha's foot]. If the Buddha had known of this matter in advance, then he should not have been walking in that place.

Additionally, the Buddha failed to know in advance that Ciñca, the brahmin woman, would slander him by accusing him of having had sexual relations with her. If the Buddha had known of this in advance, then he should have told the bhikshus that, in the future, there would be just such an occurrence.

Also, there was the case of the *brahmacārin* who, because he was jealous of the Buddha, killed a *brahmacārin* woman named Sundarī in another place and then buried her in a trench in the vicinity of the Jeta Grove. The Buddha did not know of this matter. If he had known of this, then he should have sought among the brahmins to [find a way to] see that her life would be saved.

The Buddha went to that place beneath which Devadatta was about to set loose the falling boulder, failed to announce in advance the incidents having to do with the brahmin woman and the *brahmacārin* woman. Because he did not know of these matters, one should realize that the Buddha did not exhaustively know the future. Therefore he could not possibly have been omniscient.

Furthermore, the Buddha once entered a brahmin village seeking food on the alms round but then had to leave with an empty bowl. He was unable then to know in advance that Māra would so turn the minds of the villagers against him that he would be unable to obtain anything to eat. If the Buddha had known of this matter, then he should not have entered that brahmin village. Therefore one knows that the Buddha did not exhaustively know how matters would transpire in the future.

Moreover, because King Ajātaśatru wished to harm the Buddha, he released a drunken elephant used to guard the treasury.[34] Because the Buddha did not know of this matter, he entered the city of Rājagṛha on his alms round. If he had known of this matter in advance, then he should not have gone into the city. Therefore he did not have

正體字

074c07 ‖ 不知未來事。不知未來事故則非一切智
074c08 ‖ 人。復次佛不知惡涅達多請佛因緣。即受
074c09 ‖ 其請將諸比丘詣韋羅闍國。是婆羅門忘
074c10 ‖ 先請故。使佛食馬麥。若佛豫[13]知則不應
074c11 ‖ 受請三月食馬麥。是故知佛不知未來事。
074c12 ‖ 不知未來事故則非一切智人。復次佛受
074c13 ‖ 須涅叉多羅為弟子故則不知未來事。是
074c14 ‖ 人惡心堅牢難化不信佛語。佛若知者云何
074c15 ‖ 受為弟子。受為弟子故則不知未來事。不
074c16 ‖ 知未來事故則非一切智人。復次若佛是
074c17 ‖ 一切智人則應防護未有犯罪者當為結
074c18 ‖ 戒。以先不知結戒因緣有作罪已方乃結
074c19 ‖ 戒則不知未來事。不知未來事故則非一
074c20 ‖ 切智人。復次佛法但以出家受戒[14]歲數處
074c21 ‖ 在上座恭敬禮拜。不以耆年貴族諸家功德
074c22 ‖ 智慧多聞禪定果斷神通為大。若是一切智
074c23 ‖ 者。

简体字

不知未来事。不知未来事故则非一切智人。复次佛不知恶涅达多请佛因缘。即受其请将诸比丘诣韦罗阇国。是婆罗门忘先请故。使佛食马麦。若佛豫知则不应受请三月食马麦。是故知佛不知未来事。不知未来事故则非一切智人。复次佛受须涅叉多罗为弟子故则不知未来事。是人恶心坚牢难化不信佛语。佛若知者云何受为弟子。受为弟子故则不知未来事。不知未来事故则非一切智人。复次若佛是一切智人则应防护未有犯罪者当为结戒。以先不知结戒因缘有作罪已方乃结戒则不知未来事。不知未来事故则非一切智人。复次佛法但以出家受戒岁数处在上座恭敬礼拜。不以耆年贵族诸家功德智慧多闻禅定果断神通为大。若是一切智者。

knowledge of future matters. Because he did not have knowledge of future matters, he therefore could not have been omniscient.

Additionally, the Buddha did not know of the causal circumstances involved in Agnidatta's invitation to the Buddha. Consequently he immediately accepted that invitation and then led the bhikshus to the state of Verañjā. Because this brahmin had forgotten his prior issuance of that invitation, he caused the Buddha to eat only horse fodder. If the Buddha had known of this matter in advance, then he should not have accepted that invitation on account of which he spent the entire three months [of the rains retreat] surviving only on horse fodder. We know therefore that the Buddha did not have knowledge of future matters. Because he did not have knowledge of future matters, he therefore could not have been omniscient.

Also, because the Buddha accepted Sunakṣatra as a disciple, he could not have had knowledge of future matters. This man possessed an obdurately evil mind, made himself difficult to teach, and did not believe the words of the Buddha. If the Buddha had known of this, how could he have accepted him as a disciple? Because he accepted him as a disciple, then he could not have known future matters. Because he did not have knowledge of future matters, he therefore could not have been omniscient.

Furthermore, if the Buddha had been omniscient, then, in order to prevent inevitable future instances of moral transgressions, he would have formulated his moral precepts in advance. Because he had no prior knowledge of the causal circumstances that eventually led to the formulation of each particular moral precept, it was only after someone had committed such a transgression that he then subsequently laid down these moral regulations. This being the case, he could not have known of future matters. Because he did not have knowledge of future matters, he therefore could not have been omniscient.

Moreover, in the Dharma set forth by the Buddha, it is solely on the basis of seniority in years of monastic ordination that, within the community, one sits more toward the front and is accorded reverence and obeisance [by those of fewer years of seniority]. One is not acknowledged as of greater eminence merely on the basis of one's venerable age, one's noble birth, the stature of one's clan, one's meritorious qualities, the level of wisdom one has developed, the degree of learning one has achieved, the particular *dhyāna* absorptions one has entered, the fruits of the path one has gained, the fetters one has cut off, or the spiritual powers one has acquired.

If the Buddha had really been someone possessed of all-knowledge, then he would have accorded eminence, higher priority in the receipt

正體字

應以耆年貴族諸家功德智慧多聞禪定
074c24 ‖ 果斷神通為大供養恭敬。若如是者名為
074c25 ‖ 善制。歲數者受戒年數。如五歲道人禮六
074c26 ‖ 歲者。貴族者世間有四品眾生。婆羅門剎利
074c27 ‖ [15]韋舍首陀羅。首陀羅應恭敬韋舍剎利婆
074c28 ‖ 羅門。韋舍應恭敬剎利婆羅門。剎利應恭
074c29 ‖ 敬婆羅門。諸家者。工巧家商[16]估家居士家長
075a01 ‖ 者家大臣家王家等。於諸家中。其小家應
075a02 ‖ 恭敬大家。如是於貧賤中出家者。應恭
075a03 ‖ 敬富貴中出家者。功德者毀戒人應恭敬禮
075a04 ‖ 拜持戒[1]者。持戒者不應禮毀戒者。不行
075a05 ‖ 十二頭陀者。應禮行十二頭陀者。不具足
075a06 ‖ 行頭陀者。應禮具足行頭陀者。智慧者。
075a07 ‖ 無智慧人應禮敬有智慧者。多聞者。少聞
075a08 ‖ 人應禮多聞者。不多誦者應禮敬多誦者。
075a09 ‖ 果者。須陀洹應禮敬斯陀含。如是展轉應

简体字

应以耆年贵族诸家功德智慧多闻禅定果断神通为大供养恭敬。若如是者名为善制。岁数者受戒年数。如五岁道人礼六岁者。贵族者世间有四品众生。婆罗门刹利韦舍首陀罗。首陀罗应恭敬韦舍刹利婆罗门。韦舍应恭敬刹利婆罗门。刹利应恭敬婆罗门。诸家者。工巧家商估家居士家长者家大臣家王家等。于诸家中。其小家应恭敬大家。如是于贫贱中出家者。应恭敬富贵中出家者。功德者毁戒人应恭敬礼拜持戒者。持戒者不应礼毁戒者。不行十二头陀者。应礼行十二头陀者。不具足行头陀者。应礼具足行头陀者。智慧者。无智慧人应礼敬有智慧者。多闻者。少闻人应礼多闻者。不多诵者应礼敬多诵者。果者。须陀洹应礼敬斯陀含。如是展转应

of offerings, and stature in receipt of reverential obeisance on the basis of one's venerable age, one's noble birth, the stature of one's clan, one's meritorious qualities, the level of wisdom one has developed, the degree of learning one has achieved, the particular *dhyāna* absorptions one has entered, the fruits of the path one has gained, the fetters one has cut off, and the spiritual powers one has acquired. If the Buddha had made stipulations of this sort, then that would qualify as having established a well-regulated community.

Regarding the matter of years of monastic ordination seniority, this is the principle by which a practitioner of the path ordained for only five years is enjoined to accord reverential obeisance to a monk ordained for six years.

As for the issue of nobility of birth caste, the world has four classes of beings: *brahmans, kṣatriyas, vaiśyas,* and *śūdras. Śūdras* are enjoined to revere *vaiśyas, kṣatriyas,* and *brahmans. Vaiśyas* ought to pay obeisance to *kṣatriyas* and *brahmans. Kṣatriyas* are supposed to pay reverential obeisance to *brahmans.*

As for the status of clans, there are the artisan clans, the business-and-trade clans, the merchant clans, the clans led by those of senior status, the clans of great officials, royal clans, and so forth. Among them, the members of lesser-status clans are supposed to revere members of the eminent clans. This being the case, when those from poor and base clans leave the home life to become monks, they should be enjoined to pay reverence to monks from wealthy and noble clans.

With respect to meritorious qualities, whoever has broken moral precepts should be enjoined to revere and bow in formal obeisance to those who uphold the moral precepts. Those who strictly observe the moral precepts should not be bowing in reverence to anyone who has broken the moral precepts.

Those who do not practice the twelve *dhūta* austerities[35] should bow in reverence to those who are practitioners of the twelve *dhūta* austerities. Those who are not perfectly complete in their practice of the *dhūta* practices should bow in reverence to those who are perfect in their practice of the *dhūta* austerities.

As for the matter of wisdom, people devoid of wisdom should bow in reverence to those possessed of wisdom. With regard to learning, those of shallow learning should bow in reverence to those who have achieved a high level of learning. Those who do not recite many scriptures should bow in reverence to those who are able to recite many sutras from memory.

As for the fruits of the path, the stream enterer should bow in reverence to the *sakṛdāgāmin* and it should proceed in this fashion on up to

正體字

075a10 ‖ 禮阿羅漢。一切凡夫應禮得果者。斷者。少
075a11 ‖ 斷結使及未斷者應禮多斷者。神通者。若
075a12 ‖ 未具神通者應禮[2]具神通者。佛若如是
075a13 ‖ 次第善說供養恭敬法者。是為上說。而實
075a14 ‖ 不爾。是故知非一切智人。復次佛尚不能
075a15 ‖ 知現在事。汝若謂我云何知佛不知現在
075a16 ‖ 事者。今當說之。有眾生結使薄者。無業
075a17 ‖ 障者。離八難者。堪行深法者。能成正法
075a18 ‖ 者。而佛不知。佛成道已初欲說法。生如是
075a19 ‖ 疑。我所得法甚深玄遠微妙寂滅難知難解。
075a20 ‖ 唯有智者可以內知。世間眾生貪著世事。
075a21 ‖ 此中除斷一切煩惱滅愛厭離第一難見。若
075a22 ‖ 我說法眾生不解。徒自疲苦。生如是疑。而
075a23 ‖ 實眾生有薄結使無業障者。有離八難
075a24 ‖ 者。堪行深法者。能成正法者。佛不能知
075a25 ‖ 如是眾生。是故當知不知現在事。

简体字

礼阿罗汉。一切凡夫应礼得果者。断者。少断结使及未断者应礼多断者。神通者。若未具神通者应礼具神通者。佛若如是次第善说供养恭敬法者。是为上说。而实不尔。是故知非一切智人。复次佛尚不能知现在事。汝若谓我云何知佛不知现在事者。今当说之。有众生结使薄者。无业障者。离八难者。堪行深法者。能成正法者。而佛不知。佛成道已初欲说法。生如是疑。我所得法甚深玄远微妙寂灭难知难解。唯有智者可以内知。世间众生贪着世事。此中除断一切烦恼灭爱厌离第一难见。若我说法众生不解。徒自疲苦。生如是疑。而实众生有薄结使无业障者。有离八难者。堪行深法者。能成正法者。佛不能知如是众生。是故当知不知现在事。

[the circumstance where realizers of the first three fruits of the path are enjoined to] bow in reverence to the arhat. As for all of the common people, they should bow in reverence to anyone who has gained any of the fruits of the path.

Those who have severed fewer of the fetters as well as those who have not yet severed any of the fetters should all bow in reverence to those who have severed many of the fetters.

Regarding the matter of spiritual powers, if one has not yet acquired any of the spiritual powers, he should then be bowing in obeisance to whomever has already acquired spiritual powers.

If the Buddha had skillfully set forth such sequentially ranked protocols regarding the making of offerings and the according of reverence, then his proclamations on these matters would be of a superior order. But, in truth, he did not do so. One can therefore know that the Buddha was not omniscient.

Furthermore, the Buddha was not even able to know all matters having to do with the present. If you were to ask me how I know that the Buddha did not have knowledge of present-era matters, then I would now inform you as follows:

There were beings whose fetters were but slight, who had no karmic obstacles, who were free of the eight difficulties, who were capable of practicing deep dharmas, and who were able to be successful in the cultivation of right Dharma, and yet the Buddha did not realize this. After the Buddha had attained enlightenment and was first on the verge of proclaiming the Dharma, he gave rise to the following doubt:

> The Dharma that I have gained is extremely profound, recondite, far-reaching, sublime, quiescent, difficult to know, difficult to comprehend, and such as only the wise might be able to realize inwardly. The beings in this world are attached by their desires to worldly matters. That there might be any among them who might be able to cut off their afflictions, extinguish craving, and develop renunciation—this would be the rarest of possibilities. If I were to expound the Dharma, beings would fail to comprehend it. Such an endeavor would be but a useless experiencing of wearisome hardship.

And so the Buddha generated just such a doubt even though there were in fact beings whose fetters were but slight, who had no karmic obstacles, who were free of the eight difficulties, who were capable of practicing deep dharmas, and who were able to be successful in the cultivation of right Dharma. Because the Buddha was unable to know of the existence of such beings, one should therefore know that the Buddha failed to know matters having to do with the present time.

正體字

又作是 075a26 ‖念。昔我苦行。五比丘供養執侍應先利益。今
075a27 ‖ 在何處。作是念已時有天告。今在波羅捺
075a28 ‖ 鹿野苑中。是故當知佛不知現在事。不知
075a29 ‖ 現在事故。則非一切智人。復次佛得道已
075b01 ‖ 受請說法而作是念。我今說法誰應先聞。
075b02 ‖ 即復念言。欝頭藍弗。此人利[3]智易可開悟。
075b03 ‖ 爾時此人先[4]已命終。而佛[5]訪求。時天告言。
075b04 ‖ 昨夜命終。佛又思惟迴心欲度阿羅[6]邏。天
075b05 ‖ 復白言。是人亡來七日。若佛是一切智者先
075b06 ‖ 應知此諸人命終。而實不知。不知過去事
075b07 ‖ 故則不名一切智人。一切智人法應度可度
075b08 ‖ 者。不可則置。復次佛處處有疑語。如巴
075b09 ‖ [7]蓮弗城。是事當以三因緣壞。若水若火若
075b10 ‖ 內人與外人謀。若佛是一切智人者則不
075b11 ‖ 應有疑惑語。是故知非一切智人。復次佛
075b12 ‖ 問比丘。汝等聚會為說何事。如是等問。若
075b13 ‖ 一切智人者則不應問如是等事。以問他
075b14 ‖ 故非一切智人。

简体字

又作是念。昔我苦行。五比丘供养执侍应先利益。今在何处。作是念已时有天告。今在波罗捺鹿野苑中。是故当知佛不知现在事。不知现在事故。则非一切智人。复次佛得道已受请说法而作是念。我今说法谁应先闻。即复念言。郁头蓝弗。此人利智易可开悟。尔时此人先已命终。而佛访求。时天告言。昨夜命终。佛又思惟回心欲度阿罗逻。天复白言。是人亡来七日。若佛是一切智者先应知此诸人命终。而实不知。不知过去事故则不名一切智人。一切智人法应度可度者。不可则置。复次佛处处有疑语。如巴莲弗城。是事当以三因缘坏。若水若火若内人与外人谋。若佛是一切智人者则不应有疑惑语。是故知非一切智人。复次佛问比丘。汝等聚会为说何事。如是等问。若一切智人者则不应问如是等事。以问他故非一切智人。

The Buddha also thought as follows: "Previously, when I was practicing ascetic austerities, the five bhikshus made offerings to me and supported me. It is only appropriate that I first benefit them. Where are they now?"

After he had this thought, a deva informed him: "They are now in Benares, in the place known as 'Deer Park.'"

On account of this, one knows that the Buddha did not even know of matters having to do with the present. If he failed to know of matters having to do with the present, then we can know from this that the Buddha could not have been omniscient.

Furthermore, after he had attained enlightenment, the Buddha accepted the invitation to expound on Dharma and then had this thought, "As I now proceed to proclaim the Dharma, who is it that ought to be the first to hear it?" He then had another thought: "Udraka Rāmaputra—this is a man of sharp wisdom, one who might easily become enlightened."

By this time, that man had already died and yet the Buddha nonetheless went in search of him. A deva then informed him: "His life came to an end just last night." The Buddha thought again and, having reflected, he decided he wanted to liberate Ārāḍa Kālāma. A deva then told him, "This man died seven days ago."

If the Buddha had been omniscient, he should have known beforehand that these men had already died, but in truth he did not know these events had happened. Because the Buddha did not know about past matters, he could not have been omniscient.

The methods employed by an omniscient man would be such that he should strive to bring about the liberation of those capable of achieving liberation while setting aside those incapable of success in this.

Moreover, in place after place, the Buddha spoke in terms revealing the presence of doubts on his part. Take for example the city of Pāṭaliputra that he said was bound to be destroyed by one of three causes: by flood, by fire, or by a conspiracy between insiders and outsiders. If the Buddha had really been omniscient, then he should not have had instances where his speech was marked by the presence of doubts. One knows therefore that he could not have been omniscient.

Additionally, the Buddha inquired of the bhikshus, "What matter have you all come together to discuss?" He asked questions of this sort. If he were omniscient, then he should not have asked about matters of this sort. Because he was compelled to ask others [in order to know of these matters], then he could not have been omniscient.

正體字

復次佛自稱讚身毀[8]呰他
075b15 ‖ 人。如經中說。佛告阿難。唯我一人第一無
075b16 ‖ 比無與等者。告諸比丘尼[*]犍子等是弊惡
075b17 ‖ 人成就五邪法。諸尼[*]犍子等無信無慚無愧
075b18 ‖ 寡聞懈怠少念薄智。又說梵志尼[*]犍諸外道
075b19 ‖ 弟子等諸不可事。若自稱讚毀[*]呰他人。世
075b20 ‖ 人尚愧。何況一切智人。有此事故非一切
075b21 ‖ 智人。復次佛經始終相違如經中說。諸比丘
075b22 ‖ 我新得道。又言我得往古諸佛所得道。世
075b23 ‖ 間有智尚離終始相違。何況出家一切智人
075b24 ‖ 而有相違。以終始相違故。當知非一切智
075b25 ‖ 人。是故汝說金剛三昧唯一切智人得。是事
075b26 ‖ 不然。無一切智人故。一切智三昧亦不成。
075b27 ‖ 答曰。汝莫說此。佛實是一切智人。何以故。
075b28 ‖ 凡一切法有五法藏。所謂過去法。未來法。現
075b29 ‖ 在法。出三世法。不可說法。唯佛如實遍知
075c01 ‖ 是法。如汝先難所知法無量無邊故無一切
075c02 ‖ 智人者。我今當答。

简体字

复次佛自称赞身毁呰他人。如经中说。佛告阿难。唯我一人第一无比无与等者。告诸比丘尼犍子等是弊恶人成就五邪法。诸尼犍子等无信无惭无愧寡闻懈怠少念薄智。又说梵志尼犍诸外道弟子等诸不可事。若自称赞毁呰他人。世人尚愧。何况一切智人。有此事故非一切智人。复次佛经始终相违如经中说。诸比丘我新得道。又言我得往古诸佛所得道。世间有智尚离终始相违。何况出家一切智人而有相违。以终始相违故。当知非一切智人。是故汝说金刚三昧唯一切智人得。是事不然。无一切智人故。一切智三昧亦不成。答曰。汝莫说此。佛实是一切智人。何以故。凡一切法有五法藏。所谓过去法。未来法。现在法。出三世法。不可说法。唯佛如实遍知是法。如汝先难所知法无量无边故无一切智人者。我今当答。

Also, the Buddha engaged in self-praise while deprecating others. This is as described in the sutras, "The Buddha told Ānanda, 'I alone am foremost, without a peer, unequaled by anyone.'"[36]

He told the bhikshus, "The Nirgranthas and others of that sort are base and evil people who have perfected the five types of deviant dharmas. The Nirgranthas and such have no faith, have no sense of shame, have no dread of blame, and are men of but little learning who are indolent, possessed of only scant mindfulness and shallow wisdom."

He also discussed all manner of impermissible endeavors engaged in by *brahmacārins*, by Nirgranthas, and by the disciples and other followers of the non-Buddhist traditions.

Self-praise and deprecation of others is a behavior of which even common people of the world are ashamed. How much the more so should this be the case for someone who is omniscient. Because the Buddha engaged in behaviors of this sort, he could not have been omniscient.

Furthermore, comparing beginnings and endings, one finds that the Buddhist scriptures are self-contradictory. Take for instance the statements in the sutras wherein, on the one hand, the Buddha claims, "Bhikshus, I am one who has newly discovered the path." Then, on the other hand, he claims: "I have attained that path which has previously been attained by all buddhas of antiquity."

Even wise worldly people abandon any tendency to contradict themselves through chronological inconsistencies. How much the less should it be that a monastic possessed of all-knowledge could stumble into such chronological self-contradictions. Because the Buddha fell into chronological inconsistencies, one should realize that he could not possibly have been omniscient. Therefore your claim that the vajra samādhi is only acquired by omniscient men is wrong, this because there is no such thing as an omniscient person. Nor can one establish any case for the existence of some sort of omniscience samādhi.

B. A: Wrong. As I Shall Now Explain, The Buddha Truly Is Omniscient

Response: You should not speak this way. The Buddha truly is omniscient. And how is this so? In general, all dharmas are comprised of five categorical repositories of dharmas, namely: past dharmas, future dharmas, present dharmas, dharmas that transcend the three periods of time, and ineffable dharmas. It is only a buddha who completely knows all these dharmas in accordance with reality.

I shall now respond to your earlier challenge that asserts, because knowable dharmas are measureless and boundless, there are no

正體字

若所知法無量無邊。智
075c03 ‖ 亦無量無邊。以無量無邊智知無量無邊法
075c04 ‖ 無咎。若謂是知亦應以智知是則無窮者。
075c05 ‖ 今當答。[9]法應以智知。[10]智如世間人言。我
075c06 ‖ 是智者我是無智者。我是麁智者。我是細智
075c07 ‖ 者。以是因緣以智知[*]智故。則無無窮過。
075c08 ‖ 如以現在[*]智知過去智則盡知一切法
075c09 ‖ 無有遺餘。復次如人數他通身為十知亦
075c10 ‖ 如是。自知亦[11]知他則無有咎。如燈自照
075c11 ‖ 亦照他。如汝所說和合百千萬億智人尚
075c12 ‖ 不能盡知一切法。何況一人知者。是事不
075c13 ‖ 然。何以故。一[12]切智慧人能知眾事。雖復眾
075c14 ‖ 多無有智慧不能有所知。如百千盲人
075c15 ‖ 不[13]任作導。一人有眼任為導師。是故汝
075c16 ‖ 以一人為難。雖復多智於佛則無智。是
075c17 ‖ 事不然。

简体字

若所知法无量无边。智亦无量无边。以无量无边智知无量无边法无咎。若谓是知亦应以智知是则无穷者。今当答。法应以智知。智如世间人言。我是智者我是无智者。我是粗智者。我是细智者。以是因缘以智知智故。则无无穷过。如以现在智知过去智则尽知一切法无有遗余。复次如人数他通身为十知亦如是。自知亦知他则无有咎。如灯自照亦照他。如汝所说和合百千万亿智人尚不能尽知一切法。何况一人知者。是事不然。何以故。一切智慧人能知众事。虽复众多无有智慧不能有所知。如百千盲人不任作导。一人有眼任为导师。是故汝以一人为难。虽复多智于佛则无智。是事不然。

omniscient people. Insofar as knowable dharmas might be measureless and boundless, the corresponding knowledge is also measureless and boundless. There is no fault in claiming that it is by means of measureless and boundless knowledge that one may know measureless and boundless dharmas.

As for your earlier assertion that knowing should somehow also involve a knowledge that knows [itself] and that this would entail the fallacy of infinite regress, I shall now respond, as follows:

It should be the case that dharmas are known by one's cognition. This cognition is similar to what is referenced when the world's common people describe themselves in this way: "I am a knowledgeable person," "I am someone with no knowledge," "I am someone possessed of only a coarse type of knowledge," or "I am someone who possesses subtle knowledge."

One should realize from these circumstances that it is with one's own cognitive ability that one knows [the character of one's own] knowledge. This being the case, there is no fallacy of infinite regress involved here. This is just a case of using one's own present cognitive ability to know one's past knowledge. It is in this way that one can exhaustively know all dharmas without any omissions.

Also, this is just like when someone counts others [in addition to oneself], thus reaching [for instance a total of] ten [people in all]. The capacity to know is just like that. For knowing to thereby know both itself and others is thus a concept free of any fault. This is also analogous to when a lamp is able to illuminate both itself and other things as well.

As for your contention that even the aggregated knowing capacity of a hundred thousand myriads of *koṭis* of wise people could not exhaustively know all dharmas, how much the less might a single person be able to know them—this is wrong. How is this so? An omniscient person is able to know the many things. Although there may be some additional multitude of people, if they have no cognitive ability, they won't know much of anything.

This is comparable to a situation in which there was a group of a hundred thousand blind men. [Even together], they still could not get hired as guides, but just one single person with good eyes might well be able to serve as a guide. Consequently, as regards your challenge to [the plausibility of omniscience on the part of] a single person, even in a situation where many knowers might be involved, they would still have no knowledge at all compared to the Buddha's capacities in this regard. Therefore your position as stated is erroneous.

正體字

汝謂佛不說[14]韋陀等外經故非
075c18 ‖ 一切智人者。今當答。韋陀中無善寂滅法。
075c19 ‖ 但有種種諸戲論事。諸佛所說皆為善寂滅
075c20 ‖ 故。佛雖知韋陀等經。不能令人得善寂
075c21 ‖ 滅。是故不說。問[15]曰。韋陀中亦有善寂滅解
075c22 ‖ 脫說。世間先皆幽闇都無所有。初有大人出
075c23 ‖ 現如日。若有見者得度死難。更有餘[16]導。
075c24 ‖ 又說。人身小則神小。人大則神大。身為神
075c25 ‖ 宅常處其中。若以智慧開解神縛則得解
075c26 ‖ 脫。是故當知韋陀中有寂滅解脫。答曰。無
075c27 ‖ 是事也。何以[17]故。韋陀[18]經中有四顛倒。世間
075c28 ‖ 無常而別有常世間。如說一作天祠墮落
075c29 ‖ 再亦墮落三作則不墮。是為無常中常顛倒。
076a01 ‖ 世間苦而說有常樂處。是為苦中樂顛倒。
076a02 ‖ 又說我神轉為子願使壽百歲。子是他身云
076a03 ‖ 何為我。是為無我中我顛倒。

简体字

汝谓佛不说韦陀等外经故非一切智人者。今当答。韦陀中无善寂灭法。但有种种诸戏论事。诸佛所说皆为善寂灭故。佛虽知韦陀等经。不能令人得善寂灭。是故不说。问曰。韦陀中亦有善寂灭解脱说。世间先皆幽闇都无所有。初有大人出现如日。若有见者得度死难。更有余导。又说。人身小则神小。人大则神大。身为神宅常处其中。若以智慧开解神缚则得解脱。是故当知韦陀中有寂灭解脱。答曰。无是事也。何以故。韦陀经中有四颠倒。世间无常而别有常世间。如说一作天祠堕落再亦堕落三作则不堕。是为无常中常颠倒。世间苦而说有常乐处。是为苦中乐颠倒。又说我神转为子愿使寿百岁。子是他身云何为我。是为无我中我颠倒。

As for your contention that, because the Buddha does not discuss the Vedas and other such non-Buddhist scriptures, he must therefore not be omniscient—I shall now respond to that as follows:

The Vedas are entirely lacking in the dharma of [liberation achieved through] skillful realization of nirvāṇa.[37] They contain only all manner of conceptual elaboration. Since what the Buddhas proclaim is all entirely devoted to the skillful realization of nirvāṇa, even though the Buddha is already well aware of the contents of the Vedas and other such scriptures, the Buddha does not discuss such things because those [Vedic] teachings have no capacity to lead anyone to the skillful realization of nirvāṇa.

Question: The Vedas *do* contain discussions of the skillful realization of nirvāṇa. Before the arising of this world, all was darkness and nothing whatsoever existed. In the beginning there existed a great man who appeared like the rising of the sun. If one was able to see him, then one could be liberated from the difficulty of being subject to dying.

[The Vedas] contain yet more guidance on these matters. They state that, because one's person is but small, then one's spiritual soul is correspondingly small. However, if one's person is great, then one's spiritual soul will be correspondingly great in scope, for the body is the home of the spiritual soul that always abides within it. If one uses wisdom to untie the bonds restraining one's spiritual soul, one will then gain liberation. Therefore one should realize from this that the Vedas *do* contain teachings leading to liberation through attainment of nirvāṇa.

Response: This is simply not so. Why not? The Vedic scriptures are tied up with the four inverted views. The world is impermanent and yet they posit the existence of a separate and permanent world. They claim that only one or two sacrifices to their deva [is insufficient and] conduces to falling away from it, but with a third sacrifice, one will not be subject to falling away from it. This scenario involves the inverted view that falsely ascribes permanence to what is itself impermanent.

The world is a place of suffering and yet the Vedas claim the existence of a sphere of eternal bliss. This is just an instance of the inverted view that falsely ascribes bliss to what is inherently bound up with suffering.

The Vedas also claim that one's soul may transform into one's son and be subject through prayer to an extended lifetime of a hundred years. But a "son" is another person, so how could it constitute a self? This is just an instance of the inverted view that falsely ascribes selfhood to what is not actually a self.

正體字

說身清淨
076a04 ‖ 第一無比。金銀珍寶無及身者。是名[1]無淨
076a05 ‖ 中淨顛倒。顛倒則無實。無實云何有寂滅。
076a06 ‖ 是故韋陀中無善寂滅法。問曰。韋陀中說。能
076a07 ‖ 知韋陀者清淨安隱。云何言無善寂滅法。
076a08 ‖ 答曰。知韋陀者雖說安隱非畢竟解脫。
076a09 ‖ 於異身中生解脫想。是說因長壽天。說為
076a10 ‖ 解脫。是故韋陀中實無解脫。復次韋陀中。略
076a11 ‖ 說有三義。一者呪願。二者稱讚。三者法則。
076a12 ‖ 呪願名為令我得妻子牛馬金銀珍寶。稱讚
076a13 ‖ 名為汝火神頭黑頸赤體黃常在眾生五大
076a14 ‖ 中。法則名為是事應作是不應作。如從昴
076a15 ‖ 星初受火法而實呪願稱讚法。則無有寂
076a16 ‖ 滅解脫。何以故。貪著世樂然蘇呪願無真
076a17 ‖ 智慧。不斷煩惱何有解脫。問曰。韋陀法自
076a18 ‖ 古有之第一可信。汝言無善寂滅故不可
076a19 ‖ 信者。是事不然。何以故。

简体字

说身清净第一无比。金银珍宝无及身者。是名无净中净颠倒。颠倒则无实。无实云何有寂灭。是故韦陀中无善寂灭法。问曰。韦陀中说。能知韦陀者清净安隐。云何言无善寂灭法。答曰。知韦陀者虽说安隐非毕竟解脱。于异身中生解脱想。是说因长寿天。说为解脱。是故韦陀中实无解脱。复次韦陀中。略说有三义。一者咒愿。二者称赞。三者法则。咒愿名为令我得妻子牛马金银珍宝。称赞名为汝火神头黑颈赤体黄常在众生五大中。法则名为是事应作是不应作。如从昴星初受火法而实咒愿称赞法。则无有寂灭解脱。何以故。贪着世乐然苏咒愿无真智慧。不断烦恼何有解脱。问曰。韦陀法自古有之第一可信。汝言无善寂灭故不可信者。是事不然。何以故。

They also claim that one's body is possessed of the foremost level of purity and so incomparable in this respect that not even the purity of gold, silver, or precious gems can approach the purity of the body. This is just an instance of the inverted view that falsely ascribes purity to what is devoid of purity.

If one holds inverted views, then [one's views] are devoid of reality. [If such teachings] are devoid of reality, how could they possess [a path to] nirvāṇa? Therefore the Vedas are devoid of any good methods for attaining nirvāṇa.

Question: The Vedas assert that whoever is able to know the Vedas becomes purified and possessed of peace and security. How then can you state that they have no good methods for attaining nirvāṇa?

Response: Although the Vedas assert that whoever knows the Vedas will gain peace and security, this is not ultimate liberation. Rather, this is but an envisioning of liberation projected onto another body. This claim bases itself on the idea that existence in the long-life heavens constitutes liberation. Therefore the Vedas truly contain no means to achieve liberation.

Furthermore, the teachings in the Vedas generally embody three types of concepts: The first involves chants and prayers. The second involves the utterance of praises. The third involves the principles of their dharma.

"Chants and prayers" refers to praying, "May I be caused to obtain a wife and sons, cows, horses, gold, silver, and precious jewels."

"Utterance of praises" refers to statements such as, "Oh, you, the spirit of fire with your black head, your red neck, and your yellow body—you abide eternally in the five great elements of living beings."

"Principles of their dharma" refers to teachings stating that one should do this and abstain from doing that.

Just as with their [erroneous teaching that] fire was first received from the Pleiades, so too, in truth, their methods of using chants and prayers and utterances of praises are all devoid of [any means to achieve] nirvāṇa's liberation. How is this so? Covetous attachment to worldly pleasures, [offerings of] burning ghee, spells, and incantations—these are all devoid of genuine wisdom. Since these do not cut off the afflictions, how could [the Vedas] have [the means to achieve] liberation?

Question: The dharmas in the Vedas have come forth from antiquity and are deserving of the foremost degree of faith. As for your contention that they have no good methods by which one might reach nirvāṇa, they are therefore not fit to be believed, this is wrong. Why?

正體字

佛法近乃出世。韋
076a20 ‖ 陀自古久遠常在世間。是故古法可信近法
076a21 ‖ 不可信。汝言韋陀中無善寂滅法。是事不
076a22 ‖ 然。答曰。時不可信。[2]無明先出正智後出。邪
076a23 ‖ 見先出正見後出。不可以無明邪見先出故
076a24 ‖ 可信。正智正見後出不可信。如先有污泥
076a25 ‖ 後有蓮花。先有[3]病後有藥。如是不可以
076a26 ‖ 在先出者為貴。是故韋陀先出。佛法後出。
076a27 ‖ 謂不可信者。是事不然。復次過去[4]錠光等
076a28 ‖ 諸佛皆先出世。其法則古出。韋陀是後出。若
076a29 ‖ 汝以先久為貴者。此諸佛及法則應是貴。
076b01 ‖ 問曰。韋陀不能作善寂滅。是故佛法中不
076b02 ‖ 說。若佛知不能作寂滅。何用知為。若不知
076b03 ‖ 則非一切智人。二俱有過。答曰。汝語非也。
076b04 ‖ 佛先知韋陀不能善寂滅故不說亦不修
076b05 ‖ 行。問曰。若佛知韋陀無有利益故而說不
076b06 ‖ 修習者何用知為。答曰。大智之人應悉分別
076b07 ‖ 是正道是邪道。欲令無量人眾度險惡道故
076b08 ‖ 行於正道。

简体字

佛法近乃出世。韦陀自古久远常在世间。是故古法可信近法不可信。汝言韦陀中无善寂灭法。是事不然。答曰。时不可信。无明先出正智后出。邪见先出正见后出。不可以无明邪见先出故可信。正智正见后出不可信。如先有污泥后有莲花。先有病后有药。如是不可以在先出者为贵。是故韦陀先出。佛法后出。谓不可信者。是事不然。复次过去锭光等诸佛皆先出世。其法则古出。韦陀是后出。若汝以先久为贵者。此诸佛及法则应是贵。问曰。韦陀不能作善寂灭。是故佛法中不说。若佛知不能作寂灭。何用知为。若不知则非一切智人。二俱有过。答曰。汝语非也。佛先知韦陀不能善寂灭故不说亦不修行。问曰。若佛知韦陀无有利益故而说不修习者何用知为。答曰。大智之人应悉分别是正道是邪道。欲令无量人众度险恶道故行于正道。

Whereas the Buddha's Dharma has only recently emerged into the world, the Vedas have come down from long distant antiquity and have always prevailed in the world. Therefore, given that ancient dharmas are deserving of belief and newly arisen dharmas are not deserving of belief, your claim that the Vedas are devoid of any good methods by which one might realize nirvāṇa—this is wrong.

Response: Their relative antiquity is no justification for faith. Ignorance tends to come first whereas right knowledge comes only later. Erroneous views emerge first whereas right views emerge later. One cannot have faith in ignorance and erroneous views simply because they happened to emerge first nor can one deem right knowledge and right views to be unbelievable simply because they emerged later. This is analogous to there first being mud and only later lotuses, first being disease and only later a cure. Matters of these sorts are not worthy of being valued simply because they happened to appear first. Therefore, as for your contention that, because the Vedas came first and the Buddha's Dharma came later, the latter is unworthy of belief, this is a fallacy.

Furthermore, Dīpaṃkara Buddha and the other buddhas of the past all came into the world earlier. Their Dharma principles emerged in antiquity whereas the Vedas actually came forth only later. If you insist on relying on chronological primacy and long history as your bases for according esteem, then the Buddhas and their Dharma should be most highly valued.

Question: You claim it is because the Vedas have no good methods for reaching nirvāṇa that they are therefore not discussed in the Buddha's Dharma. But if the Buddha had really already known they are unable to lead to nirvāṇa, why did he bother to become knowledgeable about them? If in fact he was not *already* knowledgeable about them, he could not have been omniscient. Both stances are faulty.

Response: Your claim is wrong. The Buddha knew from early on that the Vedas have no good methods for reaching nirvāṇa. It is for this reason that he neither discussed them nor practiced what they teach.

Question: If it really was because the Buddha already knew there is no benefit to be had through the Vedas that he therefore instructed others not to cultivate their teaching, what was the point in his acquiring knowledge about them?

Response: People possessed of great knowledge should thoroughly distinguish between the correct path and the erroneous path. It is because one wishes to cause countless beings to go beyond dangerous and bad paths that one takes up the practice of the right path. This

正體字

譬如導師善分別邪道正道。佛亦
076b09 ‖ 如是。既自得出生[5]老死險道。亦復欲令
076b10 ‖ 眾生出故。善知八[6]真聖道。亦知韋陀等邪
076b11 ‖ 險惡道。為離邪惡道故。行於正道[7]故。但
076b12 ‖ 知而不說。猶如農夫為穀種植至秋收穫
076b13 ‖ 亦得草[麩-夫+戈]。佛亦如是。為無上道故勤行精
076b14 ‖ 進得菩提[8]道。亦知韋陀等諸邪道。是故無
076b15 ‖ 咎。如汝先說無人能有具知四韋陀者。
076b16 ‖ 此難不然。世間人各有念力。有人一日能
076b17 ‖ 誦五偈。有誦百偈。有誦二百偈。若人一日
076b18 ‖ 不誦十偈則謂無能誦百偈出百偈者。
076b19 ‖ 此非實語。汝等不能盡知故。便言都無智
076b20 ‖ 者。若人見一人不能度河便言無能度
076b21 ‖ 者。是人不名正說。何以故。自有餘大力者
076b22 ‖ 能度。此亦如是。設使餘人不能盡知。一切
076b23 ‖ 智者知之何咎。復次脾娑仙人。皆讀韋陀亦
076b24 ‖ 應成一切智。若有盡讀韋陀。何以言無一
076b25 ‖ 切智。

简体字

譬如导师善分别邪道正道。佛亦如是。既自得出生老死险道。亦复欲令众生出故。善知八真圣道。亦知韦陀等邪险恶道。为离邪恶道故。行于正道故。但知而不说。犹如农夫为谷种植至秋收获亦得草[麩-夫+戈]。佛亦如是。为无上道故勤行精进得菩提道。亦知韦陀等诸邪道。是故无咎。如汝先说无人能有具知四韦陀者。此难不然。世间人各有念力。有人一日能诵五偈。有诵百偈。有诵二百偈。若人一日不诵十偈则谓无能诵百偈出百偈者。此非实语。汝等不能尽知故。便言都无智者。若人见一人不能度河便言无能度者。是人不名正说。何以故。自有余大力者能度。此亦如是。设使余人不能尽知。一切智者知之何咎。复次脾娑仙人。皆读韦陀亦应成一切智。若有尽读韦陀。何以言无一切智。

is analogous to a guide who skillfully distinguishes between errant paths and the right path.

The Buddha is just the same in this respect. Since he himself had already succeeded in escaping the dangerous path of birth, aging, and death and also wished to cause other beings to escape from it as well, he knew well the genuine eightfold path of the Āryas and also knew the dangerous and bad paths of the Vedas and other such teachings. It was in order to facilitate others' abandonment of deviant and bad paths and in order to encourage their practice of the correct path that, [with regard to the Vedas], he merely became knowledgeable about them, but did not discuss them.

This is analogous to the situation with farmers who plant their fields and then, with the arrival of autumn, reap a harvest that may also happen to include a few useless weeds. The Buddha is like this as well. For the sake of achieving success in the unsurpassable path, he cultivates assiduously and vigorously and consequently gains the path of bodhi while incidentally gaining knowledge of the Vedas and other such erroneous paths. Hence there is no fault on his part in any of this.

As for your previous statement claiming that no single person can completely know the four Vedas, this challenge of yours is false. People of the world each have the power of memory. There are those who, in a single day, can only recite five verses from memory, whereas others can recite one or two hundred verses from memory. If a particular person who cannot even recite ten verses from memory then holds the opinion that nobody could be able to recite from memory a hundred or more than a hundred verses, this would be an untruthful claim. It is because people such as yourself are unable to completely know the Vedas that you then claim nobody knows them.

If someone observes that some other person was unable to ford a particular river and then claims that nobody can cross that river, this person's statement on the matter does not qualify as correct speech. Why not? It is because there will naturally be some other person possessed of great strength who can indeed cross that river. This case is just like that. Even if one supposes that other [ordinary people] would be unable to entirely know [the Vedas], what fault is there in stipulating that someone possessed of all-knowledge would know them?

Furthermore, the *pisuo*[38] rishis all study the Vedas and ought themselves to be able to reach all-knowledge. Thus if there are these persons who have completely studied the Vedas, how can you say that nobody can have all-knowledge?

正體字

若汝言有經書能生貪欲瞋恚者。我
076b26 ‖ 今當答。若人欲長壽。應離死因緣。佛亦如
076b27 ‖ 是欲斷一切眾生貪欲瞋恚。應知貪欲[9]瞋
076b28 ‖ 恚因緣。復次如汝[10]說能知生貪欲瞋恚
076b29 ‖ 經書則有貪欲瞋恚者。無有是[11]處也。佛
076c01 ‖ 雖知是不用不行故無過咎。如人知死因
076c02 ‖ 緣則不死。若行死因緣則死。是事亦爾。若
076c03 ‖ 汝說不知未來事故不名一切智者。我今
076c04 ‖ 當答。此則非難。我等亦知有難一切智者
076c05 ‖ 如經中說。佛告諸比丘。凡夫無[12]智有三相。
076c06 ‖ 不應思而思。不應說而說。不應作而作。
076c07 ‖ 是故皆已總說。汝等未來世凡夫皆在其中
076c08 ‖ 無利益故。何用分別說其名字等。若謂佛
076c09 ‖ 知有難不[＊]豫答者亦不須此。今現四眾
076c10 ‖ 中亦有善斷疑難者。今亦有能破諸難問
076c11 ‖ 者。何用先答。如汝今日現見比丘之中能
076c12 ‖ 破婆羅門者。是故不須先答。

简体字

若汝言有经书能生贪欲嗔恚者。我今当答。若人欲长寿。应离死因缘。佛亦如是欲断一切众生贪欲嗔恚。应知贪欲嗔恚因缘。复次如汝说能知生贪欲嗔恚经书则有贪欲嗔恚者。无有是处也。佛虽知是不用不行故无过咎。如人知死因缘则不死。若行死因缘则死。是事亦尔。若汝说不知未来事故不名一切智者。我今当答。此则非难。我等亦知有难一切智者如经中说。佛告诸比丘。凡夫无智有三相。不应思而思。不应说而说。不应作而作。是故皆已总说。汝等未来世凡夫皆在其中无利益故。何用分别说其名字等。若谓佛知有难不豫答者亦不须此。今现四众中亦有善断疑难者。今亦有能破诸难问者。何用先答。如汝今日现见比丘之中能破婆罗门者。是故不须先答。

I shall now respond to your [above-stated] claim that there are scriptures which [by their explication of the causes and conditions conducing to desire] are capable of causing one to feel desire or hatred. If one wishes to have a long life, he should abandon causes and conditions conducive to death. The Buddha, too, in this same way, wished to influence beings to cut off their desires and hatreds. This required that he know the causes and conditions that initiate the arising of desire and hatred.

Additionally, as for your contention that, if one is able to know the classical texts concerned with generating desire or hatred, one will then become afflicted with desire and hatred—this is a baseless claim. Although the Buddha had knowledge of these texts, because he did not use them or implement their practices, he was without fault in this respect. So too, if a person merely knows the causes and conditions that precipitate death, this does not entail his dying [as a result]. Only if he were to implement the causes and conditions that precipitate death would he then die as a result. This case is just the same as that one.

I shall now address your contention that, if one does not know future matters, then one does not qualify as omniscient. This does not constitute as a valid challenge. We already know of instances involving challenges to the plausibility of omniscience. As stated in the sutras: "The Buddha told the bhikshus, 'The common person bereft of wisdom has three characteristics: He contemplates what he should not contemplate, discusses what he should not discuss, and does what he should not do.'"[39]

Everything of relevance is already comprehensively mentioned in that statement. You common people of this future time are all included in it. As it would have no particular benefit, what would be the point in his having distinguished and mentioned names and such [related to future events]?

If one were to claim [that there is a contradiction] if the Buddha knew there would be these challenges, yet failed to reply to them in advance, there would really have been no need for this, for, in this presently existing fourfold assembly there are already those well able to cut off doubts in their responses to challenges [such as this]. We now already have those well able to refute challenging inquiries. What then would be the point in [the Buddha himself] responding in advance to such things? Right now, among the bhikshus you encounter in the present day, there are already those well able to refute the tenets posited by brahmins. Therefore there is no need [for the Buddha] to have responded in advance to such challenges.

正體字

又先時亦有
076c13 ‖ 答。散在眾經。人不能具知佛法故。不知
076c14 ‖ 處所。若言受調達出家事。我今當答。謂
076c15 ‖ 受調達出家則非一切智人者。是[13]語不然。
076c16 ‖ 調達出家非佛所度。問曰。若餘人度者佛何
076c17 ‖ 以聽。答曰。善惡各有時。不必出家便惡。調
076c18 ‖ 達出家之後有持戒諸功德。是故出家無
076c19 ‖ 過。復次調達於十二年清淨持戒誦六萬
076c20 ‖ 法藏。此果報者當來不空必有利益。汝說調
076c21 ‖ 達機關激石[14]者。我今當說。諸佛成就無殺
076c22 ‖ 法故。一切世間無能奪命者。問曰。若成就
076c23 ‖ 不殺法者。何故迸石而來。答曰。佛於先世
076c24 ‖ 種壞身業定報應受。示眾生業報不可捨故
076c25 ‖ 現受。是故自來。汝言旃遮女佛不先說者。
076c26 ‖ 我今當答。以旃遮女故譏佛者。不能壞
076c27 ‖ 一切智人因緣。若佛先說旃遮女當來

简体字

又先时亦有答。散在众经。人不能具知佛法故。不知处所。若言受调达出家事。我今当答。谓受调达出家则非一切智人者。是语不然。调达出家非佛所度。问曰。若余人度者佛何以听。答曰。善恶各有时。不必出家便恶。调达出家之后有持戒诸功德。是故出家无过。复次调达于十二年清净持戒诵六万法藏。此果报者当来不空必有利益。汝说调达机关激石者。我今当说。诸佛成就无杀法故。一切世间无能夺命者。问曰。若成就不杀法者。何故迸石而来。答曰。佛于先世种坏身业定报应受。示众生业报不可舍故现受。是故自来。汝言旃遮女佛不先说者。我今当答。以旃遮女故讥佛者。不能坏一切智人因缘。若佛先说旃遮女当来

Furthermore, there have already been prior responses to such challenges that are scattered in various places throughout the many sutras. Because people are unable to completely know the Dharma of the Buddha, they do not know where those passages are located.

I shall now address your challenge on the matter of the Buddha's having allowed Devadatta to leave the home life and become a monk. As for your opinion that, if the Buddha allowed Devadatta to leave the home life, he could not have been omniscient, this statement is wrong. When Devadatta left the home life to become a monk, it was not the Buddha who was involved in allowing him to become a monastic.

Question: Even if it was someone else who allowed him to become a monastic, why did the Buddha allow this to happen?

Response: The doing of good and the doing of evil each have the season in which they occur. It was not necessarily the case that, having left home, he would immediately embark on doing evil. After Devadatta left home to become a monk, he had all of the meritorious qualities that are associated with upholding the moral precepts. Therefore there was no fault in [permitting] his leaving the home life.

Additionally, for twelve years, Devadatta was pure in his observance of the moral precepts and also became able then to recite from memory sixty-thousand lines from the treasury of Dharma. The karmic reward from this is such that, in the future, [such cultivation] will not have been in vain. In fact, it will definitely benefit him later on.

I will now reply to your statement regarding Devadatta's prying loose of a boulder [in an attempt to murder the Buddha]. Because all buddhas have already perfected the dharma of not killing, nobody in any world can ever rob them of life.

Question: If the Buddha had actually perfected the dharma of not killing, why did the boulder shatter and [allow a piece of it] to come down [and strike him in the foot]?

Response: The Buddha had planted karmic causes associated with damage to the body for which he was bound to undergo this fixed retribution. He manifested the appearance of having to undergo it in order to demonstrate to beings that karmic retributions cannot be escaped. It was for this reason that he voluntarily came to that place.

I shall now respond to your contention that there was some problem in the Buddha's not having spoken in advance about the incident involving that woman, Ciñcā. There is nothing in that woman, Ciñcā's, disparaging of the Buddha that can serve as a causal basis for impugning his qualification as omniscient. If the Buddha had announced in advance: "In the future, that woman, Ciñca, will come forth and

正體字

謗我 076c28 ‖者。旃遮女則不來。復次佛先世謗人罪業
076c29 ‖ 因緣。今必應受。汝說佛何以不遮孫陀利
077a01 ‖ 入祇洹事。我今當答。此事不能壞一切智
077a02 ‖ 人因緣。佛無有力令一切眾生盡作樂人。
077a03 ‖ 又諸佛離一切諍訟不自高身不著持戒。
077a04 ‖ 是故不遮。復次佛先世業熟故。必應受七
077a05 ‖ 日謗。又眾生見佛聞謗不憂。[1]雪明不喜故。
077a06 ‖ 發無上道心。作是願言。我等亦當得如是
077a07 ‖ 清淨心。是故無咎。汝先說佛入婆羅門聚
077a08 ‖ 落空鉢而出非一切智人者。今當答。佛不
077a09 ‖ 以[2]飲食先觀人心入聚落已魔轉其意。
077a10 ‖ 問曰。是事佛應先知。我入聚落魔當轉人
077a11 ‖ 心。答曰。佛亦先知此事。為大利益眾生。諸
077a12 ‖ 佛非但以受人食故。以為利益度脫眾
077a13 ‖ 生。有以清淨心迎逆敬禮和顏瞻視。此皆大
077a14 ‖ 利何必飲食。以種種門利益眾生。非空入
077a15 ‖ 聚落。

简体字

谤我者。旃遮女则不来。复次佛先世谤人罪业因缘。今必应受。汝说佛何以不遮孙陀利入祇洹事。我今当答。此事不能坏一切智人因缘。佛无有力令一切众生尽作乐人。又诸佛离一切诤讼不自高身不着持戒。是故不遮。复次佛先世业熟故。必应受七日谤。又众生见佛闻谤不忧。雪明不喜故。发无上道心。作是愿言。我等亦当得如是清净心。是故无咎。汝先说佛入婆罗门聚落空钵而出非一切智人者。今当答。佛不以饮食先观人心入聚落已魔转其意。问曰。是事佛应先知。我入聚落魔当转人心。答曰。佛亦先知此事。为大利益众生。诸佛非但以受人食故。以为利益度脱众生。有以清净心迎逆敬礼和颜瞻视。此皆大利何必饮食。以种种门利益众生。非空入聚落。

slander me," then that woman, Ciñca, would not in fact have come forth as she did. Furthermore, it was due to the karmic causes and conditions associated with the Buddha's having slandered others in a previous lifetime that he was now definitely bound to undergo [the corresponding retribution]. [40]

I shall now address your challenge as to how it could have been that the Buddha failed to prevent the incident that occurred when Sundarī entered the Jeta Grove.[41] This incident does not constitute a reason for impugning the Buddha's qualification as omniscient. The Buddha does not have some power by which he is able to cause every being's life to be an entirely happy one. Also, the Buddhas have all left behind disputation, do not elevate themselves, and are not attached to [making others] uphold moral precepts, consequently he did not act to prevent this incident.

Additionally, it was because of the ripening of karma from a previous life that he was definitely bound to undergo that seven days of slander. Moreover, when beings observed that the Buddha was neither perturbed over hearing himself slandered nor joyful when his innocence was made clear, they brought forth the resolve to follow the unsurpassable path, uttering this vow, "We too shall acquire just such a pure mind as this." Therefore there was no fault [in the Buddha's having acted as he did].

I shall now respond to your contention that, because the Buddha entered a brahmin village and then left with an empty bowl, he was therefore not omniscient.[42] The Buddha [did not go to that village] for the sake of food and drink, [but rather because] he had contemplated the minds of the people there. It was only after he entered the village that Māra changed the villagers' minds.

Question: This is a matter about which the Buddha should have become aware in advance, thinking, "If I go into this village, Māra will change these peoples' minds."

Response: The Buddha in fact *did* know about this matter in advance [and entered that village anyway] in order to bring great benefit to those beings. It is not solely on the basis of receiving alms food from them that the Buddhas benefit beings and facilitate their liberation. There were those who welcomed him there with pure minds, bowed in reverence to him, and looked up to him with congenial gazes. All of these things already served great benefit. Why should it be an essential requirement that he be given food and drink? There are many different sorts of methods by which he was able to be of benefit to beings. Thus it was not in vain that he entered that village.

正體字

汝說佛逆趣醉象者。今當答。佛雖知
077a16 ‖ 此事。以因緣故往以此醉象必應得度。又
077a17 ‖ 能障其害佛罪業。復次此象身如黑山。眾
077a18 ‖ 人見此低頭禮佛皆起恭敬。以是因緣故
077a19 ‖ [3]佛故往趣。復次佛趣此象無有過失。若
077a20 ‖ 有惡事可作此難。汝難至隨蘭若者。為
077a21 ‖ 受先世業果報故。汝說畜須[4]洹叉多羅
077a22 ‖ 為弟子者。今當說。佛身口意命不須守護。
077a23 ‖ 無所畏故聽為弟子。復次是人常近佛故
077a24 ‖ 得見種種大神力。見諸天龍夜叉乾闥婆阿
077a25 ‖ 修羅等諸王來供養佛請問種種甚深要法
077a26 ‖ 心得清淨。心清淨故得利益因緣。是故雖
077a27 ‖ 惡聽為弟子。問曰。此人於佛多生惡心。是
077a28 ‖ 故不應聽為弟子。答曰。若不聽為弟子亦
077a29 ‖ 有惡心。是故聽為弟子無咎。汝說先未作
077b01 ‖ 罪時何以不制戒。今當答。

简体字

汝说佛逆趣醉象者。今当答。佛虽知此事。以因缘故往以此醉象必应得度。又能障其害佛罪业。复次此象身如黑山。众人见此低头礼佛皆起恭敬。以是因缘故佛故往趣。复次佛趣此象无有过失。若有恶事可作此难。汝难至随兰若者。为受先世业果报故。汝说畜须洹叉多罗为弟子者。今当说。佛身口意命不须守护。无所畏故听为弟子。复次是人常近佛故得见种种大神力。见诸天龙夜叉乾闼婆阿修罗等诸王来供养佛请问种种甚深要法心得清净。心清净故得利益因缘。是故虽恶听为弟子。问曰。此人于佛多生恶心。是故不应听为弟子。答曰。若不听为弟子亦有恶心。是故听为弟子无咎。汝说先未作罪时何以不制戒。今当答。

I shall now respond to your statement about the Buddha's having gone up the road on which there was a drunken elephant.[43] Although the Buddha already knew of this matter, there was a reason he deliberately went there. It was because this drunken elephant was definitely at a point where he could be brought across to liberation. The Buddha was also intent on preventing his falling into the karmic offense of harming a buddha.

Additionally, this elephant's body had the appearance of a black mountain. When the population there saw this elephant bow down its head in reverence to the Buddha, they all brought forth thoughts of reverence. It was for these reasons that the Buddha deliberately went up that road. Also, there was no error involved in the Buddha's having entered that road to encounter that elephant. Only if some unfortunate incident had transpired would you have a basis for bringing up this challenge.

As for your challenge regarding the Buddha's having gone to Verañjā, that was simply a case of having to undergo retribution for karmic deeds committed in a previous life.[44]

I shall now address your statement on the issue of the Buddha's having accepted Sunakṣatra as a disciple.[45] The Buddha has no need to guard against errors in actions of body, speech, mind, or livelihood.[46] It was because he is utterly without fear that he permitted Sunakṣatra to become a disciple.

Also, because this man always dwelt in close proximity to the Buddha, he was thus able to observe the display of all manner of spiritual powers and also saw the arrival of devas, dragons, *yakṣas, gandharvas, asuras,* kings, and others, all coming to make offerings to the Buddha and to pose respectful questions to him on all manner of extremely profound and essential dharmas. Hence his mind was thereby able to become purified. Because he was able to achieve purification of mind, this was a causal basis for his [eventual] benefit. Therefore, even though he was an evil man, the Buddha nonetheless accepted him as a disciple.

Question: This man had many evil thoughts about the Buddha. Therefore the Buddha should not have permitted him to become a disciple.

Response: Even if the Buddha had not accepted him as a disciple, the man still would have had those evil thoughts. Therefore there was no fault in the Buddha's permitting him to become a disciple.

I shall now respond to your challenge as to why the Buddha did not formulate the moral precepts in advance of [his disciples'] commission

正體字

佛先結戒。說 077b02 ‖八聖道正見正思惟正語正業正命正精進正
077b03 ‖ 念正定。說是至涅槃道故。已說一切諸戒。
077b04 ‖ 復次佛說三學。善學戒善學心善學慧。當
077b05 ‖ 知已說一切諸戒。復次佛告諸比丘。一切
077b06 ‖ 惡決定不應作。是不名先結戒耶。復次佛
077b07 ‖ 說十善道。離殺盜婬兩舌惡罵妄言綺語貪
077b08 ‖ 嫉瞋恚邪見。不名先結戒耶。佛先十二年
077b09 ‖ 中說一偈為布薩法。所謂一切惡莫作。一
077b10 ‖ 切善當行。自淨其志意。是則諸佛教。是故
077b11 ‖ 當知先已結戒。復次佛說諸小惡因緣皆應
077b12 ‖ 當離。如說。
077b13 ‖ 　離身諸惡行　　亦離口諸惡
077b14 ‖ 　離意諸惡行　　餘惡悉遠離
077b15 ‖ 如是說者當知先[5]已結戒。復次佛先已說
077b16 ‖ 諸守護法。如說。
077b17 ‖ 　護身為善哉　　能護口亦善
077b18 ‖ 　護意為善哉　　護一切亦善

简体字

佛先结戒。说八圣道正见正思惟正语正业正命正精进正念正定。说是至涅槃道故。已说一切诸戒。复次佛说三学。善学戒善学心善学慧。当知已说一切诸戒。复次佛告诸比丘。一切恶决定不应作。是不名先结戒耶。复次佛说十善道。离杀盗淫两舌恶骂妄言绮语贪嫉嗔恚邪见。不名先结戒耶。佛先十二年中说一偈为布萨法。所谓一切恶莫作。一切善当行。自净其志意。是则诸佛教。是故当知先已结戒。复次佛说诸小恶因缘皆应当离。如说。

离身诸恶行　　亦离口诸恶
离意诸恶行　　余恶悉远离

如是说者当知先已结戒。复次佛先已说诸守护法。如说。

护身为善哉　　能护口亦善
护意为善哉　　护一切亦善

of the corresponding transgressions. The Buddha did in fact formulate moral precepts in advance. He set forth the eightfold path of the Āryas that consist of right views, right thought, right speech, right action, right livelihood, right effort, right mindfulness, and right meditative concentration. Because he did describe this path leading to the attainment of nirvāṇa, he in fact had already formulated all of the precepts.

Furthermore, the Buddha described the three trainings wherein one thoroughly trains in moral virtue, thoroughly trains in [focusing] the mind, and thoroughly trains in wisdom. One should then realize from this that he had in fact already set forth all of the moral precepts.

Additionally, the Buddha told the bhikshus that they should definitely not do any sort of evil. Does this not constitute prior formulation of moral precepts?

Also, the Buddha spoke of the path of the ten courses of good karmic action, namely abandoning killing, stealing, sexual misconduct, divisive speech, harsh speech, false speech, frivolous speech, covetousness, ill will, and wrong views. Does this not constitute prior formulation of moral precepts?

Twelve years earlier, the Buddha described in a single verse the *upoṣadha* dharma,[47] namely:

To refrain from doing any sort of evil deed,
to respectfully engage in every sort of good deed,
and to purify one's own mind—
This is the teaching of all Buddhas.[48]

One should therefore realize that the Buddha in fact *did* formulate the moral precepts in advance.

Also, the Buddha stated that one should abandon even all of the most minor causes and conditions associated with evil, as stated in these lines:

Abandon all evil actions of the body.
Also abandon all evil speech,
abandon all evil actions of the mind,
and utterly abandon all other forms of evil.

On the basis of statements such as these, one should realize that the Buddha had already formulated the moral precepts in advance. Additionally, the Buddha had already described in advance the dharmas through which one guards against transgressions, as stated in these lines:

To guard the body is good indeed.
To be able to guard one's speech is also good.

正體字

077b19 ‖ 　比丘護一切　得遠離諸[6]惡
077b20 ‖ 如是說者當知先已結戒。復次佛先說善
077b21 ‖ 相。如說。
077b22 ‖ 　手足勿妄犯　節言慎所行
077b23 ‖ 　當樂守定意　是名真比丘
077b24 ‖ 如是說者當知先已結戒。復次說沙門法
077b25 ‖ 故。當知先已結戒。沙門有四法。一於瞋不
077b26 ‖ 報。二於罵默然。三杖捶能受。四害者忍之。
077b27 ‖ 復次佛說四念處。觀身觀受觀心觀法。是
077b28 ‖ 涅槃道住處故。當知先[7]已結戒。若微小惡
077b29 ‖ 尚不聽。何況身口惡業。如是等因緣當知
077c01 ‖ 先已結戒。如王者立制。不應作惡。後有
077c02 ‖ 犯者隨事輕重作如是罪如是治之。佛
077c03 ‖ 亦如是。先總說戒。後有犯者說其罪相。如
077c04 ‖ 有作惡者教令懺悔。作如是罪

简体字

　比丘护一切　得远离诸恶

如是说者当知先已结戒。复次佛先说善相。如说。

　手足勿妄犯　节言慎所行
　当乐守定意　是名真比丘

如是说者当知先已结戒。复次说沙门法故。当知先已结戒。沙门有四法。一于嗔不报。二于骂默然。三杖捶能受。四害者忍之。复次佛说四念处。观身观受观心观法。是涅槃道住处故。当知先已结戒。若微小恶尚不听。何况身口恶业。如是等因缘当知先已结戒。如王者立制。不应作恶。后有犯者随事轻重作如是罪如是治之。佛亦如是。先总说戒。后有犯者说其罪相。如有作恶者教令忏悔。作如是罪

To guard one's mind is good indeed,
and to guard against all errors is good as well.[49]
The bhikshu guards against all errors
and thereby succeeds in abandoning all evil.

One should realize on the basis of these statements that the Buddha in fact *did* formulate the moral precepts in advance. Moreover, the Buddha also described in advance the characteristics of goodness, as stated in these lines:

Do not allow hands or feet to carelessly commit transgressions.
Restrain your words and take care in actions done.
One should take pleasure in guarding and focusing the mind.
It is on these bases that one is rightfully called a bhikshu.[50]

One should realize on the basis of statements such as this that the Buddha in fact *did* formulate the moral precepts in advance.

Furthermore, because the Buddha described the dharmas by which one is a *śramaṇa*, one should realize he did in fact formulate the moral precepts in advance. There are four dharmas by which one is a *śramaṇa*: First, one does not respond in kind to hate-filled actions. Second, one remains silent in the face of scolding. Third, one is able to endure even being beaten with staves. And fourth, one maintains patience with those who have dealt one harm.

Moreover, the Buddha taught the four stations of mindfulness, namely the contemplation of the body, the contemplation of feelings, the contemplation of thoughts, and the contemplation of dharmas, doing so because they constitute the abode of the path to nirvāṇa. Hence one should realize that he *did* formulate the moral precepts in advance.

The Buddha would not even permit the most subtle form of evil, how much the less would he condone any sort of evil karma in one's physical actions or speech. For reasons such as these, one should realize that he did indeed formulate the moral precepts in advance.

This is analogous to a king's establishment of laws in which one is forbidden to do evil deeds. When, later on, there are transgressions against those laws, it is according to the relative gravity of the crime that corresponding punishments are imposed. The Buddha is just the same in this respect. He first made general statements describing the moral precepts. Later on, when offenses occurred, he described the specific characteristic factors by which the given action constituted an offense.

Where there were those who committed evil deeds, they were instructed and caused to repent. He instructed that, for a given offense,

正體字

應如是
077c05 ‖ 懺。不見擯滅擯不共住等。成如是事故。後
077c06 ‖ 乃結戒。[8]
077c07 ‖ 十住毘婆沙論卷第十 077c10 ‖ 十住毘婆沙論卷第十一
077c11 ‖ 077c12 ‖ 聖者龍樹造
077c13 ‖ 後秦龜茲國三藏鳩摩羅什譯
077c14 ‖ 四十不共法中難一切智人品之餘
077c15 ‖ [9]汝說耆年貴族家等應為上座。今當答。道
077c16 ‖ 法中耆年貴族家等於道無益。何以故。生
077c17 ‖ 佛法中名為貴族好家中生。從受大戒數
077c18 ‖ 其年數名為耆年。汝謂耆年應供養者。先
077c19 ‖ 出家受戒非是大耶。[10]又從受戒以後無
077c20 ‖ 有諸姓等差別。諸比丘受大戒。名為生在
077c21 ‖ 佛家。是則失先大小家名皆為一家。汝說
077c22 ‖ 持戒者。出家在先持戒日久長夜護持。年歲
077c23 ‖ 多故應為上座。如結戒中說。汝說持戒之
077c24 ‖ 人不應禮破戒者。今當答。破戒人尚不
077c25 ‖ 應共住。何況禮拜供養。以其自言是比丘
077c26 ‖ 故。隨其大小而為作禮。如禮泥木天像。以
077c27 ‖ 念真天故。

简体字

应如是忏。不见摈灭摈不共住等。成如是事故。后乃结戒。

汝说耆年贵族家等应为上座。今当答。道法中耆年贵族家等于道无益。何以故。生佛法中名为贵族好家中生。从受大戒数其年数名为耆年。汝谓耆年应供养者。先出家受戒非是大耶。又从受戒以后无有诸姓等差别。诸比丘受大戒。名为生在佛家。是则失先大小家名皆为一家。汝说持戒者。出家在先持戒日久长夜护持。年岁多故应为上座。如结戒中说。汝说持戒之人不应礼破戒者。今当答。破戒人尚不应共住。何况礼拜供养。以其自言是比丘故。随其大小而为作礼。如礼泥木天像。以念真天故。

a given corresponding form of penance was to be performed or that either temporary expulsion or complete expulsion was stipulated so that the miscreant could not to dwell together with the community, and so forth. It was only with the establishment of these sorts of cases that we came to have the subsequent formulation of moral precepts.

I shall now address your contention that superior position in the monastic community should be accorded on the basis of age, nobility of birth caste, status of one's clan, and so forth. In the dharmas of the path, issues of age, nobility of birth caste, status of one's clan, and so forth afford no benefit. How is this so? It is on the basis of being born into the Dharma of the Buddha that one qualifies as being born into nobility and into a fine clan. Seniority is determined on the basis of the number of years one has received the higher ordination and this is the rationale for being referred to as an elder.

As for your opinion that those who are merely older in years should be given priority in the receipt of offerings, is it not the case that those who first left the home life and received the ordination precepts are better regarded as of greater eminence?

Furthermore, from the time one receives the ordination precepts onward, there are no longer any distinctions on the basis of one's caste and such. It is only when bhikshus receive the precepts of the higher ordination that they then qualify as having been born into the family of the Buddhas. It is at this point that one loses any name associated with prior birth into a greater or lesser clan and everyone then belongs to this one single family.

As for your statements on upholding the precepts—those who first left the home life to become monastics and who have observed the moral precepts for the longest time and then proceed to uphold those moral precepts for a long time—it is because of their years of seniority in this that they should be accorded a superior position within the monastic community. This is as set forth in the original formulation of the moral precept code.

I shall now address your contention that those who are most strictly observant in their upholding of the moral precepts should not bow in reverence to those who have broken the moral precepts. Those who truly have broken the moral precepts should not even be allowed to dwell together with the community, how much the less should they receive reverential obeisance or offerings.

It is on the basis of their claim to be a bhikshu that one pays reverence to them according to their order of seniority. This is similar to when one bows in reverence before a deity's image made of clay or wood, doing so as a means of bearing in mind that actual deity.

正體字

佛勅年少應禮上座。順佛教
077c28 ‖ 故則便得福。汝說以頭陀故應敬禮者。今
077c29 ‖ 當答。若頭陀[11]人有五種故難得分別。一者
078a01 ‖ 愚癡無所知故貪受難法。二者鈍根悕望
078a02 ‖ 得利。三者惡意欺誑於人。四者狂亂。五者
078a03 ‖ 作念。頭陀法者。諸佛賢聖所共稱讚。以其
078a04 ‖ 隨順涅槃道故。是五種人。行頭陀法真偽
078a05 ‖ 難別。多聞者。多聞之人亦如頭陀難可分
078a06 ‖ 別。何以故。或以樂道故多聞。或以利養故
078a07 ‖ 多聞。如是等亦難分別。又佛法貴如說行。
078a08 ‖ 不貴多讀多誦。又如佛說行一法句能自
078a09 ‖ [1]利益名為多聞。智慧亦如是。若不能如
078a10 ‖ 所說行何用智慧為。是故不以智慧故說
078a11 ‖ 為上座。

简体字

佛敕年少应礼上座。顺佛教故则便得福。汝说以头陀故应敬礼者。今当答。若头陀人有五种故难得分别。一者愚痴无所知故贪受难法。二者钝根悕望得利。三者恶意欺诳于人。四者狂乱。五者作念。头陀法者。诸佛贤圣所共称赞。以其随顺涅槃道故。是五种人。行头陀法真伪难别。多闻者。多闻之人亦如头陀难可分别。何以故。或以乐道故多闻。或以利养故多闻。如是等亦难分别。又佛法贵如说行。不贵多读多诵。又如佛说行一法句能自利益名为多闻。智慧亦如是。若不能如所说行何用智慧为。是故不以智慧故说为上座。

The Buddha decreed that those of fewer years seniority should revere those who are seated in a superior position within the monastic order. It is through according with the Buddha's instructions in this that one acquires karmic merit.

I shall now respond to your statement that the according of reverence should be based on one's practice of the *dhūta* austerities. In this matter of those who take up the *dhūta* practices, there are five general types of practitioners among which it is difficult to make clear distinctions:[51]

First, there are those who are deluded and who, due to an absence of right knowledge, are driven by desire to practice these difficult dharmas;

Second, there are those possessed of only dull faculties who wish to acquire benefits as a result;

Third, there are those with evil intentions focused on deceiving others;

Fourth, there are those who are mentally ill;

And fifth, there are those who [take them up], thinking, "The dharmas of the *dhūta* austerities are praised by all buddhas, worthies, and *āryas* because they accord with the path to nirvāṇa."

Among these five classes of practitioners of the *dhūta* austerities, it is difficult to distinguish which are genuine and which are false.

Now, as for this matter of one's level of learning, just as with the *dhūta* austerities, it is difficult to distinguish clearly among those who have acquired abundant learning. How is this so? It could be that it is on the basis of delighting in the path that one has accrued much learning. Or perhaps it is only for the sake of receiving offerings that one has accrued much learning. It is difficult to make clear distinctions in matters such as these.

Additionally, in the Dharma of the Buddha, it is practice in accordance with one's words that is accorded esteem. One does not accord esteem merely on the basis of having engaged in much study or having become able to recite many scriptures. Also, according to the statements of the Buddha himself, if one practices but a single sentence of Dharma and is thereby able to derive self-benefit from that, this itself qualifies as abundant learning.

So too it is with this matter of wisdom. If one remains unable to implement a level of practice consistent with one's level of discourse, of what use is this wisdom? Consequently, it is not on the basis of one's degree of wisdom that one determines who is accorded a superior position in the monastic order.

正體字

譬如世間現事弟雖多聞多智而
078a12 ‖ 兄不為作禮。是故不以智慧故先受供養
078a13 ‖ 禮拜如是。雖多聞智慧應禮先受戒者。若
078a14 ‖ 先供養多聞智慧者則為鬪亂。餘[2]得沙門
078a15 ‖ 果斷結。得神通最難知。是人得果是不
078a16 ‖ 得果。是多[3]斷結是少[*]斷結。是得神通是
078a17 ‖ 不得神通。不可以此為上座。若同得道
078a18 ‖ 果斷結神通誰為上座。是故隨佛教行最
078a19 ‖ 為第一。汝說佛於說法生疑。今當答。佛
078a20 ‖ 於深法尚不有疑。何況應說不應說中而
078a21 ‖ 有疑乎。佛不言我都不說法。但云心樂閑
078a22 ‖ 靜不務[4]興事。而後於說法中無咎。復次
078a23 ‖ 諸外道言。佛為大聖寂默無戲論。何用畜
078a24 ‖ 眾而教化為。設使教化亦不可盡。似如分
078a25 ‖ 別何用說法畜養弟子是貪著相。是故佛自
078a26 ‖ 思惟。我法甚深智慧方便

简体字

譬如世间现事弟虽多闻多智而兄不为作礼。是故不以智慧故先受供养礼拜如是。虽多闻智慧应礼先受戒者。若先供养多闻智慧者则为斗乱。余得沙门果断结。得神通最难知。是人得果是不得果。是多断结是少断结。是得神通是不得神通。不可以此为上座。若同得道果断结神通谁为上座。是故随佛教行最为第一。汝说佛于说法生疑。今当答。佛于深法尚不有疑。何况应说不应说中而有疑乎。佛不言我都不说法。但云心乐闲静不务兴事。而后于说法中无咎。复次诸外道言。佛为大圣寂默无戏论。何用畜众而教化为。设使教化亦不可尽。似如分别何用说法畜养弟子是贪着相。是故佛自思惟。我法甚深智慧方便

This is analogous to the current way of doing things in the world. Although a younger brother may indeed be more learned or more wise, the elder brother is still not enjoined to pay him reverence. Therefore, after this same fashion, it is not on the basis of one's level of wisdom that one gains priority in the receipt of offerings or reverence. So it is then that, even though one may indeed have accrued much learning or wisdom, one should still accord reverence on the basis of who first received the ordination precepts. Were one to accord priority in the receipt of offerings to those of greater learning or a higher level of wisdom, this would inevitably result in discord within the community.

As for the other [criteria you propose for priority in according reverence], namely realization of the *śramaṇa's* fruits of the path, severance of fetters, and acquisition of spiritual powers, those are the most difficult matters to know. Whether or not this person has attained a fruit of the path, whether he has cut off more fetters or fewer fetters [than this other person], and whether or not he has acquired spiritual powers—one cannot use such matters as the basis for superior position in the monastic order. Consider for instance those who have realized the same fruits of the path, cut off the same fetters, and acquired the same spiritual powers. Who among them should be accorded superior position in the monastic order? Consequently, it is by far the best to simply accord with the Buddha's instructions on these matters.

I shall now address your contention that the Buddha himself was beset by doubt about whether he should expound the Dharma.[52] The Buddha had no doubts at all even with regard to the most profound sorts of dharmas, how much the less might he have had doubts with regard to whether or not he should expound the Dharma. The Buddha never said that he would entirely forego his teaching of the Dharma. He merely indicated a preference for continuing to abide in serenity, refraining from becoming involved in numerous endeavors. There was no fault in his having simply waited till later to begin expounding the Dharma.

Also, the non-Buddhist partisans would say, "If the Buddha is such a great *ārya* that he remains silent and declines to involve himself in conceptual elaboration, what use could he have for assembling a following and offering to give teachings?" Then again, once he started teaching, this would inevitably turn into an endless endeavor. It was as if he was weighing the utility of proceeding to teach the Dharma and assemble a group of disciples when this could appear outwardly as if it were a mark of covetous attachment.

Due to these factors, the Buddha reflected, "Though my Dharma is extremely deep, the wisdom and skillful means that might be

正體字

無量無邊。而可度
078a27 ‖ 者少。是故自言不如默然。又防外道所譏
078a28 ‖ 呵故。令梵天王求請說法。即時梵天王等
078a29 ‖ 白佛言。眾生可愍。中有利根結使薄者易
078b01 ‖ 可化度。是故受諸梵王等請。如人得大寶
078b02 ‖ 藏應示餘人。如是諸聖自得法利亦應利
078b03 ‖ 人。如汝所說佛不知阿蘭迦蘭等先已命
078b04 ‖ 終欲為說法者。今當答。佛不念其死與
078b05 ‖ 不死。但念此人結使微薄堪[5]任化度。隨所
078b06 ‖ 念處則有智生。是故佛先自說。而後天告理
078b07 ‖ 故宜然。又佛先出家。就此二人曾經宿止。
078b08 ‖ 諸天人民[6]儻能疑佛受其妙法餘處得道。
078b09 ‖ 佛欲斷彼疑故。即時唱言彼人長衰如此。妙
078b10 ‖ 法如何不聞。推如是義。五比丘事亦復可
078b11 ‖ 知。但念其可度因緣。不念其住止所在。後
078b12 ‖ 念住處即便得知。

简体字

无量无边。而可度者少。是故自言不如默然。又防外道所讥呵故。令梵天王求请说法。即时梵天王等白佛言。众生可愍。中有利根结使薄者易可化度。是故受诸梵王等请。如人得大宝藏应示余人。如是诸圣自得法利亦应利人。如汝所说佛不知阿兰迦兰等先已命终欲为说法者。今当答。佛不念其死与不死。但念此人结使微薄堪任化度。随所念处则有智生。是故佛先自说。而后天告理故宜然。又佛先出家。就此二人曾经宿止。诸天人民傥能疑佛受其妙法余处得道。佛欲断彼疑故。即时唱言彼人长衰如此。妙法如何不闻。推如是义。五比丘事亦复可知。但念其可度因缘。不念其住止所在。后念住处即便得知。

employed in teaching it would be measureless and boundless. Still, those who are actually amenable to gaining liberation are but few." Consequently, he thought to himself, "It would be better to remain silent." It was also to defend against the potential for mocking deprecation by non-Buddhist partisans that he instead influenced the Brahma Heaven King to [first] request the proclamation of Dharma. The Brahma Heaven King and others then immediately addressed the Buddha, saying, "Beings are surely worthy of pity. There are among them those of sharp faculties and but few fetters who would be easy to teach and bring across to liberation."

Because of this, the Buddha acceded to the request of the Brahma Heaven King and others. It was as if someone who had just found a great treasury of jewels felt he should reveal their presence to others. In this same way, when *āryas* themselves gain the benefits of the Dharma, they feel they should also use it to benefit others.

I shall now address your contention that, because the Buddha expressed a wish to speak the Dharma for Ārāḍa Kālāma and others, not realizing that they had in fact already died, [this contradicts the plausibility of his being omniscient]. The Buddha had not brought to mind the issue of whether or not they had already died, but rather was only considering the fact that, because these men's fetters were but scant, they would be capable of being instructed and brought across to liberation. It is in correspondence with the point upon which one's thought is focused that a corresponding knowledge arises. It was as a consequence of this that the Buddha first said this to himself and a deva then appropriately informed him.[53]

Also, since earlier on, when the Buddha had just abandoned the home life, he had gone to those men, [Arāda Kālāma and Udraka Rāmaputra], and had spent time with them, the devas and other people could have entertained doubts in which they thought the Buddha had perhaps received the sublime Dharma from them and had then become enlightened in another location. Because the Buddha wished to cut off any doubts that they might have had, he immediately exclaimed, "Oh, those men—they have for so long suffered such misfortune as this. How can it be that they have still not heard this sublime Dharma?"

By inferring the implications of this idea, one can deduce the nature of the matter of the five bhikshus. It was because the Buddha had only brought to mind the causes and conditions associated with their capacity to gain liberation that he had not yet considered precisely where they were currently dwelling. Afterward, once he had thought about where they were dwelling, he then knew where they were.

正體字

是故不應破一切智人。
078b13 ‖ 汝言疑說巴連弗城壞者。今當答。是城破因
078b14 ‖ 緣不定。不定因緣而定說者是則為過。又我
078b15 ‖ 先說四十不共法中諸佛善知不定。答者則
078b16 ‖ 不受此難。汝說佛問諸比丘。汝等聚會為
078b17 ‖ 何所說。今當答。佛將欲說法門故。作如是
078b18 ‖ 問。或欲結戒故。[7]命其自說如是種種說
078b19 ‖ 法故。問而無咎。世間亦有知而復問。如見
078b20 ‖ 人食問言食耶。如天寒時問言寒耶。佛亦
078b21 ‖ 如是知而復問隨俗無咎。汝言自讚毀他
078b22 ‖ 非一切智人者。今當答。佛不貪身不貪
078b23 ‖ 供養。不恚他人不增上慢。所以自說我
078b24 ‖ 於世間最第一者。有信眾生諸根猛利捨
078b25 ‖ 惡知識。以我為師是人長夜當得安隱。是
078b26 ‖ 故佛自讚身。復次有人求第一樂道。而有
078b27 ‖ 懈怠不能精進。

简体字

是故不应破一切智人。汝言疑说巴连弗城坏者。今当答。是城破因缘不定。不定因缘而定说者是则为过。又我先说四十不共法中诸佛善知不定。答者则不受此难。汝说佛问诸比丘。汝等聚会为何所说。今当答。佛将欲说法门故。作如是问。或欲结戒故。命其自说如是种种说法故。问而无咎。世间亦有知而复问。如见人食问言食耶。如天寒时问言寒耶。佛亦如是知而复问随俗无咎。汝言自赞毁他非一切智人者。今当答。佛不贪身不贪供养。不恚他人不增上慢。所以自说我于世间最第一者。有信众生诸根猛利舍恶知识。以我为师是人长夜当得安隐。是故佛自赞身。复次有人求第一乐道。而有懈怠不能精进。

Therefore one should not look upon these issues as refuting the plausibility of there being an omniscient person.

I shall now address your stated doubt with regard to the causes for the destruction of the city of Pāṭaliputra. The precise causes and conditions by which this city would meet its destruction were still unfixed. To make a fixed pronouncement on the unfolding of unfixed causes and conditions would itself be a fault.

Also among the forty exclusive dharmas listed earlier, I stated that all buddhas are thoroughly cognizant of dharmas that are unfixed. In response then, I do not accept this challenge as valid.

I shall now address your contention about the Buddha's querying the bhikshus as to the contents of their conversation by asking, "So, what are you all gathered together to discuss?" It was because the Buddha was about to hold forth on some aspect of Dharma that he initiated the discussion by asking a question of this sort. It could have been that, because he wished to formulate another of the moral prohibitions, he directed them to talk about what they were discussing. Because he took all sorts of such instances as occasions for speaking Dharma, the Buddha's posing a question was free of any fault [in relation to the issue of his omniscience].

Furthermore it is a commonplace in the world, even when one is already well aware of what is happening, for one to go ahead and ask a question. For instance, on observing someone eating, one may ask, "Oh, so you're eating, are you?" Or, for instance, on a particularly cold day, one may ask, "Isn't it cold?"

In this same way, even though he already knew, the Buddha would nonetheless pose a question. Being but a means of conforming to convention, this is entirely free of fault.

I shall now address your judgment that anyone who praises himself and criticizes others could not possibly be an omniscient person. The Buddha entertained no desires with respect to himself and so was not the least bit covetous of receiving offerings. He did not hate other men and was not possessed of overweening pride. As for the reason for his having declared himself to be foremost among everyone in the world, it was because there were beings who were amenable to faith and possessed of acutely sharp faculties who, if they cast aside bad spiritual guides and took the Buddha as their teacher, they could then gain that peace and security that would see them through the long night [of subsequent rebirths]. It was for this reason that the Buddha did in fact praise his own personal qualities.

Additionally, there were those who, although they sought the path to the supreme bliss, were still indolent and unable to bring forth

正體字

是故佛言無上利中不應
078b28 ‖ 懈怠。我於世間第一導師善說正法。宜勤
078b29 ‖ 精進可得道果。如是等因緣自讚其身。非
078c01 ‖ 為自貴輕賤他人。呵惡人者欲令除滅
078c02 ‖ 惡法。非為憎恚眾生。有人求如法利。其心
078c03 ‖ 清淨質直。而與惡知識和合。欲令遠離此
078c04 ‖ 故而呵罵之。未得佛時尚以髓腦施人。何
078c05 ‖ 況成佛而當呵罵。汝說佛法初後相違。今當
078c06 ‖ 答。佛法中無有始終相違事。汝等不知佛
078c07 ‖ 法義故以為相違。是涅槃道者。從迦葉佛
078c08 ‖ 滅已來。無復人說。亦無人得。是故言我新
078c09 ‖ 得道。餘處復說我得故道。是道錠光等諸佛
078c10 ‖ 所得。所謂八聖道能至涅槃。一道一因緣故名
078c11 ‖ 為故道。是故當知佛成一切智。問曰。所言
078c12 ‖ 一切智者。云何名為一切智。為知一切故
078c13 ‖ 名為一切智耶。答曰。一切智者知可知。可
078c14 ‖ 知者五法藏。

简体字

是故佛言无上利中不应懈怠。我于世间第一导师善说正法。宜勤精进可得道果。如是等因缘自赞其身。非为自贵轻贱他人。呵恶人者欲令除灭恶法。非为憎恚众生。有人求如法利。其心清净质直。而与恶知识和合。欲令远离此故而呵骂之。未得佛时尚以髓脑施人。何况成佛而当呵骂。汝说佛法初后相违。今当答。佛法中无有始终相违事。汝等不知佛法义故以为相违。是涅槃道者。从迦葉佛灭已来。无复人说。亦无人得。是故言我新得道。余处复说我得故道。是道锭光等诸佛所得。所谓八圣道能至涅槃。一道一因缘故名为故道。是故当知佛成一切智。问曰。所言一切智者。云何名为一切智。为知一切故名为一切智耶。答曰。一切智者知可知。可知者五法藏。

vigorous effort. Consequently the Buddha declared, "In this matter of gaining the most supreme benefit, one must not be indolent. I am the supreme spiritual guide in this world, the one who well proclaims right Dharma. It is only fitting then that you become assiduous and vigorous, for it is only then that you may gain the fruits of the path." And so it was that, for reasons such as these, the Buddha did indeed praise his own personal qualities. It was not out of a wish to be accorded esteem, nor was it out of a wish to slight and deprecate others.

In cases where the Buddha rebuked evil men, it was for the sake of inducing them to get rid of evil dharmas. It was not because he detested other beings. In some cases, there were those seeking to achieve benefit through Dharma, people whose minds were pure and of straightforward character, but who were locked in relationships with bad spiritual guides. In order to induce them to abandon these bad teachers, the Buddha would sometimes criticize and rebuke them. Even before he had achieved buddhahood, [in earlier lifetimes] he even sacrificed his own brain and the very marrow of his bones as gifts to others. How much the less could it be that, once he had already attained buddhahood, he would be inclined to berate and scold others?

I shall now respond to your contention that there were chronologically contradictory tenets in the Buddha's Dharma. There are no contradictions present in the Dharma of the Buddha between what came at the beginning and what followed later on. It is only because you and your cohorts do not understand the concepts involved in the Buddha's Dharma that you have the opinion that it is inherently contradictory.

This path leading to the realization of nirvāṇa had not been either proclaimed or realized by anyone during the entire time between Kāśyapa Buddha's nirvāṇa on forward to the present. It was for this reason that the Buddha declared, "I am he who has newly attained the path." In other places, he also said, "I have attained the ancient path." The path is that which was previously realized by Dīpaṃkara Buddha and the other buddhas of the past, namely the eightfold path of the Āryas that is able to lead one to nirvāṇa. It is because, in all these cases, it is but a single path relying on but a single set of causes and conditions that it is referred to it as "the ancient path." One should realize from this that the Buddha did obtain all-knowledge.

Question: As for the so-called "all-knowledge," precisely what is it that constitutes all-knowledge? Is it really on the basis of knowing absolutely everything that it is referred to as "all-knowledge"?

Response: "All-knowledge" refers to knowing all that can be known. "What can be known" refers to the five categorical repositories of

正體字

過去未來現在出三世不可說
078c15 ‖ 所用。知此五藏者名為知。是故知及所知
078c16 ‖ 名為一切。問曰。知可知[8]名一切者。是事不
078c17 ‖ 然。何以故。是法但是一。可知知亦是可知
078c18 ‖ 故。如世間言是人知利是人知鈍。答曰。若
078c19 ‖ 一切是一者則寒熱相違皆應是一。明闇苦
078c20 ‖ 樂諸相違事亦應是一。但是事不然。是故不
078c21 ‖ 得言一切皆是一。問曰。汝所執亦同此過。
078c22 ‖ 若可知是一者。苦樂等亦應是一而實不
078c23 ‖ 一。答曰。我不言一切可知是一。汝所執一
078c24 ‖ 切皆是一。是故不與汝同過。復次汝說同有
078c25 ‖ 過故。汝自執中有過。若人自受所執中過
078c26 ‖ 即墮負處。汝知所執有過。不應復說他過。
078c27 ‖ 是故汝說同有過者。是事不然。復次若謂
078c28 ‖ 知可知二法為一者。應用可知法知瓶衣
078c29 ‖ 等物而實用知知一切物。

简体字

过去未来现在出三世不可说所用。知此五藏者名为知。是故知及所知名为一切。问曰。知可知名一切者。是事不然。何以故。是法但是一。可知知亦是可知故。如世间言是人知利是人知钝。答曰。若一切是一者则寒热相违皆应是一。明闇苦乐诸相违事亦应是一。但是事不然。是故不得言一切皆是一。问曰。汝所执亦同此过。若可知是一者。苦乐等亦应是一而实不一。答曰。我不言一切可知是一。汝所执一切皆是一。是故不与汝同过。复次汝说同有过故。汝自执中有过。若人自受所执中过即堕负处。汝知所执有过。不应复说他过。是故汝说同有过者。是事不然。复次若谓知可知二法为一者。应用可知法知瓶衣等物而实用知知一切物。

dharmas, namely all past, future, and present dharmas, the dharmas that transcend the three periods of time, and the ineffable dharmas. That which is used in knowing these five categories of dharmas is cognition. Hence it is both cognition and those things that it knows that are referred to as the "all" [in the term "all-knowledge."]

Question: As for this contention that it is both the faculty of cognition and those things it knows that together comprise the "all" [of all-knowledge], this is wrong. How so? This is but a singular dharma, this because that cognition that is capable of knowing is itself knowable as when people of the world speak of this person's cognitive ability as sharp whereas that person's cognitive ability is dull.

Response: Well, if as you state that "all" is itself just a singular entity, then it should be that those polar opposites such as "hot" and "cold" are but one thing. And so too it should be that "bright" and "dark," "suffering" and "happiness," and all polar opposites should in each case be but a single thing. But this is not the case. Therefore, one cannot claim that "all" is but a singular entity.

Question: That idea to which you are clinging is itself possessed of this same fault. If the faculty of cognition is one thing, then [that which it knows, namely] "suffering," "happiness," and so forth—those should all also be but singular entities, but in truth, they are not.

Response: I never claimed that everything that can be known is, [in aggregate], but one single thing. Now that idea to which *you* are clinging is indeed that everything [that can be known] *is* somehow, [in its collective aggregate], but a single thing. Therefore, [what I am saying] is not the same as that faulty concept you are proposing.

Furthermore, since you claim that [both of] these positions are equally at fault, that idea to which you are clinging is faulty. In a case where someone accepts that the idea he is proposing is faulty, his position is thereby refuted. Now, when you understand that the idea to which you have been clinging is faulty, you should not continue to claim that someone else is the party whose position is faulty. Hence, as for your contention that what I have set forth here is somehow possessed of the same fault that characterizes your position—this is wrong.

Moreover, if you claim that the two dharmas consisting of the faculty of cognition on the one hand and that which is known on the other are somehow but a single entity, then one should be able to use any particular knowable dharma to know phenomena like vases and robes and such, but in truth it is solely the faculty of cognition that can be used in the knowing of all things.

正體字

若謂瓶衣等於
079a01 ‖ 知無異者。今瓶衣等不能知物。即應有
079a02 ‖ 異而實用知知一切物。如是處處有過故
079a03 ‖ 不得言一切[1]皆是一。復次知所知是二名
079a04 ‖ 為一切知。是一切法故。名如來名一切
079a05 ‖ 智者。是一切智人因金剛三昧。是故金剛
079a06 ‖ 三昧成。汝先言金剛三昧不成一切智不成
079a07 ‖ 者。是事不然。[2]

简体字

若谓瓶衣等于知无异者。今瓶衣等不能知物。即应有异而实用知知一切物。如是处处有过故不得言一切皆是一。复次知所知是二名为一切知。是一切法故。名如来名一切智者。是一切智人因金刚三昧。是故金刚三昧成。汝先言金刚三昧不成一切智不成者。是事不然。

If you are going to claim that phenomena like vases and robes and such are no different from the faculty of cognition—this vase and robe and so forth—they are entirely unable to know any phenomenon at all. It immediately follows that it ought to be the case that they are different [from the faculty of cognition] and it is truly the case that one uses the faculty of cognition to know everything.

Because your position is faulty in these ways in place after place, you cannot thus claim that the constituent phenomena forming the "all" of all-knowledge are all collectively but a single thing.

So, again, the faculty of cognition and that which is known, these two things—they are what constitute the "all" of "all-knowledge," this because they together constitute all dharmas. It is because of the Buddha's knowing of all of these dharmas that he is known as the Tathāgata and is renowned as one who is possessed of all-knowledge. This omniscient man became possessed of all-knowledge because of the *vajra* samādhi. Therefore the *vajra* samādhi is indeed something that can be established. As for your initial contentions that the *vajra* samādhi cannot be established and that "all-knowledge" is also not something that can be established, these contentions are both wrong.

The End of Chapter Twenty-Two

正體字

079a08 ‖ [3]四十不共法中善知不定品第二十三
079a09 ‖ 善知不定法者。諸法未生未出未成未定
079a10 ‖ 未分別。是中如來智慧得力。如佛分別業經
079a11 ‖ 中說。佛告阿難。有人身行善業。口行善業。
079a12 ‖ 意行善業。是人命終而墮地獄。有人身行
079a13 ‖ 惡業。口行惡業。意行惡業。是人命終而生
079a14 ‖ 天上。阿難白佛言。何故如是。佛言。是人或
079a15 ‖ 先世罪福因緣已熟。今世罪福因緣未熟。或
079a16 ‖ 臨命終生正見邪見善惡心。垂終之心其
079a17 ‖ 力大故。又[4]首迦經中說。叔迦婆羅門子白
079a18 ‖ 佛言。瞿曇。諸婆羅門在家白衣。能修福德
079a19 ‖ 善根勝出家者。是事云何。佛言。我於此中
079a20 ‖ 不定答。出家或有不修善則不如在家。

简体字

十住毗婆沙论卷第十

四十不共法中善知不定品第二十三

善知不定法者。诸法未生未出未成未定未分别。是中如来智慧得力。如佛分别业经中说。佛告阿难。有人身行善业。口行善业。意行善业。是人命终而堕地狱。有人身行恶业。口行恶业。意行恶业。是人命终而生天上。阿难白佛言。何故如是。佛言。是人或先世罪福因缘已熟。今世罪福因缘未熟。或临命终生正见邪见善恶心。垂终之心其力大故。又首迦经中说。叔迦婆罗门子白佛言。瞿昙。诸婆罗门在家白衣。能修福德善根胜出家者。是事云何。佛言。我于此中不定答。出家或有不修善则不如在家。

Chapter 23:[54] Forty Dharmas Exclusive to Buddhas (Part 3)

IV. Chapter 23: Forty Dharmas Exclusive to Buddhas (Part 3)

A. 10) Thorough Knowing of Matters That Are Unfixed

As for knowing well the unfixed dharmas, the Tathāgata's wisdom has achieved power within the sphere of all dharmas even at that point when they have not yet arisen, have not yet come forth, have not yet reached completion, have not become definitively fixed, and have not yet become clearly distinguishable. This is as stated in the *Sutra on the Buddha's Distinguishing of Karma* wherein it states:

> The Buddha told Ānanda, "There are people who practice good deeds with the body, who practice good deeds through speech, and who practice good deeds with the mind, and yet, when their lives come to an end, they then fall into the hells. There are yet other people who practice evil deeds with the body, who practice evil deeds through speech, and who practice evil deeds with the mind, and yet, when their lives come to an end, they are nonetheless reborn in the heavens."
>
> Ānanda addressed the Buddha and asked, "Why do events occur in this way?"
>
> The Buddha replied, "It may have been that the causes and conditions associated with previous life karmic offenses or meritorious deeds had already ripened, whereas the karmic offenses or meritorious deeds of the present life had not yet ripened. Or, alternatively, when approaching the end of life, they gave rise to either right views or erroneous views that precipitated either wholesome or evil thoughts, this because the power of the thoughts produced as one approaches the moment of death—their power is immense."[55]

Additionally, in the *Śuka Sutra,* it states:

> Śuka, son of a brahmin, addressed the Buddha and asked, "Gotama, why is it that the brahmin laity are in some cases able to cultivate meritorious deeds and roots of goodness in a manner superior to that of some of those who have left the home life and become monastics?"
>
> The Buddha replied, "For these sorts of matters, I do not present a fixed reply. There may be cases in which someone who has left behind the home life does not cultivate goodness and, as a consequence, in this endeavor, he does not equal the efforts of a given

正體字

在
079a21 ‖ 家能修善則勝出家。又大涅槃經中說。巴
079a22 ‖ 連弗城當以三事壞。或[5]水或火或內人與
079a23 ‖ 外人謀。又因波梨末梵志說。是裸形波梨末
079a24 ‖ 梵志。若不捨是語。若是心若是邪見。到我
079a25 ‖ 目前無有是處。若皮繩斷。若身斷。終不來
079a26 ‖ 到佛前。又筏喻經中說。我此法甚深。以方
079a27 ‖ 便說令淺易解。若有直心如教行者得二
079a28 ‖ 種利。若今世盡漏。若不盡漏當得不還道。
079a29 ‖ 又增一阿含舍迦梨經中。佛告阿難。若人故
079b01 ‖ 起業。無有不受報而得道者。若現受報
079b02 ‖ 若生受若後受。又增一阿浮羅經中說。佛告
079b03 ‖ 諸比丘。諸惡人死若作畜生若墮地獄。善
079b04 ‖ 人生處若天若人。又無畏王子經中說。無畏
079b05 ‖ 白佛言。佛有所說能令他瞋不。佛言。王子
079b06 ‖ 是事不定。佛或憐愍心故。令他人瞋

简体字

在家能修善则胜出家。又大涅槃经中说。巴连弗城当以三事坏。或水或火或内人与外人谋。又因波梨末梵志说。是裸形波梨末梵志。若不舍是语。若是心若是邪见。到我目前无有是处。若皮绳断。若身断。终不来到佛前。又筏喻经中说。我此法甚深。以方便说令浅易解。若有直心如教行者得二种利。若今世尽漏。若不尽漏当得不还道。又增一阿含舍迦梨经中。佛告阿难。若人故起业。无有不受报而得道者。若现受报若生受若后受。又增一阿浮罗经中说。佛告诸比丘。诸恶人死若作畜生若堕地狱。善人生处若天若人。又无畏王子经中说。无畏白佛言。佛有所说能令他嗔不。佛言。王子是事不定。佛或怜愍心故。令他人嗔

householder. This is a case in which a householder is able to cultivate goodness in a manner superior to that of a particular monastic."

Furthermore, the *Great Nirvāṇa Sutra* states that the city of Pāṭaliputra is bound to be destroyed by one of three circumstances: by flood, by fire, or by a conspiracy between insiders and outsiders.

Also, [another example of an unfixed statement] arose because of a *brahmacārin* named Patikaputra about which the Buddha said:

> As for this naked ascetic, the *brahmacārin* named Patikaputra, if he fails to relinquish this statement, these thoughts, and these wrong views, then it will be impossible for him to come and appear before me. He will either be trapped by a broken rope or prevented from leaving by a broken body. In any case, he will never be able to arrive here in the presence of the Buddha.

Additionally, in the *Sutra on the Analogy of the Raft*, the Buddha said:

> This Dharma of mine is extremely deep. It is by resort to expedients that I enable even those who are shallow to easily reach an understanding of it. If there be anyone possessed of a straightforward mind who is willing to practice in accordance with the teachings, he will gain one of two kinds of benefit from this, either the cessation of the contaminants in this present lifetime or, in the event that he doesn't achieve the cessation of the contaminants, he will still succeed in attaining the path of the non-returner (*anāgāmin*).[56]

Also, in the *Ekottara Āgama*'s *Shejiali Sutra*,[57] the Buddha told Ānanda:

> As for whosoever deliberately undertakes the requisite karmic actions, none among them will fail to gain the karmic rewards and thus achieve success in the path, whether that be through receiving the results of present-life karma in this present life, whether that be through receiving them in the next birth, or whether that be through receiving them in subsequent lives.[58]

In addition, we also have this statement in the *Ekottara Āgama*'s *Afuluo Sutra*:[59] "The Buddha told the bhikshus, 'When evil people die, they may become animals or they may fall into the hells. Good people will be reborn either in the heavens or among humans.'"

Also, in the *Prince Fearless Sutra*, it states:

> Prince Fearless addressed the Buddha, saying, "Does the Buddha not have instances in which what he proclaims is able to cause others to become angry?"
>
> The Buddha replied, "Prince, this is an unfixed matter. It may happen that the Buddha, motivated by pity, will influence someone to become angry with the intended result that they will there-

正體字

得種
079b07 ‖ 善因緣。如乳母以曲指鉤出小兒口中惡
079b08 ‖ 物雖傷無患。又阿毘曇中說。眾生三品。從
079b09 ‖ 不定聚或墮邪定。或墮正定。如是等四法
079b10 ‖ 藏中無定事。數千萬種。問曰。若人智慧不定
079b11 ‖ 無決定心。於事中或爾或不爾則不名一
079b12 ‖ 切智人。一切智人者不二語者。決定語者。明
079b13 ‖ 了語者。是故善知不定。不得[6]名為佛不共
079b14 ‖ 法。答曰。不定事。若爾若不爾。隨屬眾因緣
079b15 ‖ 故。是中不應定說。[7]又若不定事而作定
079b16 ‖ [8]答不名一切智人。是故於不定事中必
079b17 ‖ 應用不定智。是故有不定智不共法。復次
079b18 ‖ 若人於一切法中決定知。是人即墮必定
079b19 ‖ 邪論中。若一切法必定則諸所[9]作為則不
079b20 ‖ 須人功方便而得。如說。
079b21 ‖ 　若好醜已定　　人功則應定
079b22 ‖ 　不須諸因緣　　方便而修習
079b23 ‖ 復次現見不自守護身則有眾苦。若自防
079b24 ‖ 護身則安利。

简体字

得种善因缘。如乳母以曲指钩出小儿口中恶物虽伤无患。又阿毗昙中说。众生三品。从不定聚或堕邪定。或堕正定。如是等四法藏中无定事。数千万种。问曰。若人智慧不定无决定心。于事中或尔或不尔则不名一切智人。一切智人者不二语者。决定语者。明了语者。是故善知不定。不得名为佛不共法。答曰。不定事。若尔若不尔。随属众因缘故。是中不应定说。又若不定事而作定答不名一切智人。是故于不定事中必应用不定智。是故有不定智不共法。复次若人于一切法中决定知。是人即堕必定邪论中。若一切法必定则诸所作为则不须人功方便而得。如说。

若好丑已定　　人功则应定
不须诸因缘　　方便而修习

复次现见不自守护身则有众苦。若自防护身则安利。

> by plant the causes and conditions for goodness. This is analogous to a wet-nurse having to use a crooked finger to clear an infant's mouth of some dangerous object. Although it may inflict injury, it is done in order to prevent a calamity."[60]

There is also the statement recorded in the Abhidharma: "Beings fall into three groups. From the [karmically] indefinite group, they may fall into the definitely deviant group or the definitely righteous group."[61]

There are several thousand or even myriads of similar such types of unfixed phenomena that are cited within the four repositories of the Dharma.[62]

Question: If a person's wisdom is unfixed and characterized by indefinite thought that takes a given circumstance to perhaps be this way or perhaps not be this way, then this is not someone who is omniscient. One who is omniscient would not make two different statements [with regard to a single matter], but rather would instead be able to make definitive pronouncements, pronouncements that are utterly clear. Because of this, "thoroughly knowing unfixed matters" cannot be referred to as a dharma exclusive to the Buddha.

Response: Unfixed matters are such that they may either be this way or not this way. It is because they develop in accordance with a multiplicity of causes and conditions that one should not make definite pronouncements about them.

Moreover, were one to offer definite answers regarding indefinite phenomena, then that itself would indicate that one is *not* omniscient. Consequently, in assessing unfixed phenomena, it is essential to employ the knowledge of unfixed matters. Hence there is this exclusive dharma referred to as "the knowledge of unfixed matters."

Additionally, if one were to claim definitive knowledge with respect to all dharmas, then one would fall into the erroneous determinist fallacy. If all dharmas really were already definitely fixed, then all that one does would not require any human effort and skillful means to bring it about. This idea is as set forth here:

> If good or bad experiences were already definitely determined,
> then the character of a person's efforts should be fixed as well.
> There would be no need for any of the causal factors
> involved in the skillful means that one uses in one's cultivation.

Moreover, it is already manifestly clear that if one fails to take care with regard to one's personal behavior, then one will bring about manifold sufferings, whereas, if one is guarded with respect to one's personal behavior, then one will enjoy peace and benefit as a result of doing so.

正體字

又如種種作業事中受諸疲
079b25 || 苦後得種種富樂果報。或復有人今世靜默
079b26 || 都無所作而得果報。是故有是不定事。為
079b27 || 知是不定事故。知有不定智。問曰。汝守護
079b28 || 不守護。施功不施功。而亦有不定事成者。
079b29 || 有人好自防護而得苦惱。不自防護不
079c01 || 得苦惱。又勤自疲苦不得功果。不勤施
079c02 || 功而得功果。是事不定。答曰。汝所說則成
079c03 || 我不定義。若有不定事應有不定智。我不
079c04 || 言若人不自防護悉皆受苦。又不言離
079c05 || 功業有果報。有人雖作功夫先世罪障故
079c06 || 不得受樂。不言一切皆爾。是故汝難非也。
079c07 || 是名諸佛於不定事中獨有不定智具足。
079c08 || 知無色處者。聲聞辟支佛。知生無色處眾
079c09 || 生及法少分。諸佛世尊

简体字

又如种种作业事中受诸疲苦后得种种富乐果报。或复有人今世静默都无所作而得果报。是故有是不定事。为知是不定事故。知有不定智。问曰。汝守护不守护。施功不施功。而亦有不定事成者。有人好自防护而得苦恼。不自防护不得苦恼。又勤自疲苦不得功果。不勤施功而得功果。是事不定。答曰。汝所说则成我不定义。若有不定事应有不定智。我不言若人不自防护悉皆受苦。又不言离功业有果报。有人虽作功夫先世罪障故不得受乐。不言一切皆尔。是故汝难非也。是名诸佛于不定事中独有不定智具足。知无色处者。声闻辟支佛。知生无色处众生及法少分。诸佛世尊

Also, this is just as in all sorts of endeavors involved in carrying on one's livelihood wherein, on the one hand, one is required to endure a good deal of weariness and suffering to later acquire a reward in the form of all manner of wealth and happiness, whereas, on the other hand, someone else is able to simply remain still and silent in this present life, doing nothing whatsoever, only to then reap karmic rewards. So it is that there are these unfixed circumstances. It is because they are cognizant of these unfixed circumstances that we can know that the Buddhas possess the knowledge of what is unfixed.

Question: Whether or not you personally take care and whether or not you make a direct personal effort, these unfixed circumstances will still occur. On the one hand there are those who skillfully defend against untoward developments and yet still end up being subjected to intense anguish while on the other hand there are those who do not defend against such exigencies at all and yet do not encounter any intense anguish at all. Also, there are those who, in their diligence, undergo much weariness and pain, but still do not obtain the fruits of their efforts, whereas there are others who are not the least bit diligent and make no particular effort and, even so, they still manage to gain fruits [otherwise] associated with making an effort. These matters are all unfixed.

Response: Your statement simply serves to cooperate in the establishment of my position regarding unfixed matters. If these unfixed matters do indeed exist, then this wisdom that is cognizant of whatsoever is unfixed should exist. I never claimed that, if someone failed to guard against untoward events they would always be subjected to suffering. Nor did I ever claim that, without the expenditure of effortful action, one would necessarily be able to enjoy fruitful results. There are those people who, despite making an effort, are still blocked from the enjoyment of happiness by karmic obstacles originating in earlier lifetimes. I never claimed that all cases were necessarily this way. Therefore the challenges that you have posed on this topic are wrong.

This is what is meant [when it is said] with regard to unfixed circumstances that it is the Buddhas alone who possess complete knowledge of what is unfixed.

B. 11) Thorough Knowing of Formless Absorption Phenomena

As for knowing the formless realm stations, *śrāvaka* disciples and *pratyekabuddhas* know a lesser portion of the beings and dharmas associated with the formless realm stations of existence whereas the Buddhas, the Bhagavats, have a perfectly complete knowledge of the

正體字

於無色處眾生及法
079c10 ‖ 具足悉知。是無色處有若干眾生生此處。
079c11 ‖ 若干眾生生彼處。若干眾生生初無色定處。
079c12 ‖ 若干眾生生第二處。若干眾生生第三處。
079c13 ‖ 若干眾生生第四處。若干眾生生來爾所
079c14 ‖ 時。若干眾生經爾所時當退沒。若干眾
079c15 ‖ 生極壽爾所時。若干眾生畢定壽命。若干
079c16 ‖ 眾生不畢定壽命。若干眾生從欲界命終
079c17 ‖ 來生此中。若干眾生從色界命終來生此
079c18 ‖ 中。若干眾生從無色界命終還生此中。若
079c19 ‖ 干眾生人中命終即來生此。若干眾生天中
079c20 ‖ 命終即來生此。是諸眾生於此命終。若生
079c21 ‖ 欲界若生色界若生無色界。是諸眾生此
079c22 ‖ 中命終。若生天道若生人道若生阿修羅
079c23 ‖ 道。若生地獄[10]畜生餓鬼道中。是諸眾生
079c24 ‖ 於彼處入涅槃。

简体字

于无色处众生及法具足悉知。是无色处有若干众生生此处。若干众生生彼处。若干众生生初无色定处。若干众生生第二处。若干众生生第三处。若干众生生第四处。若干众生生来尔所时。若干众生经尔所时当退没。若干众生极寿尔所时。若干众生毕定寿命。若干众生不毕定寿命。若干众生从欲界命终来生此中。若干众生从色界命终来生此中。若干众生从无色界命终还生此中。若干众生人中命终即来生此。若干众生天中命终即来生此。是诸众生于此命终。若生欲界若生色界若生无色界。是诸众生此中命终。若生天道若生人道若生阿修罗道。若生地狱畜生饿鬼道中。是诸众生于彼处入涅槃。

beings and dharmas associated with the formless realm stations of existence.

Regarding these formless realm stations of existence, the Buddhas know:

That a certain number of beings are born into this station;

That a certain number of beings are born into that station;

That a certain number of beings are born into the station associated with the first formless absorption;

That a certain number of beings are born into the second station;

That a certain number of beings are born into the third station;

That a certain number of beings are born into the fourth station;

That a certain number of beings have dwelt there for a particular amount of time since they were born there;

That a certain number of beings, after a particular period of time, will fall away from that realm;

That a certain number of beings will enjoy a maximum lifespan of a particular amount of time;

That a certain number of beings will have a definitely fixed lifespan;

That a certain number of beings will enjoy a lifespan the length of which is not definitely fixed;

That a certain number of beings will be born here after their lifetimes in the desire realm have come to an end;

That a certain number of beings will be born here after their lifetimes in the form realm have come to an end;

That a certain number of beings will return to be reborn here after their lifetimes in this formless realm have come to an end;

That a certain number of beings will be born here directly after their lives in the human realm come to an end;

That a certain number of beings will be reborn here directly after their lives in the heavens have come to an end;

That, when the lives of these particular beings end here, they will then take birth in the desire realm, that they will then take birth in the form realm, or that they will then take birth in the formless realm;

That, when the lives of these particular beings end here, they will then take birth in the celestial realm rebirth destiny, that they will then take birth in the human realm rebirth destiny, that they will then take birth in the *asura* realm rebirth destiny, or that they will then take birth in the rebirth destinies of the hell realms, the animal realms, or the hungry ghost realms;

That these particular beings will enter nirvāṇa in that particular place;

正體字

若干眾生皆是凡夫。若
079c25 ‖ 干眾生是佛賢聖弟子。若干眾生凡夫弟子。
079c26 ‖ 若干眾生成聲聞乘。若干眾生成辟支佛
079c27 ‖ 乘。若干眾生皆成大乘。若干眾生不成
079c28 ‖ 聲聞乘。若干眾生不成辟支佛乘。不成大
079c29 ‖ 乘。若干眾生行滅者。若干眾生不行滅者。若
080a01 ‖ 干眾生上行。若干眾生某佛弟子。諸佛又知
080a02 ‖ 是定受味。是定不受味。是善是無記。是定
080a03 ‖ 中斷若干結。是定上中下。略說無色諸定。
080a04 ‖ 唯有諸佛以一切種智悉能分別大小深
080a05 ‖ 淺心相[1]應不相應果報非果報等。是名

简体字

若干众生皆是凡夫。若干众生是佛贤圣弟子。若干众生凡夫弟子。若干众生成声闻乘。若干众生成辟支佛乘。若干众生皆成大乘。若干众生不成声闻乘。若干众生不成辟支佛乘。不成大乘。若干众生行灭者。若干众生不行灭者。若干众生上行。若干众生某佛弟子。诸佛又知是定受味。是定不受味。是善是无记。是定中断若干结。是定上中下。略说无色诸定。唯有诸佛以一切种智悉能分别大小深浅心相应不相应果报非果报等。是名

That a particular group of beings are all merely common people;
That a particular group of beings are *ārya* disciples of buddhas;
That a particular group of beings are [buddhas'] disciples who are common people [that have not yet become *āryas*];
That a particular group of beings will achieve success in the Śrāvaka Disciple Vehicle;
That a particular group of beings will achieve success in the Pratyekabuddha Vehicle;
That a particular group of beings will all achieve success in the Great Vehicle;
That a particular group of beings will fail to achieve success in the Śrāvaka Disciple Vehicle;
That a particular group of beings will fail to achieve success in the Pratyekabuddha Vehicle and will also fail to achieve success in the Great Vehicle;
That a particular group of beings will develop their practice to the point of reaching nirvāṇa;
That a particular group of beings will fail to develop their practice to the point where they reach nirvāṇa;
That a particular group of beings will pursue a superior level of practice;
And that a particular group of beings are all disciples of a particular buddha.

The Buddhas also know:

That this particular meditative absorption is one in which one is exposed to delectably blissful experiences;[63]
That in this particular meditative absorption there will be no exposure to delectably blissful experiences;
[That this particular meditative absorption] is wholesome or is merely neutral;
That in this particular meditative absorption one may successfully sever a certain number of fetters;
And that this particular meditative absorption is superior, is middling, or is inferior.

To summarize, only the Buddhas, by employing their knowledge of all modes are able to clearly distinguish which of these formless-realm meditative absorptions are greater or lesser, which are deeper or shallower, which involve mental dharmas, which involve dharmas not associated with the mind, which are acquired as resultant effects [of previous karma], which are not acquired as resultant effects [of previous karma], and so forth. This is what is meant when it is said that the

正體字

諸佛
080a06 ‖ 具足悉知無色定處通達。滅法者。諸辟支佛
080a07 ‖ 諸阿羅漢。過去現在滅度者。諸佛通達如經
080a08 ‖ 中說。諸比丘是賢劫前九十一劫。毘婆尸佛
080a09 ‖ 出至三十一劫。有二佛出。一名尸棄。二名
080a10 ‖ 毘式婆。此賢劫中鳩樓孫迦那含牟尼迦葉佛
080a11 ‖ 出。如是過去諸佛大知見。[2]經此中應說。及
080a12 ‖ 諸聲聞弟子滅度入無餘涅槃。及辟支佛。號
080a13 ‖ 曰成。號曰華相。號曰見法。號曰法篋。號
080a14 ‖ 曰喜見。號曰無垢。號曰無得。如是等諸辟
080a15 ‖ 支佛。入無餘涅槃佛悉通達。復次未滅度
080a16 ‖ 在有餘涅槃。生緣都盡通達是事。亦名通
080a17 ‖ 達知滅。如經說。佛告阿難。我於此人悉知
080a18 ‖ 無有微闇。是人畢定盡是內法。是人命終
080a19 ‖ 當入涅槃。亦名知滅。又於餘人通達四
080a20 ‖ 諦能知其事。亦名知滅。如經說。我何不
080a21 ‖ 方便。令此人即於此處漏盡解脫。

简体字

诸佛具足悉知无色定处通达。灭法者。诸辟支佛诸阿罗汉。过去现在灭度者。诸佛通达如经中说。诸比丘是贤劫前九十一劫。毗婆尸佛出至三十一劫。有二佛出。一名尸弃。二名毗式婆。此贤劫中鸠楼孙迦那含牟尼迦葉佛出。如是过去诸佛大知见。经此中应说。及诸声闻弟子灭度入无余涅槃。及辟支佛。号曰成。号曰华相。号曰见法。号曰法箧。号曰喜见。号曰无垢。号曰无得。如是等诸辟支佛。入无余涅槃佛悉通达。复次未灭度在有余涅槃。生缘都尽通达是事。亦名通达知灭。如经说。佛告阿难。我于此人悉知无有微闇。是人毕定尽是内法。是人命终当入涅槃。亦名知灭。又于余人通达四谛能知其事。亦名知灭。如经说。我何不方便。令此人即于此处漏尽解脱。

Buddhas thoroughly know the stations of existence corresponding to the formless meditative absorptions.

C. 12) The Knowledge of All Matters Related to Eternal Cessation

As for [the completely penetrating knowledge of all] dharmas pertaining to cessation, the Buddhas possess a penetrating knowledge of the *pratyekabuddhas* and arhats who have entered nirvāṇa either in the past or present eras. This is as recorded in the sutras where it states:

> Bhikshus, ninety-one kalpas prior to this "Worthy Kalpa" (*bhadrakalpa*), Vipaśyin Buddha appeared. After thirty-one kalpas, there followed two more buddhas, the first of whom was Śikhin and the second of whom was Viśvabhū. Then, in this Worthy Kalpa, Krakucchanda, Kanakamuni, and Kāśyapa Buddha emerged.[64]

Just such great knowledge and vision regarding all buddhas of the past should be discussed [more extensively] herein in relation to this sutra.[65] It also reaches to those *śrāvaka* disciples who have entered the nirvāṇa without residue and extends also to the *pratyekabuddha* named "Success," to the one named "Floral Insignia," to the one named "Seer of Dharma," to the one named "Dharma Basket," to the one named "Delightful Vision," to the one named "Stainless," to the one named "Free of Gain," and to the other such *pratyekabuddhas* as well. So it is that the Buddhas possess a completely penetrating knowledge of those who have entered the nirvāṇa without residue.[66]

Additionally, in cases where they have not yet entered final nirvāṇa, but rather still abide in the nirvāṇa with residue, the Buddhas possess a penetratingly comprehensive knowledge with regard to the utter ending of all conditions associated with taking birth. [These matters] also pertain to their penetrating knowledge of [the phenomena associated with] cessation.

This is as recorded in the sutras wherein it states, "The Buddha told Ānanda, 'I entirely know with respect to this person that he no longer has even the slightest darkness. This person has definitely put an end to these particular inward dharmas. When this person reaches the end of this life, he will enter nirvāṇa.'" This too is included in what is meant by "having knowledge of cessation."[67]

Also, regarding other people's penetrating comprehension of the four truths, he is able to know their circumstances. This too is included in what is meant by "having knowledge of cessation."

As it is said in the sutras, "Why should I not simply resort to expedients to cause this person in this very place to gain the liberation associated with ending the contaminants?"

正體字

如佛告
080a22 ‖ 阿難。汝樂禪定樂斷結使。亦名通達知
080a23 ‖ 滅。如佛告舍利弗。我知涅槃知至涅槃
080a24 ‖ 道。知至涅槃眾生。如是等諸經。此中應
080a25 ‖ 說。是名諸佛通達知滅。善知心不相應非
080a26 ‖ 色法者。戒善根使善律儀不善律儀等諸心
080a27 ‖ 不相應非色法。聲聞辟支佛不能通達。諸佛
080a28 ‖ 善能通達如現目前。於心不相應諸法中。
080a29 ‖ 成就第一智慧力故。問曰。戒善律儀不善律
080b01 ‖ 儀是色法。何以言非色法。答曰。戒善律儀
080b02 ‖ 不善律儀有二種。有作有無作。作是色。無作
080b03 ‖ 非色。無作非[3]色。佛以不共力故現前能知。
080b04 ‖ 餘人以比智知。問曰。諸佛但善知心不相
080b05 ‖ 應非色法。不善知相應法耶。答曰。若通達
080b06 ‖ 不相應法。相應法無所復論。如人能

简体字

如佛告阿难。汝乐禅定乐断结使。亦名通达知灭。如佛告舍利弗。我知涅槃知至涅槃道。知至涅槃众生。如是等诸经。此中应说。是名诸佛通达知灭。善知心不相应非色法者。戒善根使善律仪不善律仪等诸心不相应非色法。声闻辟支佛不能通达。诸佛善能通达如现目前。于心不相应诸法中。成就第一智慧力故。问曰。戒善律仪不善律仪是色法。何以言非色法。答曰。戒善律仪不善律仪有二种。有作有无作。作是色。无作非色。无作非色。佛以不共力故现前能知。余人以比智知。问曰。诸佛但善知心不相应非色法。不善知相应法耶。答曰。若通达不相应法。相应法无所复论。如人能

And as the Buddha told Ānanda, "You delight in *dhyāna* concentration and delight in cutting off the fetters." These circumstances too are associated with what is meant by having a completely penetrating knowledge of cessation.

This is also as illustrated in the Buddha's statement to Śāriputra, "I know nirvāṇa, know the path leading to the realization of nirvāṇa, and know those beings who will arrive at the realization of nirvāṇa."[68]

Such sutras as we have cited herein should all be discussed at greater length. The ideas cited above are indicative of what is meant by all buddhas possessing the penetrating comprehension of all matters having to do with cessation.

D. 13) Thorough Knowing of Non-Form Dharmas Unrelated to Mind

As for thorough knowing of the non-form dharmas unassociated with the mind, roots of goodness associated with the moral precepts influence all of those non-form dharmas unassociated with the mind such as the moral regulations requiring wholesome actions and the moral regulations prohibiting bad actions. *Śrāvaka* disciples and *pratyekabuddhas* are unable to possess a completely penetrating comprehension of such matters. The Buddhas, however, are so well able to penetratingly comprehend them that these become as manifestly clear to them as if they were right before their very eyes. This is because they have perfected the foremost power of wisdom with respect to dharmas unassociated with the mind.

Question: Moral regulations requiring wholesome actions and moral regulations prohibiting bad actions are form dharmas. Why do you refer to them as "non-form" dharmas?

Response: Moral regulations requiring wholesome actions and moral regulations prohibiting bad actions are of two kinds, namely those involving actions and those not involving actions. Those involving actions are within the sphere of form dharmas whereas those not involving actions are "non-form" dharmas. As for those non-form dharmas not involving actions, employing his exclusive power of knowing, the Buddha is able to have a clear and present knowledge of them whereas others are compelled to rely upon inferential knowledge to understand them.

Question: Are the Buddhas only able to thoroughly know the non-form dharmas unassociated with the mind while not being able to thoroughly know the dharmas associated with the mind?

Response: If one already possesses a penetrating comprehension of the unassociated dharmas, then there is no need even to bring up the associated dharmas. It is as if we were speaking of an archer able to

正體字

射毫 080b07 ‖毛。麁物則不論。復次七百不相應法中。聲聞
080b08 ‖ 辟支佛以第六識能知七法。一名二相三
080b09 ‖ 義四無常五生六不生七度。佛以第六識皆
080b10 ‖ 悉能知。佛知四諦相及知世俗法。是故言
080b11 ‖ 諸佛善知心不相應無色法。勢力波羅蜜者。
080b12 ‖ 於一切所知法無餘中得一切種智勢力十
080b13 ‖ 力四無所畏四功德處助成故。又善得[4]十
080b14 ‖ 力故。是故佛能成就勢力波羅蜜。是勢力
080b15 ‖ 在第十六心中得增益。一切智常在佛身。
080b16 ‖ 乃至無餘涅槃。因是事故。於一切法中得
080b17 ‖ 無礙智。無礙智波羅蜜者。法義辭樂說。於此
080b18 ‖ 四法勢力無量通達無礙。如經中說。佛告
080b19 ‖ 諸比丘。如來四[5]弟子成就第一念力智慧
080b20 ‖ 力堪受力。如善射射樹葉即過無難。是諸
080b21 ‖ 弟子以四念處來問難。我常不休息。除飲
080b22 ‖ 食便利睡眠。於百年中如來常答。樂說智慧
080b23 ‖ 無有窮盡。

简体字

射毫毛。粗物则不论。复次七百不相应法中。声闻辟支佛以第六识能知七法。一名二相三义四无常五生六不生七度。佛以第六识皆悉能知。佛知四谛相及知世俗法。是故言诸佛善知心不相应无色法。势力波罗蜜者。于一切所知法无余中得一切种智势力十力四无所畏四功德处助成故。又善得十力故。是故佛能成就势力波罗蜜。是势力在第十六心中得增益。一切智常在佛身。乃至无余涅槃。因是事故。于一切法中得无碍智。无碍智波罗蜜者。法义辞乐说。于此四法势力无量通达无碍。如经中说。佛告诸比丘。如来四第子成就第一念力智慧力堪受力。如善射射树叶即过无难。是诸弟子以四念处来问难。我常不休息。除饮食便利睡眠。于百年中如来常答。乐说智慧无有穷尽。

pierce a single fine feather [floating through the air]. One would have no need in such a case to inquire if his arrow might be able to hit something large.

Furthermore, *śrāvaka* disciples and *pratyekabuddhas* are able to employ their sixth consciousness to know but seven among the seven hundred unassociated dharmas, namely: first, names; second, characteristic marks; third, meanings; fourth, impermanence; fifth, production; sixth, non-production; and seventh, crossing on beyond. The Buddhas, however, are able to employ their sixth consciousness to know every one of them. The Buddhas also know the marks of the four truths as well as the mundane dharmas. It is for these reasons that it is said that the Buddhas thoroughly know the non-form dharmas unassociated with the mind.

E. 14) The Great Powers Pāramitā

As for the powers *pāramitā*, [the Buddhas] gain the power of the knowledge of all modes with respect to all knowable dharmas without exception and are assisted in this by the ten powers, the four fearlessnesses, and the four bases of meritorious qualities. Also, it is due to having gained the ten powers that the Buddhas are therefore able to perfect the powers *pāramitā*. This power is increased in the sixteenth mind-moment [involved in achieving the direct seeing of the path]. All-knowledge is always present in the person of the Buddha until he attains the nirvāṇa without residue. It is because of this that he gains the unimpeded knowledge of all dharmas.

F. 15) The Four Unimpeded Knowledges Pāramitā

As for the *pāramitā* of the [four] unimpeded knowledges (*pratisaṃvid*), they are unimpeded knowledge with respect to: dharmas (*dharma-pratisaṃvid*), meaning (*artha-pratisaṃvid*), language (*nirukti-pratisaṃvid*), and eloquence (*pratibhāna-pratisaṃvid*). [The Buddhas] possess an unlimited penetrating comprehension of these four dharmas that is unimpeded in its implementation. As described in the sutras:[69]

> The Buddha told the bhikshus, "There are four of the Tathāgata's disciples who have perfected the foremost power of mindfulness, power of wisdom, and power of endurance so consummately that they are like a skilled archer who can shoot any single tree leaf without difficulty. Even if these disciples were to all come forth and pose challenging questions on the four stations of mindfulness, setting aside the time required for drink, food, toilet and sleep, I could always and incessantly respond to their questions for a hundred years during which the Tathāgata would always reply with inexhaustible eloquence and wisdom."

正體字

佛於此中以少欲相自論智
080b24 ‖ 慧。若三千大千世界所有四天下滿中微塵。
080b25 ‖ 隨爾所塵數作爾所三千大千世界。滿中
080b26 ‖ 眾生皆如舍利弗如辟支佛。皆悉成就智
080b27 ‖ 慧樂說。壽命如上塵數大劫。是諸人等因
080b28 ‖ 四念處盡其形壽問難如來。如來還以四
080b29 ‖ 念處義答其所問。言義不重樂說無盡。法
080c01 ‖ 無礙智者。善能分別諸法名字通達無礙。
080c02 ‖ 義無礙者。於諸法義通達無礙。辭無礙者。
080c03 ‖ 隨眾生類以諸言辭令其解義通達無礙。
080c04 ‖ 樂說無礙者。問答時善巧說法無有窮盡。
080c05 ‖ [6]餘賢聖不能究盡。唯有諸佛能盡其邊。是
080c06 ‖ 故名無礙智波羅蜜。具足答波羅蜜者。一切
080c07 ‖ 問難中。佛善能具足答。何以故。於四種問答
080c08 ‖ 中無有錯亂。善知義故。具足不壞義波羅
080c09 ‖ 蜜故。樂欲深知

简体字

佛于此中以少欲相自论智慧。若三千大千世界所有四天下满中微尘。随尔所尘数作尔所三千大千世界。满中众生皆如舍利弗如辟支佛。皆悉成就智慧乐说。寿命如上尘数大劫。是诸人等因四念处尽其形寿问难如来。如来还以四念处义答其所问。言义不重乐说无尽。法无碍智者。善能分别诸法名字通达无碍。义无碍者。于诸法义通达无碍。辞无碍者。随众生类以诸言辞令其解义通达无碍。乐说无碍者。问答时善巧说法无有穷尽。余贤圣不能究尽。唯有诸佛能尽其边。是故名无碍智波罗蜜。具足答波罗蜜者。一切问难中。佛善能具足答。何以故。于四种问答中无有错乱。善知义故。具足不坏义波罗蜜故。乐欲深知

Here the Buddha, with his characteristically scant wish to do so, discussed his own implementation of these knowledges. Supposing that there were a number of great trichiliocosms as numerous as all the atoms in all four continents of all worlds in a great trichiliocosm, supposing also that all those world systems were filled with beings all of whom were the likes of Śāriputra and the *pratyekabuddhas*, and suppose too that all of these men employed their perfected knowledges and eloquence to pose difficult questions to the Tathāgata on the four stations of mindfulness, doing so to the exhaustion of lifetimes extending to a number of kalpas as numerous as all the aforementioned atoms—the Tathāgata would still be able to reply to their questions on the meanings involved in the four stations of mindfulness, expounding on their meaning without redundancy and with inexhaustible eloquence.[70]

Now, as for the unimpeded knowledge with respect to dharmas, [the Buddhas] are well able to distinguish all details involved in the designations of dharmas with an unimpededly penetrating comprehension.

As for the unimpeded knowledge with respect to meaning, they are able to bring to bear an unimpededly penetrating comprehension of the meanings associated with those dharmas.

In the case of their unimpeded knowledge with respect to language, the Buddhas are able to accord with the languages and phrases through which the various sorts of beings are caused to understand those meanings, doing so with an unimpededly penetrating comprehension.

Regarding their unimpeded knowledge as it applies to eloquence, during that entire time in which they are answering questions, they are skillful and clever in speaking on Dharma and they are able to carry on in this fashion endlessly. Whatever topic all other worthies and *āryas* are unable to treat exhaustively, it is only the Buddhas who can reach the limits of that topic.

It is on these bases that we speak of the *pāramitā* of the unimpeded knowledges.

G. 16) The Pāramitā of Perfectly Complete Replies and Predictions

Regarding the *pāramitā* of perfection in the answering of questions, the Buddha is well able to answer in all situations involving the posing of difficult questions. And why is this so? It is because, in the four types of responses, he remains utterly free of erroneous or disordered presentations, because he well knows the conceptual meanings, because he has perfected the *pāramitā* of preserving the undamaged meaning, and because he delights in a profound knowing of the natures of

正體字

一切眾生性所行所樂故。
080c10 ‖ 如舍利弗白佛言。世尊。佛為人說善法。而
080c11 ‖ 是中多有眾生得證。證已心無渴[7]愛。無
080c12 ‖ 渴愛故於世間無所受。無所受已心則
080c13 ‖ 內滅。佛於善法中無上事盡知無餘。更無
080c14 ‖ 勝者。問曰。汝言四種問答。[8]何謂為四。答曰。
080c15 ‖ 一定答。二分別答。三反問答。四置答。定答
080c16 ‖ 者。如一比丘問佛。世尊。頗有色常不變異
080c17 ‖ 不。世尊。受想行識常不變異不。佛答言。比
080c18 ‖ 丘無有色常[9]而不變。無有受想行識常而
080c19 ‖ 不[10]變。如是等名為定答。分別答者。如布
080c20 ‖ 多梨子梵志問[11]娑摩提。有人故作身口意
080c21 ‖ 業。受何等果報。娑摩提定答。有人以身口
080c22 ‖ 意故作業受苦惱報。是問應分別答。是梵
080c23 ‖ 志後來問佛是事。佛答言。布多梨子。

简体字

一切众生性所行所乐故。如舍利弗白佛言。世尊。佛为人说善法。而是中多有众生得证。证已心无渴爱。无渴爱故于世间无所受。无所受已心则内灭。佛于善法中无上事尽知无余。更无胜者。问曰。汝言四种问答。何谓为四。答曰。一定答。二分别答。三反问答。四置答。定答者。如一比丘问佛。世尊。颇有色常不变异不。世尊。受想行识常不变异不。佛答言。比丘无有色常而不变。无有受想行识常而不变。如是等名为定答。分别答者。如布多梨子梵志问娑摩提。有人故作身口意业。受何等果报。娑摩提定答。有人以身口意故作业受苦恼报。是问应分别答。是梵志后来问佛是事。佛答言。布多梨子。

all beings, what they themselves practice, and what they themselves find pleasing. This is illustrated by the instance in which Śāriputra addressed the Buddha, saying:

> Bhagavat, when the Buddha discourses on the good Dharma, many are the beings who, upon hearing this, then gain realizations. Having gained such realizations, their minds become free of all craving. And because they become free of all craving, they no longer have anything in the world that they indulge. And once they no longer have anything at all that they indulge, their minds achieve a state of inward cessation.

The Buddha exhaustively knows, without exceptions, the unsurpassable aspects of the good Dharma. There is no one who is superior to him in this regard.

Question: You spoke of the four types of replies. What are those four?

Response:

> First, the definitive reply.
> Second, the distinguishing reply.
> Third, the counter-questioning reply.
> And, fourth, the reply that sets aside the question.

In the case of the definitive reply, this is illustrated by the instance where a bhikshu asked the Buddha, "Bhagavat, is it or is it not the case that there could be some form that is eternal and unchanging? Bhagavat, is it or is it not the case that there could be any feelings, perceptions, formative factors, or consciousnesses that are permanent and unchanging?"

The Buddha replied, saying, "Bhikshu, there is no form that is permanent and unchanging. There are no feelings, perceptions, formative factors, or consciousnesses that are permanent and unchanging."

Cases such as these illustrate the "definitive reply."

The distinguishing reply is illustrated by the instance where Potaliputta,[71] the Brahmacārin, inquired of Samiddhi,[72]asking: [73] "In instances where a person deliberately performs actions of body, speech, or mind, what sorts of karmic retributions ensue therefrom?"

Samiddhi responded with a definitive reply, saying, "In instances where persons deliberately perform actions of body, speech, or mind, they are bound to undergo retributions involving suffering and anguish."

But this should have involved a distinguishing reply. This *brahmacārin* later came and asked the Buddha about this matter, to which the Buddha replied, saying, "Potaliputta, in instances where

正體字

有人
080c24 ‖ 若身口意故作業。是業或受苦報。或受樂
080c25 ‖ 報。或受不苦不樂[12]報。苦業受苦報。樂業受
080c26 ‖ 樂報。不苦不樂業受不苦不樂報。如是等諸
080c27 ‖ 經皆分別答。反問答者。如先尼梵志問佛。
080c28 ‖ [13]佛言。我還問汝。隨汝意答。先尼於汝意
080c29 ‖ 云何。色是如來不。受想行識是如來不。答言。
081a01 ‖ 非也世尊。離[1]色受想行識是如來不。答言。
081a02 ‖ 非也世尊。如是等經應廣說。是名反問答。
081a03 ‖ 置答者。十四種邪見是。所謂世間常世間無
081a04 ‖ 常。世間常無常。世間非常非無常。世間有邊。
081a05 ‖ 世間無邊。世間亦有邊[2]亦無邊。世間非有邊
081a06 ‖ 非無邊。如來滅後有。如來滅後無。如來滅後
081a07 ‖ 亦有亦無。如來滅後非有非無。[3]身即是神。
081a08 ‖ 身異[4]神異。

简体字

有人若身口意故作业。是业或受苦报。或受乐报。或受不苦不乐报。苦业受苦报。乐业受乐报。不苦不乐业受不苦不乐报。如是等诸经皆分别答。反问答者。如先尼梵志问佛。佛言。我还问汝。随汝意答。先尼于汝意云何。色是如来不。受想行识是如来不。答言。非也世尊。离色受想行识是如来不。答言。非也世尊。如是等经应广说。是名反问答。置答者。十四种邪见是。所谓世间常世间无常。世间常无常。世间非常非无常。世间有边。世间无边。世间亦有边亦无边。世间非有边非无边。如来灭后有。如来灭后无。如来灭后亦有亦无。如来灭后非有非无。身即是神。身异神异。

someone deliberately performs actions of body, speech, or mind, this karma may result in undergoing painful retributions, in undergoing pleasurable retributions, or in undergoing retributions that are neither painful nor pleasurable. Pain-inducing actions result in undergoing painful retributions. Pleasure-inducing actions result in undergoing pleasurable retributions. Actions that are neither pain-inducing nor pleasure-inducing result in undergoing karmic retributions that are neither painful nor pleasurable."

Scriptural passages such as these illustrate instances of the distinguishing reply.

The counter-questioning reply is illustrated by that instance in which the *brahmacārin* named Śreṇika inquired of the Buddha and the Buddha replied, "I shall now return the question to you whereupon you may reply in accordance with your own idea on this matter. Śreṇika, what do you think? Do physical forms constitute the Tathāgata, or not? Or is it that feelings, perceptions, formative factors, or consciousnesses constitute the Tathāgata?"

He replied, "No, Bhagavat. They do not."

[The Buddha then asked him], "Is the Tathāgata apart from form, feelings, perceptions, formative factors, or consciousnesses, or not?"

He replied, "No, Bhagavat. He is not."

These types of passages from scripture should be more extensively discussed. They illustrate what is meant by the counter-questioning reply.

As for the reply that sets aside the question, this applies to the response to questions regarding the fourteen classic erroneous views, namely:

Is the world eternal?
Is the world non-eternal?
Is the world both eternal and non-eternal?
Is the world neither eternal nor non-eternal?
Is the world bounded?
Is the world unbounded?
Is the world both bounded and unbounded?
Is the world neither bounded nor unbounded?
Does the Tathāgata exist after his nirvāṇa?
Does the Tathāgata not exist after his nirvāṇa?
Does the Tathāgata both exist and not exist after his nirvāṇa?
Does the Tathāgata neither exist nor not exist after his nirvāṇa?
Is the body identical with a spiritual soul (*jīva*)?
Is the body different from a spiritual soul?

正體字

如上一切眾生如大辟支佛智
081a09 ‖ 慧樂說以如是四種問佛。佛皆隨順答其
081a10 ‖ 所問。不多不少。是故說佛具足答波羅蜜。
081a11 ‖ 無有能害。佛者得不可殺法故。無能斷佛
081a12 ‖ 身分支節存亡自在。如經說。若人欲方便
081a13 ‖ 害佛者。無有是處。問曰。佛壽命為定為不
081a14 ‖ 定。答曰。有人言不定。若佛壽命有定者。於
081a15 ‖ 餘定壽命者有何差別。而實佛壽命不定。無
081a16 ‖ 能害者。乃為希有。有人言。佛壽命有定。餘
081a17 ‖ 人壽命雖定。而手足耳鼻可斷。佛無是事。
081a18 ‖ 問曰。云何佛不可害。是不共法。答曰。諸佛
081a19 ‖ 不可思議。假喻可知。假使一切十方世界眾
081a20 ‖ 生皆有勢力。設有一魔有爾所勢力。復令
081a21 ‖ 十方一一眾生力如惡魔。欲共害佛。尚不
081a22 ‖ 能動佛一毛。況有害者。問曰。若爾者調達
081a23 ‖ 云何得傷佛。答曰。此事先已答。佛欲示眾
081a24 ‖ 生三毒相。

简体字

如上一切众生如大辟支佛智慧乐说以如是四种问佛。佛皆随顺答其所问。不多不少。是故说佛具足答波罗蜜。无有能害。佛者得不可杀法故。无能断佛身分支节存亡自在。如经说。若人欲方便害佛者。无有是处。问曰。佛寿命为定为不定。答曰。有人言不定。若佛寿命有定者。于余定寿命者有何差别。而实佛寿命不定。无能害者。乃为希有。有人言。佛寿命有定。余人寿命虽定。而手足耳鼻可断。佛无是事。问曰。云何佛不可害。是不共法。答曰。诸佛不可思议。假喻可知。假使一切十方世界众生皆有势力。设有一魔有尔所势力。复令十方一一众生力如恶魔。欲共害佛。尚不能动佛一毛。况有害者。问曰。若尔者调达云何得伤佛。答曰。此事先已答。佛欲示众生三毒相。

As stated above, even in an instance where all beings possessed the wisdom and eloquence of the *pratyekabuddha* and they inquired of the Buddha on these four matters, the Buddha would in all cases adapt to their needs in answering their questions, offering replies that are neither excessive nor deficient. It is for these reasons that the Buddhas are said to possess the *pāramitā* of perfection in the answering of questions.

H. 17) Invulnerability to Harm by Anyone

There is no one whatsoever who can harm the Buddha. This is because he has gained that dharma by which one cannot be killed. There is no one who can cut off any part of the Buddha's body. He has sovereign mastery over whether he will live or die. This is as stated in scripture, wherein it states: "Were one to seek some method by which to inflict harm on the Buddha—there simply is no such possibility at all."

Question: Is the lifespan of a buddha fixed or is it unfixed?

Response: There are those who claim that it is unfixed. But if a buddha's lifespan were actually fixed, what difference then would there be between his case and that of all others who have fixed lifespans? Still, in truth, the lifespan of a buddha is not fixed. That there is no one who can harm a buddha—now *that* is extraordinary. There are those who say that the lifespan of a buddha is fixed. However, whereas others whose lifespans are fixed are indeed subject to having hands, feet, ears, and nose sliced off, the Buddha [is unique in that he] is entirely free of any such vulnerability.

Question: How is it that the Buddhas have this exclusive dharma of being invulnerable to being harmed?

Response: The inconceivability of the Buddhas can be understood by resort to analogy. Suppose for instance that all beings throughout the worlds of the ten directions were to have a given amount of power. Now, if a single *māra* could possess a certain amount of power, also suppose that each and every one of those beings throughout the ten directions was caused to possess powers like those of Māra, the Evil One. Even if all of those beings then joined in wishing to inflict harm on the Buddha, they would still be unable to move even a single hair on the Buddha's body. How much the less might they actually succeed in harming the Buddha.

Question: Well, if that is the case, how then could Devadatta have succeeded in injuring the Buddha?

Response: This question was already answered earlier. The Buddha wished to show beings the character of the three poisons. Even though

正體字

調達雖持戒修善貪著利養而
081a25 ‖ 作大惡。又令知佛於諸人天心無有異。
081a26 ‖ 加以慈愍視調達羅睺羅如左右眼。佛常
081a27 ‖ 說等心。是時現其平等。天人見此起希有
081a28 ‖ 心益更信樂。又長壽[5]天見佛先世有惡業
081a29 ‖ 行。若今不受謂惡行無報。佛欲斷其邪見
081b01 ‖ 故現受此報。復次佛於苦樂心無有異。無
081b02 ‖ 吾我心。畢竟空故。諸根調柔不可變故。不
081b03 ‖ 須作方便離苦受樂。如菩薩藏中說。佛
081b04 ‖ 以方便故現受此事。應當廣知。是名佛不
081b05 ‖ 可殺害不共法。說法不[6]空者。諸佛所有言說
081b06 ‖ 皆有果報。是故諸佛說法不空。何以故。諸
081b07 ‖ 佛未說法時。先觀眾生本末心在何處結
081b08 ‖ 使厚薄。知其先世所從功德。見其根性勢
081b09 ‖ 力多少。知其障礙方處時節。[7]應軟法可度

简体字

调达虽持戒修善贪着利养而作大恶。又令知佛于诸人天心无有异。加以慈愍视调达罗睺罗如左右眼。佛常说等心。是时现其平等。天人见此起希有心益更信乐。又长寿天见佛先世有恶业行。若今不受谓恶行无报。佛欲断其邪见故现受此报。复次佛于苦乐心无有异。无吾我心。毕竟空故。诸根调柔不可变故。不须作方便离苦受乐。如菩萨藏中说。佛以方便故现受此事。应当广知。是名佛不可杀害不共法。说法不空者。诸佛所有言说皆有果报。是故诸佛说法不空。何以故。诸佛未说法时。先观众生本末心在何处结使厚薄。知其先世所从功德。见其根性势力多少。知其障碍方处时节。应软法可度

Devadatta had previously upheld the moral precepts and cultivated goodness, because he was attached to receiving offerings, he committing immensely evil deeds.

[The Buddha] also allowed this to happen in order to cause [beings] to realize that the mind of the Buddha does not vary in the way it regards any human or deva. His having compassion and pity for Devadatta on the one hand and Rāhula[74] on the other was the same as his equal regard for his own left and right eyes.

The Buddha always spoke of the mind of uniformly equal regard for everyone. He revealed his equality of regard at this time. When the devas and people observed this, they were struck by the extraordinary nature of this and thus felt even stronger resolute faith.

In addition, because of this, the devas of the long-life heavens could see that the Buddha was still bound to undergo retribution for bad karmic actions done in previous lives. Had he not undergone it now, they might have thought that bad actions could be free of corresponding karmic retributions. Because the Buddha wished to cut off their wrong views, he thereby revealed his own undergoing of this karmic retribution.

Furthermore, the Buddha's mind is no different in the presence of pain or pleasure. His mind is free of any concept of a self. This is because it is ultimately empty. Because his sense faculties have all been made pliant and imperturbable by change, he has no need to use expedients to separate from pain and enjoy pleasures. This is as described in the Bodhisattva canon where it states: "It was merely as an expedient that the Buddha manifested as subject to this experience." One should infer the broader implications of this.

The above points illustrate what is meant by the Buddha's exclusive dharma of being invulnerable to being killed or harmed.

I. 18) Their Words Are Never Spoken without a Purpose

In speaking on the Dharma, their words are never empty. All words spoken by the Buddhas have a corresponding intended effect. Therefore, when the Buddhas speak on Dharma, their words are never empty. And how is this so? Before the Buddhas begin to speak on Dharma, they first contemplate from root to branch where beings' minds abide and whether their fetters are thick or only scant. Thus they know the origins of their meritorious qualities in previous lives, observe the nature and strength of their karmic roots, and know:

Where and when beings [will encounter] obstacles;
Whether they are susceptible to liberation through gentle teaching methods;

正體字

081b10 ‖ 苦事可度。或復應以軟苦事度。或[8]須小發
081b11 ‖ 度。或廣分別度。有以陰入界十二因緣而
081b12 ‖ 得度者。或以信門或以慧門而得入者。是
081b13 ‖ 人應從佛度。是人應從聲聞度。是人應
081b14 ‖ 以餘緣得度。是人應成聲聞乘。是人應成
081b15 ‖ 辟支佛乘。是人應成大乘。是人久習貪欲
081b16 ‖ 習瞋恚習愚癡。是人習貪欲瞋恚。是人習
081b17 ‖ 貪欲愚癡。如是各各分別。是人墮斷見。是
081b18 ‖ 人墮常見。是人多[9]著身見。是人多習邊見。
081b19 ‖ 是人多習戒取見取。是人多習憍慢。是人多
081b20 ‖ 習自卑諂曲。是人心多疑悔。

简体字

苦事可度。或复应以软苦事度。或须小发度。或广分别度。有以阴入界十二因缘而得度者。或以信门或以慧门而得入者。是人应从佛度。是人应从声闻度。是人应以余缘得度。是人应成声闻乘。是人应成辟支佛乘。是人应成大乘。是人久习贪欲习嗔恚习愚痴。是人习贪欲嗔恚。是人习贪欲愚痴。如是各各分别。是人堕断见。是人堕常见。是人多着身见。是人多习边见。是人多习戒取见取。是人多习憍慢。是人多习自卑谄曲。是人心多疑悔。

Whether they are susceptible to liberation through harsh teaching methods;

Whether they are susceptible to liberation through a combination of gentle and harsh teaching methods.[75]

Whether they need only a little bit of instigation to gain liberation;

Whether they require extensive distinguishing instructions to gain liberation;

That there are those who gain liberation through [teachings on] the aggregates, the sense bases, the sense realms, or the twelve links of conditioned co-production;

Whether they may gain access [to liberation] through the gateway of faith or through the gateway of wisdom;

That this person should gain liberation through the teaching of a buddha;

That this person should gain liberation through the teaching of a *śrāvaka* disciple;

That this person should gain liberation through some other set of conditions;

That this person should be able to gain success in the Śrāvaka Disciple Vehicle;

That this person should be able to gain success in the Pratyekabuddha Vehicle;

That this person should be able to gain success in the Great Vehicle;

That this person has long practiced habitual greed, habitual hatred, and habitual delusion;

That this person has practiced habitual greed and hatred;

And that this person has practiced habitual greed and delusion.

In this way, they distinguish and determine with regard to each and every situation:

That this person has fallen into an annihilationist view;

That this person has fallen into an eternalist view;

That this person is for the most part attached to the view that seizes on the existence of a real self in association with the body [or any of the other four aggregates];[76]

That this person is most often habitually attached to extreme views;

That this person is most often habitually attached to the views that seize upon either prohibitions or on opinionated views;

That this person is for the most part habitually arrogant;

That this person is for the most part habitually inclined toward feelings of inferiority and the tendency to flattery and deviousness;

That this person's mind is mostly inclined toward doubt and regret.

正體字

是人好樂言
081b21 ‖ 辭。有貴義理有樂深義有樂淺事。是人
081b22 ‖ 先世集助道法。是人今世集助道法。是人但
081b23 ‖ 集福報善根。是人但集貫穿善根。是人應
081b24 ‖ 疾得道。是人久乃得道。佛先觀察籌量隨
081b25 ‖ 應得度。而為說法而度脫之。是故一切說
081b26 ‖ 法皆悉不空。如經說。世尊先知見而說法。
081b27 ‖ 非不知見說法。無謬無失者。諸佛說法無
081b28 ‖ 謬無失。無謬者。語義不乖違故。無失者。
081b29 ‖ 不失義故。不失道因緣故名不失。不謬
081c01 ‖ 道果因緣故名不謬。不少故名不失。不過
081c02 ‖ 故名不謬。

简体字

是人好乐言辞。有贵义理有乐深义有乐浅事。是人先世集助道法。是人今世集助道法。是人但集福报善根。是人但集贯穿善根。是人应疾得道。是人久乃得道。佛先观察筹量随应得度。而为说法而度脱之。是故一切说法皆悉不空。如经说。世尊先知见而说法。非不知见说法。无谬无失者。诸佛说法无谬无失。无谬者。语义不乖违故。无失者。不失义故。不失道因缘故名不失。不谬道果因缘故名不谬。不少故名不失。不过故名不谬。

That this person has developed a fondness for refined literary expressiveness;
That there are those who prize refinement in meanings and principles;
That there are those who delight in profundities;
That there are those who enjoy topics that are merely superficial;
That, in previous lifetimes, this person has accumulated the Dharma provisions requisite to success in the path;
That this person is accumulating the Dharma provisions for the path in this present lifetime;
That this person has only accumulated roots of goodness conducive to enjoying karmic rewards [from previous meritorious actions];
That this person has only accumulated roots of goodness associated with thorough understanding;
That this person should be able to rapidly become enlightened;
And that this person will require a long time before he can become enlightened.[77]

The Buddha first engages in investigative contemplation and assessment of individual circumstances and then, according with whichever approach is appropriate to instigate someone's liberation, he then speaks Dharma for them and thereby brings about their liberation.

It is as a consequence of this that every instance of the Buddha's speaking of Dharma is free of any merely empty discourse. This is as described in a sutra: "The Bhagavat first knows and sees and only then speaks Dharma. It is not the case that he speaks Dharma without first knowing and seeing."

J. 19) Their Speech Is Free of Error

Regarding the absence of errors and mistakes [in their speech], when the Buddhas speak Dharma, they do not commit any errors or make any mistakes. "Absence of errors" refers to there being no instances in which the meaning of what they say is contradictory. "Absence of mistakes" means they make no mistakes with regard to meanings.

It is because they do not make mistakes with regard to causes and conditions as they relate to the path that they are said to not make mistakes. It is because they do not commit errors with regard to causes and conditions as they relate to the fruits of the path that they are said to not commit any error.

It is because they are not deficient that they are said to not make mistakes and it is because they are not excessive that they are said to not commit any error.

正體字

以通達四無礙智故。念安慧常
081c03 ‖ 調和故。遠離斷常無因邪因等諸見故。所說
081c04 ‖ 法中不使人有迷悶。所言初後無相違過。
081c05 ‖ 隨此義經。應此中廣說。如經說。諸比丘為
081c06 ‖ 汝說法。初善中善後善。語善義善淳一無雜
081c07 ‖ 具說梵行。以希有事說法者。隨所教化即
081c08 ‖ 得道果。是名希有。若有所答若所受記皆
081c09 ‖ 實不[10]異。是亦希有。佛有所說道。此道不
081c10 ‖ 雜煩惱能斷煩惱。是亦希有。佛有所說皆
081c11 ‖ 有利益終不空言是亦希有。若人於佛法
081c12 ‖ 中勤心精進。能斷不善法增益善法。是亦
081c13 ‖ 希有。復次有三希有。現神通希有。逆說彼
081c14 ‖ 心希有。[11]有教化希有。以是三希有說法。名
081c15 ‖ 為以希有說法。諸眾聖中最上導師者。諸佛
081c16 ‖ 知一切眾生心所行所樂。結使

简体字

以通达四无碍智故。念安慧常调和故。远离断常无因邪因等诸见故。所说法中不使人有迷闷。所言初后无相违过。随此义经。应此中广说。如经说。诸比丘为汝说法。初善中善后善。语善义善淳一无杂具说梵行。以希有事说法者。随所教化即得道果。是名希有。若有所答若所受记皆实不异。是亦希有。佛有所说道。此道不杂烦恼能断烦恼。是亦希有。佛有所说皆有利益终不空言是亦希有。若人于佛法中勤心精进。能断不善法增益善法。是亦希有。复次有三希有。现神通希有。逆说彼心希有。有教化希有。以是三希有说法。名为以希有说法。诸众圣中最上导师者。诸佛知一切众生心所行所乐。结使

This is accomplished through their possession of a penetrating comprehension of the four unimpeded knowledges, through their constant harmonization of mindfulness and stable wisdom, and through their utter abandonment of views associated with annihilationism, eternalism, acausality, erroneous causality, or other such wrong views.

In the Dharma that they speak, there is no cause by which people become perplexed. In whatsoever they say, there are no faults involving inconsistencies between what is set forth in the beginning and in the end.

Scriptures accordant with these concepts should be discussed more extensively herein. As it says in one of the sutras: "Bhikshus. When I speak Dharma for you, it is good in the beginning, good in the middle, and good in the end. The phrasings are good and the meanings are good. It possesses a singular purity free of any debasing admixture and it is perfectly complete in its proclamation of *brahmacarya*."[78]

K. 20) Complete Use of the Three Turnings in Speaking Dharma

As regards the matter of [the Buddha's] speaking of Dharma involving rarities, whomever they undertake to teach is immediately enabled to realize the fruits of the path. This is a rarity.

Whenever they provide a reply or offer a prediction, their statements are always genuine and do not differ [from actual circumstances]. This too is a rarity.

The Buddha has the path as the subject of his discourse. This path as it is proclaimed by the Buddha is not admixed with afflictions and is able to bring about the severance of the afflictions. This too is a rarity.

Whenever the Buddha speaks, benefit ensues from it and it never involves mere empty words. This too is a rarity.

Whenever a person applies mental diligence and vigor to the cultivation of the Buddha's Dharma, he can cut off the unwholesome dharmas and bring about increase in the good dharmas. This too is a rarity.

There are three additional rarities: the rarity of displaying spiritual powers, the rarity of foretelling the content of others' thoughts, and the rarity of being able to accomplish the transformational teaching of others. It is on the basis of these three sorts of rarities in the proclaiming of Dharma that the Buddha's discourse on Dharma is said to be characterized by rarities.[79]

L. 21) They Are the Great Generals among All Āryas

Regarding [the Buddha's] eminence as the most superior spiritual guide among all the Āryas, buddhas know what the minds of beings course in, know what they delight in, know whether their fetters are

正體字

深淺諸根利
081c17 ‖ 鈍。上中下智慧。善知通達故。於眾聖中最
081c18 ‖ 上導師。又能善知四諦相。善知諸法總相別
081c19 ‖ 相。又以說法不空因緣不謬不失法故。於
081c20 ‖ 眾聖中最上導師。問曰。四眾亦能說法破外
081c21 ‖ 道令入佛法。何以但稱佛為最上導師。答
081c22 ‖ 曰。當以假喻說。若一切眾生智慧勢力皆如
081c23 ‖ 辟支佛。是諸眾生若不承佛意。欲度一人
081c24 ‖ 無有是處。若是諸人說法時。乃至不[12]能
081c25 ‖ 斷無色界結使毫釐[13]分。若佛欲度眾生有
081c26 ‖ 所言說。乃至外道邪見諸龍夜叉等及餘不
081c27 ‖ 解佛語者皆悉令解。是等亦能轉化無量
081c28 ‖ 眾生。乃至今日聲聞眾令眾生住四果中。
081c29 ‖ 皆是如來最上導師相。是故佛名最上導師。
082a01 ‖ 於眾聖中不共之法。四不守護法者。諸佛
082a02 ‖ 不守護身業。不[1]護口業。不[*]護意業。不
082a03 ‖ [*]護

简体字

深浅诸根利钝。上中下智慧。善知通达故。于众圣中最上导师。又能善知四谛相。善知诸法总相别相。又以说法不空因缘不谬不失法故。于众圣中最上导师。问曰。四众亦能说法破外道令入佛法。何以但称佛为最上导师。答曰。当以假喻说。若一切众生智慧势力皆如辟支佛。是诸众生若不承佛意。欲度一人无有是处。若是诸人说法时。乃至不能断无色界结使毫厘分。若佛欲度众生有所言说。乃至外道邪见诸龙夜叉等及余不解佛语者皆悉令解。是等亦能转化无量众生。乃至今日声闻众令众生住四果中。皆是如来最上导师相。是故佛名最上导师。于众圣中不共之法。四不守护法者。诸佛不守护身业。不护口业。不护意业。不护

deep or shallow, know whether their faculties are sharp or dull, and know whether their wisdom is superior, middling, or inferior. It is because they know these matters well and know them with penetrating comprehension that they are the most superior spiritual guides among all the Āryas.

They are also able to well know the characteristics of the four truths, and to well know all the general and specific characteristics of all dharmas.

It is also because, when they speak on the Dharma, their words are not empty and because, when they speak on the Dharma, they commit no errors and make no mistakes that they are therefore the most superior spiritual guides among all the Āryas.

Question: But the other four groups are also able to speak on the Dharma and thus refute the teachings of the non-Buddhists and thereby cause them to enter into the Dharma of the Buddha. Why then does one only speak of the Buddha as the most superior spiritual guide?

Response: This should be explained by an analogy. Suppose all beings possessed the wisdom powers of a *pratyekabuddha.* If all of these beings did not receive the intentional assistance of the Buddha and yet wished somehow to bring about the liberation of but a single person, this would be a complete impossibility. When all of these persons spoke Dharma, they would still be unable to cause the severance of a tiny fraction of even one of the formless realm fetters.

If, on the other hand, the Buddha wished to bring about the liberation of some being and then proceeded to say something, even those burdened with the erroneous views of the non-Buddhists, the dragons, the *yakṣas,* and the various other sorts of beings who do not understand the language of the Buddha—these would all still be caused to understand. Then all of these would in turn be able to teach countless other beings. And so this proceeds even to the point that, today, whenever those within the community of *śrāvaka* disciples cause beings to abide in the four fruits of the path, they are all emblematically representative of the Tathāgata as the most superior of all spiritual guides.

It is for these reasons that the Buddha is known as the most superior spiritual guide, and it is for these reasons that this is regarded as an exclusive dharma not held in common with the other *āryas.*

M. 22–25) They Are Able to Remain Unguarded in Four Ways

As for the four unguarded dharmas, the Buddhas are unguarded in their physical actions, are unguarded in their verbal actions, are unguarded in their mental actions, and are unguarded with respect to

正體字

資生。何以故。是四事於他不護。不作
082a04 || 是念。我身口意命恐他人知。何以故。長夜
082a05 || 修習種種清淨業故。皆善見知斷一切煩惱
082a06 || 法故。成就一切無比善根故。善行可行法
082a07 || 無可呵故。具足行捨波羅蜜故。捨者。眼見
082a08 || 色捨憂喜心。乃至意法亦如是。婆[2]呵提欝
082a09 || 多羅等諸經應此中說。四無所畏者。問曰。一
082a10 || 法名為無畏。何以故有四。答曰。於四事中
082a11 || 無有疑畏[3]故有四。一者如佛告諸比丘。
082a12 || 我自發誠言。是一切智人。此中若有沙門婆
082a13 || 羅門諸天魔梵及餘世間智人。如法難[4]言。
082a14 || 不知此法。我於此中乃至不見有[5]微畏
082a15 || 相。不見是相故。得安隱無畏。是初無畏。如
082a16 || 實盡知一切法故。二者自發誠言。我一切
082a17 || 諸漏盡。若沙門婆羅門諸天魔梵。言是漏不
082a18 || [6]盡。

简体字

资生。何以故。是四事于他不护。不作是念。我身口意命恐他人知。何以故。长夜修习种种清净业故。皆善见知断一切烦恼法故。成就一切无比善根故。善行可行法无可呵故。具足行舍波罗蜜故。舍者。眼见色舍忧喜心。乃至意法亦如是。婆呵提郁多罗等诸经应此中说。四无所畏者。问曰。一法名为无畏。何以故有四。答曰。于四事中无有疑畏故有四。一者如佛告诸比丘。我自发诚言。是一切智人。此中若有沙门婆罗门诸天魔梵及余世间智人。如法难言。不知此法。我于此中乃至不见有微畏相。不见是相故。得安隐无畏。是初无畏。如实尽知一切法故。二者自发诚言。我一切诸漏尽。若沙门婆罗门诸天魔梵。言是漏不尽。

the means for sustaining life. And why is this? These four matters are not protected from others' [knowledge]. They do not think, "Regarding my [actions of] body, speech, and mind, and my [means of sustaining] life—I fear that others might come to know about them."

And why is this? This is because, during the long night [of previous lifetimes], they have cultivated every sort of pure karmic deed and have always well seen, well known, and well severed every one of the dharmas associated with the afflictions. And this is because they have perfected every sort of peerless root of goodness, because they have so well practiced whatever dharma is amenable to practice, because they have reached the point where there is nothing about them the least bit worthy of criticism, and because they have utterly perfected the *pāramitā* of equanimity.

Now, on this matter of their "equanimity," when their eyes view form, they relinquish any thoughts of either distress or delight. And so it goes [with the other sense faculties and objects] up to and including the mind faculty's engagement with dharmas [as objects of mind]. In this connection, one would ideally also discuss here citations from such scriptures as the *Poheti* and *Uttara* sutras.[80]

N. 26–29) They Possess the Four Types of Fearlessnesses

Now, as for the four types of fearlessness….

Question: There is a single dharma known as "fearlessness." How is it that we here have four of them?

Response: It is because there are four matters in which there is an absence of doubt or fear that we therefore speak of four of them, as follows:[81]

First, as the Buddha told the bhikshus, "I myself here utter these truthful words: 'I am a man possessed of all-knowledge.' If anyone here, whether he be a *śramaṇa*, brahmin, deva, Māra, Brahmā, or other person possessed of worldly knowledge were to challenge this statement in a manner consistent with Dharma, claiming that I do not indeed possess a direct knowledge of this Dharma, I would not then experience in this challenge even the slightest sign of fearfulness, and it is because of not experiencing any such sign that I have become established in security and fearlessness in this regard." This is the first type of fearlessness. It is a result of exhaustively knowing all dharmas in accordance with reality.

As for the second type of fearlessness, the Buddha said, "I myself here utter these truthful words: 'I have brought all of the contaminants to an end.' If any *śramaṇa*, brahmin, deva, Māra, or Brahmā were to claim that these contaminants have not indeed been brought to an end,

正體字

乃至不見有[7]是相。不見是相故安
082a19 ‖ 隱無畏。是二無畏。善斷諸煩惱及斷煩惱
082a20 ‖ 習氣故。三者我說障道法。此中若有沙門
082a21 ‖ 婆羅門諸天魔梵及餘世間智人。如法難言。
082a22 ‖ 是法雖用不能障道。我於此中不見有
082a23 ‖ 微畏相。不見是相故得安隱無有疑畏。
082a24 ‖ 是三無畏。善知障解脫法故。四者我所說
082a25 ‖ 道如法說行者。得至苦盡。若有沙門婆羅
082a26 ‖ 門諸天魔梵及餘世間智人。如法難言。[8]如
082a27 ‖ 是法雖如說行不能至盡苦道。我於此
082a28 ‖ 中無有微畏相。不見是相故得安隱無
082a29 ‖ 有疑畏。是四無畏。善知至苦盡道故。是四
082b01 ‖ 無畏皆過怖畏心驚毛竪等相故。名為無
082b02 ‖ 畏。又在大眾威德殊勝故。名為無畏。又善
082b03 ‖ 知一切問答故。名為無畏。諸天會經此中
082b04 ‖ 應廣說。

简体字

乃至不见有是相。不见是相故安隐无畏。是二无畏。善断诸烦恼及断烦恼习气故。三者我说障道法。此中若有沙门婆罗门诸天魔梵及余世间智人。如法难言。是法虽用不能障道。我于此中不见有微畏相。不见是相故得安隐无有疑畏。是三无畏。善知障解脱法故。四者我所说道如法说行者。得至苦尽。若有沙门婆罗门诸天魔梵及余世间智人。如法难言。如是法虽如说行不能至尽苦道。我于此中无有微畏相。不见是相故得安隐无有疑畏。是四无畏。善知至苦尽道故。是四无畏皆过怖畏心惊毛竖等相故。名为无畏。又在大众威德殊胜故。名为无畏。又善知一切问答故。名为无畏。诸天会经此中应广说。

I would not then experience in this challenge even the slightest sign of fearfulness.[82] It is because of not experiencing any such sign that I have become established in security and fearlessness in this regard." This is the second type of fearlessness. It is a result of having thoroughly cut off all afflictions and having also cut off the habitual propensities associated with past afflictions.

As for the third [type of fearlessness], [the Buddha said], "I have proclaimed which dharmas constitute obstacles to realization of the path. If anyone herein, whether he be a *śramaṇa*, brahmin, deva, Māra, Brahmā, or other person possessed of worldly knowledge were to challenge this statement in a manner consistent with Dharma, claiming that, even though one might avail oneself of these dharmas, they would not be able to cause an obstacle to the path, I would not then experience in this challenge even the slightest sign of fearfulness. It is because of not experiencing any such sign that I have become established in security and fearlessness in this regard." This is the third type of the fearlessness. It is a result of having thoroughly known those dharmas that constitute obstacles to the achievement of liberation.

As for the fourth [type of fearlessness, the Buddha said], "Whoever practices the path I have proclaimed, practicing it in accordance with the way I have explained the Dharma, will succeed in reaching the end of suffering. If any *śramaṇa*, brahmin, deva, Māra, Brahmā, or other person possessed of worldly knowledge were to challenge this statement in a manner accordant with Dharma, claiming that, although one might practice a dharma such as this in a manner consistent with the way it has been explained, one would be unable to reach the path that brings about the end of suffering, I would not then experience in this challenge even the slightest sign of fearfulness. It is because of not experiencing any such sign that I have become established in security and fearlessness in this regard." This is the fourth type of fearlessness. It is a result of thoroughly knowing the path leading to the extinguishing of suffering.

All four of these types of fearlessness are referred to as "fearlessnesses" because they all involve leaving behind such characteristic signs as fearfulness, terror, or horripilation. They are also termed "fearlessnesses" because they are able to maintain within the Great Assembly an awe-inspiring power of virtue extraordinary in its excellence. They are also called "fearlessnesses" because they so well know how to respond to all sorts of questions. Here, one should extensively discuss citations from *The Sutra on the Convocation of the Devas*.[83]

正體字

問曰。若佛是一切智人。應於一切
082b05 ‖ 法盡無畏。何以[9]但說四。答曰。略舉大要
082b06 ‖ 以開事端。餘亦如是。佛十力者。力名扶助。
082b07 ‖ 氣勢不可窮盡。無能沮壞。雖有十名而實
082b08 ‖ 一智。緣十事故名為十力。佛智緣一切事
082b09 ‖ 故。應有無量力。以此十力足度眾生
082b10 ‖ 故。[10]但說十力。但開此十力。餘皆可知。初
082b11 ‖ 力者。一切法因非因。決定通達智。名為初
082b12 ‖ 力。如佛說。若是狂人不捨是語不捨邪
082b13 ‖ 見不捨是心。來在佛前無有是處。如佛
082b14 ‖ 告阿難。世間二佛一時出世無有是處。一
082b15 ‖ 佛出世則有是處。是事為一佛世界故說。
082b16 ‖ 而實十方無量無邊諸世界中。百千萬億無
082b17 ‖ 數諸佛一時出世。又經說身口意惡業有妙
082b18 ‖ 愛果報無有是處。若身口意善業有妙愛
082b19 ‖ 果報則有是處。如是等五藏諸經應此中
082b20 ‖ 廣說。

简体字

问曰。若佛是一切智人。应于一切法尽无畏。何以但说四。答曰。略举大要以开事端。余亦如是。佛十力者。力名扶助。气势不可穷尽。无能沮坏。虽有十名而实一智。缘十事故名为十力。佛智缘一切事故。应有无量力。以此十力足度众生故。但说十力。但开此十力。余皆可知。初力者。一切法因非因。决定通达智。名为初力。如佛说。若是狂人不舍是语不舍邪见不舍是心。来在佛前无有是处。如佛告阿难。世间二佛一时出世无有是处。一佛出世则有是处。是事为一佛世界故说。而实十方无量无边诸世界中。百千万亿无数诸佛一时出世。又经说身口意恶业有妙爱果报无有是处。若身口意善业有妙爱果报则有是处。如是等五藏诸经应此中广说。

Question: If the Buddhas are indeed possessed of all-knowledge, then they should be fearless in relation to all dharmas. Why is it then that we speak only of these four types [of fearlessness]?

Response: These serve to raise the major essential topics in order to introduce the most important instances. All other instances are similar to these.

O. 30–39) They Possess the Ten Powers

As for the ten powers of the Buddha, "power" refers to the inexhaustible energetic strength that assists them and makes them invulnerable to interference by anyone. Although there are ten designations in this regard, in truth, this involves a single type of knowledge that, because it takes ten different circumstances as objective conditions, [these ten exemplary manifestations] are known as "the ten powers."

Because the knowledge of the Buddha takes all things as its objective conditions, it should be that there are countless powers. But it is because these ten powers are adequate to bring about the liberation of beings that we only speak of "the ten powers." Through merely introducing these ten powers, one can then know the others by inference.

1. The First Power

The first power is [the Buddha's] definite and completely penetrating knowledge with respect to all dharmas of what does and does not constitute the cause. This is the first power. [This was the basis for, as cited earlier], the Buddha's having said [in reference to the *brahmacārin* named Patikaputra], "If this crazy person does not relinquish these claims, does not relinquish these perverse views, and does not relinquish these thoughts, then, as for his being able to arrive here in the presence of the Buddha—this is an utter impossibility."

[This is also the basis for] the Buddha's having said to Ānanda:

> "It is utterly impossible that two buddhas might arise in the world at the same time. However, it is indeed possible for a single buddha to come forth into the world."[84] This was said solely with respect to the circumstance of a single buddha emerging in a single world. In truth, in all of the countless and limitless worlds throughout the ten directions, there are countless hundreds of thousands of myriads of *koṭis* of buddhas simultaneously emerging throughout those worlds.
>
> Additionally, the sutras state: "It is impossible that bad physical, verbal, and mental karmic actions might have excellent and desirable results. However, it is indeed possible that good physical, verbal, and mental karmic actions may have excellent and desirable results."[85]

Here one should extensively discuss related scriptural citations from among the five categorical repositories of Dharma.

正體字

第二力者。於過去未來現在諸業諸[11]法
082b21 ‖ 受佛如實分別知處所知事知果報。佛若
082b22 ‖ 欲知一切眾生過去諸業過去業報[12]即能
082b23 ‖ 知。或業過去報在現在。或業過去報在未
082b24 ‖ 來。或業過去報在過去。或業過去報在過去
082b25 ‖ 未來。或業過去報在過去現在。或業過去報
082b26 ‖ 在未來現在。或業過去報在過去未來現在。
082b27 ‖ 或業現在報在現在。或業現在報在未來。或
082b28 ‖ 業現在報在現在未來。或業未來報在未來。
082b29 ‖ 有如是等分別受法者。四受法。現受樂後
082c01 ‖ 世受苦。現受苦後世受樂。現受樂後受
082c02 ‖ 樂。現受苦後受苦。處者。隨業時方所在。又
082c03 ‖ 知是業受報處。

简体字

第二力者。于过去未来现在诸业诸法受佛如实分别知处所知事知果报。佛若欲知一切众生过去诸业过去业报即能知。或业过去报在现在。或业过去报在未来。或业过去报在过去。或业过去报在过去未来。或业过去报在过去现在。或业过去报在未来现在。或业过去报在过去未来现在。或业现在报在现在。或业现在报在未来。或业现在报在现在未来。或业未来报在未来。有如是等分别受法者。四受法。现受乐后世受苦。现受苦后世受乐。现受乐后受乐。现受苦后受苦。处者。随业时方所在。又知是业受报处。

2. The Second Power

The second power is [the Buddha's] knowing in accordance with reality and with distinguishing clarity the place, the circumstances, and the karmic retributions associated with all past, future, and present karmic deeds along with all the dharmas that are involved in experiencing [those retributions].

If the Buddha wishes to know with regard to any being their past karmic deeds and their past karmic retributions, he is able to immediately know them. So too, he is immediately able to know:

With respect to past karmic deeds, their retribution in the present;
With respect to past karmic deeds, their retribution in the future;
With respect to past karmic deeds, their retribution in the past;
With respect to past karmic deeds, their retribution in both the past and the future;
With respect to past karmic deeds, their retribution in both the past and the present;
With respect to past karmic deeds, their retribution in both the future and the present;
With respect to past karmic deeds, their retribution in the past, the future, and the present;
With respect to present karmic deeds, their retribution in the present;
With respect to present karmic deeds, their retribution in the future;
With respect to present karmic deeds, their retribution in both the present and the future;
And with respect to future karmic deeds, their retribution in the future.

There are all manner of such distinctions regarding the dharmas involved in undergoing karmic retributions. There are four dharmas categorizing such karmic retributions, namely:

Undergoing blissful experiences in the present followed by undergoing suffering in future lifetimes;
Undergoing suffering in the present followed by undergoing blissful experiences in future lifetimes;
Undergoing blissful experiences in the present followed by blissful experiences in the future;
And undergoing suffering in the present followed by undergoing suffering in the future as well.[86]

As regards [the Buddha's knowing] "the place," this refers to his knowing for any karmic deed the time and place [of its occurrence] as well as the precise place in which this retribution will be undergone.

正體字

事者。或隨因緣。或隨三不
082c04 ‖ 善根。或多自作。或多因他。如是等善惡業
082c05 ‖ 因緣佛盡知。報者。知諸業各各有報。善業
082c06 ‖ 或善處生或得涅槃。惡業諸惡處生。佛悉知
082c07 ‖ 是諸業本末因緣自身及他。是中智力不退
082c08 ‖ 故名為力。三力者。佛於禪定解脫三昧垢淨
082c09 ‖ 相如實知。禪者四禪。定者四無色定四無量
082c10 ‖ 心等皆名為定。解脫者八解脫。三昧者除
082c11 ‖ 諸禪解脫餘定盡名三昧。有人言。三解脫門
082c12 ‖ 及有覺有觀定。無覺有觀定。無覺無觀定。名
082c13 ‖ 為三昧。有人言。定小三昧大。是故一切諸佛
082c14 ‖ 菩薩所得定。皆名三昧。是四處皆攝在一切
082c15 ‖ 禪波羅蜜。

简体字

事者。或随因缘。或随三不善根。或多自作。或多因他。如是等善恶业因缘佛尽知。报者。知诸业各各有报。善业或善处生或得涅槃。恶业诸恶处生。佛悉知是诸业本末因缘自身及他。是中智力不退故名为力。三力者。佛于禅定解脱三昧垢净相如实知。禅者四禅。定者四无色定四无量心等皆名为定。解脱者八解脱。三昧者除诸禅解脱余定尽名三昧。有人言。三解脱门及有觉有观定。无觉有观定。无觉无观定。名为三昧。有人言。定小三昧大。是故一切诸佛菩萨所得定。皆名三昧。是四处皆摄在一切禅波罗蜜。

As regards [the Buddha's] knowing "the circumstances," this refers to knowing the corresponding causes and conditions, knowing the three corresponding types of bad karmic roots, knowing whether the deed was primarily performed by oneself, or knowing whether the deed occurred for the most part through the instigation of someone else. The Buddha entirely knows all such causes and conditions associated with good and bad karmic deeds.

As regards [the Buddha's knowing] "the karmic retributions," he knows that all karmic deeds have their corresponding karmic retributions. For instance, good karmic deeds may result in being reborn in a good place or in attaining nirvāṇa, whereas bad karmic deeds may result in being reborn in any of the wretched destinies.

The Buddha knows entirely with respect to all these karmic deeds their roots, their branches, their associated causes and conditions, and whether they were done at one's own behest or at the behest of others. It is because this power of knowledge does not diminish that it is referred to as a "power."

3. The Third Power

The third power is the Buddha's knowing in accordance with reality the *dhyānas*, the meditative concentrations, the liberations, and the samādhis, together with their corresponding marks of defilement and purity.

"*Dhyānas*" refers to the four *dhyānas*. "Meditative concentrations" refers to the four formless-realm meditative concentrations, the four immeasurable minds, and other such states, all of which are referred to as "meditative concentrations. "Liberations" refers to the eight liberations. As for "samādhis" all of the other meditative concentrations aside from the *dhyānas* and the liberations are referred to as "samādhis."

There are others who claim that the three gates to liberation, meditative concentrations still characterized by initial ideation (*vitarka*) and discursive thought (*vicāra*), meditative concentrations characterized by the absence of initial ideation and the presence of discursive thought, and meditative concentrations devoid of both initial ideation and discursive thought—these may all be referred to as "samādhis."

There are yet others who claim that "meditative concentrations" are relatively minor [meditative states] whereas "samādhis" are relatively major. Therefore, one may refer to all meditative concentrations realized by any buddha or bodhisattva as constituting a "samādhi."

All four of these constituent categories are subsumed within all explanations of "*dhyāna pāramitā*."

正體字

垢名[13]受味。淨名不[*]受味。復次
082c16 ‖ 垢名有漏定。淨名無漏[14]定。三昧解脫等分
082c17 ‖ 別者。[15]如是禪分別知他眾生他人上下諸
082c18 ‖ 根。如實知名第四力。他眾生者凡夫是。他
082c19 ‖ 人者須陀洹等諸賢聖是。或有人言。眾生名
082c20 ‖ 為凡夫。及諸學人煩惱未盡故。他人者阿羅
082c21 ‖ 漢等煩惱盡故。或有人言。眾生與人一種名
082c22 ‖ 有差別。諸根者。信精進念定慧非眼等根。上
082c23 ‖ 名猛利堪任得道。下名闇鈍不堪受道。
082c24 ‖ 佛於此二根上下如實知不錯謬。他眾生
082c25 ‖ 他人心各有所樂如實知。是第五力。所樂
082c26 ‖ 名為貴所向事。

简体字

垢名受味。净名不受味。复次垢名有漏定。净名无漏定。三昧解脱等分别者。如是禅分别知他众生他人上下诸根。如实知名第四力。他众生者凡夫是。他人者须陀洹等诸贤圣是。或有人言。众生名为凡夫。及诸学人烦恼未尽故。他人者阿罗汉等烦恼尽故。或有人言。众生与人一种名有差别。诸根者。信精进念定慧非眼等根。上名猛利堪任得道。下名闇钝不堪受道。佛于此二根上下如实知不错谬。他众生他人心各有所乐如实知。是第五力。所乐名为贵所向事。

As for "defilement," this refers to [meditative states characterized by] the experience of delectably pleasurable (*āsvādana*) sensations whereas "purity" refers here to not indulging delectably pleasurable sensations.

Then again, "defilement" may refer to any meditative concentration still characterized by the contaminants (*āsrava*) whereas "purity" may refer to any meditative concentration characterized by the absence of the contaminants.

As for the distinctions among the samādhis, liberations, and so forth, [the Buddha] knows with distinguishing clarity these sorts of *dhyāna* meditation states.

4. The Fourth Power

The fourth power is [the Buddha's] knowing in accordance with reality the relative superiority or inferiority of the faculties of other beings and other personages.

"Other beings" refers to common persons. "Other personages" refers here to the stream enterer and the other classes of worthies and *āryas*. There may be others who interpret "beings" as a reference not only to common persons, but also even to those practitioners still involved in the learning stages, this because all of these have still not succeeded in putting an end to all of the contaminants. For them, "other personages" is a reference reserved for arhats and such, this because they have utterly ended all afflictions.

Yet others point out that both "beings" and "other personages" are but a single category and it is only the designations themselves that differ.

As for their "faculties," in this context they refer to faith, vigor, mindfulness, concentration, and wisdom and *not* to the sense faculties such as the eye and so forth [as the word might otherwise signify].

"Superior," as it applies to these faculties, refers to faculties that are fiercely sharp and which have the capacity to enable the attainment of enlightenment. "Inferior," on the other hand, refers to [faculties] that are dim, dull, and inadequate to enable one to take up [the practice of] the path.

The Buddha knows the relative superiority and inferiority of these two types of faculties and knows these matters in accordance with reality and in a manner free of any sort of error.

5. The Fifth Power

The fifth power is [the Buddha's] knowing in accordance with reality that in which the minds of other beings and other personages delight. "That in which they delight" refers to whatever endeavors they esteem

正體字

如有人貴財物世樂或
082c27 ‖ 有貴重福德善法。是事佛如實知。世間種
082c28 ‖ 種性無量性。佛如實知。是第六力。種種性者
082c29 ‖ 雜性萬端。無量性者。於一一性有無量種
083a01 ‖ 分別。性者從先世來心常習用常所樂行修
083a02 ‖ 習故成性。是二善惡性佛如實知。至一切
083a03 ‖ 處道如實知。是第七力。至一切處道者。能
083a04 ‖ 得一切功德。是道名為至一切處道。所謂五
083a05 ‖ 分三昧。若五[1]知三昧。若八聖道分是。或聖
083a06 ‖ 道所攝諸法。或四如意足。如經說。比丘善
083a07 ‖ 修習四如意足無利不得。有人言四禪是。
083a08 ‖ 如經說。比丘得四禪。心安住一處清淨。除
083a09 ‖ 諸煩惱滅諸障礙。調和堪用不復動轉。若
083a10 ‖ 迴向知宿命事。即能知宿命事。是第八力。
083a11 ‖ 佛若欲念自身及一切眾生無量無邊宿命。

简体字

如有人贵财物世乐或有贵重福德善法。是事佛如实知。世间种种性无量性。佛如实知。是第六力。种种性者杂性万端。无量性者。于一一性有无量种分别。性者从先世来心常习用常所乐行修习故成性。是二善恶性佛如实知。至一切处道如实知。是第七力。至一切处道者。能得一切功德。是道名为至一切处道。所谓五分三昧。若五知三昧。若八圣道分是。或圣道所摄诸法。或四如意足。如经说。比丘善修习四如意足无利不得。有人言四禅是。如经说。比丘得四禅。心安住一处清净。除诸烦恼灭诸障碍。调和堪用不复动转。若回向知宿命事。即能知宿命事。是第八力。佛若欲念自身及一切众生无量无边宿命。

and are inclined to engage in. For instance, there are those people who esteem wealth and worldly pleasures, whereas there are others who deeply esteem karmic merit and the practice of good dharmas. The Buddha knows all of these matters in accordance with reality.

6. The Sixth Power

The sixth power is the Buddha's knowing in accordance with reality the different types of natures of beings in the world as well as the countless [distinctions among those] natures. "Different types of natures" refers to the myriad variations in these natures. "Countless natures" is a reference to the countless distinctions in each and every one of these types of natures. As for the term "nature," it is because one's mind has always habitually practiced [particular sorts of endeavors] and has always delighted in practicing and cultivating them throughout one's past lives right up until the very present—it is for this reason that they therefore form the basis of one's "nature." The Buddha knows in accordance with reality these two categories of natures, the good and the bad.

7. The Seventh Power

The seventh power is [the Buddha's] knowing in accordance with reality the paths leading to all destinations. As for "the paths leading to all destinations," those are the means by which one may succeed in acquiring all meritorious qualities. These paths are referred to as "the paths leading to all destinations."

These include, for instance, the five-factor samādhi,[87] the five-fold awareness samādhi,[88] the eight-fold path of the Āryas, all dharmas subsumed by the path of the Āryas, or the four bases of psychic power, the latter as cited in a sutra that says: "If a bhikshu cultivates the four bases of psychic power, there is no benefit that he will not acquire."

There are others who claim that this may also refer to the four *dhyānas*, as cited in a sutra that says: "When a bhikshu gains the four *dhyānas*, his mind comes to abide with stability and purity in a single place in which he then succeeds in ridding himself of all afflictions and in destroying all obstacles. It then becomes well-regulated so that it becomes serviceable and no longer subject to movement or distraction."

8. The Eighth Power

The eighth power is the [Buddha's] immediate ability to know past-life matters whenever he chooses to direct his awareness to events from previous lives. If the Buddha wishes to recall any of the countless and limitless lifetimes of either himself or all other beings, he then

正體字

083a12 ‖ 一切事皆悉知。無有不知過恒河沙等劫
083a13 ‖ 事。是人何處生。姓名貴賤飲食資生苦樂所
083a14 ‖ 作事業所受果報。心何所行本從何來。如
083a15 ‖ 是等事。以天眼清淨過於人眼。見六道眾
083a16 ‖ 生隨業受身。是第九力。大力聲聞以天眼
083a17 ‖ 見小千國土。亦見中眾生生時死時。[2]小辟
083a18 ‖ 支佛見千小千國土。見中眾生生時死時。
083a19 ‖ 中力辟支佛見百萬小千國土。見中眾生生
083a20 ‖ 時死時。大力辟支佛見三千大千國土。見
083a21 ‖ 中眾生生死所趣。諸佛世尊見無量無邊不
083a22 ‖ 可思議世間。亦見是中眾生生時死時。第十
083a23 ‖ 力者。欲漏有漏無明漏一切漏盡。諸煩惱及
083a24 ‖ 氣都盡。是名第十力。無礙解脫者。解脫有三
083a25 ‖ 種。一者於煩惱障礙解脫。二者於定障礙
083a26 ‖ 解脫。三者於一切法障礙解脫。是中得慧
083a27 ‖ 解脫阿羅漢。得離煩惱障礙解脫。

简体字

一切事皆悉知。无有不知过恒河沙等劫事。是人何处生。姓名贵贱饮食资生苦乐所作事业所受果报。心何所行本从何来。如是等事。以天眼清净过于人眼。见六道众生随业受身。是第九力。大力声闻以天眼见小千国土。亦见中众生生时死时。小辟支佛见千小千国土。见中众生生时死时。中力辟支佛见百万小千国土。见中众生生时死时。大力辟支佛见三千大千国土。见中众生生死所趣。诸佛世尊见无量无边不可思议世间。亦见是中众生生时死时。第十力者。欲漏有漏无明漏一切漏尽。诸烦恼及气都尽。是名第十力。无碍解脱者。解脱有三种。一者于烦恼障碍解脱。二者于定障碍解脱。三者于一切法障碍解脱。是中得慧解脱阿罗汉。得离烦恼障碍解脱。

knows all of these matters entirely. There are no instances in which he is unable to know some particular matter even beyond a number of kalpas equal to the number of sands in the Ganges River.

He knows where this person was born, what his name was, whether he was of noble or lowly caste, what he drank and ate, how he sustained his life, whether he experienced suffering or happiness, the types of endeavors in which he engaged, the karmic retributions that he underwent, what his mind engaged in, and from whence he originally came. He knows all such matters.

9. The Ninth Power

The ninth power is the [Buddha's] ability to see with the heavenly eye purified beyond the power of man's eyes the beings of the six destinies taking on bodies in accordance with their karmic deeds.

A *śrāvaka* disciple possessed of great powers uses the heavenly eye to see the lands contained within a small chiliocosm and also sees when the beings therein are born and when they die.

A lesser *pratyekabuddha* sees the lands of a thousand small chiliocosms and sees when the beings therein are born and when they die.

A *pratyekabuddha* possessed of middling powers sees the lands contained in a hundred myriads of small chiliocosms and sees when the beings therein are born and when they die.

A *pratyekabuddha* possessed of great powers sees the lands contained in a great trichiliocosm and sees the destinies to which they proceed when they die and are reborn.

The Buddhas, the Bhagavats, see a countless, boundless, and inconceivable number of worlds and also see when the beings therein are born and when they die.

10. The Tenth Power

As for the tenth power, it is the [Buddha's] ending of all contaminants, including the contaminant of sensual desire, the contaminant of [craving for] existence, and the contaminant of ignorance, these together with the utter ending of all afflictions or affliction-associated energetic propensities. This is the tenth power.

P. 40) They Have Achieved Unimpeded Liberation

As for unimpeded liberation, there are three types of liberations. The first is the liberation from the obstacles of the afflictions. The second is the liberation from the obstacles to meditative concentration. The third is the liberation from the obstacles to [the knowledge of] all dharmas. Among these, an arhat who has achieved liberation through wisdom gains liberation from the obstacles of the afflictions. Both the

正體字

共解脫
083a28 ‖ 阿羅漢及辟支佛。得離煩惱障礙解脫。得
083a29 ‖ 離諸禪定障礙解脫。唯有諸佛具三解脫。
083b01 ‖ 所謂煩惱障礙解脫。諸禪定障礙解脫。一切
083b02 ‖ 法障礙解脫。總是三種解脫故。佛名無礙解
083b03 ‖ 脫。常隨心共生。乃至無餘涅槃則止。是四十
083b04 ‖ 不共法。略開佛法門令眾生[3]解故說。所
083b05 ‖ 不說者無量無邊。所謂一常不離慧。二知
083b06 ‖ 時不失。三滅一切習氣。四得定波羅蜜。五
083b07 ‖ 一切功德殊勝。六隨所宜行波羅蜜。七無
083b08 ‖ 能見頂者。八無與等者。九無能勝者。十世
083b09 ‖ 間中上。十一不從他聞得道。十二不轉法
083b10 ‖ 者。十三自言是佛終不能到佛前。十四不
083b11 ‖ 退法者。十五得大[4]悲者。十六得大慈者。十
083b12 ‖ 七第一可信受者。

简体字

共解脱阿罗汉及辟支佛。得离烦恼障碍解脱。得离诸禅定障碍解脱。唯有诸佛具三解脱。所谓烦恼障碍解脱。诸禅定障碍解脱。一切法障碍解脱。总是三种解脱故。佛名无碍解脱。常随心共生。乃至无余涅槃则止。是四十不共法。略开佛法门令众生解故说。所不说者无量无边。所谓一常不离慧。二知时不失。三灭一切习气。四得定波罗蜜。五一切功德殊胜。六随所宜行波罗蜜。七无能见顶者。八无与等者。九无能胜者。十世间中上。十一不从他闻得道。十二不转法者。十三自言是佛终不能到佛前。十四不退法者。十五得大悲者。十六得大慈者。十七第一可信受者。

doubly-liberated arhat and the *pratyekabuddha* succeed in achieving both the liberation from the obstacles of the afflictions and the liberation from the obstacles to the *dhyāna* concentrations.

It is only the Buddhas who have completely achieved all three of these liberations, namely liberation from the obstacles of the afflictions, liberation from the obstacles to acquisition of the *dhyāna* concentrations, and the liberation from the obstacles to [the knowledge of] all dharmas. It is because he brings together all three of the liberations that the Buddha is designated as having achieved unimpeded liberation. This [unimpeded liberation] always accompanies the mind all the way up to the point of entry into the nirvāṇa without residue.

Q. Summary Discussion of the Dharmas Exclusive to the Buddha

These forty dharmas exclusive to the Buddhas provide a general introduction to an entryway into the dharmas of the Buddha. They are discussed here because this allows beings to thereby acquire an understanding of them. However, those [exclusive dharmas] that remain undiscussed herein are innumerable and boundless. Specifically, these include the following:

1) [The Buddha] never departs from wisdom.
2) He never errs in knowing the right time.
3) He has extinguished all habitual karmic propensities.
4) He has gained the meditative concentration *pāramitā.*
5) All of his meritorious qualities are possessed of extraordinary supremacy.
6) He has perfected the *pāramitā* of always according in his actions with what is appropriate to the circumstances.
7) No one is able to view the very top of [the light rays radiating from] the crown of his head.
8) No one is his equal.
9) No one is able to surpass him.
10) He is superior to all beings in the world.
11) His attainment of the path is not learned from anyone else.
12) He never turns away from the Dharma.
13) Whoever else might claim to be a buddha is forever unable to enter the presence of the Buddha.
14) He has perfected the dharma of never retreating.
15) He has acquired the great compassion.
16) He has acquired the great kindness.
17) He is the foremost among all whose teachings one may accept in faith.

正體字

十八第一名聞利養。十九
083b13 ‖ 與佛同止。諸師無與佛等者。二十諸師無
083b14 ‖ 有得[＊]弟子眾如佛者。二十一端正第一見
083b15 ‖ 者歡悅。二十二佛所使人無能害者。二十三
083b16 ‖ 佛欲度者無有傷害。二十四心初生時能
083b17 ‖ 斷思惟結。二十五可度眾生終不失時。二
083b18 ‖ 十六第十六[5]智得阿耨多羅三藐三菩提。二
083b19 ‖ 十七世間第一福田。二十八放無量光明。二
083b20 ‖ 十九所行不同餘人。三十百福[6]德相。三十
083b21 ‖ 一無量無邊善根。三十二入胎時。三十三生
083b22 ‖ 時。三十四得佛道時。三十五轉法輪時。三
083b23 ‖ 十六捨長壽命時。三十七入涅槃時能動三
083b24 ‖ 千大千世界。三十八擾動無量無邊諸魔宮
083b25 ‖ 殿令無威德皆使驚畏。三十九諸護世天
083b26 ‖ 王釋提桓因夜[7]摩天王兜率陀天王化樂天
083b27 ‖ 王自在天王梵天王淨居諸天等。一時來集
083b28 ‖ 請轉法輪。四十佛身堅固如那羅延。

简体字

十八第一名闻利养。十九与佛同止。诸师无与佛等者。二十诸师无有得第子众如佛者。二十一端正第一见者欢悦。二十二佛所使人无能害者。二十三佛欲度者无有伤害。二十四心初生时能断思惟结。二十五可度众生终不失时。二十六第十六智得阿耨多罗三藐三菩提。二十七世间第一福田。二十八放无量光明。二十九所行不同余人。三十百福德相。三十一无量无边善根。三十二入胎时。三十三生时。三十四得佛道时。三十五转法轮时。三十六舍长寿命时。三十七入涅槃时能动三千大千世界。三十八扰动无量无边诸魔宫殿令无威德皆使惊畏。三十九诸护世天王释提桓因夜摩天王兜率陀天王化乐天王自在天王梵天王净居诸天等。一时来集请转法轮。四十佛身坚固如那罗延。

18) He is the foremost among those [who are worthy of] fame and offerings.
19) No guru who is a contemporary of the Buddha is equal to the Buddha.
20) No guru gains a community of disciples equal to that of the Buddha.
21) The supreme refinement of his appearance causes all who see him to be delighted.
22) Whoever is sent forth as an emissary of a Buddha cannot be harmed by anyone.
23) No one is able to injure anyone whom the Buddha has set out to liberate.
24) From the very moment he first brings forth a thought, he is able to sever all thought-related fetters.
25) He never misses the right time [to provide appropriate instruction to] beings who are capable of achieving liberation.
26) In the sixteenth [mind-moment involved in the acquisition of] wisdom, a buddha attains *anuttarasamyaksaṃbodhi.*
27) He is the foremost among the world's fields of merit.
28) He emanates measureless radiant light.
29) His actions differ from those of anyone else.
30) He possesses the [physical] marks that are associated with a hundred-fold generation of merit.[89]
31) He has measureless and boundless roots of goodness.
32) When he enters the womb—
33) When he is born—
34) When he achieves buddhahood—
35) When he turns the wheel of the Dharma—
36) When he relinquishes the possibility of the long lifespan—
37) And when he enters nirvāṇa—[on all these occasions], he is able to cause all the worlds throughout the great trichiliocosm to shake.
38) [On all of the above occasions], he sets quaking the countless palaces of the *māras,* causing them to lose their awesome power and be struck with terror.
39) [When he achieves buddhahood], the world-protecting heavenly kings, Śakra, ruler of the devas, the Yāma Heaven King, the Tuṣita Heaven King, the Nirmāṇarati Heaven King, the Paranirmita Vaśavartin Heaven King, the Brahma Heaven King, the devas of the Pure Abodes, and the other devas—they all simultaneously assemble and request the turning of the Dharma wheel.
40) The Buddha's body is as solid as the body of Nārāyaṇa.[90]

正體字

四十一 083b29 ‖ 未有結戒而初結戒。四十二有所施作勢
083c01 ‖ 力勝人。四十三菩薩處胎母於一切男子
083c02 ‖ 無染著心。四十四力能救度一切眾生。佛
083c03 ‖ 不共法有如是等無量無數。妨餘事故不
083c04 ‖ 須廣說。聲聞法雖[8]似佛法。優劣不同則
083c05 ‖ 有差別。復次總說諸佛一切諸法無量無邊
083c06 ‖ 不可思議第一希有。一切眾生所不能共。
083c07 ‖ 假使十方諸三千大千世界過諸算數是中
083c08 ‖ 所有眾生智慧皆如大梵天王。皆如大辟支
083c09 ‖ 佛。皆如舍利弗。合集是諸智慧令一人得。
083c10 ‖ 欲及於佛四十不共法中微少分者。無有
083c11 ‖ 是處。若於一法百千萬億分中不及其一。
083c12 ‖ 諸佛有如是無量無邊功德之力。何以故。無
083c13 ‖ 數大劫安住四功德處。深行六波羅蜜。善能
083c14 ‖ 具足菩薩一切所行諸法。不共一切眾生
083c15 ‖ 故。果報亦不共。[9]
083c16 ‖ 十住毘婆沙論卷第十一

简体字

四十一未有结戒而初结戒。四十二有所施作势力胜人。四十三菩萨处胎母于一切男子无染着心。四十四力能救度一切众生。佛不共法有如是等无量无数。妨余事故不须广说。声闻法虽似佛法。优劣不同则有差别。复次总说诸佛一切诸法无量无边不可思议第一希有。一切众生所不能共。假使十方诸三千大千世界过诸算数是中所有众生智慧皆如大梵天王。皆如大辟支佛。皆如舍利弗。合集是诸智慧令一人得。欲及于佛四十不共法中微少分者。无有是处。若于一法百千万亿分中不及其一。诸佛有如是无量无边功德之力。何以故。无数大劫安住四功德处。深行六波罗蜜。善能具足菩萨一切所行诸法。不共一切众生故。果报亦不共。

41) When the moral precepts have not yet been formulated, he is the one who first formulates the moral precepts.
42) Whenever he takes up any endeavor, his power in accomplishing this is superior to that of any man.
43) During the entire time the Bodhisattva is residing in his mother's womb, she loses all thoughts of defiling attachment for men.
44) His power is such that he is able to bring about the rescue and liberation of all beings.

There are measurelessly and innumerably many dharmas such as these that are exclusive to the Buddha. Because it would interfere with the explanation of other matters, there is no need to present an extensive discussion of them here. Although these dharmas as found in the Dharma of the Śrāvaka Disciples do resemble dharmas of the Buddha, due to dissimilarities in the degree of superiority or inferiority, there are distinct differences [in how they are described].

Moreover, to summarize, all of the dharmas of the Buddhas are measureless, limitless, inconceivable, of the foremost degree of rarity, and such that no other being is able to have them in common [with any buddha]. Even if all the countless beings in the worlds of all the great trichiliocosms throughout the ten directions possessed wisdom comparable to the king of the Great Brahma Heaven, comparable to a great *pratyekabuddha,* or comparable to Śāriputra, and one were somehow able to collect all this wisdom together in a single person—even if that one person then wished to approach the most minutely small fraction of these forty dharmas exclusive to the Buddhas—this would still be an utter impossibility. He could not even measure up to but one part in a hundred thousand myriads of *koṭis* of parts of just a single one of those dharmas.

The Buddhas possess the power of just such an immeasurable and limitless number of meritorious qualities. And why is this so? It is because they have securely established themselves in the four bases of meritorious qualities for a countless number of great kalpas during which they have deeply practiced the six *pāramitās* and have become well able to completely equip themselves with all dharmas practiced by the bodhisattva. Because [these dharmas] are not held in common with any other beings, so too, the fruits resulting [from their practice] are not held in common with any beings, either.

The End of Chapter Twenty-Three

正體字

083c19 ‖ 十住毘婆沙論卷第十二 083c20 ‖
083c21 ‖ 聖者龍樹造
083c22 ‖ 後秦龜茲國三藏鳩摩羅什譯
083c23 ‖ [10]讚偈品第二十四
083c24 ‖ 已如是解四十不共法竟。應取是四十不
083c25 ‖ 共法相念佛。又應以諸偈讚佛。如現在
083c26 ‖ 前對面共語。如是則成念佛三昧。如偈說。
083c27 ‖ 聖主大精進　四十獨有法
083c28 ‖ 我今於佛前　敬心以稱讚
083c29 ‖ 如意及飛行　其力無邊限
084a01 ‖ 於聖如意中　無有與等者
084a02 ‖ 聲聞中自在　他心智無量
084a03 ‖ 善能調伏心　隨意而應適
084a04 ‖ 其念如大海　湛然在安隱
084a05 ‖ 世間無有法　而能擾亂者
084a06 ‖ 諸佛所稱歎　金剛三昧寶
084a07 ‖ 得之在胸中　如賢懷直心
084a08 ‖ 善知不定法　四無色定事
084a09 ‖ 微細難分別　盡知無有餘

简体字

赞偈品第二十四

已如是解四十不共法竟。应取是四十不共法相念佛。又应以诸偈赞佛。如现在前对面共语。如是则成念佛三昧。如偈说。

圣主大精进　四十独有法
我今于佛前　敬心以称赞
如意及飞行　其力无边限
于圣如意中　无有与等者
声闻中自在　他心智无量
善能调伏心　随意而应适
其念如大海　湛然在安隐
世间无有法　而能扰乱者
诸佛所称叹　金刚三昧宝
得之在胸中　如贤怀直心
善知不定法　四无色定事
微细难分别　尽知无有余

Ch. 24: Verses Offered in Praise

V. Chapter 24: Verses Offered in Praise

A. The Importance of Praises to Mindfulness-of-the-Buddha Practice

Now that, in this way, we have reached the end of this explanation of the forty dharmas exclusive to the Buddhas, one should take the aspects emblematic of these forty exclusive dharmas and use them in one's own practice of mindfulness of the Buddha. One should also use verses to praise the Buddha, doing so as if one were standing directly before him, speaking to him. If one proceeds in this manner, then one may succeed in entering the mindfulness-of-the-Buddha samādhi. Accordingly, there are verses, as follows:

B. The Praise Verses

1. Verses in Praise of the Forty Dharmas Exclusive to the Buddhas

Oh, greatly vigorous lord of the Āryas—
Now, in the presence of the Buddha,
I shall praise with reverential mind
these forty dharmas possessed only [by buddhas].[91]

As for his supernatural powers and travel through flight,
their power when enacted is utterly limitless.
Among the psychic powers of the other *āryas,*
there are none at all that can equal these.

Among the *śrāvaka* disciples, he holds sway with sovereign mastery,
using his measureless knowledge of others' thoughts.
Thus he is well able to train their thoughts
by according with their minds as he appropriately responds to them.

His mindfulness is as expansive as the great ocean
while also being tranquil and calmly secure.
In all the world, there is no dharma
able to cause him to become perturbed.

The jewel of the vajra samādhi
that is praised by all buddhas—
he has acquired it and it resides within in his heart
just as the Worthies embrace the straightforward mind.

He thoroughly knows the unfixed dharmas
and the matters associated with the four formless absorptions
that are so subtle they are difficult to distinguish.
He exhaustively knows them all without exception.

正體字

084a10 ‖ 眾生若已滅　今滅及當滅
084a11 ‖ [1]唯獨有世尊　智慧能通達
084a12 ‖ 善知不相應　非色法中事
084a13 ‖ 一切諸世間　悉皆不能知
084a14 ‖ 世尊大威力　功德不可量
084a15 ‖ 智慧無邊際　皆無與等者
084a16 ‖ 於四問答中　超絕無倫匹
084a17 ‖ 眾生諸問難　一切皆易答
084a18 ‖ 若諸世間中　欲有害佛者
084a19 ‖ 是事皆不成　以成不殺法
084a20 ‖ 若於三時中　諸有所說者
084a21 ‖ 言必不虛[2]設　常有大果報
084a22 ‖ 凡有所說法　無非是希有
084a23 ‖ 義趣尚不謬　何況於言辭
084a24 ‖ 於三聖弟子　上中下差別
084a25 ‖ 四雙八輩等　第一大導師
084a26 ‖ 身口意業命　畢竟常清淨
084a27 ‖ 是故於此中　不復須防護
084a28 ‖ 自說一切智　心無有疑畏
084a29 ‖ 若人來難我　恐有所不知

简体字

众生若已灭　今灭及当灭
唯独有世尊　智慧能通达
善知不相应　非色法中事
一切诸世间　悉皆不能知
世尊大威力　功德不可量
智慧无边际　皆无与等者
于四问答中　超绝无伦匹
众生诸问难　一切皆易答
若诸世间中　欲有害佛者
是事皆不成　以成不杀法
若于三时中　诸有所说者
言必不虚设　常有大果报
凡有所说法　无非是希有
义趣尚不谬　何况于言辞
于三圣弟子　上中下差别
四双八辈等　第一大导师
身口意业命　毕竟常清净
是故于此中　不复须防护
自说一切智　心无有疑畏
若人来难我　恐有所不知

Regarding whether a being has already died in the past,
dies now in the present, or will die at some point later in the future,
it is solely the Bhagavat, and he alone,
whose wisdom is able to fully comprehend such things.

He knows well all matters related
to the formless dharmas unassociated with the mind
that everyone else throughout all worlds
remains entirely unable to know.

The Bhagavat's great awesome powers,
his measureless meritorious qualities,
and his boundless wisdom
are all unmatched by anyone at all.

In the four types of responses to questions,
he is so preeminent that he has no peer.
As for all the challenging questions that beings present,
he replies to them all with utter ease.

If anywhere in any world
there is someone wishing to harm the Buddha,
this circumstance never comes to pass,
for he has gained the dharma by which he cannot be slain.

If at any point throughout the three periods of time
there is anything that he says,
those words are definitely not set forth in vain,
but rather always bring great fruits as a result.

Of all the dharmas that he proclaims,
none of them are not especially rare.
He is never in error as regards their significance,
how much the less might he ever err in words and phrases.

For the three types of *ārya* disciples
that differ as either superior, middling, or inferior,
and include the eight classes in four pairs,[92] and the others,
he is the foremost great spiritual guide.

In actions of body, speech, and mind, and in sustaining his life,
he is ultimately and always pure
and hence, in all of these,
he never again needs to act in a guarded way.

When he himself proclaims his possession of all-knowledge,
his mind remains utterly free of any doubt or fear
such that he might think, "If someone comes and challenges me,
I fear there may be something I do not know."

正體字

084b01 ‖	自說漏盡相	盡到無漏邊
084b02 ‖	心無有疑畏	餘漏有不盡
084b03 ‖	自說障礙法	於中無疑難
084b04 ‖	雖有用此法	不能為障礙
084b05 ‖	所說八聖道	心無有疑畏
084b06 ‖	有言是八道	不能至解脫
084b07 ‖	如實知是因	是果及與非
084b08 ‖	故號一切智	名聞流無量
084b09 ‖	三世所有業	是諸業定報
084b10 ‖	及非定果報	種種皆悉知
084b11 ‖	諸禪三昧中	麁細深淺事
084b12 ‖	皆悉能了知	禪中無等者
084b13 ‖	先知眾生根	上中下差別
084b14 ‖	種種樂及性	隨宜而說法
084b15 ‖	行道得諸利	兼以化導人
084b16 ‖	是以弟子眾	如實得[3]善利
084b17 ‖	宿命知無量	天眼見無邊
084b18 ‖	一切人[4]天中	無能知其限
084b19 ‖	住金剛三昧	滅煩惱及氣
084b20 ‖	又知人漏盡	故名漏盡力

简体字

自说漏尽相	尽到无漏边
心无有疑畏	余漏有不尽
自说障碍法	于中无疑难
虽有用此法	不能为障碍
所说八圣道	心无有疑畏
有言是八道	不能至解脱
如实知是因	是果及与非
故号一切智	名闻流无量
三世所有业	是诸业定报
及非定果报	种种皆悉知
诸禅三昧中	粗细深浅事
皆悉能了知	禅中无等者
先知众生根	上中下差别
种种乐及性	随宜而说法
行道得诸利	兼以化导人
是以弟子众	如实得善利
宿命知无量	天眼见无边
一切人天中	无能知其限
住金刚三昧	灭烦恼及气
又知人漏尽	故名漏尽力

When declaring his characteristic of having ended the contaminants,
thus reaching the utmost elimination of the contaminants,
his mind remains utterly free of any doubt or fear
that there might be residual contaminants that are not yet ended.

When proclaiming his knowledge of the obstructive dharmas,
he has no doubt at the prospect of being challenged
that, though one might indulge in these dharmas,
they might not actually then constitute an obstacle.

As for the eight-fold path of the Āryas that he has proclaimed,
his mind is free of any doubt or fear
that someone might rightly claim of this eight-fold path
that it is unable to lead one to reach liberation.

He knows in accordance with reality that this is a cause,
this is its result, and this other factor does not constitute [a cause].
It is for these reasons that he is said to be omniscient
and that his fame spreads immeasurably far.

All actions carried out throughout the three periods of time,
the fixed retribution associated with these actions,
and their unfixed karmic results—
He thoroughly knows all of these different matters.

As for all coarse, subtle, deep, and shallow phenomena
within all of the *dhyāna* absorptions and samādhis,
he is able to entirely know them all.
In the realm of *dhyāna* absorptions, no one is his equal.

He first knows with regard to the faculties of beings,
their distinctions as either superior, middling, or inferior,
knows what they delight in, and knows their individual natures,
whereupon, adapting to what is fitting, he teaches them the Dharma.

He cultivated the path and gained its benefits
while also teaching and guiding others.
It is in this manner that the community of disciples
gains the wholesome benefit that accords with reality.

His knowledge of past lives is measurelessly vast
and the vision of his heavenly eye has no bounds.
Among all humans and devas,
no one is able to know their limits.

He abides in the vajra samādhi,
having extinguished the afflictions and karmic propensities,
and also knows the utter ending of the human contaminants.
Hence this is known as the power of having ended the contaminants.

正體字

084b21 ‖	煩惱諸禪障	一切法障礙
084b22 ‖	三礙得解脫	號無礙解脫
084b23 ‖	四十不共法	功德不可量
084b24 ‖	無能廣說者	我已略說竟
084b25 ‖	世尊若一劫	稱說此佛法
084b26 ‖	猶尚不[5]可盡	況我無此智
084b27 ‖	世尊大慈[6]蔭	無量業善集
084b28 ‖	四功德處故	得佛無量法
084b29 ‖	世尊所稱說	四功德勝處
084c01 ‖	我今還以此	稱讚於如來
084c02 ‖	三十二相具	相有百福德
084c03 ‖	八十種妙好	三界誰能有
084c04 ‖	三千大千界	眾生所有福
084c05 ‖	果報為百倍	相有如是德
084c06 ‖	如此諸福德	并及其果報
084c07 ‖	復以為百倍	成一白毫相
084c08 ‖	三十相一一	福德及果報
084c09 ‖	復以為千倍	成一肉髻相
084c10 ‖	世尊諸功德	不可得度量
084c11 ‖	如人以尺寸	量空不可盡

简体字

烦恼诸禅障	一切法障碍
三碍得解脱	号无碍解脱
四十不共法	功德不可量
无能广说者	我已略说竟
世尊若一劫	称说此佛法
犹尚不可尽	况我无此智
世尊大慈荫	无量业善集
四功德处故	得佛无量法
世尊所称说	四功德胜处
我今还以此	称赞于如来
三十二相具	相有百福德
八十种妙好	三界谁能有
三千大千界	众生所有福
果报为百倍	相有如是德
如此诸福德	并及其果报
复以为百倍	成一白毫相
三十相一一	福德及果报
复以为千倍	成一肉髻相
世尊诸功德	不可得度量
如人以尺寸	量空不可尽

The obstacle of afflictions, the obstacles to *dhyāna* absorptions,
and the obstacles to the knowledge of all dharmas—
he has gained liberation from all three obstacles
and hence is known as one who has gained unimpeded liberation.

The forty exclusive dharmas
have measureless meritorious qualities
of which no one could present an expansive explanation.
I have hereby now concluded this general explanation.

Even if, for an entire kalpa, the Bhagavat
spoke in praise of these dharmas of the Buddhas,
he would still be unable to completely describe them.
How much the less might I do so in the absence of such wisdom.

2. Verses Praising the Four Bases of Meritorious Qualities

The shade of the Bhagavat's great kindness
has been thoroughly gathered together through countless deeds.
It is because of the four bases of meritorious qualities
that he has gained the Buddha's measureless Dharma.

As for these four supreme bases of meritorious qualities
of which the Bhagavat has spoken with praise—
I shall now return to these
in setting forth praises of the Tathāgata.

He is completely endowed with the thirty-two marks,
each mark of which requires a hundred-fold generation of merit.
As for the eighty marvelous secondary characteristics,
who residing in the three realms could possibly possess them?

Were one to multiply by a hundred all the karmic rewards
produced by the merit created by all the beings
residing within a great trichiliocosm,
each of the marks has just such a quantity of merit [as its cause].

It would require just such a quantity of merit
as well as its associated karmic rewards,
multiplied yet another hundred times
to produce a buddha's mid-brow white hair mark.

It would require for each and every one of thirty marks
all of their corresponding merit and karmic rewards,
multiplied yet again a thousand more times,
to produce the fleshy *uṣṇīṣa* sign atop a buddha's crown.

The meritorious qualities of the Bhagavat
are such that they could never be measured.
Any attempt to do so would be like someone using a ruler
to measure the endless expanse of empty space.

正體字

084c12 ‖	從初發大心	為度眾生故
084c13 ‖	堅心無量劫	是故成佛道
084c14 ‖	精勤欲成滿	如此之大願
084c15 ‖	無量劫數中	行諸難苦行
084c16 ‖	如諸往古佛	說四功德處
084c17 ‖	無量劫乃成	今得安住中
084c18 ‖	本為護實諦	捨身及親愛
084c19 ‖	財寶諸富樂	是故得具足
084c20 ‖	無量劫數中	見聞覺知法
084c21 ‖	每先善思惟	而後為人說
084c22 ‖	若於不見等	及於中有疑
084c23 ‖	而能如實說	所益無有量
084c24 ‖	不說他匿事	[7]嫌譏而拒逆
084c25 ‖	念常在安慧	順化令安隱
084c26 ‖	第一真妙諦	涅槃實為最
084c27 ‖	餘者皆虛妄	世尊[8]德具足
084c28 ‖	飲食臥具等	堂閣妙樓觀
084c29 ‖	名好象馬車	端嚴諸婇女
085a01 ‖	金銀珍寶等	聚落諸城邑

简体字

从初发大心	为度众生故
坚心无量劫	是故成佛道
精勤欲成满	如此之大愿
无量劫数中	行诸难苦行
如诸往古佛	说四功德处
无量劫乃成	今得安住中
本为护实谛	舍身及亲爱
财宝诸富乐	是故得具足
无量劫数中	见闻觉知法
每先善思惟	而后为人说
若于不见等	及于中有疑
而能如实说	所益无有量
不说他匿事	嫌讥而拒逆
念常在安慧	顺化令安隐
第一真妙谛	涅槃实为最
余者皆虚妄	世尊德具足
饮食卧具等	堂阁妙楼观
名好象马车	端严诸婇女
金银珍宝等	聚落诸城邑

From the moment he brought forth the great resolve
for the sake of bringing about the liberation of all beings,
he persevered for countless kalpas with solid resolve.
It was because of this that he then achieved buddhahood.

Intensely diligent in his zeal to achieve the fulfillment
of such a magnanimous vow,
throughout an immeasurably great number of kalpas,
he has cultivated all the difficult ascetic practices.

Just as with all buddhas of the ancient past
who taught these four bases of meritorious qualities,
only after countless kalpas were they then perfected
so that now he has succeeded in securely abiding within them.

a. Verses Praising the Truth Basis of Meritorious Qualities

Their foundation lies in preservation of the actual truth,
for which he relinquished even his own body and loved ones,
his riches, treasures, and the happiness associated with wealth.
It is through this that he achieved its complete fulfillment.

Throughout measurelessly many kalpas,
in every instance, he has first thoroughly contemplated
the dharmas that are seen, heard, sensed, and known,[93]
and then, afterward, has explained them for the sake of others.

Where others had not observed (some aspect of Dharma) and such,
as well as in situations where they were beset by doubts,
he was then able to explain these matters in accordance with reality.
Those whom he benefited in this way were measurelessly many.

He would not discuss the confidential matters of others.
Even if resented or ridiculed for this, he still refused to betray them.
His thoughts always dwelt in a state of stable wisdom
as he adapted his teachings to lead others to peace and security.

As for the foremost and most genuinely sublime truth,
nirvāṇa is truly supreme,
for all else, in every case, is false.
The Bhagavat has achieved[94] its complete fulfillment.

b. Verses Praising the Relinquishment Basis of Meritorious Qualities

[He made gifts of] beverages, food, bedding, and such,
halls, buildings, marvelous residences, viewing terraces,
highly prized elephants, horses, and vehicles, and also
relinquished female companions of especially fine appearance.

[He gave away] gold, silver, pearls, jewels, and such,
villages, cities, and towns,

正體字	085a02 ‖	國土及榮位	并以四天下
	085a03 ‖	愛子[1]所親婦	支節及頭目
	085a04 ‖	割肉出[2]骨髓	及以舉身施
	085a05 ‖	憐愍諸眾生	悉施無所惜
	085a06 ‖	為求出生死	不以求自樂
	085a07 ‖	虛空諸星宿	地上所有沙
	085a08 ‖	世尊菩薩時	布施數過是
	085a09 ‖	終不以非法	求財而布施
	085a10 ‖	無有不知施	無侵惱人施
	085a11 ‖	不貪惜好物	而以惡者施
	085a12 ‖	無諂曲心施	無惜而強施
	085a13 ‖	無恚無疑心	無邪無輕笑
	085a14 ‖	無厭無不信	[卑*頁]面等布施
	085a15 ‖	無有分別心	此應彼不應
	085a16 ‖	但以悲心故	平等而行施
	085a17 ‖	不輕於眾生	以為非福田
	085a18 ‖	見聖心恭敬	破戒者憐愍
	085a19 ‖	不自高其身	卑下於他人
	085a20 ‖	亦不為稱讚	不求報等施
	085a21 ‖	無悔無憂愁	無惡賤心施

简体字	国土及荣位	并以四天下
	爱子所亲妇	支节及头目
	割肉出骨髓	及以举身施
	怜愍诸众生	悉施无所惜
	为求出生死	不以求自乐
	虚空诸星宿	地上所有沙
	世尊菩萨时	布施数过是
	终不以非法	求财而布施
	无有不知施	无侵恼人施
	不贪惜好物	而以恶者施
	无谄曲心施	无惜而强施
	无恚无疑心	无邪无轻笑
	无厌无不信	[卑*頁]面等布施
	无有分别心	此应彼不应
	但以悲心故	平等而行施
	不轻于众生	以为非福田
	见圣心恭敬	破戒者怜愍
	不自高其身	卑下于他人
	亦不为称赞	不求报等施
	无悔无忧愁	无恶贱心施

entire states, and exalted official positions,
and gave away [his dominion over] the four continents as well.

[He relinquished] cherished sons, beloved wives,
his limbs, his head, and his eyes,
and made gifts by slicing off his flesh, removing bones and marrow,
or even giving away his entire body.

Doing so out of pity for beings,
he gave them all, having none that he continued to cherish.
He did so aspiring to go beyond *saṃsāra*
and not out of some quest to secure his own bliss.

All of the stars and constellations throughout empty space,
and all the grains of sand in this entire earth—
when the Tathāgata was still a bodhisattva,
the number of times he gave in such ways exceeded even these.

He never resorted to actions contrary to Dharma
as he sought out wealth to be used in giving.
He never engaged in giving unaccompanied by knowledge and
never engaged in giving that was invasive or distressing to others.

He never gave bad things as gifts
because he coveted some other fine thing [in return].
He never gave with an ingratiating deviousness
and never engaged in forceful giving because of coveting something.

He never gave with a hate-filled or doubting mind,
never did so with perverse intent or with derisive laughter,
never did so out of disgust or disbelief,
and never gave with the face turned away, or in other such ways.

He had no discriminating mind [by which he judged],
"This one is worthy and that one is unworthy."
Because he only relied on the mind of compassion,
it was with equal regard for everyone that he practiced giving.

He did not slight other beings,
considering them to not qualify as fields of merit.
On seeing *āryas*, his mind was reverential.
On seeing those who have broken the precepts, he felt pity for them.

He did not elevate himself above others,
treat others as mere inferiors,
engage in giving for the sake of praise,
give in expectation of rewards, or give in other such ways.

He never gave with regrets or with worry-filled misgivings
and never gave with thoughts of disdain or disrespect.

正體字

085a22 ‖	無待急恨心	無法應當施
085a23 ‖	無不敬心施	無棄著地施
085a24 ‖	[3]無[4]求惱者施	無[5]垢競勝施
085a25 ‖	無戲弄求者	無不自手施
085a26 ‖	不輕於少物	以多自高施
085a27 ‖	不以聲聞乘	辟支佛乘施
085a28 ‖	不限一世施	無有非時施
085a29 ‖	世尊無數劫	行諸希有施
085b01 ‖	皆為無上道	不為求自樂
085b02 ‖	於諸佛法中	出家行遠離
085b03 ‖	修習諸佛法	為諸人天說
085b04 ‖	說如是施法	於諸施中上
085b05 ‖	猶如日光明	星月中殊勝
085b06 ‖	如是勝捨處	超越諸天人
085b07 ‖	猶亦如世尊	一切世間上
085b08 ‖	是故能具足	如是勝捨處
085b09 ‖	名聞無量劫	流布無窮已
085b10 ‖	世尊無量劫	護持清淨戒
085b11 ‖	開諸禪定門	為得深寂處

简体字

无待急恨心	无法应当施
无不敬心施	无弃着地施
无求恼者施	无垢竞胜施
无戏弄求者	无不自手施
不轻于少物	以多自高施
不以声闻乘	辟支佛乘施
不限一世施	无有非时施
世尊无数劫	行诸希有施
皆为无上道	不为求自乐
于诸佛法中	出家行远离
修习诸佛法	为诸人天说
说如是施法	于诸施中上
犹如日光明	星月中殊胜
如是胜舍处	超越诸天人
犹亦如世尊	一切世间上
是故能具足	如是胜舍处
名闻无量劫	流布无穷已
世尊无量劫	护持清净戒
开诸禅定门	为得深寂处

He never gave with a mind affected by irritability or hostility
and never gave simply as a protocol-dictated formality.

He never gave with a disrespectful mind,
never gave by simply tossing the gift on the ground,
never gave deliberately seeking to cause distress,
and never gave out of a jealousy-driven struggle for supremacy.

He would never tease a supplicant,
never failed to present a gift with his own hands,
did not slight the recipient with a merely paltry gift,
and did not give excessively in order to enhance his own esteem.

His giving was never motivated by intentions associated with
either the Śrāvaka Disciple Vehicle or the Pratyekabuddha Vehicle.
His giving was never limited to concern for only a single lifetime
and he never engaged in giving done at the wrong time.

For countless kalpas, the Bhagavat
practiced every form of rare giving,
always doing so for the sake of the unsurpassable path
and not merely in order to seek his own happiness.

Throughout the duration of all buddhas' Dharma,
he became a monastic, practiced renunciation,
cultivated the Dharma of all buddhas,
and proclaimed the Dharma for the sake of all humans and devas.

He taught just such a dharma of giving as this
that is supreme among all types of giving,
just as, among all the stars and the moon,
it is the light of the sun that is supreme.

Such supremacy in the relinquishment basis [of meritorious qualities]
surpasses that of any deva or human,
just as it is the Bhagavat
who is superior to everyone in the world.

He was therefore able to perfect
such supreme practice of the relinquishment basis.
His fame shall endure for countless kalpas,
flowing on and spreading ceaselessly.

c. Verses Praising the Quiescence Basis of Meritorious Qualities

For countless kalpas, the Bhagavat
preserved and upheld the precepts of moral purity
and opened the gates of the *dhyāna* absorptions
for the sake of acquiring the deep quiescence basis.

正體字

085b12 ‖ 先離於五相　後行八解脫
085b13 ‖ 入淨三三昧　亦[6]住三解脫
085b14 ‖ 世尊善分別　六十五種禪
085b15 ‖ 無有一禪定　先來不生者
085b16 ‖ 於此諸定中　亦不受其味
085b17 ‖ 世尊因諸[7]定　得三種神通
085b18 ‖ 以此度眾生　是故一切勝
085b19 ‖ 世尊無量劫　等心弘慈化
085b20 ‖ 阿僧祇眾生　令住於梵世
085b21 ‖ 能以巧方便　善說禪定故
085b22 ‖ 世尊菩薩時　常於無量世
085b23 ‖ 無貪煩惱纏　而往來世間
085b24 ‖ 過去得值者　無量生天上
085b25 ‖ 過去諸菩薩　所可行寂滅
085b26 ‖ 世尊菩薩時　亦等無有異
085b27 ‖ 是故於寂滅　勝處悉充滿
085b28 ‖ 世尊菩薩時　所有諸智慧
085b29 ‖ 以慧求菩提　今成是慧報
085c01 ‖ 一切所資食　如人依地生
085c02 ‖ 世尊於世世　捨十闇惡道

简体字

先离于五相　后行八解脱
入净三三昧　亦住三解脱
世尊善分别　六十五种禅
无有一禅定　先来不生者
于此诸定中　亦不受其味
世尊因诸定　得三种神通
以此度众生　是故一切胜
世尊无量劫　等心弘慈化
阿僧祇众生　令住于梵世
能以巧方便　善说禅定故
世尊菩萨时　常于无量世
无贪烦恼缠　而往来世间
过去得值者　无量生天上
过去诸菩萨　所可行寂灭
世尊菩萨时　亦等无有异
是故于寂灭　胜处悉充满
世尊菩萨时　所有诸智慧
以慧求菩提　今成是慧报
一切所资食　如人依地生
世尊于世世　舍十闇恶道

He began by abandoning five characteristics[95]
and later practiced the eight liberations.
He entered and purified the three samādhis,
and also dwelt in the three liberations.

The Bhagavat well distinguishes
the sixty-five kinds of *dhyānas*.
There is no *dhyāna* whatsoever
that he has not formerly produced.

Even when abiding in these meditative absorptions,
he did not indulge in their delectably pleasurable states.
Due to the various meditative absorptions,
the Bhagavat gained three types of spiritual superknowledges.

He used these in the liberation of beings
and so became supreme in all things.
For countless kalpas, with a mind of equal regard,
the Bhagavat widely spread his kindly transformative teaching.

An *asaṃkhyeya* of beings
was thereby caused to abide in the Brahma World Heavens
because he was able to use skillful means
in thoroughly teaching the *dhyāna* absorptions.

While still a bodhisattva, the Bhagavat
for incalculably many lifetimes, always
remained free of any entanglement in the affliction of covetousness.
Thus he was able to come and go in the world.

Of those who succeeded in encountering him in the past,
countless such beings thereby achieved rebirth in the heavens.
As for that quiescence that
all bodhisattvas of the past were able to practice,

when still a bodhisattva, the Bhagavat
also practiced, doing so in a manner no different from theirs.
Thus, as regards the realization of quiescence,
that supreme basis [of meritorious qualities], it was entirely fulfilled.

d. Verses Praising the Wisdom Basis of Meritorious Qualities

All those forms of wisdom
possessed by the Bhagavat while he was still a bodhisattva—
He relied on such wisdom in his quest for bodhi
so that, as a karmic result, he has now developed this wisdom.

Just as people rely on the earth for the production
of all the food that it supplies,
[so, too], as in life after life, the Bhagavat
relinquished the ten courses of dark and bad actions

正體字

085c03 ‖	常行十善道	斯由慧氣[8]分
085c04 ‖	捨五欲五蓋	得種種禪定
085c05 ‖	無量劫數世	不從他人受
085c06 ‖	善哉大聖尊	悉是慧[9]勢力
085c07 ‖	眾生因世尊	無量生六天
085c08 ‖	亦令至梵世	斯皆由慧力
085c09 ‖	世尊於生死	苦樂所迷悶
085c10 ‖	不失菩提心	斯皆是慧力
085c11 ‖	世尊於生死	不樂而常在
085c12 ‖	樂涅槃不取	斯皆是慧力
085c13 ‖	安坐道場時	降魔及軍眾
085c14 ‖	度脫諸群生	斯皆是慧力
085c15 ‖	本求菩提時	集無量助法
085c16 ‖	聞者常迷悶	何況能受行
085c17 ‖	世尊能堪忍	斯皆是慧力
085c18 ‖	經書諸技術	世世生自知
085c19 ‖	亦能兼教人	斯皆是慧力
085c20 ‖	親近無量佛	悉飲甘露教
085c21 ‖	種種諮請問	亦隨而分別
085c22 ‖	經法智慧中	未曾有悋惜

简体字

常行十善道	斯由慧气分
舍五欲五盖	得种种禅定
无量劫数世	不从他人受
善哉大圣尊	悉是慧势力
众生因世尊	无量生六天
亦令至梵世	斯皆由慧力
世尊于生死	苦乐所迷闷
不失菩提心	斯皆是慧力
世尊于生死	不乐而常在
乐涅槃不取	斯皆是慧力
安坐道场时	降魔及军众
度脱诸群生	斯皆是慧力
本求菩提时	集无量助法
闻者常迷闷	何况能受行
世尊能堪忍	斯皆是慧力
经书诸技术	世世生自知
亦能兼教人	斯皆是慧力
亲近无量佛	悉饮甘露教
种种咨请问	亦随而分别
经法智慧中	未曾有吝惜

and always practiced the path of the ten good actions,
these [deeds] were all due to the power of wisdom.[96]

He renounced the five desires and the five hindrances
and thus acquired all the various *dhyāna* absorptions.
He accomplished this for the number of lifetimes in countless kalpas
and did not acquire this from others.
This is excellent indeed, O Great Honored One of the Āryas.
All of this was due to the power of wisdom.

It is because of the Bhagavat that beings,
countless in number, have taken rebirth in the six heavens.
So too has he enabled them to reach the Brahma World.
All of this was due to the power of wisdom.

Throughout the course of his births and deaths, the Bhagavat,
even when confused and perturbed by sufferings and pleasures,
never lost the resolve to attain bodhi.
All of this was due to the power of wisdom.

Throughout the course of *saṃsāra,* the Bhagavat
did not delight [in worldly existence] and yet still always remained.
He delighted in nirvāṇa, yet did not seize on its [final] realization.
All of this was due to the power of wisdom.

When sitting peacefully there in the *bodhimaṇḍa,*
he overcame Māra and his armies
and proceeded to liberate all the classes of beings.
All of this was due to the power of wisdom.

When he originally strove in quest of bodhi,
he accumulated countless provisions for the path.
If merely hearing of them causes one to be confused and perturbed,
how much the less might one be able to take on their practice.
That the Bhagavat was able to patiently endure such things
was in every case due to the power of wisdom.

That, in lifetime after lifetime, he was able to naturally know
the classic texts as well as all the arts and skills
while also being able to teach them to others
was in every case due to the power of wisdom.

He drew close to countless buddhas
and from them all drank the sweet-dew nectar of their teachings,
He consulted them and inquired about the many different topics
and then also pursued additional distinguishing [clarifications].

He was never the least bit miserly
with the wisdom of the sutras' Dharma,

正體字

085c23 ‖ 乃至僕僮奴　亦諮受善語
085c24 ‖ 世尊以是故　慧勝處流布
085c25 ‖ 世尊於前世　求是菩提時
085c26 ‖ 於[10]一切眾生　行大慈悲心
085c27 ‖ 以第一智慧　常出大勢力
085c28 ‖ 悉作無量種　希有諸難事
085c29 ‖ 一切諸世間　盡共無量劫
086a01 ‖ 說之不可盡　亦非算數及
086a02 ‖ 如是等諸事　超越於人天
086a03 ‖ 一切世間中　奇特無有比
086a04 ‖ 大業所獲果　具足一切智
086a05 ‖ 能破生死王　安住法王處[1]

简体字

乃至仆僮奴　亦咨受善语
世尊以是故　慧胜处流布
世尊于前世　求是菩提时
于一切众生　行大慈悲心
以第一智慧　常出大势力
悉作无量种　希有诸难事
一切诸世间　尽共无量劫
说之不可尽　亦非算数及
如是等诸事　超越于人天
一切世间中　奇特无有比
大业所获果　具足一切智
能破生死王　安住法王处

but rather offered it even to servants, youths, and menials,
allowing them to freely receive his fine explanations.
Because of this, [the fame of] the Bhagavat's
supreme wisdom basis [of meritorious qualities] spreads on afar.

Throughout his former lifetimes, as the Bhagavat
pursued his quest for the realization of bodhi,
he practiced the great kindness and compassion
toward all beings.

Relying on the foremost wisdom,
he always marshalled his great strength
to take up and do all the countless kinds
of rare and difficult endeavors.

3. Concluding Praise Verses

In all of the many worlds,
he exhaustively contributed all his efforts for countless kalpas.
One could never come to the end of them through verbal description,
nor could one even reach it through mathematical calculation.

All of his endeavors of such sorts
surpass those done by any human or deva.
Even in all the many worlds,
there is nothing comparable to his extraordinary marvels.

The fruits reaped through such great deeds
reach complete fulfillment in the realization of all-knowledge.
He is the king of those able to destroy *saṃsāra*
and dwells securely in the place of the Dharma king.

The End of Chapter Twenty-Four

正體字

086a06 ‖ [2]助念佛三昧品第二十五
086a07 ‖ 菩薩應以此　四十不共法
086a08 ‖ 念諸佛法身　佛非色身故
086a09 ‖ 是偈次第略解四十不共法六品中義。是故
086a10 ‖ 行者先念色身佛。次念法身佛。何以故。新
086a11 ‖ 發意菩薩。應以三十二相八十種好念佛。
086a12 ‖ 如先說。轉深入得中勢力。應以法身念佛
086a13 ‖ 心轉深入得上勢力。應以實相念佛而不
086a14 ‖ 貪著。
086a15 ‖ 不[3]染著色身　法身亦不著
086a16 ‖ 善知一切法　永寂如虛空
086a17 ‖ 是菩薩得上勢力。不以色身法身深貪著
086a18 ‖ 佛。何以故。信樂空法故。知諸法如虛空。虛
086a19 ‖ 空者無障礙故。障礙因緣者。

简体字

十住毗婆沙论卷第十一

助念佛三昧品第二十五

菩萨应以此　四十不共法
念诸佛法身　佛非色身故

是偈次第略解四十不共法六品中义。是故行者先念色身佛。次念法身佛。何以故。新发意菩萨。应以三十二相八十种好念佛。如先说。转深入得中势力。应以法身念佛心转深入得上势力。应以实相念佛而不贪着。

不染着色身　法身亦不着
善知一切法　永寂如虚空

是菩萨得上势力。不以色身法身深贪着佛。何以故。信乐空法故。知诸法如虚空。虚空者无障碍故。障碍因缘者。

Ch. 25: Teachings to Aid the Mindfulness-of-the-Buddha Samādhi

VI. Chapter 25: Teachings Aiding Mindfulness-of-the Buddha Samādhi

A. Initial Instructions on the Mindfulness-of-the Buddha Samādhi

The bodhisattva should rely on these
forty exclusive dharmas
in his mindfulness of the Buddhas' Dharma body,
for the Buddhas are not their form bodies.

These [preceding] verses have sequentially and summarily explained six categories of meanings associated with the forty exclusive dharmas.[97] In doing so, the practitioner therefore first takes up the mindfulness of the Buddha's form body and then takes up the mindfulness of the Buddha's Dharma body.

Why is this the case? The bodhisattva who has only recently brought forth the resolve [to attain buddhahood] should first take up the practice of mindfulness of the Buddha in reliance on the thirty-two marks and eighty secondary characteristics [of the Buddha's form body], doing so in the manner described earlier.

Then, as one's practice progressively penetrates more deeply, one will develop a middling degree of strength in that practice. One should then rely on the Dharma body in his mindfulness of the Buddha.

Then, as one's mind progressively penetrates yet more deeply, one will then achieve a supreme degree of power in the development of this practice. At that point, one should then take up mindfulness of the Buddha in accordance with the true character of [all dharmas][98] and remain free of any sort of attachment in doing so.

One must not become deeply attached to the form body.[99]
One also refrains from becoming attached to the Dharma body.
One should thoroughly realize that all dharmas
are as eternally quiescent as empty space.

As this bodhisattva develops a superior degree of power [in this practice], he refrains from developing a deep attachment to the Buddha on the basis of either the form body or the Dharma body. Why not? Through one's resolute belief in the dharma of emptiness, one understands that all dharmas are like empty space.

Empty space is defined by the absence of obstruction. The causal circumstances associated with obstruction include phenomena like

正體字

諸須彌山由乾
086a20 ‖ 陀等十寶山。鐵圍山黑山石山等。如是無量
086a21 ‖ 障礙因緣。何以故。是人未得天眼故。念他
086a22 ‖ 方世界佛。則有諸山障礙。是故新發意菩薩。
086a23 ‖ 應以十號妙相念佛。如說。
086a24 ‖ 新發意菩薩　以十號妙相
086a25 ‖ 念佛無毀失　猶如鏡中像
086a26 ‖ 十號妙相者。所謂如來應[4]供正遍知明行足
086a27 ‖ 善逝世間解無上士調御丈夫天人師佛世
086a28 ‖ 尊。無毀失者。所觀事空如虛空。於法無
086a29 ‖ 所失。何以故。諸法本來無生寂滅故。如是一
086b01 ‖ 切諸法皆亦如是。是人以緣名號增長禪
086b02 ‖ 法則能緣相。是人爾時[5]即於禪法得相。所
086b03 ‖ 謂身得殊異

简体字

诸须弥山由乾陀等十宝山。铁围山黑山石山等。如是无量障碍因缘。何以故。是人未得天眼故。念他方世界佛。则有诸山障碍。是故新发意菩萨。应以十号妙相念佛。如说。

新发意菩萨　以十号妙相
念佛无毁失　犹如镜中像

十号妙相者。所谓如来应供正遍知明行足善逝世间解无上士调御丈夫天人师佛世尊。无毁失者。所观事空如虚空。于法无所失。何以故。诸法本来无生寂灭故。如是一切诸法皆亦如是。是人以缘名号增长禅法则能缘相。是人尔时即于禅法得相。所谓身得殊异

Mount Sumeru, Yugaṃdhara Mountain, the rest of the ten jeweled mountains, the Iron Ring Mountains, Black Mountain, Stone Mountain, and the others. There are all sorts of other such causal bases for the existence of obstructions.

Why is this [a point at issue]? Because this person has still not yet gained the heavenly eye, if he brings to mind buddhas abiding in the worlds off in the other directions, the various mountains will block them from his view. Consequently, The bodhisattva who has only recently brought forth the resolve [to attain buddhahood] should use the sublime characteristics described by the ten names as bases for his mindfulness of the Buddha. This is as described in these lines:

> The bodhisattva who has only recently brought forth the resolve
> uses the sublime features described by the ten names
> in practicing mindfulness of the Buddhas that is free of fault,
> seeing them just as if they were images in a mirror.

As for "the sublime features described in the ten names," those ten names are:

Tathāgata;[100]
Worthy of Offerings;
The Right and Universally Enlightened One;
Perfect in the Clear Knowledges and Conduct;
Well Gone One;
Knower of the Worlds;
Unsurpassable Trainer of Those to Be Tamed;
Teacher of Devas and Humans;
Buddha;
Bhagavat.

As for "free of fault," the phenomena that one contemplates are beheld as empty and like space itself. Thus [one's contemplation] is free of any fault with regard to the Dharma. And how is this so? It is because all dharmas, from their very origin on forward to the present, have been unproduced and quiescent. Just as this is true [with respect to these dharmas], so too is this also true of all other dharmas.

By taking these names as the object [of his contemplation], this person develops his practice of the dharma of *dhyāna* meditation. Having done so, he is then able to take these characteristic signs themselves as the object of his contemplation.

At this time, this person then immediately acquires these signs in his practice of the dharma of *dhyāna* meditation and experiences what is referred to as the direct personal experience of an especially

正體字

快樂。當知得成般舟三昧。三
086b04 ‖ 昧成故得見諸佛。如鏡中像者。若菩薩成
086b05 ‖ 此三昧已。如淨明鏡自見面像。如清澄水
086b06 ‖ 中見其身相。初時隨先所念佛見其色像。
086b07 ‖ 見是像已後。若欲見他方諸佛隨所念方
086b08 ‖ 得見諸佛無所障礙。是故此人。
086b09 ‖ 　雖未有神通　　飛行到[6]于彼
086b10 ‖ 　而能見諸佛　　聞法無障礙
086b11 ‖ 是新發意菩薩於諸須彌山等諸山無能為
086b12 ‖ 作障礙。亦未得神通天眼天耳。未能飛行
086b13 ‖ 從此國至彼國。以是三昧力故。住此國
086b14 ‖ 土得見他方諸佛世尊。聞所說法常修習
086b15 ‖ 是三昧故。得見十方真實諸佛。問曰。如是
086b16 ‖ [7]定以何法能生。云何可得。答曰。
086b17 ‖ 　親近善知識　　精進無懈退
086b18 ‖ 　智慧甚堅牢　　信力不妄動
086b19 ‖ 以是四法能生是三昧。親近善知識者。能
086b20 ‖ 以是三昧教誨人者名為善知識。應加
086b21 ‖ 恭敬

简体字

快乐。当知得成般舟三昧。三昧成故得见诸佛。如镜中像者。若菩萨成此三昧已。如净明镜自见面像。如清澄水中见其身相。初时随先所念佛见其色像。见是像已后。若欲见他方诸佛随所念方得见诸佛无所障碍。是故此人。

　虽未有神通　　飞行到于彼
　而能见诸佛　　闻法无障碍

是新发意菩萨于诸须弥山等诸山无能为作障碍。亦未得神通天眼天耳。未能飞行从此国至彼国。以是三昧力故。住此国土得见他方诸佛世尊。闻所说法常修习是三昧故。得见十方真实诸佛。问曰。如是定以何法能生。云何可得。答曰。

　亲近善知识　　精进无懈退
　智慧甚坚牢　　信力不妄动

以是四法能生是三昧。亲近善知识者。能以是三昧教诲人者名为善知识。应加恭敬

extraordinary bliss. One should realize that when this occurs, one has acquired the *pratyutpanna* samādhi. Because of developing this samādhi, one is then able to see the Buddhas.

As for "as if they were images in a mirror," once the bodhisattva has developed this samādhi, it is as if one is seeing one's own face in a clean, brightly-lit mirror or like seeing the image of one's own body in a clear, still pool of water.

Initially, whichever buddha one first brings to mind, it is that very image that one sees. After one has seen this image, if one wishes to see buddhas in other regions, then, in accordance with whichever region one brings to mind, one obtains an unimpeded vision of those very buddhas. Hence, regarding this person:

> Although he does not yet possess the spiritual superknowledges
> by which he could fly to visit them,
> he is nonetheless able to see those buddhas
> and has an unimpeded ability to listen to their Dharma.

For this bodhisattva who has only recently brought forth the resolve [to attain buddhahood], neither Mount Sumeru nor any other mountain can present an obstacle and, even though he has not yet acquired any of the spiritual superknowledges, the heavenly eye, or the heavenly ear, and even though he has not yet developed the ability to fly from this country to that country, through the power of this samādhi, even while still abiding in this country, he is able to see the Buddhas, the Bhagavats, abiding in the other regions and is able to hear the Dharma as they are speaking it. Through always cultivating this samādhi, he becomes able to see all of the buddhas throughout the ten directions just as they really are.

B. Four Dharmas Capable of Bringing Forth This Samādhi

Question: Through which dharmas is one able to bring forth this meditative absorption and how can one acquire it?

Response:

> One draws close to the good spiritual guide,
> brings forth non-retreating vigor,
> develops extremely solid and durable wisdom,
> and develops the power of unshakeable faith.

It is through utilizing these four dharmas that one is able to bring forth this samādhi.

As for "drawing close to the good spiritual guide," someone able to instruct a person in the acquisition of this samādhi qualifies here as "the good spiritual guide." One should bring forth reverential respect

正體字

勤心親近莫有懈怠廢退捨離則得
086b22 ‖ 聞是深三昧義利智通達智不失智。名為堅
086b23 ‖ 牢信根深固。若沙門婆羅門若天魔梵及餘
086b24 ‖ 世人無能傾動。名為信力不可動。如是四
086b25 ‖ 法。能生三昧。復次。
086b26 ‖ 慚愧愛恭敬　供養說法者
086b27 ‖ 猶如諸世尊　能生是三昧
086b28 ‖ 慚愧愛恭敬者。於說法者深生慚愧。恭[8]恪
086b29 ‖ 愛樂供養如佛。如是四法能生是三昧。復
086c01 ‖ 次初四法者。一於三月未[9]甞睡眠。唯除便
086c02 ‖ 利飲食坐起。二於三月乃至彈指不生我
086c03 ‖ 心。三於三月經行不息。四於三月兼以法
086c04 ‖ 施不求利養。是為四。復有四法。一能見
086c05 ‖ 佛。

简体字

勤心亲近莫有懈怠废退舍离则得闻是深三昧义利智通达智不失智。名为坚牢信根深固。若沙门婆罗门若天魔梵及余世人无能倾动。名为信力不可动。如是四法。能生三昧。复次。

慚愧爱恭敬　供养说法者
犹如诸世尊　能生是三昧

慚愧爱恭敬者。于说法者深生慚愧。恭恪爱乐供养如佛。如是四法能生是三昧。复次初四法者。一于三月未尝睡眠。唯除便利饮食坐起。二于三月乃至弹指不生我心。三于三月经行不息。四于三月兼以法施不求利养。是为四。复有四法。一能见佛。

and assiduous diligence and, in drawing close [to the good spiritual guide], one must not allow any indolence, diminishment in motivation, or relinquishing of effort to take place. If one acts accordingly, one will then be able to hear the teaching of the deep meaning of this samādhi.

Sharp wisdom, wisdom characterized by penetrating comprehension, and undiminishing wisdom are what qualify as "solid and durable" [wisdom]. One's faculty of faith is deeply and firmly established, so much so that, no matter whether it be a *śramaṇa* or a brahmin or a celestial *māra* or Brahmā or anyone else in the world—none of them could cause it to quaver even slightly. This is what is meant by an unshakeable power of faith. It is these very four dharmas described here that are able to bring forth this samādhi.

C. Four More Dharmas Capable of Bringing Forth This Samādhi

Furthermore:

> With a sense of shame, dread of blame, cherishing reverence,
> and offerings to those who proclaim the Dharma
> presented as if they were given to the Bhagavats themselves,
> one thereby becomes able to bring forth this samādhi.

As for "with a sense of shame, dread of blame, and cherishing reverence," one brings forth a profound sense of shame and dread of blame in relation to those who teach the Dharma. With sincere reverence and affectionate delight, one makes offerings to them as if they were the Buddhas themselves. In this way, these four dharmas are able to produce this samādhi.

D. Four More Dharmas Capable of Bringing Forth This Samādhi

Another preliminary set of fourfold dharmas is as follows:

First, for a period of three months, one strives to refrain from sleeping and, with the exception of using the toilet and eating and drinking, one refrains from sitting down;

Second, for that period of three months, one avoids, even for the duration of a finger snap, indulgence in any thought seizing on the existence of a self;

Third, for that entire three months, one strives to always walk and never rest;

Fourth, for that entire three months, when also engaged in the giving of Dharma, one refrains from seeking offerings from others.

These are the four. There are four more such dharmas, as follows:

E. Four More Dharmas Capable of Bringing Forth This Samādhi

First, one becomes able to see the Buddhas;

正體字

二安慰勸人聽是三昧。三常不貪嫉行
086c06 || 菩提心者。四能集菩薩所行道法。是為四。
086c07 || 復有四法。一造作佛像乃至畫像。二當善
086c08 || 書寫是三昧經。令信樂者得[10]已誦讀。三教
086c09 || 增上慢人令離[11]憎上慢法。使得阿耨多羅
086c10 || 三藐三菩提。四當護持諸佛正法。是為四。
086c11 || [12]復有四法。一少語言。二在家出家不與共
086c12 || 住。三常繫心取所緣相。四樂遠離空閑靜
086c13 || 處。是為四。初五法者。一無生[13]忍法。厭離一
086c14 || 切諸有為法。不樂一切諸所生處。不受一
086c15 || 切諸外道法。惡厭一切世間諸欲乃至不念
086c16 || 何況身近。二心常修習無量諸法定在一
086c17 || 處。

简体字

二安慰劝人听是三昧。三常不贪嫉行菩提心者。四能集菩萨所行道法。是为四。复有四法。一造作佛像乃至画像。二当善书写是三昧经。令信乐者得已诵读。三教增上慢人令离憎上慢法。使得阿耨多罗三藐三菩提。四当护持诸佛正法。是为四。复有四法。一少语言。二在家出家不与共住。三常系心取所缘相。四乐远离空闲静处。是为四。初五法者。一无生忍法。厌离一切诸有为法。不乐一切诸所生处。不受一切诸外道法。恶厌一切世间诸欲乃至不念何况身近。二心常修习无量诸法定在一处。

Second, one reassures and encourages others to listen to the teaching of this samādhi;

Third, one is never envious or jealous of anyone who is putting the resolve to attain bodhi into practice;

Fourth, one is able to accumulate the dharmas of the bodhisattva path.

These are the four. There are four more such dharmas, as follows:

F. Four More Dharmas Capable of Bringing Forth This Samādhi

First, one makes buddha images that may also include painted images;

Second, one should carefully write out copies of the sutra that discusses this samādhi and then encourage others who have a resolute faith in it to study and recite it aloud once they have obtained it;[101]

Third, teach those of overweening pride[102] to abandon their overweening pride[103] and then influence them to pursue the attainment of *anuttarasamyaksaṃbodhi;*

Fourth, one should devote oneself to the protection and preservation of the right Dharma of all buddhas.

These are the four. There are four more such dharmas, as follows:

G. Four More Dharmas Capable of Bringing Forth This Samādhi

First, one avoids speaking;

Second, both lay and monastic practitioners are to refrain from dwelling together with others;

Third, one always anchors one's mind on the characteristic sign that has been chosen as the object of one's mental focus;[104]

Fourth, one delights in dwelling far apart from others, in a location that is vacant, serene, and silent.

These are the four. The first of the five-fold sets of associated dharmas is as follows:

H. Five More Dharmas Capable of Bringing Forth This Samādhi

First, abiding in the unproduced-dharmas patience (*anutpattika-dharma-kṣānti*), one renounces all conditioned dharmas, does not delight in any of the destinies of rebirth, refuses to accept any of the non-Buddhist dharmas, and remains so disgusted with all worldly desires that one does not even bring them to mind, how much the less might one draw physically close to them;

Second, even as one's mind always cultivates and practices countless dharmas, it remains in a state of one-pointed concentration;

正體字

於諸眾生無有瞋礙。心常隨順行四攝
086c18 ‖ 法。三能成就慈悲喜捨不[14]出他過。四能多
086c19 ‖ 集佛所說法如所說行。五清淨身口意業
086c20 ‖ 及見。是為五。復有五法。一樂如經所讚布
086c21 ‖ 施無有慳心。樂說深法無所悋惜亦能
086c22 ‖ 自住。二忍辱柔和同住歡喜。惡口罵詈鞭捶
086c23 ‖ 縛等。但推業緣不恚他人。三常樂聽是三
086c24 ‖ 昧讀誦通利為人解說令流布增廣勤行修
086c25 ‖ 習。四心無妬嫉。不自高身不下他人。除
086c26 ‖ [15]眠睡蓋。五於佛法僧寶信心清淨。於上中
086c27 ‖ 下坐深心供奉。他有小恩常憶不忘。常住
086c28 ‖ 真實語中。是為五復次。
086c29 ‖ 出家諸菩薩　所學三昧法
087a01 ‖ 在家菩薩者　是法應當知

简体字

于诸众生无有嗔碍。心常随顺行四摄法。三能成就慈悲喜舍不出他过。四能多集佛所说法如所说行。五清净身口意业及见。是为五。复有五法。一乐如经所赞布施无有悭心。乐说深法无所吝惜亦能自住。二忍辱柔和同住欢喜。恶口骂詈鞭捶缚等。但推业缘不恚他人。三常乐听是三昧读诵通利为人解说令流布增广勤行修习。四心无妒嫉。不自高身不下他人。除眠睡盖。五于佛法僧宝信心清净。于上中下坐深心供奉。他有小恩常忆不忘。常住真实语中。是为五复次。

出家诸菩萨　所学三昧法
在家菩萨者　是法应当知

One remains free of the obstacle of hatred toward any being and one's mind always accords with the practice of the four means of attraction;

Third, one becomes able to perfect kindness, compassion, sympathetic joy, and equanimity while also refraining from exposing others' transgressions;

Fourth, one becomes able to accumulate a multitude of dharmas proclaimed by the Buddha while also being able to carry them out in accordance with the way they were taught;

Fifth, one purifies one's physical, verbal, and mental actions as well as one's views.

These are the five. There are five more associated dharmas, as follows:

I. Five More Dharmas Capable of Bringing Forth This Samādhi

First, one delights in according with the practice of giving as praised in the sutras, doing so without miserly thoughts. One delights in speaking on profound dharmas, withholds nothing due to stinginess, and also remains able to dwell in those very dharmas oneself;

Second, one abides in patience, mental pliancy, and delight when abiding in close proximity to others and, if subjected to harsh speech, scolding and cursing, whippings, beatings, being tied up, or other such experiences, one simply attributes it to one's own karmic conditions and does not hate others for doing this;

Third, one always delights in listening to teachings that explain this samādhi, in reading and reciting them, in thoroughly understanding them, in explaining them for others, and in causing them to circulate and spread ever more widely even as one diligently practices and cultivates [this samādhi];

Fourth, one's mind remains free of any jealous feelings toward others, one refrains from elevating oneself and looking down on others, and one strives to rid oneself of the hindrance of drowsiness;

Fifth, one maintains a mind of pure faith in the Buddha Jewel, the Dharma Jewel, and the Sangha Jewel, offers up deeply sincere service to those of senior, middling, and lower station, always remembers and never forgets even the smallest kindnesses of others, and always abides in truthful speech.

These are the five. In addition, there are the following lines:

J. The Guidelines for Lay and Monastic Cultivation of This Samādhi

As for those samādhi dharmas
in which monastic bodhisattvas train,
householder bodhisattvas
should also know these dharmas.

正體字

087a02 ‖ 若在家菩薩欲修習是三昧一當深以信
087a03 ‖ 心。二不求業果報。三當捨一切內外物。四
087a04 ‖ 歸命三寶。五淨持五戒無有毀缺。六具足
087a05 ‖ 行十善道。亦令餘人住此法中。七斷除婬
087a06 ‖ 欲。八毀[1]呰五欲。九不嫉妬。十於妻子中
087a07 ‖ 不生愛著。十一心常願出家。十二常受[2]齊
087a08 ‖ 戒。十三心樂住寺廟。十四具足慚愧。十五
087a09 ‖ 於淨戒比丘起恭敬心。十六不慳悋法。十
087a10 ‖ 七於說法者深愛敬心。十八於說法者生
087a11 ‖ 父母大師想。十九於說法者以諸樂具敬
087a12 ‖ 心供養。二十知恩報恩。如是在家菩薩。住
087a13 ‖ 如是等功德者。則能學是三昧。出家菩薩
087a14 ‖ 修習是三昧法者。所謂

简体字

若在家菩萨欲修习是三昧一当深以信心。二不求业果报。三当舍一切内外物。四归命三宝。五净持五戒无有毁缺。六具足行十善道。亦令余人住此法中。七断除淫欲。八毁呰五欲。九不嫉妒。十于妻子中不生爱着。十一心常愿出家。十二常受齐戒。十三心乐住寺庙。十四具足惭愧。十五于净戒比丘起恭敬心。十六不悭吝法。十七于说法者深爱敬心。十八于说法者生父母大师想。十九于说法者以诸乐具敬心供养。二十知恩报恩。如是在家菩萨。住如是等功德者。则能学是三昧。出家菩萨修习是三昧法者。所谓

1. Twenty Guidelines for Lay Cultivators of This Samādhi

If a householder bodhisattva wishes to cultivate this samādhi, [he should observe the following twenty guidelines]:

1) One should proceed with a mind of deep faith;
2) One should not seek any sort of karmic reward;
3) One should give up all personal and extra-personal things;
4) One should take refuge in the Three Jewels;
5) One should uphold the five moral precepts purely and in a manner free of any transgression or deficiency;
6) One should perfect the practice of the ten courses of good karmic action while also influencing others to abide in these dharmas;
7) One should cut off all sexual desire;
8) One should repudiate the five types of desire;
9) One should refrain from any feelings of jealousy toward others;
10) One should not nurture an affectionate attachment for either one's spouse or one's children;
11) One should always maintain an aspiration to leave the householder's life to become a monastic;
12) One should always take on and observe the layperson's precepts of abstinence;[105]
13) One's mind should delight in the opportunity to abide within the precincts of a temple;[106]
14) One should be well possessed of a sense of shame and a dread of blame;
15) One should bring forth thoughts of reverential respect toward bhikshus who are pure in upholding the moral precepts;
16) One should not act in a miserly way with the Dharma;
17) One should maintain a mind of deep affection and reverence toward those who teach the Dharma;
18) One should think of teachers of Dharma as if they were one's father, mother, or great teaching master;
19) One should respectfully present all manner of delightful gifts as offerings to the Dharma teaching masters;
20) One should feel gratitude for the kindnesses that have been bestowed upon one and one should repay those kindnesses accordingly.

If a householder bodhisattva abides in meritorious qualities such as these, he will then be able to learn this samādhi.

2. Sixty Guidelines for Monastic Cultivators of This Samādhi

As for [the guidelines appropriate to] a monastic bodhisattva's cultivation of dharmas pertaining to this samādhi, they are as follows:

正體字

一於戒無[3]毀疵。二
087a15 ‖ 持戒不雜污。三持戒不濁。四清淨戒。五無
087a16 ‖ 損戒。六不取戒。七不依戒。八不得戒。九
087a17 ‖ 不退戒。十持聖所讚戒。十一持智所稱
087a18 ‖ 戒。十二隨波羅提木叉戒。十三具足威儀行
087a19 ‖ 處。十四乃至微小罪心大怖畏。十五淨身口
087a20 ‖ 意業。十六淨命。十七所有戒盡受持。十八
087a21 ‖ 信樂甚深法。十九於無所得法心能忍。空
087a22 ‖ 無相無願法中心不驚。二十勤發精進。二十
087a23 ‖ 一念常在前。二十二信心堅固。二十三具足
087a24 ‖ 慚愧。二十四不貪利養。二十五無嫉妬。二
087a25 ‖ 十六住頭陀功德。二十七住細行法中。二十
087a26 ‖ 八不樂說世間俗語。

简体字

一于戒无毁疵。二持戒不杂污。三持戒不浊。四清净戒。五无损戒。六不取戒。七不依戒。八不得戒。九不退戒。十持圣所赞戒。十一持智所称戒。十二随波罗提木叉戒。十三具足威仪行处。十四乃至微小罪心大怖畏。十五净身口意业。十六净命。十七所有戒尽受持。十八信乐甚深法。十九于无所得法心能忍。空无相无愿法中心不惊。二十勤发精进。二十一念常在前。二十二信心坚固。二十三具足惭愧。二十四不贪利养。二十五无嫉妒。二十六住头陀功德。二十七住细行法中。二十八不乐说世间俗语。

1) One remains free of any defect as regards observance of the moral precepts;
2) One maintains uncorrupted observance of the moral precepts;
3) One maintains unsullied observance of the moral precepts;
4) One maintains pure observance of the moral precepts;
5) One maintains undiminished observance of the moral precepts;
6) One does not seize on the moral precepts themselves [as constituting the very essence of moral virtue];
7) One does not rely on the moral precepts [alone as the sole component of one's practice];
8) One realizes that the moral precepts cannot finally be apprehended at all [as inherently existent entities];
9) One never retreats from one's observance of the moral precepts;
10) One upholds the moral precepts in the manner that is praised by the Āryas;
11) One upholds the moral precepts in the manner that is extolled by the wise;
12) One accords with the *prātimokṣa* precepts;
13) One perfects the bases for the awe-inspiring deportment;
14) One remains immensely fearful of committing even the most minor transgression of the precepts;
15) One purifies the actions of body, speech, and mind;
16) One maintains purity in right livelihood;
17) One completely upholds all of the moral precepts;
18) One maintains resolute belief in the extremely profound dharmas;
19) One is able to patiently acquiesce in the dharma of the non-apprehension [of any dharma whatsoever] and is able to not be frightened even by the dharmas of emptiness, signlessness, and wishlessness;
20) One remains diligent in bringing forth vigor [in one's practice];
21) One always maintains ever-present mindfulness;
22) One maintains a mind of solid faith;
23) One is well possessed of a sense of shame and a dread of blame;
24) One does not covet offerings;
25) One remains free of jealousy toward others;
26) One abides in the meritorious qualities associated with practicing the *dhūta* austerities;
27) One abides in the subtleties of Dharma practice;
28) One takes no delight in speaking the coarse language of the world;

正體字

二十九遠離聚語。三
087a27 ‖ 十知報恩。三十一知作恩報恩[4]者。三十二
087a28 ‖ 於和[5]上阿闍梨所[6]生恭敬忌難心。三十三
087a29 ‖ 破除憍慢。三十四降伏我心。三十五善知識
087b01 ‖ 難遇故勤心供給。三十六所從聞是法處。
087b02 ‖ 若得經卷若口誦處。於此人所生父母想
087b03 ‖ 善知識想大師想大慚愧愛敬想。三十七常
087b04 ‖ 樂阿練若。三十八不樂住城邑聚落。三十
087b05 ‖ 九不貪著檀越善知識家。四十不惜身命。
087b06 ‖ 四十一心常念死。四十二不存利養。四十
087b07 ‖ 三於諸物中心不染著。四十四無所渴愛。
087b08 ‖ 四十五守護正法。四十六不著衣鉢。四十
087b09 ‖ 七不畜遺餘。四十八但欲乞食。四十九次
087b10 ‖ 第乞食。五十常知慚愧心常有悔。五十一
087b11 ‖ 不畜金銀珍寶錢財。離諸不善悔。五十二
087b12 ‖ 心無纏垢。五十三常行慈心。

简体字

二十九远离聚语。三十知报恩。三十一知作恩报恩者。三十二于和上阿阇梨所生恭敬忌难心。三十三破除憍慢。三十四降伏我心。三十五善知识难遇故勤心供给。三十六所从闻是法处。若得经卷若口诵处。于此人所生父母想善知识想大师想大惭愧爱敬想。三十七常乐阿练若。三十八不乐住城邑聚落。三十九不贪着檀越善知识家。四十不惜身命。四十一心常念死。四十二不存利养。四十三于诸物中心不染着。四十四无所渴爱。四十五守护正法。四十六不着衣钵。四十七不畜遗余。四十八但欲乞食。四十九次第乞食。五十常知惭愧心常有悔。五十一不畜金银珍宝钱财。离诸不善悔。五十二心无缠垢。五十三常行慈心。

29) One avoids gathering in groups for [idle] conversation;
30) One knows to repay kindnesses one has received;
31) One acknowledges those who bestow kindnesses and those who repay kindnesses;
32) Toward one's monastic preceptors and monastic Dharma teachers, one brings forth thoughts of sincere reverence and appreciation for the rarity of being able to encounter them;[107]
33) One does away with any arrogance one might be harboring;
34) One overcomes the self-cherishing mind;
35) Because a good spiritual guide can only rarely be encountered, one strives with diligence to look after his needs;
36) With regard to the source from which one first learned about this Dharma, whether by obtaining a sutra text from someone or by hearing someone recite it, one thinks of them with the same regard as one would maintain for one's own father or mother, one's good spiritual guide, or a great teaching master, and with regard to them, one also feels a sense of shame, dread of blame, affection, and reverence;
37) One always delights in dwelling in a forest hermitage;
38) One does not delight in dwelling in a city or village;
39) One does not covet the opportunity to frequent the homes of benefactors[108] and good spiritual friends;
40) One does not maintain a stinting covetousness for one's own physical survival;
41) One remains ever mindful of death;
42) One does not hoard offerings;
43) One does not indulge any defiling attachment for possessions.
44) One remains free of cravings;
45) One guards and preserves right Dharma;
46) One is not attached to one's robes or bowl;
47) One does not hoard leftover things;
48) One prefers to eat only food that has been obtained on the alms round;
49) On the alms round, one moves along seeking alms according to the proper sequence;[109]
50) One always maintains a sense of shame and dread of blame and always feels remorse [for one's past transgressions];
51) One refrains from hoarding gold, silver, precious jewels, or money and also avoids indulging in unwholesome remorsefulness;[110]
52) One's mind remains free of entangling defilements;
53) One always puts the mind of kindness into practice;

正體字

五十四除斷
087b13 ‖ 瞋恚。五十五常行悲心。五十六除斷愛著。
087b14 ‖ 五十七常求利安一切世間。五十八常憐愍
087b15 ‖ 一切眾生。五十九常樂經行。六十除却睡
087b16 ‖ 眠。出家菩薩住如是等法中。應修習是三
087b17 ‖ 昧。復次。
087b18 ‖ 餘修三昧法　　亦應如是學
087b19 ‖ 能生是般舟三昧。餘助法亦應修習。何等
087b20 ‖ 是。一緣佛恩常[7]念在前。二不令心散亂。
087b21 ‖ 三繫心在前。四守護根門。五飲食知止足。
087b22 ‖ 六初夜後夜常修三昧。七離諸煩惱障。八
087b23 ‖ 生諸禪定。九禪中不[8]受味。十散壞色相。
087b24 ‖ 十一得不淨相。十二不貪五陰。十三不著
087b25 ‖ 十八界。十四不染十二入。十五不恃族姓。
087b26 ‖ 十六破憍慢。十七於一切法心常空寂。

简体字

五十四除断嗔恚。五十五常行悲心。五十六除断爱着。五十七常求利安一切世间。五十八常怜愍一切众生。五十九常乐经行。六十除却睡眠。出家菩萨住如是等法中。应修习是三昧。复次。

余修三昧法　　亦应如是学

能生是般舟三昧。余助法亦应修习。何等是。一缘佛恩常念在前。二不令心散乱。三系心在前。四守护根门。五饮食知止足。六初夜后夜常修三昧。七离诸烦恼障。八生诸禅定。九禅中不受味。十散坏色相。十一得不净相。十二不贪五阴。十三不着十八界。十四不染十二入。十五不恃族姓。十六破憍慢。十七于一切法心常空寂。

54) One cuts off all feelings of anger;
55) One always puts the mind of compassion into practice;
56) One cuts off affectionate attachments;
57) One always seeks ways to benefit and bring peace to the entire world;
58) One always feels pity for all beings;
59) One always delights in [meditative] walking;
60) One does away with lethargy and sleepiness.

The monastic bodhisattva who abides in dharmas such as these should cultivate and practice this samādhi. Additionally:

3. Fifty Dharmas Supporting Cultivation of This Samādhi

One should also train in this same manner
in the other dharmas pertaining to the cultivation of samādhi.

In order to be able to bring forth this *pratyutpanna* samādhi, one should also cultivate the other supportive dharmas. And what are these? They are:

1) One takes the Buddha's kindness as one's objective focus and always mindfully contemplates him as if he were directly before one;
2) One does not allow one's mind to become scattered;
3) One anchors one's attention directly before one;
4) One guards the gates of the sense faculties;
5) With respect to food and drink, one is easily satisfied;
6) One always cultivates samādhi in both the first and last watches of the night;
7) One abandons the obstacle of the afflictions;
8) One brings forth all of the *dhyāna* absorptions;
9) In one's practice of *dhyāna* meditation, one does not indulge in the delectably pleasurable meditation states;
10) One demolishes through separation the appearance of attractive forms;[111]
11) One acquires the sign of unloveliness;[112]
12) One does not desire the five aggregates;
13) One does not become attached to the eighteen sense realms;
14) One does not indulge any defilement in relation to the twelve sense bases;
15) One does not presumptuously rely on one's [superior] caste origins;
16) One destroys any arrogance;
17) One's mind always remains empty and quiescent in relation to all dharmas that one encounters;

正體字

十
087b27 ‖ 八於諸眾生生親族想。十九不取戒。二十
087b28 ‖ 不分別定。二十一應勤多學。二十二以是
087b29 ‖ 多學而不憍慢。二十三於諸法無疑。二十
087c01 ‖ 四不違諸佛。二十五不逆法。二十六不壞
087c02 ‖ 僧。二十七常詣諸賢聖。二十八遠離凡夫。
087c03 ‖ 二十九樂出世間論。三十修六和敬法。三十
087c04 ‖ 一常修習五解脫處。三十二除九瞋惱事。三
087c05 ‖ 十三斷八懈怠法。三十四修八精進。三十五
087c06 ‖ 常觀九[9]相。三十六得大人八覺。三十七具
087c07 ‖ 足諸禪定三昧。三十八於此禪定無所貪
087c08 ‖ 無所得。三十九聽法專心。四十壞五陰
087c09 ‖ [*]相。四十一不住事[*]相。四十二深怖畏生
087c10 ‖ 死。四十三於五陰生怨賊想。四十四於諸
087c11 ‖ 入中。生空聚想。四十五於四大中生毒蛇
087c12 ‖ 想。四十六於涅槃中生寂滅想安隱樂想。
087c13 ‖ 四十七於五欲中生涎唾想。心樂出離。

简体字

十八于诸众生生亲族想。十九不取戒。二十不分别定。二十一应勤多学。二十二以是多学而不憍慢。二十三于诸法无疑。二十四不违诸佛。二十五不逆法。二十六不坏僧。二十七常诣诸贤圣。二十八远离凡夫。二十九乐出世间论。三十修六和敬法。三十一常修习五解脱处。三十二除九嗔恼事。三十三断八懈怠法。三十四修八精进。三十五常观九相。三十六得大人八觉。三十七具足诸禅定三昧。三十八于此禅定无所贪无所得。三十九听法专心。四十坏五阴相。四十一不住事相。四十二深怖畏生死。四十三于五阴生怨贼想。四十四于诸入中。生空聚想。四十五于四大中生毒蛇想。四十六于涅槃中生寂灭想安隐乐想。四十七于五欲中生涎唾想。心乐出离。

18) One imagines all beings as one's close relatives;
19) One does not seize on the moral precepts themselves [as constituting the very essence of moral virtue];
20) One does not make discriminating distinctions regarding the meditative absorptions;
21) One should diligently pursue abundant learning;
22) One does not become arrogant because of this abundant learning;
23) One remains free of doubts with respect to any of the dharmas.
24) One does not oppose the Buddhas;
25) One does not act in a manner that is contrary to the Dharma;
26) One does not do anything that contributes to the destruction of the Sangha;
27) One always goes to pay one's respects to worthies and *āryas;*
28) One distances oneself from foolish common people;
29) One delights in discussion of world-transcending topics;
30) One cultivates the six dharmas of mutual harmony;[113]
31) One always cultivates the five bases of liberation;[114]
32) One rids himself of the nine bases for generating the affliction of anger;[115]
33) One cuts off the eight dharmas associated with indolence;[116]
34) One cultivates the eight types of vigor;[117]
35) One always contemplates the nine signs [of the deterioration of the corpse];[118]
36) One has realized for himself the eight realizations of great men;[119]
37) One perfects all of the *dhyāna* concentrations and samādhis;
38) One has no covetous attachment to these *dhyāna* concentrations and realizes they have no apprehensible reality;[120]
39) When listening to Dharma, one does so with a focused mind;
40) One demolishes the perception of the five aggregates [as inherently existent phenomena];
41) One does not abide in the perception of phenomena [as inherently existent];
42) One is deeply fearful of *saṃsāra*'s births and deaths;
43) One contemplates the five aggregates as like enemies;[121]
44) One contemplates the sense bases as like an empty village;
45) One contemplates the four great elements as like venomous serpents;
46) One brings forth the contemplation of nirvāṇa as quiescent, secure, and happy;[122]
47) One contemplates the five desires as worthy of being spat upon and one's mind delights in escaping from them;

正體字

四
087c14 ‖ 十八不違佛教。四十九於一切眾生無所
087c15 ‖ 諍訟。五十教化眾生令安住一切功德。復
087c16 ‖ 次。
087c17 ‖ 如是三昧報　　菩薩應當知
087c18 ‖ 菩薩行是般舟三昧。果報亦應知。問曰。修
087c19 ‖ 習是三昧得何果報。答曰。於無上道得不
087c20 ‖ 退轉報。復次如經所說果報。佛語[10]颰陀婆
087c21 ‖ 羅菩薩。譬如有人能摧[11]碎三千世界地皆
087c22 ‖ 如微塵。又三千大千世界中所有草木花葉
087c23 ‖ 一切諸物皆為微塵。颰陀婆羅。以一微塵
087c24 ‖ 為一佛世界。有爾所世界皆滿中上妙珍
087c25 ‖ 寶以用布施。跋陀婆羅於意云何。是人以
087c26 ‖ 是布施因緣得福多不。甚多世尊。佛言。颰
087c27 ‖ 陀婆羅。我今實語汝。若有善男子。得聞諸
087c28 ‖ 佛現前三昧。不驚不畏其福無量。何況信受
087c29 ‖ 持讀[12]諷誦為人解說。何況定心修習。如一
088a01 ‖ [1]搆牛乳頃。颰陀婆羅。我說此人福德尚無
088a02 ‖ 有量。何況能得成是三昧者。

简体字

四十八不违佛教。四十九于一切众生无所诤讼。五十教化众生令安住一切功德。复次。

如是三昧报　　菩萨应当知

菩萨行是般舟三昧。果报亦应知。问曰。修习是三昧得何果报。答曰。于无上道得不退转报。复次如经所说果报。佛语颰陀婆罗菩萨。譬如有人能摧碎三千世界地皆如微尘。又三千大千世界中所有草木花叶一切诸物皆为微尘。颰陀婆罗。以一微尘为一佛世界。有尔所世界皆满中上妙珍宝以用布施。跋陀婆罗于意云何。是人以是布施因缘得福多不。甚多世尊。佛言。颰陀婆罗。我今实语汝。若有善男子。得闻诸佛现前三昧。不惊不畏其福无量。何况信受持读讽诵为人解说。何况定心修习。如一构牛乳顷。颰陀婆罗。我说此人福德尚无有量。何况能得成是三昧者。

48) One never opposes the teachings of the Buddha;
49) One has no disputes or quarrels with any other being;
50) In teaching beings, one influences them to dwell securely in all of the meritorious qualities.

K. The Benefits of Cultivating This Pratyutpanna Samādhi

In addition:

> The bodhisattva should understand
> the benefits that result from such a samādhi.

The bodhisattva should also understand the benefits that result from practicing this *pratyutpanna* samādhi.

Question: What are the resulting benefits gained by cultivating this samādhi?

Response: One obtains the resulting benefit of becoming irreversible with respect to the unsurpassable path. Additionally, as for what the sutra says about these resulting benefits, we have the following:[123]

> The Buddha told Bhadrapāla Bodhisattva, "By way of analogy, suppose there was a person who was able to crush to dust all the earth in all worlds in a trichiliocosm and was also able also to crush to dust all the grasses, trees, flowers, leaves, and everything else throughout all of the worlds in a great trichiliocosm.
>
> "Bhadrapala, let us consider now that each and every one of those motes of dust were to constitute one world in which a single buddha dwells and suppose then that one filled to overflowing just such a number of worlds with sublimely marvelous precious jewels and presented all of these jewels as an offering to them.
>
> "Bhadrapāla, what do you think? By performing such an act of giving, would this person gain a great deal of merit or not?"
>
> "Indeed, O Bhagavat, he would reap a great deal."
>
> The Buddha said, "Bhadrapāla, I will now tell you truthfully that if there was a son of good family who heard of this samādhi in which all buddhas appear before one and he were then to be neither startled nor frightened by hearing of it, the merit he would reap from that alone would be immeasurably vast. How much the more so would this be the case if he were to have faith in it, accept it, uphold it, read [teachings in which it is explained], recite them, and explain them for others. How much the more so yet would this be the case if he were to actually cultivate it with concentrated mind even for the time it takes to tug a single squirt of milk from the udder of a cow.
>
> "Bhadrapāla, let me tell you: Even this person's merit would surpass one's ability to measure it. How much the more so would this be so in the case of someone who was actually able to succeed in acquiring this samādhi."

正體字

佛又告颰陀
088a03 ‖ 婆羅。若有善男子善女人。受持讀誦為他
088a04 ‖ 人說。若劫盡時設墮此火火即尋滅。颰陀
088a05 ‖ 婆羅。持是三昧者。若有官事。若遇怨賊師
088a06 ‖ 子虎狼惡獸惡龍諸毒虫等。若夜叉羅剎鳩
088a07 ‖ 槃[2]荼毘舍闍等。若人非人等。若害身若害
088a08 ‖ 命若毀戒。無有是處。若讀誦為人說時亦
088a09 ‖ 無衰惱。唯除業報必應受者。復次颰陀婆
088a10 ‖ 羅。菩薩受持讀誦是三昧時。若得眼耳鼻
088a11 ‖ 舌口齒病風寒冷病如是等種種餘病。以是
088a12 ‖ 病故而失壽命無有是處唯除業報必應
088a13 ‖ 受者。復次颰陀婆羅。若人受持讀誦是三
088a14 ‖ 昧者。諸天守護諸龍夜叉摩睺羅伽人非人
088a15 ‖ 四天王帝釋梵天王諸佛世尊皆共護念。復
088a16 ‖ 次是人皆為諸天所共愛念乃至諸佛皆共
088a17 ‖ 愛念。復次是人皆為諸天所共稱讚乃至諸
088a18 ‖ 佛皆共稱讚。復次諸天皆欲見是菩薩來
088a19 ‖ 至其所。乃至諸佛皆欲見是菩薩來至其
088a20 ‖ 所。

简体字

佛又告颰陀婆罗。若有善男子善女人。受持读诵为他人说。若劫尽时设堕此火火即寻灭。颰陀婆罗。持是三昧者。若有官事。若遇怨贼师子虎狼恶兽恶龙诸毒虫等。若夜叉罗刹鸠槃荼毗舍阇等。若人非人等。若害身若害命若毁戒。无有是处。若读诵为人说时亦无衰恼。唯除业报必应受者。复次颰陀婆罗。菩萨受持读诵是三昧时。若得眼耳鼻舌口齿病风寒冷病如是等种种余病。以是病故而失寿命无有是处唯除业报必应受者。复次颰陀婆罗。若人受持读诵是三昧者。诸天守护诸龙夜叉摩睺罗伽人非人四天王帝释梵天王诸佛世尊皆共护念。复次是人皆为诸天所共爱念乃至诸佛皆共爱念。复次是人皆为诸天所共称赞乃至诸佛皆共称赞。复次诸天皆欲见是菩萨来至其所。乃至诸佛皆欲见是菩萨来至其所。

The Buddha continued, telling Bhadrapāla, "If a son or daughter of good family who receives, upholds, reads, recites, and explains [teachings on this samādhi] for others were on the verge of falling into the fires arising at the end of the kalpa, those fires would immediately become extinguished.

"Bhadrapāla, whosoever sustains this samādhi—supposing that he were to encounter some difficulty with officialdom, or supposing that he were to encounter hostile thieves, lions, tigers, wolves, fearsome beasts, fearsome dragons, any of the venomous serpents, or any other such threat, whether from *yakṣas, rākṣasas, kumbhāṇḍas, piśācis,* and such, or from humans, non-humans, or any other sort of entity—that any of those entities might succeed in physically harming him, taking his life, or causing him to break the precepts—this would be an utter impossibility.

So too would this also be the case with respect to those who might be reading, reciting, or teaching this to others. In those cases too they would remain free of any destructive affliction, with the sole exception of instances where they were already bound to undergo compulsory karmic retributions.[124]

"Furthermore, Bhadrapala, when a bodhisattva accepts, upholds, reads, or recites the sutra on this samādhi, if he happens to contract some sickness of the eye, ear, nose, tongue, mouth, or teeth, some disease instigated by wind or cold, or any other such disease, that he might then lose his life because of any of these diseases would be an utter impossibility with the sole exception of instances where he was already bound to undergo compulsory karmic retributions.

"Also, Bhadrapāla, if a person were to accept, uphold, read, or recite the sutra on this samādhi, the devas themselves would protect him. So too would he be protected by the dragons, *yakṣas, mahoragas,* humans, non-humans, the Four Heavenly Kings, Śakra, ruler of the devas, the Brahma Heaven King, and the Buddhas, the Bhagavats. They would all join in remaining protectively mindful of this practitioner.

"Furthermore, this person would be one of whom the devas would all be affectionately mindful, and so too would this be so for other such beings up to and including the Buddhas themselves who would also remain affectionately mindful of this practitioner.

"Additionally, this person would be one whom the devas praise, and so too, he would be one whom other beings up to and including all buddhas would praise as well.

"Also, this bodhisattva would be one whom the devas would all wish to see coming to visit them, and so too with the others on up to the Buddhas themselves who would all wish to see him coming to visit them.

正體字

復次是菩薩受持是三昧者。所未聞經
088a21 ‖ 自然得[3]聞。復次是菩薩得是三昧者。乃至
088a22 ‖ 夢中皆得如是諸利益事。颰陀婆羅。菩薩若
088a23 ‖ 我一劫若減一劫。說受持讀誦是三昧者
088a24 ‖ 功德不可得盡。何況得成就者。颰陀婆羅。
088a25 ‖ 如人於百歲中身力輕健其疾如風。是人百
088a26 ‖ 歲行不休息。常至東方南西北方四維上下。
088a27 ‖ 於汝意云何。是人所詣十方有人能數知
088a28 ‖ 里數不。颰陀婆羅言。不可數[4]也。唯除
088a29 ‖ 如來舍利弗阿惟越致餘不能知。颰陀婆
088b01 ‖ 羅。若有善男子善女人以是人所行處滿中
088b02 ‖ 真金布施。若有人但聞是三昧。以四種隨
088b03 ‖ 喜迴向阿耨多羅三藐三菩提。常求多聞。
088b04 ‖ 如過去諸佛行菩[5]薩道時隨喜是三昧。我
088b05 ‖ 亦如是。如今現在菩薩隨喜是三昧。我亦
088b06 ‖ 如是。如未來諸佛行菩薩道時隨喜是三
088b07 ‖ 昧。我亦如是。如過去未來現在菩薩所行
088b08 ‖ 三昧。我亦隨喜皆為得多聞。我亦如是求
088b09 ‖ 多聞故。隨喜是三昧。颰陀婆羅。是[6]隨喜
088b10 ‖ 福德。於上福德百分不及一。百千萬億分
088b11 ‖ 不及一。

简体字

复次是菩萨受持是三昧者。所未闻经自然得闻。复次是菩萨得是三昧者。乃至梦中皆得如是诸利益事。颰陀婆罗。菩萨若我一劫若减一劫。说受持读诵是三昧者功德不可得尽。何况得成就者。颰陀婆罗。如人于百岁中身力轻健其疾如风。是人百岁行不休息。常至东方南西北方四维上下。于汝意云何。是人所诣十方有人能数知里数不。颰陀婆罗言。不可数也。唯除如来舍利弗阿惟越致余不能知。颰陀婆罗。若有善男子善女人以是人所行处满中真金布施。若有人但闻是三昧。以四种随喜回向阿耨多罗三藐三菩提。常求多闻。如过去诸佛行菩萨道时随喜是三昧。我亦如是。如今现在菩萨随喜是三昧。我亦如是。如未来诸佛行菩萨道时随喜是三昧。我亦如是。如过去未来现在菩萨所行三昧。我亦随喜皆为得多闻。我亦如是求多闻故。随喜是三昧。颰陀婆罗。是随喜福德。于上福德百分不及一。百千万亿分不及一。

"Furthermore, the bodhisattva who accepts and upholds the sutra on this samādhi will naturally become able to hear whichever other sutras he has not yet heard.

"Additionally, this bodhisattva who gains this samādhi will become able to acquire all of these beneficial experiences even in his dreams.

"Bhadrapāla, were I to attempt to describe the merit of this bodhisattva who accepts, uphold, reads, and recites the sutra on this samādhi, doing so even for an entire kalpa or somewhat less than a kalpa, I would still be unable to come to the end of it. How much the less would this be possible in the case of someone who actually succeeds in perfecting this samādhi.

"Bhadrapāla, if some man with strong body and speed like the wind ran for a hundred years without resting, always proceeding to the east, south, west, north, the four midpoints, above, and below, what do you think? Would anyone be able to know the number of miles he traveled in all those regions throughout the ten directions?"

Bhadrapāla replied, "That would be an incalculable number. Except for the Tathāgata, someone like Śāriputra, or an *avaivartika* [bodhisattva], nobody would be able to know such a number."

"Bhadrapāla, suppose that, on the one hand, there was a son or daughter of good family who filled up with real gold all the area traveled by that man and then give it all away as gifts. Suppose too that, on the other hand, there was someone who merely heard of this samādhi and then engaged in four types of rejoicing and dedication of merit to *anuttarasamyaksaṃbodhi* and the constant pursuit of abundant learning, [doing so by reflecting as follows]:

> Just as all buddhas of the past when practicing the bodhisattva path rejoiced in this samādhi, so too do I now rejoice in it;
>
> Just as the bodhisattvas of the present now rejoice in this samādhi, so too do I now rejoice in it;
>
> Just as all future buddhas during their practice of the bodhisattva path shall rejoice in this samādhi, so too do I now rejoice in it;
>
> And in just that fashion as this samādhi was practiced by all past, future, and present bodhisattvas, so too do I now also rejoice in all of that, and just as they all did so for the sake of pursuing abundant learning [essential to the path], so too do I now rejoice in this samādhi for the sake of the quest for such abundant learning.

"Bhadrapāla, if one were to attempt to compare the previously described merit with the merit from this rejoicing, it could not approach a hundredth part or even one part in a hundred thousand

正體字

乃至算數譬喻所不能及。是三昧
088b12 ‖ 得如是無量無邊果報。復次。
088b13 ‖ 是三昧住處　　少中多差別
088b14 ‖ 如是種種相　　皆當須論[7]義
088b15 ‖ 是三昧所住處。少相中相多相。如是等應分
088b16 ‖ 別。知是事應當解釋。住處者。是三昧或於
088b17 ‖ 初禪可得。或第二禪或第三禪或第四禪可
088b18 ‖ 得。或初禪中間得勢力。能生是三昧。或少
088b19 ‖ 者人勢力少故名為少。又少時住故名為
088b20 ‖ 少。又見少佛世界故。名為少。中多亦如
088b21 ‖ 是。說是三昧或說有覺有觀。或無覺有
088b22 ‖ 觀。或無覺無觀。或喜相應。或樂相應。或不
088b23 ‖ 苦不樂相應。或有入出息。或無入出息。或
088b24 ‖ 定是善性。或有漏。或無漏。

简体字

乃至算数譬喻所不能及。是三昧得如是无量无边果报。复次。

是三昧住处　　少中多差别
如是种种相　　皆当须论义

是三昧所住处。少相中相多相。如是等应分别。知是事应当解释。住处者。是三昧或于初禅可得。或第二禅或第三禅或第四禅可得。或初禅中间得势力。能生是三昧。或少者人势力少故名为少。又少时住故名为少。又见少佛世界故。名为少。中多亦如是。说是三昧或说有觉有观。或无觉有观。或无觉无观。或喜相应。或乐相应。或不苦不乐相应。或有入出息。或无入出息。或定是善性。或有漏。或无漏。

myriads of *koṭis* of parts. The futility of this comparison simply could not be adequately described through any form of calculation or analogy. The benefits resulting from this samādhi are just so immeasurable and boundless as this."

L. This Samādhi's Various Stations and Levels of Cultivation

In addition:

> As for the stations in which one may abide in this samādhi
> as well as the distinctions pertaining to lesser, middling, and greater,
> the many different characteristics such as these
> should all be taken up for a discussion of their meaning.

The stations in which one may abide in this samādhi as well as its lesser, middling, and greater characteristics—all such things should be distinguished and known and these matters should then be explained.

Regarding "the stations in which one may abide in it," this samādhi may be acquired in the first *dhyāna*, the second *dhyāna*, the third *dhyāna*, or the fourth *dhyāna* and one may acquire strength in it while in the first *dhyāna*.

It may be that someone who is "lesser" is able to bring forth this samādhi. Here, "lesser" may refer to the fact that a person is possessed of only a lesser degree of strength [in this practice]. "Lesser" may also refer to abiding [in the samādhi] for a shorter period of time. "Lesser" may also refer to the practitioner's seeing a relatively smaller number of buddha worlds. Distinctions regarding "middling" and "greater" may be made in just the same way.

M. Various Qualitative Variations in How This Samādhi Manifests

In discussing this samādhi, one may speak of it as:

Sometimes involving the presence of ideation (*vitarka*) and the presence of discursion (*vicāra*);
Sometimes involving the absence of ideation and the presence of discursion;
Sometimes involving the absence of ideation and the absence of discursion;
Sometimes involving the presence of joy (*prīti*);
Sometimes involving the presence of bliss (*sukha*);
Sometimes involving neither suffering nor bliss;
Sometimes involving the presence of breathing;
Sometimes involving the absence of breathing;
Sometimes definitely being of a wholesome nature;
Sometimes involving the presence of the contaminants;
Sometimes involving the absence of the contaminants;

正體字

或欲界繫。或色界
088b25 ‖ 繫。或無色界繫。或非欲界。或非色界。或非無
088b26 ‖ 色界繫。是三昧是心數法。心相應。隨心行法。
088b27 ‖ 共心生法。非色。非現。能緣。非業。業相應。隨
088b28 ‖ 業行。非先世業果報。除因報。可修可知可證。
088b29 ‖ 亦以身證亦以慧證。或可斷或不可斷。有
088c01 ‖ 漏應斷。無漏不可斷。知見亦如是。不與
088c02 ‖ 七覺合。如是一切諸分別三昧義。皆應此
088c03 ‖ 中說。復次修習是三昧得見諸佛。如說。
088c04 ‖ 得見諸佛已　勤心而供養
088c05 ‖ 善根得增長　能疾化眾生
088c06 ‖ 供養名心意清淨。恭敬歡喜念佛有無量功
088c07 ‖ 德。以種種讚歎名[8]口供養。

简体字

或欲界系。或色界系。或无色界系。或非欲界。或非色界。或非无色界系。是三昧是心数法。心相应。随心行法。共心生法。非色。非现。能缘。非业。业相应。随业行。非先世业果报。除因报。可修可知可证。亦以身证亦以慧证。或可断或不可断。有漏应断。无漏不可断。知见亦如是。不与七觉合。如是一切诸分别三昧义。皆应此中说。复次修习是三昧得见诸佛。如说。

得见诸佛已　勤心而供养
善根得增长　能疾化众生

供养名心意清净。恭敬欢喜念佛有无量功德。以种种赞叹名口供养。

Sometimes connected with the desire realm;
Sometimes connected with the form realm;
Sometimes connected with the formless realm;
Sometimes not connected with the desire realm;
Sometimes not connected with the form realm;
And sometimes not connected with the formless realm.

N. Various Abhidharmic Classifications of This Samādhi

This samādhi;

Is a mental dharma;
Is [a dharma] associated with the mind;
Is a dharma that occurs along with the mind;
Is a non-form [dharma];
Is a non-manifest [dharma];
Is able to take an object;
Is not karma [*per se*];
Is associated with karmic activity;
Is coexistent with karmic activity;
Is not the result of karmic actions from a previous life except when it is the result of a particular cause;[125]
Can be cultivated, can be known, and can be realized;
Can be realized both with the body and by means of wisdom;
Can be subject to severance or may be invulnerable to severance;
Should be severed when contaminants are present;
And is invulnerable to severance when free of the contaminants.

Similar distinctions of this sort may also made with respect to the knowledge and vision associated with this samādhi. Also, it is not necessarily conjoined with the seven limbs of enlightenment.[126] Ideally, all of these distinctions should be discussed herein.

O. The Practitioner's Offerings, Roots of Goodness, and Teaching

Furthermore, it is through the cultivation of this samādhi that one may succeed in seeing the Buddhas. Accordingly, it is said that:

After one has succeeded in seeing the Buddhas,
one proceeds with diligent resolve to present offerings [to them].
As one's roots of goodness are thus able to grow,
one becomes able to rapidly teach beings.

"Making offerings" refers to having a pure mind imbued with reverence and delight as one brings to mind the countless meritorious qualities of the Buddha. When one praises him in various ways, this constitutes the making of verbal offerings. When one makes formal

正體字

敬禮華香等
088c08 ‖ 名身供養。是故福德轉更增長。如穀子在
088c09 ‖ 地雨潤生長。疾教化者令眾生住三乘中。
088c10 ‖ 如是菩薩增長善根。
088c11 ‖ 以初二攝法　　攝取諸眾生
088c12 ‖ 後餘二攝法　　未盡能信受
088c13 ‖ 初二者布施愛語。利益同事名為後二。是
088c14 ‖ 菩薩在初地。不能具解故。但能信受。
088c15 ‖ 爾時諸善根　　迴向於佛道
088c16 ‖ 如彼成[9]煉金　　調熟則堪用
088c17 ‖ 智慧火所[*]煉故。於菩薩所行事中。善根成
088c18 ‖ 熟則堪任用。

简体字

敬礼华香等名身供养。是故福德转更增长。如谷子在地雨润生长。疾教化者令众生住三乘中。如是菩萨增长善根。

以初二摄法　　摄取诸众生
后余二摄法　　未尽能信受

初二者布施爱语。利益同事名为后二。是菩萨在初地。不能具解故。但能信受。

尔时诸善根　　回向于佛道
如彼成炼金　　调熟则堪用

智慧火所炼故。于菩萨所行事中。善根成熟则堪任用。

reverential bows and presents flowers, incenses, and other such things, this constitutes the making of physical offerings.

Because of these actions, one's karmic merit grows ever greater just as a seed starts to grow when it is planted in earth and receives moisture from the rain. "Rapidly teaching" refers to influencing beings to abide in the Three Vehicles. It is in this way that the bodhisattva brings about the growth of his roots of goodness.

P. The Practitioner's Use of the Four Means of Attraction

Through availing oneself of the first two dharmas of attraction,
one is able to attract beings [to the Dharma].
One resorts to the latter two dharmas of attraction
for those not yet fully able to believe and accept [Dharma teachings].

"The first two" refers to "giving" and to "pleasing words" whereas "beneficial actions" and "joint endeavors" constitute "the latter two dharmas" [of the four means of attraction]. Because this bodhisattva who abides on the first ground is as yet unable to completely comprehend everything, [there may be certain aspects of the teaching] that he can only accept on faith.

Q. The Practitioner's Dedication of Roots of Goodness

He then takes all of his roots of goodness
and dedicates them to the realization of buddhahood.
This is comparable to when others smelt gold
and then refine it, whereupon it thereby becomes amenable to use.

It is through being smelted by the fire of wisdom that, in all the endeavors undertaken by the bodhisattva, his roots of goodness ripen and then finally become amenable to use.

The End of Chapter Twenty-Five

Part Two Endnotes

1. Although the arrangement of the *Taisho* text does not make this clear, it is obvious that these first four five-character phrases form a quatrain upon which the following paragraph comments. Hence I have formatted the text accordingly.
2. This most likely refers to "The Pratyutpanna Samādhi Sūtra" preserved in the *Taisho* Canon as the *Banzhou Sanmei Jing* (般舟三昧經 / T13.no. 0418.902c23–919c05). Paul Harrison has produced a translation of this text for the BDK English Tripitaka.
3. I emend the reading of the text here (but still keep the emendation in brackets since there are no supporting variants in any of the other editions), this to correct an obvious scribal error wherein the name of the third of these "four bases of meritorious qualities" is missing from this sentence. The missing "basis" here is *mie* (滅), "quiescence" (*upaśamādhiṣṭhāna*).
4. These four bases of meritorious qualities (四功德處: 諦, 捨, 滅, 慧; *satyādhiṣṭhāna, tyāgādhiṣṭhāna, upaśamādhiṣṭhāna, prajñādhiṣṭhāna;* truth, relinquishment [generosity], quiescence, and wisdom) are brought up repeatedly in this and other Nāgārjunian treatises, sometimes in slightly varying order and sometimes, as in the present case, with the Chinese translation using slightly variant terminological choices for one of the four list components.
5. "Arms appearing like golden gate bars" is a rather obscure simile that I have never encountered. The SYMG editions have *chan* (鋋) which would be the equally obscure "like golden spears."
6. To correct an apparent graphic-similarity scribal error, I emend the reading of the *Taisho* text here by preferring the SYMG editions' *sheng* (生), "growth," to the *Taisho* edition's *zhu* (主), "ruler."
7. The "reply that sets aside the question" is one of polite refusal to provide an answer, not because the answer is not known, but because the question involves a false premise making the query absurd on the face of it, because providing the answer would only promote endless frivolous and fruitless speculation on the part of the questioner (as with the fourteen imponderables), or because providing an answer would in no way serve the goal of spiritual liberation.
8. More specifically, the component lists comprising the thirty-seven wings of enlightenment are: the five faculties, the five powers, the seven limbs of bodhi, the eight-fold path, the four stations of mindfulness, the four right efforts, and the four foundations of psychic power.

9. "Foes" refers here to the three poisons, i.e. the afflictions. An arhat has completely destroyed them. VB points out that this pronouncement references the word play in the word *"arahant"* where it is explained that they are those who are enemy (*ari*) destroyers (*hanta*).
10. Perhaps due to corruption of the manuscript at some point in its long history, the following list contains only 74 of the 80 secondary characteristics.
11. The *saṃkakṣikā* is the monastic's robe that is worn over the left shoulder and under the right arm.
12. The *nivāsana* is the monastic's skirt-like inner robe.
13. The *saṃghāṭī* is the monastic's outer robe.
14. "Eight kinds of *āryas*" usually refers to those eminences who reside at the four candidate stages and the four realization stages on the Śrāvaka Vehicle path. The first is candidate for stream-entry and the eighth is the fully realized arhat.
15. *Garuḍa* birds prey on young dragons, hence the mention that, at least when attending Dharma teachings by buddhas, they manage to remain uncharacteristically free of any mutual hostility.
16. Although the *Taisho* text has *xiang* (相), "appearance," here it is as an often-encountered and more-or-less standard short-form abbreviation for *xiang* (想), "thought."
17. VB notes that this is a stock description of the Buddha's teaching of the Dharma as found in the *suttas* of the Nikāyas, as for example: *"ādikalyāṇaṃ majjhe kalyāṇaṃ pariyosāne kalyāṇaṃ sātthaṃ sabyañjanaṃ,* etc.," and *"sandiṭṭhiko akālika ehipassiko opanayako paccattaṃ veditabbo viññūhi."*
18. KJ transliterated rather than translated these fruits of the path (*srota-āpanna, sakṛdāgāmin, anāgamin*) that, with the exception of *"arhat,"* I have elected to translate.
19. The emendation proposed by the 2009 edition of CBETA ([和>知]) involving a supposed graphic-similarity scribal error is itself erroneous and irrelevant. This verse simply restates an idea clearly articulated late in Chapter 18: "Through not allowing estrangement to occur among other beings or among one's relatives, and through being able to cause those who have become estranged to be reunited, one acquires the mark of male genital ensheathment. Due to having [planted the karmic causes that result in] this mark, one acquires many disciples." See 65b18-20: 能善調人不令眾生親里遠離。若有乖離還令和合故得陰藏相。有是相故多得弟子。
20. "Genital ensheathment" of course also associates with transcendence of sensual desire and, as an incidental implication, that there

may therefore be no biological sons via which the patrilineal lineage might continue on.

Here, the metaphoric interpretation points out that it is the pure wisdom eye (pure by virtue of an absence of attachments) that leads to the continuance of the lineage of the Buddhas, this because it is a buddha's wise teachings flowing from his possession of the wisdom eye that beget "the sons of the Buddha," i.e. the bodhisattvas who will themselves become the buddhas of the future who carry on his Dharma lineage.

21. These are eight voice qualities possessed only by the Buddhas: 1) Extremely fine; 2) Gentle; 3) Appropriate; 4) Possessed of venerable wisdom; 5) Non-feminine; 6) Unmistaken; 7) Deep and far-reaching; and 8) Inexhaustible. These are discussed at length in Section 59 of "A Sequential Explanation of the Initial Gateway into the Dharma Realm" (法界次第初門 / T46n1925_p0697a15–b20) composed by the famous meditation master and immensely prolific Tiantai hermeneutic school exegete Zhiyi (沙門釋智顗, a.k.a. 陳隋國師智者大師).

22. Because the received text's listing of these 40 exclusive dharmas presents them in a somewhat different order than occurs as they are actually presented and discussed in the text, I reorder and renumber them here to follow the actual order of their presentation. I do so based on the usually factual assumption that the section titles and preliminary lists in translations of Sanskrit texts are for the most part *not* part of the original text, but rather are added by the Sanskrit-to-Chinese translator to assist the reader, or, in this case, perhaps by the editors and scribes in Kumārajīva's translation bureau. For those interested in the erroneously ordered and numbered list found here in the received text, it is as follows:

    1) Sovereign mastery of the ability to fly;
    2) [The ability to manifest] countless transformations;
    3) Boundless psychic powers of the sort possessed by *āryas*;
    4) Sovereign mastery of the ability to hear sounds;
    5) Immeasurable power of knowledge to know others' thoughts;
    6) Sovereign mastery in [training and subduing] the mind;
    7) Constant abiding in stable wisdom;
    8) Never forgetting;
    9) Possession of the powers of the *vajra* samādhi;
    10) Thorough knowing of matters that are unfixed
    11) Thorough knowing of matters pertaining to the formless realm's meditative absorptions;
    12) The completely penetrating knowledge of all matters associated with eternal cessation;

13) Thorough knowing of the non-form dharmas unassociated with the mind;
14) The great powers *pāramitā;*
15) The [four] unimpeded [knowledges] *pāramitā;*
16) The *pāramitā* of perfectly complete replies and predictions in response to questions;
17) Perfectly complete implementation of the three turnings in speaking Dharma;
18) Their words are never spoken without a purpose;
19) Their speech is free of error;
20) Invulnerability to harm by anyone;
21) They are the great generals among all *āryas;*
22–25) They are able to remain unguarded in four ways;
26–29) They possess the four fearlessnesses;
30–39) They possess the ten powers;
40) They possess the unimpeded liberations.

23. VB notes: "This is a category in Sarvāstivāda Abhidharma (not in the Theravāda Abhidharma), which indicates the author is familiar with the Sarvāstivāda system."

24. "Without a purpose" here is literally "empty" (in the sense of "in vain" or "fruitlessly").

25. VB notes: "See Anguttara Nikaya 7:58. The four are: conduct of body, speech, and mind, and livelihood."

26. To correct an apparent graphic-similarity scribal error, I emend the reading of the *Taisho* text here by preferring the SYMG editions' *neng* (能), "able to," to the *Taisho* edition's *suo* (所), "that which."

27. VB notes: "See *Anguttara Nikaya,* Sevens, no. 40 (see, too, Sixes, no. 24):

    'Bhikkhus, possessing seven qualities, a bhikkhu exercises mastery over his mind and is not a servant of his mind. What seven? Here, (1) a bhikkhu is skilled in concentration; (2) skilled in the attainment of concentration; (3) skilled in the duration of concentration; (4) skilled in emergence from concentration; (5) skilled in fitness for concentration; (6) skilled in the range of concentration; and (7) skilled in resolution regarding concentration. Possessing these seven qualities, a bhikkhu exercises mastery over his mind, and is not a servant of his mind.'"

28. This appears to be yet another instance of KJ's use of *xing* (性), usually translated as "nature," as a translation for *dhātu* which is more ordinarily translated into Sino-Buddhist Classical Chinese as *jie* (界), "realm."

29. VB notes: "In the above [passage: '諸相諸觸諸覺諸念亦知起知住知生知滅'], 相 is clearly another instance of the confusion between 相 and 想

so common in Chinese texts. The Pali part parallel has *saññā*. See the end of Majjhima Nikāya 123, where the Buddha says he knows the arising, persistence, and passing away of *vedanā*, *saññā*, and *vitakka*."

30. In response to my earlier draft translation of *emo* (惡魔) here as "an evil demon," VB notes: Here there is no doubt that 惡魔 is none other than the infamous Māra, a particular individual, not just any "evil demon." See *Samyutta Nikāya* 4:24 "Seven Years of Pursuit":

    "On one occasion the Blessed One was dwelling at Uruvelā on the bank of the river Nerañjarā at the foot of the Goatherd's Banyan Tree. Now on that occasion Māra the Evil One had been following the Blessed One for seven years, seeking to gain access to him but without success....

    "Then Māra the Evil One, in the presence of the Blessed One, recited these verses of disappointment:

    "There was a crow that walked around
    A stone that looked like a lump of fat.
    'Let's find something tender here,' [he thought,]
    'Perhaps there's something nice and tasty.'

    But because he found nothing tasty there,
    The crow departed from that spot.
    Just like the crow that attacked the stone,
    We leave Gotama disappointed."

31. These five are: past dharmas, present dharmas, future dharmas, unconditioned dharmas (referred to below as "those that transcend the three periods of time"), and ineffable dharmas.

32. I emend the text here to correct an apparent graphic-similarity scribal error, preferring SYMG's *san* (三), "three," to the *Taisho* text's *er* (二), "two." The rationale for the emendation is evident in the paragraph's discussion of "three" dharmas that are "strung together," not merely "two."

33. I have made the same emendation here as in the immediately previous note.

34. VB notes that this incident involving the elephant named Nālagiri is described in the Vinaya, Cūlavagga, II 194 foll. of PTS Pali edition.

35. As described later in the text, "The twelve *dhūta* austerities" are:

    Adopting the dharma of dwelling in a forest hermitage;
    Obtaining one's food through the alms round;
    Wearing robes made of cast-off rags;
    [Taking one's daily meal in but] a single sitting;
    Always sitting to sleep, [never lying down];

Having taken the meal, not accepting food or drink at the wrong times;
Possessing only a single set of three robes;
Wearing only an animal-hair robe;
Laying out one's sitting mat wherever one happens to be;
Dwelling at the foot of a tree;
Dwelling out in the open (lit. "on empty ground");
Dwelling in a charnel field.

36. VB notes: "In the Pali these are laid out as parallel descriptive terms. The Pali actually has nine synonymous terms. See AN 1:174."

37. Based on VB's very sensible suggestion that "quiescent cessation" (寂滅) is probably here as elsewhere simply a somewhat opaque sounding sino-Buddhist translation of *"nirvāṇa,"* I have gone ahead and rendered it as such throughout this entire passage as well as in other places throughout the text where the context demands it.

38. I have been unable to find a Sanskrit antecedent for this Chinese transliteration of a type of rishi, a *"pisuo"* (脾娑) rishi. VB suggests that this may be a transliteration of *viśvarśi* (*viś ṛṣi*).

39. VB notes that one can find approximate Pali Canon parallels at MN 110.4, MLDB p. 892, and AN 3:3.

40. VB notes: "The story of Ciñcā the brahmin girl occurs in the Dhammapada Commentary, commenting on verse 176. See Burlingame, *Buddhist Legends* III 19 foll."

41. VB notes: "In the Pali Canon, this incident is referred to in Udāna Section 38."

42. VB notes: "The incident is at SN 4:18 (PTS ed. I 113–14)."

43. VB notes: "The story is in the Pāli Vinaya in Cullavagga, chapter 7; PTS ed II 194–96."

44. VB notes: "This [story] is at the beginning of the Pārājika chapter of the Vinaya."

45. VB notes: "His departure from the Sangha and denunciation of the Buddha are mentioned at the beginning of MN 12. MN 105 is spoken to him, and his arguments with the Buddha about arahants are at DN 23."

46. VB notes: "See AN 7:58: Four things that the Tathāgata does not have to guard: conduct of body, speech, and mind, and livelihood."

47. "The *upoṣadha* dharma" is a reference to spiritual purification, in particular the two days of the month when monastics recite the precepts and the days of the month in which pious lay people voluntarily take on a semi-monastic level of moral precept observance.

48. This is verse 183 of the *Dhammapada.*
49. The first four lines here correspond to *Dhammapada* 361.
50. This corresponds to verse 362 of the *Dhammapada.*
51. VB notes: "See AN 5:181 foll.: 'Bhikkhus, there are these five kinds of forest dwellers. What five? (1) One who becomes a forest dweller because of his dullness and stupidity; (2) one who becomes a forest dweller because he has evil desires, because he is driven by desire; (3) one who becomes a forest dweller because he is mad and mentally deranged; (4) one who becomes a forest dweller, [thinking]: "It is praised by the Buddhas and the Buddhas' disciples"; (5) and one who becomes a forest dweller for the sake of fewness of desires, for the sake of contentment, for the sake of eliminating [defilements], for the sake of solitude, for the sake of simplicity. The fifth is pronounced the best.'"
52. VB notes: "I think the author here is referring to the Buddha's hesitation, immediately after his enlightenment, about going out and teaching the Dharma. See MN 26.19, SN 6:1, etc."
53. VB notes: "This is at MN 26.22–23. Interestingly the author here takes a similar perspective on *sarvajñatā* as the Theravāda commentaries, that knowledge arises when the Buddha directs his attention to some issue (*āvajjanapaṭibaddhaṃ buddhassa bhagavato ñāṇaṃ*), in contrast to the later Mahāyāna view that the Buddha perpetually knows everything simultaneously."
54. The second part of the Chinese text's title, "Forty Dharmas Exclusive to Buddhas: The Exclusive Dharma of Thoroughly Knowing What is Unfixed," is misleading because "the exclusive dharma of thoroughly knowing what is unfixed" only describes the first few pages of this long chapter that in fact discusses all of the remaining exclusive dharmas (nos. 10–40). I have therefore dropped this misleading phrase from the chapter title. One should be aware that these chapter titles almost certainly do not originate with Nāgārjuna but rather with Kumārajīva's translation team.
55. VB notes: "The above corresponds to Majjhima Nikaya no. 136."
56. Commenting on the corresponding passages as preserved in the Pali canon, VB notes: "The Pāli sutta with the simile of the raft mentions all four fruits (MN 22; see the end). But the proposition about one of two fruits occurs in a number of other suttas, such as the Satipaṭṭhāna Sutta (see end of MN 10)."
57. Regarding this "*Ekottara Āgama*'s *Shejiali Sutra*" (舍迦梨經), I have so far been unable to locate the Sanskrit for its title.

58. VB comments: "The above corresponds to Anguttara Nikāya 10:217 (also 10:218). Note that there are three modes in which the karmic results may be received, both in Pāli and Chinese versions: in the present life (現受報), upon rebirth (that is, the next life; 生受), or in a subsequent life (after the next one; 後受). Here is the Pāli followed by my rendering:

 217. *"Nāhaṃ, bhikkhave, sañcetanikānaṃ kammānaṃ katānaṃ upacitānaṃ appaṭisaṃviditvā byantībhāvaṃ vadāmi. Tañca kho diṭṭheva dhamme upapajje vā apare vā pariyāye. Na tvevāhaṃ, bhikkhave, sañcetanikānaṃ kammānaṃ katānaṃ upacitānaṃ appaṭisaṃveditvā dukkhass'antakiriyaṃ vadāmi."*

 "Bhikkhus, I do not say that there is a termination of volitional kamma that has been done and accumulated so long as one has not experienced [its results], and that may be in this very life, or in the [next] rebirth, or on some subsequent occasion. But I do not say that there is making an end of suffering so long as one has not experienced [the results of] volitional kamma that has been done and accumulated."

59. Again, I have so far been unable to find the Sanskrit name for this transliterated title.

60. VB notes: "The Pāli parallel is *Majjhima* 58: *Abhayarājakumāra Sutta.*"

61. These "three groups" refers to the *tri-skandha* (三聚) as that term is used to categorize the karmic destinies of beings. Those who are "definitely deviant" or "erroneous" are definitely bound to be unsuccessful in reaching enlightenment whereas those who are "definitely righteous" or "correct" are definitely bound to succeed in becoming enlightened. In his Mppu, in commenting on a passage in the Great Perfection of Wisdom Sutra that brings up the topic of these three groups, N points out that it is the ability or inability to destroy the inverted views that is pivotal in determining one's position in this threefold categorization. It is those who may or may not encounter the karmic conditions enabling the destruction of these inverted views who are categorized as "indefinite." (See T25.n1509.647c27–648a01.)

62. These four "repositories of Dharma" (*dharma-piṭaka*) are identified by Nāgārjuna in his Mppu as: 1) the Sutra Piṭaka; 2) the Vinaya Piṭaka; 3) the Abhidharma Piṭaka; and 4) the Kṣudraka-piṭaka (T12; No. 1509; 143c23–25).

63. These are "delectable absorptions" (*āsvādana-samādhi*) which are characterized by the arising of extremely pleasurable meditation states to which the unskilled or unwise meditator is vulnerable to becoming attached.

64. VB notes: "The Pāli parallel is the opening passage of Dīgha Nikāya no. 14, almost verbatim the same."

65. I emend the reading of the *Taisho* text here by preferring on sensibility grounds the SYMG editions' *ci jing* (此經), "this sutra," to the *Taisho* edition's *jing ci* (經此), "sutra this."

    The sutra to which this text refers is obviously the Ten Grounds Sutra upon which Nāgārjuna's SZPPS comments. This topic of the expansiveness of the Buddha's knowledge and vision is treated at great length in the sutra itself.

66. VB notes: "The names of *pratyekabuddhas* are mentioned in MN 116. I would posit the following equivalents [for a few of the *pratyekabuddhas* mentioned here]:

    無垢 = Ariṭṭha
    華相 = Tagarasikhī
    喜見 = Piyadassī

67. VB notes: "Parallel to the above is AN 6:62 Section 6: (6) 'Then, Ānanda, having encompassed his mind with my own mind, I understand some person thus: "Wholesome qualities and unwholesome qualities are found in this person." On a later occasion, having encompassed his mind with my own mind, I understand him thus: "This person does not have even a mere fraction of a hair's tip of an unwholesome quality. This person possesses exclusively bright, blameless qualities. He will attain *nibbāna* in this very life."'"

68. VB notes: "[This passage is found] in MN 12."

69. VB notes: "The following passage comes toward the end of MN 12."

70. This long paragraph (beginning with "Supposing…") has the appearance of language quoted from a sutra. However, having failed to locate it, I frame it here as simply Nāgārjuna's amplification of the meaning of the immediately preceding passage that VB recognized as having a Pali analogue in MN 12.

71. This is the name as recorded in the Pali canon. I'm not sure about the Sanskrit for this name.

72. Ibid.

73. VB notes that the following passage is found in the beginning of MN 136.

74. Rāhula was the Buddha's son whereas Devadatta was someone intent on killing the Buddha.

75. VB suggest that this passage may be alluding to AN 4:111, "Kesi the Horse Trainer."

76. This refers to *satkāyadṛṣṭi*.

77. Again, although in these last two cases, the Chinese is literally "gain the path" (得道), per Hirakawa (p. 451, column 2) this corresponds to: *"bodhi, abhisaṃbuddha, saṃbodhi-prāpta."* Edgerton in turn suggests "becoming perfectly enlightened" for *abhisambuddhana* (Page 58, column 2).

78. Although *"brahmacarya"* (梵行) generally refers to celibate spiritual practice, it may just as well be thought of as "the holy life" or "the spiritual life. VB notes that this scriptural quote "is found in many places in the Nikāyas: e.g., beginning of MN 148: *"Bhagavā etadavoca – 'dhammaṃ vo, bhikkhave, desessāmi ādikalyāṇaṃ majjhe kalyāṇaṃ pariyosānakalyāṇaṃ sātthaṃ sabyañjanaṃ, kevalaparipuṇṇaṃ parisuddhaṃ brahmacariyaṃ pakāsessāmi.'"*

79. VB notes: "In the Pali suttas, the second wonder is being able to declare another person's thoughts. For the three wonders, see AN 3:60: "There are, brahmin, these three kinds of wonders. What three? The wonder of psychic potency, the wonder of mind-reading, and the wonder of instruction (*iddhipāṭihāriyaṃ ādesanāpāṭihāriyaṃ anusāsanīpāṭihāriyaṃ;* also at DN 11.3–8, I 212–14). The second is explained thus: There is one who ... declares: 'Your thought is thus, such is what you are thinking, your mind is in such and such a state.' And even if he makes many declarations, they are exactly so and not otherwise."

80. I have been unable to locate either the Sanskrit or Pali antecedents for the titles of these scriptures. VB also notes: "I'm not sure of the references here. Perhaps the former is the Potaliya Sutta, MN 54, but I'm not sure."

81. VB notes: "[The Pali canon analogue for] the following is at MN 12 and AN 4:8."

82. I emend the reading of the *Taisho* text here by preferring on sensibility grounds the SYMG editions' *wei wei* (微畏, "slightest fear," to the *Taisho* edition's *shi* (是), "this."

83. VB notes that the analogue passage in the Pali canon is found at DN no. 20.

84. VB notes: "See MN 115 and AN 1:277."

85. VB notes: "The above, too, is in MN 115 and AN 1:284 foll."

86. VB notes: "On this, see MN 45, 46."

87. VB notes: "This may be an allusion to AN 5:28."

88. VB notes: "This may be an allusion to AN 5:27."

89. This is a concept with numerous similar alternative explanations, most of which refer to the immense amount of merit and time required to acquire the thirty-two marks and eighty minor characteristics of a

buddha's body and finally achieve buddhahood. This is discussed in greater detail in Nāgārjuna's commentary on the Great Perfection of Wisdom Sutra. See T25.1509.57b05–27.

90. Nārāyaṇa is a powerful celestial eminence regarded as a Dharma protector in Buddhism.

91. As is quite common with the syntax of multi-line Classical Chinese verses, this quatrain has require the rearrangement of its lines to produce a sensible and naturally flowing statement in English.

92. "Eight classes in four pairs" (四雙八輩) refers to the four preliminary phases and four fruition stages on the individual-liberation path of the *śrāvaka* disciples.

93. VB notes: "見聞覺知 = Pāḷi *diṭṭhaṃ, sutaṃ, mutaṃ, viññātaṃ,* where mutaṃ is explained as things sensed through the other three sense faculties: smell, taste, and touch."

 Hence, in "seen, heard, sensed, and known," (per Hirakawa's BCSD: *dṛṣṭa-śruta-mata-jñāta* or *dṛṣṭa-śruta-mata-vijñāta*) "sensed" (*mata*) refers to the sensory function of the olfactory, gustatory, and tactile sense faculties. Therefore this series is intended to refer to the functions of all six sense faculties and their corresponding consciousnesses.

94. To correct an apparent scribal error very likely originating in homophony, I emend the reading of the text here, preferring on sensibility grounds the homophonous *de* (得), "achieved" of the SYMG editions to the *Taisho* text's *de* (德), "qualities."

95. "Five characteristics" here is slightly ambiguous. It could refer particularly to the five types of desire which together constitute the first of the five hindrances (visible forms, sounds, smells, tastes, and touchables, or wealth, sex, fame, food, and leisure). Alternatively, it may be intended to refer to all five of the "five hindrances" that must be eliminated to access deep states of meditation (desire, ill will, lethargy-and-sleepiness, excitedness-and-regretfulness, and afflicted doubtfulness).

96. To correct an apparent graphic-similarity scribal error, I emend the reading of the *Taisho* text here by preferring the SYMG editions' *li* (力), "power," to the *Taisho* edition's *fen* (分), "portion."

97. I am not sure precisely what Nāgārjuna intended by "the six categories of meanings associated with the forty exclusive Dharmas," set forth in his preceding praise verses.

98. The Sanskrit antecedent of *shixiang* (實相) in KJ translations is usually *dharmatā,* i.e. the true nature of all dharmas, i.e. *śūnyatā,* i.e. the utter absence of inherent existence in any and all phenomena.

99. To correct an apparent graphic-similarity scribal error, I emend the reading of the *Taisho* text here by preferring the SYMG editions' *shen* (深), "deep" or "profound," to the *Taisho* edition's *ran* (染), "defiled." Nāgārjuna's discussion of this line corroborates the correctness of the emendation.

100. When translated into Chinese, "Tathāgata" means "Thus Come One."

101. Again, this most likely refers to "The Pratyutpanna Samādhi Sūtra" preserved in the *Taisho* Canon as the *Banzhou Sanmei Jing* (般舟三昧經 / T13.no. 0418.902c23–919c05).

102. "Overweening pride," *zeng shang man* (增上慢), corresponds to the Sanskrit *adhimāna.*

103. To correct an obvious graphic-similarity scribal error, I emend the reading of the *Taisho* text here by preferring the SYMG editions' *zeng* (增), "increase," to the *Taisho* edition's *zeng* (憎), "detest."

104. "Characteristic sign" refers here to any of the signs associated with three sequential levels of practice described at the very beginning of this chapter:
    1) The thirty-two marks and eighty secondary characteristics of a buddha's form body;
    2) The Dharma body of the Buddhas;
    3) The true character [of all dharmas], i.e. "emptiness of inherent existence" (*śūnyatā*). This "emptiness of inherent existence" is evidenced by: a) their being merely composite constructs of subsidiary conditions; b) their being merely evanescently transient states in a chain of serial causality; and c) their being mere names attached to a) and b) to which one falsely imputes individual reality.

105. To correct an obvious graphic-similarity scribal error, I emend the reading of the *Taisho* text here by preferring the SYMG editions' *zhai* (齋), "ritual purification," to the *Taisho* edition's *qi* (齊), "uniform."

    Also, "Precepts of abstinence" refers here to the *aṣṭāṅgasamanvāgataṃ upavāsaṃ,* the laity's formal acceptance and observance of the practice of upholding the eight precepts that include celibacy and not eating after midday. One observes this enhanced level of lay precept practice either continuously or on the eighth, fourteenth, fifteenth, twenty-third, twenty-ninth, and thirtieth days of each lunar month.

106. This reference to laypeople staying in a monastery probably refers most usually to the not uncommon practice of allowing laypeople to live in separate quarters on monastery grounds when they are continuously training in these eight lay precepts for a predetermined period of time.

107. I translate here as "monastic preceptor" and "monastic Dharma teacher" what the KJ text retains in transliteration as *"upādhyāya"* and *"ācārya"* respectively.

108. KJ retained the Sanskrit term for "benefactor" (*dānapati*) which I have opted to translate here.

109. VB notes: "This is the practice of seeking alms at every door, without skipping over houses where the people do not give or give poor quality food." The rationale for observing this "proper sequence" is that, since providing alms to monks and nuns produces karmic merit, one would not want to deny that opportunity to anyone.

110. Lest "unwholesome remorsefulness" seem somewhat opaque, this would refer first and foremost to regretting having done something good or regretting not having done something bad.

111. "Demolishing through separation" most likely refers to the "deconstructive analysis" involved in such contemplations as the contemplation of the thirty-two (or 36) parts of the body, the nine stages of the decomposition of a rotting corpse, the white-boned skeleton contemplation, etc. All of these contemplations serve as powerful antidotes to sensual desire.

112. This attainment of the sign of unloveliness refers to directly perceiving the unloveliness of sensually attractive physical forms so completely that the image of their unloveliness is retained even in the absence of the initially contemplated meditation object. This is often accomplished by deeply practicing the contemplations of the parts of the body, the stages of decomposition of a rotting corpse, or the white-boned skeleton.

113. Hirakawa gives the Sanskrit as: *"saṃrañjanīyaṃ dharmam."* These six dharmas refer to mutual harmoniousness, respect, equality, and fairness in matters pertaining to: body, speech, mind, precepts, views, and benefits received (food, robes, shelter, etc.).

114. These five bases of liberation (Skt. *vimukty-āyatanāni*) are five different circumstances under which, with or without the advantage of correct teaching from a qualified Dharma teacher or fellow practitioner, a practitioner may come to engage with and find success in cultivation, establish his mind in concentration, and then finally achieve liberation. VB refers us to AN 5:26 for the precise canonical explanation.

115. VB refers us to AN 9:29.

116. VB refers us to AN 8:80.

117. VB refers us to AN 8:80, noting that this is found in the second part of that sutta.

118. These are the *navasaṃjñā* for which VB refers us to AN 9:16.
119. VB refers us to AN 8:30.
120. "No apprehensible reality" (無所得) refers to emptiness of inherent existence, i.e. there is nothing in or about these *dhyāna* absorptions that can be gotten at as ultimately real.
121. VB notes: "Items 43-45 are at SN 35:238, 'The Simile of the Vipers.'"
122. VB notes: "This may also be in SN 35:238: 'The further shore, which is safe and free from danger': this is a designation for Nibbāna."
123. This appears to be a quotation from the "Pratyutpanna Samādhi Sūtra."
124. "Compulsory karmic retributions" most likely refers here to heinous karmic offenses that entail immediate retribution during or at the end of this very life such as: patricide, matricide, killing an arhat, drawing the blood of a buddha, or causing a schism in the monastic sangha.
125. This statement seems contradictory. As such, I am not particularly confident that this sentence is not corrupted or that I have interpreted its intent correctly.
126. The immediately preceding abhidharmic analytic categories are in some cases phrased so tersely in the Chinese as to be mildly obscure. Hence I may not have rendered all of them with definitively precise accuracy.

Part Two Variant Readings in Other Chinese Editions

Fascicle Nine Variant Readings

[0068009] 竟＝盡【宋】【元】【明】【宮】
[0068010] 降＝調【宋】【元】【明】【宮】
[0068011] 〔三昧〕－【宋】【元】【明】【宮】
[0069001] 高＝毫【明】
[0069002] 泥＝尼【宋】【元】【明】【宮】
[0069003] 闢＝鋋【宋】【元】【明】【宮】
[0069004] 畏＝界【宋】【元】【明】【宮】
[0069005] 禪＝緻【宋】【元】【明】，＝穉【宮】
[0069006] 緻＝穉【宮】＊ [＊ 1]
[0069007] 主＝生【宋】【元】【明】【宮】
[0069008] （能）＋破【宋】【元】【明】【宮】
[0069009] 〔師〕－【宋】【元】【明】【宮】
[0069010] 〔可〕－【宮】
[0069011] 大＋（法）【宋】【元】【明】【宮】
[0069012] 〔所謂〕－【宋】【元】【明】【宮】
[0069013] 岐＝祇【宋】【元】【明】
[0069014] 授＝受【宋】【元】【宮】
[0069015] 憂＝優【宋】【元】【明】【宮】
[0069016] （毘佛略未曾有論議）＋如是【明】， 明註曰如是上有如是諸經佛羅未曾有論議十一字
[0069017] 〔斐肥儸未曾有經〕－【明】
[0069018] 儸＝似【宮】
[0069019] 主＝王【宋】【元】【宮】
[0069020] 纖＝[月*鐵]【宋】【元】【宮】＊， 明註曰纖南藏作[月*鐵]＊ [＊ 1]
[0069021] 念＝命【宋】【元】【明】【宮】
[0069022] 踝＝[蹲-酋+(十/田)]【宋】【元】【明】【宮】
[0069023] 墮＝脱【宋】【元】【明】【宮】
[0069024] 身＋（行）【宋】【元】【明】【宮】
[0069025] 邊＝過【宮】
[0069026] 山＝心【宋】【元】【明】【宮】
[0069027] 順＝煩【宮】
[0069028] 鮮＝淨【宮】
[0069029] 文＝又【元】
[0070001] 度脱＝廣度【宋】【元】【宮】，＝廣受【明】
[0070002] 深紅＝染染【宋】【元】【明】【宮】
[0070003] 鮮淨＝淨鮮【宋】【元】【明】【宮】
[0070004] 已＝以【宋】【元】【明】【宮】

[0070005] 輭=懦【宋】【元】【明】【宮】
[0070006] （智）+者【宋】【元】【明】【宮】
[0070007] 講=稱【宮】
[0070008] 枕=机【宋】【元】【宮】，=几【明】*
[0070009] 幃=帷【宋】【元】【明】【宮】
[0070010] 以=有【宋】【元】【明】【宮】
[0070011] 虎=琥【宋】【元】【明】【宮】
[0070012] 車璩=硨磲【宋】【元】【明】【宮】
[0070013] 八+（部）【宋】【元】【明】【宮】
[0070014] 恨=恚【宋】【元】【明】【宮】
[0070015] 齗=齶【宋】【元】【明】【宮】
[0070016] 震=振【宋】【元】【宮】
[0070017] 不故=事不【宋】【元】【明】【宮】
[0070018] 智=知【宋】【元】【明】【宮】* [* 1]
[0070019] 〔如〕－【宋】【元】【明】【宮】
[0070020] 恚=意【宮】
[0070021] 傭=傭【宮】
[0071001] 泥=尼【明】
[0071002] 滿=端【宋】【元】【明】【宮】
[0071003] 人=仁【宋】【元】【明】【宮】
[0071004] 病=患【宋】【元】【明】【宮】
[0071005] 緻=穉【宮】下同
[0071006] 脈平=膝平【宋】【元】【明】，=膝手【宮】
[0071007] 極柔輭=柔懦輭【宋】【元】【明】【宮】
[0071008] 緻=穉【宋】【元】【宮】*，明註曰緻南藏作穉* [* 1]
[0071009] 正=整【宋】【元】【明】【宮】
[0071010] 九=八【宋】【元】【明】【宮】

Fascicle Ten Variant Readings

[0071011] 十=九【宋】【元】【明】【宮】
[0071012] 聞聲=聲聞【明】
[0071013] （受）+記【宋】【元】【明】【宮】
[0071014] 轉=輪【宋】【元】【明】【宮】
[0072001] 〔無量〕－【宋】【元】【明】【宮】
[0072002] 〔而〕－【宋】【元】【明】【宮】
[0072003] 〔百千〕－【宋】【元】【明】【宮】
[0072004] 王天=天王【宋】【元】【明】【宮】
[0072005] 劫=河【宋】【元】【明】【宮】
[0072006] 〔王〕－【宋】【元】【明】【宮】
[0072007] 相=想【宋】【元】【明】【宮】

[0072008] 羅＋（迦樓羅）【明】
[0072009] 猶如＝光猶【宋】【元】【明】【宮】
[0072010] 不＝復【宋】【元】【明】
[0072011] 末＝抹【明】
[0072012] 車璖馬瑙＝硨磲瑪瑙【宋】【元】【明】【宮】
[0072013] 〔化〕－【宋】【元】【明】【宮】
[0072014] 技＝伎【宋】【元】【明】【宮】
[0073001] 所＝能【宋】【元】【明】【宮】
[0073002] 聞＝音【宋】【元】【明】【宮】
[0073003] 力＋（勢）【宋】【元】【明】【宮】
[0073004] 犍＝揵【宋】【元】【宮】＊ [＊ 1 2 3]
[0073005] 量＝上【宋】【元】【明】【宮】
[0073006] 諸＝心【宋】【元】【明】【宮】
[0073007] 行＋（生）【宋】【元】【明】【宮】
[0073008] 〔有〕－【宋】【元】【明】【宮】
[0073009] 閡＝礙【宋】【元】【明】【宮】下同
[0073010] 出＝去【宋】【元】【明】【宮】
[0073011] 二＝三【宋】【元】【明】【宮】＊ [＊ 1]
[0074001] 〔如〕－【宋】【元】【明】【宮】＊ [＊ 1]
[0074002] 分＋（分）【宋】【元】【明】【宮】
[0074003] 大＝但【宋】【元】【明】【宮】
[0074004] 智＝知【宋】【元】【明】【宮】＊ [＊ 1 2 3]
[0074005] 智＋（知不）【宋】【元】【明】【宮】
[0074006] 〔故〕－【宋】【元】【明】【宮】
[0074007] 〔人〕－【宋】【元】【明】【宮】
[0074008] 〔者〕－【宋】【元】【明】【宮】
[0074009] 豫＝預【宋】【元】【明】【宮】＊ [＊ 1 2 3 4]
[0074010] （是）＋故【明】
[0074011] 〔城〕－【宋】【元】【明】【宮】
[0074012] 故＋（佛）【宋】【元】【明】【宮】
[0074013] 知＋（婆羅門忘請佛及僧者）【宋】【元】【明】【宮】
[0074014] 歲數＝數歲【宋】【元】【明】【宮】
[0074015] 韋＝毘【宋】【元】【明】【宮】
[0074016] 估＝賈【宋】【元】【明】【宮】
[0075001] 〔者〕－【宋】【元】【明】【宮】
[0075002] 具＋（足）【宋】【元】【明】【宮】
[0075003] 智＝根【宋】【元】【明】【宮】
[0075004] 已＝以【宋】【元】【明】【宮】下同
[0075005] 訪＝方【宋】【元】【明】【宮】
[0075006] 邏＝羅【宋】【元】【明】【宮】

[0075007] 蓮=連【宋】【元】【明】【宮】
[0075008] 喈=呰【宋】【元】【明】【宮】＊ [＊ 1]
[0075009] 法=汝【宋】【元】【明】【宮】
[0075010] 〔智〕－【宋】【元】【明】【宮】
[0075011] 知他=他知【宋】【元】【明】【宮】
[0075012] 〔切〕－【宋】【元】【明】【宮】
[0075013] 任=住【宋】【元】【明】
[0075014] 韋陀=韋大【宋】【元】【明】【宮】下同
[0075015] 〔曰〕－【宋】【元】【明】【宮】
[0075016] 導=道【宋】【元】【明】【宮】
[0075017] 〔故〕－【宮】
[0075018] 〔經〕－【宋】【元】【明】【宮】
[0076001] 無=不【宋】【元】【明】【宮】
[0076002] 無明+（邪見自古亦然有無明）【宋】【元】【明】【宮】
[0076003] 病=疾【宋】【元】【明】【宮】
[0076004] 錠=定【宋】【元】【明】【宮】
[0076005] 〔老〕－【宋】【元】【明】【宮】
[0076006] 真=直【宋】【元】【明】【宮】
[0076007] 〔故〕－【宋】【元】【明】【宮】
[0076008] 〔道〕－【宋】【元】【明】【宮】
[0076009] 〔瞋恚〕－【宋】【元】【明】【宮】
[0076010] （所）+說【宋】【元】【明】【宮】
[0076011] 〔處〕－【宋】【元】【明】【宮】
[0076012] 智=能【宋】【元】【明】【宮】
[0076013] 語=謂【宋】【元】【明】【宮】
[0076014] 〔者〕－【宮】
[0077001] 雪=宣【明】
[0077002] 飲=飯【宋】【元】【明】【宮】
[0077003] 〔佛故〕－【宋】【元】【明】【宮】
[0077004] 洹=涅【宮】
[0077005] 已=以【宮】下同
[0077006] 惡=苦【宮】
[0077007] 〔已〕－【宋】【元】【明】【宮】
[0077008] 不分卷及品【宋】【元】【明】【宮】

Fascicle Eleven Variant Readings

[0077009] 不分卷及品【宋】【元】【明】【宮】
[0077010] 〔又〕－【宋】【元】【明】【宮】
[0077011] 人+（人）【宋】【元】【明】【宮】
[0078001] 利=行【宋】【元】【宮】

[0078002] 〔得〕－【宋】【元】【明】【宮】
[0078003] （聞）＋斷【宋】【元】【明】【宮】＊ [＊ 1]
[0078004] 興＝多【宋】【元】【明】【宮】
[0078005] 任＝住【元】
[0078006] 儻＝倘【明】
[0078007] 命＝令【宋】【元】【明】【宮】
[0078008] 名＋（為）【宋】【元】【明】【宮】
[0079001] 皆＝智【宋】【元】【明】【宮】
[0079002] 卷第九終【宋】【元】【明】【宮】
[0079003] 卷第十首【宋】【元】【明】【宮】，譯號同異如首卷 【宋】【元】【明】【宮】[0079004] 首＝百【元】【明】
[0079005] 水或火＝火或水【宋】【元】【明】【宮】
[0079006] 名為＝為名【宋】【元】【明】【宮】
[0079007] 又若＝若人【宋】【元】【明】【宮】
[0079008] 答＋（曰）【宋】【元】【明】【宮】
[0079009] 〔作〕－【宋】【元】【明】【宮】
[0079010] 畜生餓鬼＝餓鬼畜生【宋】【元】【明】【宮】
[0080001] 應＋（心）【宋】【元】【明】【宮】
[0080002] 經此＝此經【宋】【元】【明】【宮】
[0080003] 色＋（故）【宋】【元】【明】【宮】
[0080004] 十＝七【宮】
[0080005] 第＝弟【宋】＊【元】＊【明】＊【宮】＊【CB】＊ [＊ 1]
[0080006] 餘＋（諸）【宋】【元】【明】【宮】
[0080007] 愛＋（心）【宋】【元】【明】【宮】
[0080008] 何＝可【元】【明】
[0080009] 而不變＝不變異【宋】【元】【明】【宮】
[0080010] 變＋（異）【宋】【元】【明】【宮】
[0080011] 娑＝婆【元】
[0080012] 報＋（若作）【宋】【元】【明】【宮】
[0080013] 〔佛言〕－【宋】【元】【明】【宮】
[0081001] 色＋（離）【宋】【元】【明】【宮】
[0081002] （世間）＋亦【宋】【元】【明】【宮】
[0081003] （如來）＋身【宋】【元】【明】【宮】
[0081004] 神＝身【明】
[0081005] （諸）＋天【宋】【元】【明】【宮】
[0081006] 空＝害【宮】
[0081007] 應＋（以）【宋】【元】【明】【宮】
[0081008] 須＝復【宋】【元】【明】【宮】
[0081009] 著＝習【宋】【元】【明】【宮】
[0081010] 異＝果【宮】

[0081011] 〔有〕－【宋】【元】【明】【宮】
[0081012] 能＋（全）【宋】【元】【明】【宮】
[0081013] （之）＋分【宋】【元】【明】【宮】
[0082001] （守）＋護【宋】【元】【明】【宮】＊ [＊ 1 2]
[0082002] 呵＝阿【元】【明】
[0082003] （是）＋故【宋】【元】【明】【宮】
[0082004] 言＋（如來）【宋】【元】【明】【宮】
[0082005] 微＝疑【宋】【元】【明】【宮】
[0082006] 盡＋（我於此中）【宋】【元】【明】【宮】
[0082007] 是＝微畏【宋】【元】【明】【宮】
[0082008] 〔如〕－【宋】【元】【明】【宮】
[0082009] 〔但〕－【宋】【元】【明】【宮】
[0082010] 但＝俱【宋】
[0082011] 法受＝受法【宋】【元】【明】【宮】
[0082012] 即＋（時）【宋】【元】【明】【宮】
[0082013] 受＝愛【宋】[>＊]【元】[>＊]【明】[>＊] [＊ 1]
[0082014] （禪）＋定【宋】【元】【明】【宮】
[0082015] 如＝知【宋】【元】【明】【宮】
[0083001] 知＝智【宋】【元】【明】【宮】
[0083002] 小＋（力）【明】【宮】
[0083003] 解＋（脫）【宮】
[0083004] 悲＝慧【宋】【元】【明】【宮】
[0083005] 智＝知【宋】【元】【明】【宮】
[0083006] 德＝田【宋】【元】【明】【宮】
[0083007] 摩＝魔【明】
[0083008] 似＝以【宋】【元】【明】【宮】
[0083009] 不分卷【宋】【元】【明】【宮】

Fascicle Twelve Variant Readings

[0083010] 不分卷【宋】【元】【明】【宮】
[0084001] 唯＝惟【宋】【元】【明】【宮】
[0084002] 設＝妄【宋】【元】【明】【宮】
[0084003] 善＝此【宋】【元】【宮】
[0084004] 天中＝中天【宋】【元】【明】【宮】
[0084005] 可＝能【宋】【元】【明】【宮】
[0084006] 蔭＝音【宋】【元】【明】
[0084007] 嫌譏而拒＝譏刺而巨【宋】【元】【明】【宮】
[0084008] 德＝得【宋】【元】【明】【宮】
[0085001] 所＝并【宋】【元】【明】【宮】
[0085002] 骨＝血【宋】【元】【明】【宮】

[0085003] 明註曰南藏無無求惱者施
[0085004] 求惱＝惱求【明】【宮】
[0085005] 垢＝妬【宋】【元】【明】【宮】
[0085006] 住＝性【宋】【元】【明】，＝往【宮】
[0085007] 定＝禪【宋】【元】【明】【宮】
[0085008] 分＝力【宋】【元】【明】【宮】
[0085009] 勢＝施【宋】【元】【明】【宮】
[0085010] 一切眾生＝諸眾生中【宋】【元】【明】【宮】
[0086001] 卷第十終【宋】【元】【明】【宮】
[0086002] 卷第十一首【宋】【元】【明】【宮】， 譯號同異如首卷【宋】【元】【明】【宮】
[0086003] 染＝深【宋】【元】【明】【宮】
[0086004] 〔供〕－【宋】【元】【明】【宮】
[0086005] 〔即〕－【宋】【元】【明】【宮】
[0086006] 于＝於【宋】【元】【明】【宮】
[0086007] （大）＋定【宋】【元】【明】【宮】，定＝寶【宮】
[0086008] 恪＝敬【明】
[0086009] 甞＝常【宋】【元】【明】【宮】
[0086010] 已＝以【宋】【元】【明】【宮】
[0086011] 憎＝增【宋】【元】【明】【宮】
[0086012] 復＋（次）【宮】
[0086013] 忍法＝法忍【宋】【元】【明】【宮】
[0086014] 出＝說【宮】
[0086015] 眠睡＝睡眠【明】
[0087001] 呰＝訾【宋】【元】【明】【宮】
[0087002] 齊＝齋【宋】【元】【明】【宮】
[0087003] 毀＝瑕【宋】【元】【明】【宮】
[0087004] 〔者〕－【宋】【元】【明】【宮】
[0087005] 上＝尚【宋】【元】【明】【宮】
[0087006] 〔生〕－【宋】【元】【明】【宮】
[0087007] 念＝令【宮】
[0087008] 受＝愛【宮】
[0087009] 相＝想【宋】【元】【明】【宮】＊ [＊ 1 2]
[0087010] 颰＝跋【宋】【元】【明】【宮】下同
[0087011] 碎＝破【宋】【元】【明】【宮】
[0087012] 諷誦＝誦諷【宋】【元】【明】【宮】
[0088001] 搆＝[毄-心+牛]【明】
[0088002] 荼＝茶【明】
[0088003] 聞＝問【明】
[0088004] 〔也〕－【宋】【元】【明】【宮】

[0088005] 薩＝提【宋】【元】【明】【宮】
[0088006] 隨喜＝菩薩【宮】
[0088007] 義＝議【宋】【元】【明】【宮】
[0088008] 口＝曰【宋】【元】【明】【宮】
[0088009] 煉＝練【宋】【元】【明】【宮】＊ [＊ 1]

Nāgārjuna
on
Mindfulness of the Buddha

Part 3: Recollection of the Buddha

Nāgārjuna's *Exegesis on the Mahāprajnāpāramitā Sūtra*
Chapter 1, Part 36-1

As Translated into Chinese by Tripiṭaka Master Kumārajīva
English Translation by Bhikshu Dharmamitra

正體字

T25n1509_p0218c19‖ [16]大智[17]度論釋初品中八念[18]義第三十
218c20‖ 六之一
218c28‖ 說。佛告諸比丘。若於阿蘭若處空舍塚間山
218c29‖ 林曠野。在中思惟。若有怖畏衣毛為竪。爾
219a01‖ 時當念佛。佛是多陀阿伽度阿羅呵三藐三
219a02‖ 佛陀乃至婆伽婆。恐怖則滅。..............
219b02‖ ....問曰。云何是念佛。
219b03‖ 答曰。行者一心念佛。得如實智慧。大慈大悲
219b04‖ 成就。是故言無錯謬。麁細多少深淺皆無不
219b05‖ 實。皆是實故名[6]為多陀阿伽度。亦如過去
219b06‖ 未來現在十方諸佛。於眾生中起大悲心。
219b07‖ 行六波羅蜜得諸法相。來至阿耨多羅三
219b08‖ 藐三菩提中。此佛亦如是。是名多陀阿伽
219b09‖ 度。如三世十方諸佛身。放大光明遍照十
219b10‖ 方破諸黑闇。心出智慧光明。破眾生無明
219b11‖ 闇冥。功德名聞亦遍滿十方。去至涅槃[7]中。
219b12‖ 此佛亦如是去。以是故亦名多陀阿伽度。

简体字

佛告诸比丘："若于阿兰若处，空舍、冢间，山林、旷野，在中思惟，若有怖畏，衣毛为竖，尔时当念佛：佛是多陀阿伽度、阿罗诃、三藐三佛陀，乃至婆伽婆。恐怖则灭。..........................

....

问曰：云何是念佛？

答曰：行者一心念佛，得如实智慧，大慈大悲成就，是故言无错谬，粗细、多少、深浅，皆无不实；皆是实故，名多陀阿伽度。亦如过去、未来、现在十方诸佛，于众生中起大悲心，行六波罗蜜，得诸法相，来至阿耨多罗三藐三菩提中；此佛亦如是，是名多陀阿伽度。如三世十方诸佛，身放大光明，遍照十方，破诸黑闇；心出智慧光明，破众生无明闇冥；功德、名闻亦遍满十方，去至涅槃；此佛亦如是去，以是故亦名多陀阿伽度。

Part Three
Recollection of the Buddha[1]

Nāgārjuna on Recollection of the Buddha

I. Recollection of the Buddha

A. The Purpose of the Practice

The Buddha told the bhikshus: "If one is engaging in contemplations in a forest hermitage,[2] an empty building, a charnel ground, the mountains, the forests, or the desolate wilderness, and if one becomes so fearful that the hairs on one's body stand on end, at just such a time, one should engage in recollection of the Buddha, recalling that the Buddha is a *tathāgatha*, an *arhat*, *samyaksaṃbuddha*, and so forth until we come to a *bhagavat*.[3] One's fearfulness will then disappear."[4]

B. Explanation of the Practice

Question: What is meant by "recollection of the Buddha"?

Response: The practitioner single-mindedly recalls that the Buddha has gained the wisdom which accords with reality and also possesses perfectly realized great loving-kindness and great compassion. Thus he is said to be free of mistakes or errors. There is nothing about him which is not genuine, regardless of whether it be concerned with the gross, the subtle, the manifold, the few, the deep, or the shallow.

C. The Ten Names of the Buddha

Because in every case he accords with reality, he is referred to as "*tathāgata*" (the "Thus Come One"). Also, just as all buddhas of the ten directions throughout the past, future, and present, in the midst of beings, give rise to the mind of great compassion, practice the six perfections, realize the true character of all dharmas, and come forth to arrive at *anuttura-samyak-saṃbodhi* ("the utmost, right, and perfect enlightenment"), so too is this case with this Buddha. This is what is meant by "*tathāgata*."

Just as the bodies of all buddhas of the three periods of time throughout the ten directions radiate great brilliant light which pervasively illuminates the ten directions, breaking up all darkness, just as their minds put forth the brilliant light of wisdom that dispels the darkness of beings' ignorance, and just as the fame of their meritorious qualities everywhere fills the ten directions as they go forth to nirvāṇa, so too does this Buddha also go forth in the same manner. It is for this reason that he too is referred to as "the *Tathāgata*" ("the Thus Come One").

正體字

219b13|| 有如是功德故。應受一切諸天世人最上
219b14|| 供養。是故名阿羅呵。若有人言。何以故。但
219b15|| 佛如實說。如來如去故。應受最上供養。以
219b16|| 佛得正遍智慧故。正名諸法不動不壞相。
219b17|| 遍名不為一法二法。故以悉知一切法無
219b18|| 餘不盡。是名三藐三佛陀。是正遍智慧。不
219b19|| 從無因而得。亦不從[8]無緣得。是中依智
219b20|| 慧持戒具足故。得正遍智慧。智慧名菩薩
219b21|| 從初發意乃至金剛三昧相應智慧。持戒名
219b22|| 菩薩從初發意乃至金剛三昧身業口業清
219b23|| 淨隨意行[9]已。是故名鞞闍遮羅那三般那
219b24|| 若。行是二行得善去。如車有兩輪善去
219b25|| 者。如先佛所去處。佛亦如是去。故名修伽
219b26|| 陀。若有言。佛自修其法不知我等事。以是
219b27|| 故知世間知世間因知世間盡知世間盡
219b28|| 道。故名為路迦憊。知世間已調御眾生。於
219b29|| 種種師中最為無上。以是故名阿耨多[10]羅
219c01|| 富樓沙曇藐婆羅提。能以三種道滅三毒。
219c02|| 令眾生行三乘道。

简体字

有如是功德故，应受一切诸天世人最上供养，是故名阿罗诃。若有人言："何以故但佛如实说，如来如去故，应受最上供养？"以佛得正遍智慧故；正名诸法不动不坏相，遍名不为一法二法故，以悉知一切法无余不尽，是名三藐三佛陀。是正遍智慧，不从无因而得，亦不从天得；是中依智慧、持戒具足故，得正遍智慧。智慧名菩萨从初发意，乃至金刚三昧相应智慧；持戒名菩萨从初发意，乃至金刚三昧身业、口业清净随意行；是故名鞞阇遮罗那三般那。若行是二行得善去，如车有两轮；善去者，如先佛所去处，佛亦如是去，故名修伽陀。若有言佛自修其法，不知我等事，以是故知世间；知世间因，知世间尽，知世间尽道故，名为路迦惫。知世间已，调御众生，于种种师中最为无上，以是故名阿耨多罗富楼沙昙藐婆罗提。能以三种道灭三毒，令众生行三乘道，

Because he possesses merit such as this, he is worthy to receive the most supreme offerings from all gods and people of the World. Hence he is referred to as *"arhat"* ("Worthy of Offerings"). If someone were to ask why it is that it is only the Buddha who speaks in accordance with reality, it is because he is "thus" in his coming and "thus" in his going. He is worthy to receive the most supreme offerings because the Buddha has realized the right and universal awakening.

"Right" refers to all dharmas' mark of unshakability and indestructibility. "Universal" refers to not being limited in scope to just one or two dharmas. Thus, because in his complete knowing of all dharmas, there are none not included and none not exhaustively known, he is referred to as *"samyaksaṃbuddha"* ("Of Right and Universal Enlightenment"). This right and universal wisdom is not acquired without a cause, nor is it realized in the absence of conditions. Here it is in reliance upon the perfection of wisdom and observance of moral precepts that he acquires this right and universal wisdom.

"Wisdom" refers to the bodhisattva's wisdom from the time of first generating the resolve [to attain buddhahood] on up to the acquisition of the *vajra* samādhi. "Upholding the moral precepts" refers to the bodhisattva's bodily actions and verbal actions which are pure and corresponding to his intentions from the time of first generating the resolve on up to the acquisition of the *vajra* samādhi. He is therefore known as *"vidyā-caraṇa-saṃpanna"* ("Perfect in Practice of Cognition").[5]

In his practice of these two practices, he achieves the state of being "well gone." This is just as when a cart that is possessed of two wheels is said to be one which is "well gone." The Buddha also goes to those places to which the former buddhas have gone. Hence he is referred to as *"sugata"* ("the Well Gone One").

There may be those who claim, "The Buddha cultivated his own dharma. However, he is unaware of the endeavors of people such as ourselves." For the sake of these, [it may be explained that] he knows the World, knows the causes in the World, knows the cessation of [the dharmas of] the World, and knows the path to the cessation of [the dharmas of] the World. Hence he is referred to as *"lokavid"* ("the World Knower").

Having already understood the World, he is able to train and guide beings. Among all teachers he is the most unsurpassed. It is for this reason that he is referred to as *"anuttaraḥ-puruṣa-damya-sārathiḥ"* ("the Unsurpassed Guide of Men to be Tamed").

He is able to employ the three kinds of paths to extinguish the three poisons and thus causes beings to practice the path of the

正體字

以是故名貰多提婆魔
219c03‖ [少/兔][11]舍。若有言。以何事故能自利益無量。復
219c04‖ 能利益他人無量。佛一切智慧成就故。過去
219c05‖ 未來現在。盡不盡動不動。一切世間了了悉
219c06‖ 知。故名為佛陀。得是九種名號。有大名稱
219c07‖ 遍滿十方。以是故名[12]為婆伽婆。經中佛自
219c08‖ 說。如是名號應當作是念佛。復次一切種
219c09‖ 種功德。盡在於佛。佛是劫初轉輪聖王摩訶
219c10‖ 三[13]磨陀等種。閻浮提中智慧威德。諸釋子
219c11‖ 中生貴[14]性憍曇氏。生時光明遍[15]照三千大
219c12‖ 千世界。梵天王持寶蓋。釋提桓因以天寶
219c13‖ 衣承接。阿那婆蹋多龍王婆伽多龍王。以妙
219c14‖ 香湯澡浴。生時地六種動。行至七步安詳
219c15‖ 如象王。觀視四方作師子吼。[16]我是末後身。
219c16‖ 當度一切眾生。阿私[17]陀仙人相之告淨飯
219c17‖ 王。是人足下千輻輪相指合縵網。當自於法
219c18‖ 中安平立。無能動無能壞者。手中德字縵
219c19‖ 網莊嚴。當以此手安慰眾生令無所畏。

简体字

以是故名贳多提婆魔[少/兔]舍喃。若有言，以何事故能自利益无量？复能利益他人无量？佛一切智慧成就故，过去、未来、现在，尽不尽，动不动，一切世间了了悉知故，名为佛陀。得是九种名号，有大名称，遍满十方，以是故名婆伽婆。经中佛自说如是名号，应当作是念佛。

复次，一切种种功德，尽在于佛。佛是劫初转轮圣王摩诃三摩陀等种，阎浮提中智慧威德，诸释子中生，贵姓憍昙氏。生时光明遍三千大千世界，梵天王持宝盖、释提桓因以天宝衣承接，阿那婆蹋多龙王、婆伽多龙王以妙香汤澡浴。生时地六种动，行至七步，安详如象王，观视四方，作师子吼："我是末后身，当度一切众生！"阿私仙人相之，告净饭王："是人足下千辐轮相，指合缦网，当自于法中安平立，无能动、无能坏者。手中德字，缦网庄严，当以此手安慰众生，令无所畏。

Three Vehicles. It is for this reason that he is referred to as *"śāstā devamanuṣyāṇām"* ("the Teacher of Gods and Men").

Suppose someone were to ask, "Because of what endeavor is he able to create incalculable self benefit while also being able to create incalculable benefit for others?" It is because of having perfected comprehensive wisdom which utterly knows everything in all the worlds of the past, future, and present, knowing them whether [those objects of knowledge] are already ended or not, and knowing them whether they abide in a state of flux or not. It is on this basis that the Buddha is known as *"buddha"* ("the Enlightened One").

Having acquired these nine types of names, he is possessed of a great reputation which extends everywhere throughout the ten directions. It is because of this that he is referred to as *"bhagavat"* (the "Venerated One").

In the scriptures, the Buddha himself indicated that one should employ these names in one's recollection of the Buddha.

D. The Illustrious Lineage and Marvelous Birth of the Buddha

Also, all of the various sorts of meritorious qualities are exhaustively present in the Buddha. The Buddha belongs to the lineage of the wheel-turning sage king at the very beginning of the kalpa, Mahāsaṃmata. He is from the wise and awesomely virtuous Śākyans, born in the noble house of Gautama.

When he was born, brilliant light everywhere illuminated the worlds of the great trichiliocosm. Brahmā, king of the gods, held a jeweled canopy [over him]. Śakra Devānām Indra received him with a jeweled cloak. The dragon king Anavatapta and the dragon king Sāgara bathed him with marvelously scented waters. When he was born, the earth moved and shook in six ways. He walked seven steps, peaceful and stable as the king of elephants, gazed contemplatively at the four quarters, and roared the lion's roar, declaring, "This is my very last incarnation. I am destined to liberate all beings."

E. The Physical Characteristics of the Buddha

Asita, the Rishi, examined [the Buddha's] physiognomy and told Pure Rice King, "This person possesses the thousand-spoked wheel mark on the bottom of his feet and the mark of webbing between [the bases of] his fingers. He is one who is destined to stand, peacefully and evenly, within the Dharma, remaining immovable and unrefuted by anyone.

"His hands are adorned with the signs indicating virtue and with proximal webs [at the base of his fingers]. He is destined to use these hands to bring comfort to beings and cause them to be free of fear.

正體字

219c20|| 如是乃至肉骨髻相。如青珠山頂。青色光明
219c21|| 從四邊出。頭中頂相無能見上。若天若人
219c22|| 無有勝者。白毫眉間跱。白光踰[18]頗梨。淨眼
219c23|| 長廣其色紺青。鼻高直好甚可愛樂。口四十
219c24|| 齒白淨利好。四牙上白其光最勝。脣上下等
219c25|| 不大不小不長不短。舌薄而大[19]軟赤紅色
219c26|| 如天蓮華。梵聲深遠聞者悅樂聽無厭足。身
219c27|| 色[20]好妙勝閻浮檀金。[21]大光周身種種雜色
219c28|| 妙好無比。[22]如是等三十二相具足。是人不
219c29|| 久出家得一切智成佛。佛身功德如是應
220a01|| 當念佛。復次佛身功德身力。勝於十萬白
220a02|| 香象寶。是為父母遺體力。若神通功德力無
220a03|| 量無限。佛身以三十二相八十隨形好莊
220a04|| 嚴。內有無量佛法功德故視之無厭。見佛
220a05|| 身者忘世五欲萬事不憶。若見佛身。一處
220a06|| 愛樂無厭不能移觀佛身功德如是。應當
220a07|| 念佛

简体字

如是乃至肉骨髻相，如青珠山顶，青色光明从四边出，头中顶相无能见上，若天、若人无有胜者。白毫眉间峙，白光逾玻璃。净眼长广，其色绀青。鼻高直好，甚可爱乐。口四十齿，白净利好；四牙上白，其光最胜。唇上下等，不大不小，不长不短。舌薄而大，软赤红色，如天莲华。梵声深远，闻者悦乐，听无厌足。身色妙好，胜阎浮檀金。大光周身，种种杂色，妙好无比。以如是等三十二相具足，是人不久出家，得一切智成佛。”佛身功德如是，应当念佛。

复次，佛身功德身力，胜于十万白香象宝，是为父母遗体力；若神通功德力，无量无限。佛身以三十二相、八十随形好庄严，内有无量佛法功德故，视之无厌。见佛身者，忘世五欲，万事不忆；若见佛身一处，爱乐无厌，不能移观。佛身功德如是，应当念佛。

He possesses signs such as these up to and including the "flesh cowl" mark [atop his head] which is like a blue pearl at the summit of a mountain. The blue-colored light emanates from its four sides. The summit mark in the middle of his head is such that no one is able to see to the top of it. Whether one be a god or a man, there are none who are superior to him.

"He is possessed of the white hair-tuft mark placed between his brows, the white light from which surpasses that of crystal. He has pure eyes which are wide and broad and which are purple-blue in color. His nose is prominent, straight, and fine in a way which is extremely attractive and pleasing. His mouth contains forty teeth which are white, pure, sharp, and fine. His four front teeth are supremely white and possessed of the most superior brilliance.

"His upper and lower lips are equal, being neither large nor small nor long nor short. His tongue is thin and yet large. It is red in color like a heavenly lotus blossom. His brahman voice is deep and far-reaching. Those who hear it are delighted by it and never grow weary of listening to it. The color of his body is fine and marvelous, superior in hue to that of Jāmbu River gold. A great light surrounds his body, displaying all manner of varied colors. It is marvelous, fine and incomparable.

"He is complete with thirty-two marks of this sort. Before long, this person will leave behind the home life, realize all-knowledge and attain buddhahood."

The physical qualities of the Buddha's body are such as this. One should [contemplate them] in one's recollection of the Buddha.

Moreover, it is a quality of the Buddha's body that his physical strength is superior to that of one hundred thousand precious perfumed white elephants. This is [just] the physical strength passed on to him by his parents. As for the power which is a quality arising from the spiritual superknowledges, it is incalculable and unlimited.

The body of the Buddha is adorned with the thirty-two marks and the eighty subsidiary characteristics. Because, internally, he is possessed of the incalculable number of meritorious qualities of the Buddha Dharma, one gazes upon him tirelessly. One who looks upon the Buddha's body forgets the five desires of the World and does not bear in mind any of the myriad matters. If one looks at any single place on the body of the Buddha, one experiences fondness and bliss, never feels that one has seen enough, and remains unable to avert one's gaze. The meritorious qualities of the Buddha's body are of such as this. Hence one should take up the practice of mindfulness of the Buddha.

正體字

220a08‖ 復次佛持戒具足清淨。從初發心修戒增積
220a09‖ 無量。與憐愍心俱不求果報。不向聲聞
220a10‖ 辟支佛道。不雜諸結使。[1]但為自心清淨不
220a11‖ 惱眾生故。世世持戒。以是故得佛道時戒
220a12‖ 得具足。應如是念佛戒眾。復次佛定眾具
220a13‖ 足。問曰。持戒以身口業清淨故可知。智慧
220a14‖ 以分別說法能除眾[2]生疑故可知。定者餘
220a15‖ 人修定尚不可知。何況於佛云何得知。答
220a16‖ 曰。大智慧具足故當知禪定必具足。譬如
220a17‖ 見蓮華大必知池亦深大。又如燈明大者
220a18‖ 必知[3]蘇油亦多。亦以佛神通變化力無量
220a19‖ 無比故。知禪定力亦具足。亦如見果大故
220a20‖ 知因亦必大。復次有時佛自為人說。我禪定
220a21‖ 相甚深。如經中說。

简体字

复次，佛持戒具足清净，从初发心修戒，增积无量，与怜愍心俱，不求果报，不向声闻、辟支佛道，不杂诸结使，但为自心清净，不恼众生故，世世持戒。以是故，得佛道时，戒得具足，应如是念佛戒众。

复次，佛定众具足。

问曰：持戒以身、口业清净故可知；智慧以分别说法，能除众疑故可知。定者，余人修定尚不可知，何况于佛？云何得知？

答曰：大智慧具足故，当知禅定必具足。譬如见莲华大，必知池亦深大；又如灯明大者，必知酥油亦多；亦以佛神通变化力无量无比故，知禅定力亦具足；亦如见果大故，知因亦必大。

复次，有时佛自为人说："我禅定相甚深。"如经中说：

F. The Buddha's Accumulation of Moral Precepts

Also, the Buddha is pure in his perfection of the upholding of the moral precepts. From the very time he first brought forth the resolve [to attain bodhi], he cultivated the moral precepts and increased his accumulation of an incalculable number [of excellent qualities]. In his extending [toward beings] a mind imbued with pity, there is never any seeking after any resulting reward. He never tends toward the path of the Hearers or the Pratyekabuddhas. There is never any admixture of any of the fetters.

He is only concerned that his own mind be pure and free of anything which might be distressing to beings. In life after life, he upholds the moral precepts. It is on account of this that, when he gains the Buddha Path, his observance of the moral precepts has achieved perfection. One should take up mindfulness of the Buddha's accumulation of the precepts in just this way.

G. The Buddha's Accumulation of Meditative Absorptions

Furthermore, the Buddha's accumulation of the meditative absorptions is entirely perfect.

Question: As for his upholding of precepts, one is able to know of this because of the purity of his bodily and verbal karma. As for his wisdom, one is able to know of it because of his making of distinctions in his explanations of Dharma and through his ability to dispel the doubts of beings. But, as for the meditative absorptions, one is not even able to know about this in the case of other persons, how much the less would one be able to know about it in the case of the Buddha?

Response: Because his great wisdom is perfect, one should know that his *dhyāna* absorptions must be entirely perfect. This is analogous to when one sees a lotus blossom which is huge: One necessarily knows that the pool [in which it grew] must also be very large. It is also just as when there is a lamp whose brightness is great. One necessarily knows that it must also contain a lot of *perilla* lamp oil. Also, because the powers of the Buddha's superknowledges and spiritual transformations are incalculable and incomparable, one knows that the power of his *dhyāna* absorptions is also entirely complete. This is also just as when one sees a result which is grand, one therefore knows that the cause must be great as well.

Furthermore, there are times when the Buddha himself has explained this matter for the sake of others, saying, "The qualities of my *dhyāna* absorptions are extremely profound." This is just as set forth in the scriptures where it is stated:

正體字

佛在阿頭摩國林樹下
220a22‖ 坐入禪定。是時大雨雷電霹靂。有四特牛耕
220a23‖ 者二人。聞聲怖死。須臾便晴。佛起經行。有
220a24‖ 一居士禮佛足已。隨從佛後白佛言。世
220a25‖ 尊。向者雷電霹靂。有四特牛耕者二人聞聲
220a26‖ 怖死。世尊聞不。佛言。不聞。居士言。佛時睡
220a27‖ 耶。佛言不睡。[4]問曰。入無心想定耶。佛言。
220a28‖ 不也。我有心想但入定耳。居士言。未曾有
220a29‖ 也。諸佛禪定大為甚深。有心想在禪定。如
220b01‖ 是大聲覺而不聞。如餘經中。佛告諸比丘。
220b02‖ 佛入出諸定。舍利弗目揵連[5]尚不聞其名。
220b03‖ 何況能知何者是。如三昧王三昧師子遊戲
220b04‖ 三昧等。佛入其中能令十方世界六種[6]震
220b05‖ 動。放大光明化為無量諸佛遍滿十方。如
220b06‖ 阿難一時心生念。過去然燈佛時。時世好
220b07‖ 人壽長易化度。今釋迦牟尼佛時世惡人壽
220b08‖ 短難教化。

简体字

佛在阿头摩国林树下坐，入禅定。是时大雨，雷电霹雳，有四特牛、耕者二人，闻声怖死。须臾便晴，佛起经行。有一居士礼佛足已，随从佛后，白佛言：“世尊，向者雷电霹雳，有四特牛、耕者二人，闻声怖死。世尊闻不？”佛言：“不闻！”居士言：“佛时睡耶？”佛言：“不睡！”曰：“入无心想定耶？”佛言：“不也！我有心想，但入定耳！”居士言：“未曾有也！”诸佛禅定大为甚深，有心想在禅定，如是大声觉而不闻。如余经中，佛告诸比丘：“佛入、出诸定，舍利弗、目揵连尚不闻其名，何况能知？何者是？如三昧王三昧、师子游戏三昧等；佛入其中，能令十方世界六种震动，放大光明，化为无量诸佛，遍满十方。”如阿难一时心生念：“过去燃灯佛时，时世好，人寿长，易化度。今释迦牟尼佛时世恶，人寿短，难教化，

> The Buddha was once in the country of Ādumā, sitting beneath a tree in the forest, having entered into *dhyāna* absorption. There arose at that time a huge rainstorm attended by crashing thunder and lighting bolts. A team of four bull oxen and two plowmen all died from fright on hearing the sound, after which, in a just a brief moment, the sky became clear again. The Buddha arose and began to walk about.
>
> There was a layman who, having bowed reverently at the feet of the Buddha, followed on along behind the Buddha and addressed the Buddha, saying, "World Honored One, there was just now such a crashing of thunder and flashing of lightning bolts that a team of four bull oxen and two plowmen all died from fright on hearing the sound. Did the World Honored One hear it or not?"
>
> The Buddha said, "I did not hear it."
>
> That layman continued, "Was the Buddha sleeping during this time?"
>
> The Buddha replied, "I was not sleeping."
>
> The layman next asked, "Was he entered into the no-thought absorption?"
>
> The Buddha said, "No. I was possessed of thought. It was just that I had entered into absorption, that's all."
>
> The layman said, "This is an unprecedented event."

The greatness of a Buddha's *dhyāna* absorption is extremely profound. He may be possessed of thought and be abiding in *dhyāna* absorption, whereupon there occurs such a great sound as this which, even while entirely awake, he nonetheless does not hear.

This is just as described in yet another scripture:

> The Buddha told the bhikshus, "The absorptions which the Buddha enters into and comes out of are such that Śāriputra and Maudgalyāyana have not even heard their names. How much the less would they be able to know what they are all about."

There are, for example, the Samādhi King Samādhi, the Lion's Sport Samādhi, and so forth. When the Buddha enters into them, he is able to cause the worlds of the ten directions to shake and move in six ways. He emits a great brilliant light that transforms into an incalculable number of buddhas who fill the ten directions. As a case in point, Ananda once thought to himself:

> "In the past, at the time of Burning Lamp Buddha, the world was a fine one, the lifespan of the people was long, and they were easy to teach and bring across to liberation. Now, in the time of Śākyamuni Buddha, the world is an evil one, the lifespan of the people is short, and they are difficult to teach. Will the Buddha nonetheless go ahead

正體字

佛事未訖而入涅槃耶。清旦以
220b09|| 是事白[7]佛。已日出。佛時入日出三昧。如
220b10|| 日出光明照閻浮提。佛身如是毛孔普出光
220b11|| 明。遍照十方恒河沙等世界。一一光中出七
220b12|| 寶千葉蓮華。一一華上皆有坐佛。一一諸佛
220b13|| 皆放無量光明。一一光中皆出七寶千葉蓮
220b14|| 華。一一華上皆有坐佛。是諸佛等遍滿十方
220b15|| 恒河沙等世界教化眾生。或有說法或有
220b16|| 默然或以經行。或神通變化身出水火。如
220b17|| 是等種種方便。度脫十方五道眾生。阿難
220b18|| 承佛威神悉見是事。佛攝神足從三昧
220b19|| 起。告阿難。見是事不。聞是事不。阿難言。
220b20|| 蒙佛威神已見已聞。佛言。佛有如是力能
220b21|| 究竟佛事不。阿難言。世尊。若眾生滿十
220b22|| 方恒河沙等世界中。佛壽一日用如[8]是力必
220b23|| 能究竟施作佛事。阿難歎言。未曾有也。世
220b24|| 尊。諸佛法無量不可思議。

简体字

佛事未讫而入涅槃耶？”清旦以是事白佛，言已，日出。佛时入日出三昧，如日出光明照阎浮提；佛身如是，毛孔普出光明，遍照十方恒河沙等世界。一一光中出七宝千叶莲华，一一华上皆有坐佛，一一诸佛皆放无量光明；一一光中皆出七宝千叶莲华，一一华上皆有坐佛。是诸佛等遍满十方恒河沙等世界，教化众生：或有说法，或有默然，或以经行，或神通变化，身出水、火。如是等种种方便，度脱十方五道众生。阿难承佛威神，悉见是事。佛摄神足，从三昧起，告阿难：“见是事不？闻是事不？”阿难言：“蒙佛威神，已见、已闻！”佛言：“佛有如是力，能究竟佛事不？”阿难言：“世尊，若众生满十方恒河沙等世界中，佛寿一日，用如此力，必能究竟施作佛事。”阿难叹言：“未曾有也！世尊，诸佛法无量不可思议！”

and enter nirvāṇa even though the Buddha's work will not have been completed?"

Early in the morning, he expressed this concern to the Buddha. The sun had already risen. The Buddha then entered into the sunrise samādhi. Just as when the sun rises, its light illuminates all of Jambudvīpa, so too it was with the body of the Buddha. His hair pores all sent forth light which illuminated all of the worlds as numerous as the Ganges' sands throughout the ten directions.

Each and every one of the rays of light put forth a seven-jeweled thousand-petaled lotus blossom. Atop each and every one of the blossoms, there was a seated buddha. Each and every one of those buddhas sent forth an immeasurable number of rays of light. From within each and every one of those rays of light there was put forth a seven-jeweled, thousand-petaled lotus blossom. Atop each and every one of those blossoms, there was a seated buddha.

All of these buddhas filled up all of the worlds as numerous as Ganges' sands throughout the ten directions and carried on with the transformative teaching of beings. In some cases, they spoke Dharma. In some other instances, they remained silent. In yet other instances, they were engaged in meditative walking. Sometimes they displayed transformations wrought by the spiritual superknowledges in which their bodies poured forth water or fire. In ways such as these, they used all sorts of skilful means with which they led across to liberation the beings of the five destinies of rebirth throughout the ten directions.

By receiving assistance from the awesome spiritual power of the Buddha, Ānanda was able to completely observe these phenomena. The Buddha then withdrew his manifestation of spiritual powers, emerged from samādhi, and asked Ānanda, "Did you see these things, or not? Did you hear these things, or not?

Ānanda replied, "Having received the assistance of the Buddha's awesome spiritual powers, I have indeed seen these things and heard these things."

The Buddha asked, "Given that the Buddha possesses power such as this, is he or is he not thereby able to bring the Buddha's work to ultimate completion?"

Ānanda replied, "World Honored One, even if beings filled up worlds of the ten directions as numerous as the Ganges' sands, were the Buddha to employ powers such as these for just a single day of his life, he would certainly be able to completely implement the work of the Buddha." Ānanda exclaimed, "This is something that has never been before. World Honored One, the Dharma of the Buddhas is measureless, inconceivable, and ineffable."

正體字

以是故知佛禪定
220b25|| 具足。復次佛慧眾具足。從初發心於阿僧
220b26|| 祇劫中無法不行。世世集諸功德。一心專
220b27|| 精不惜身命以求智慧。如薩陀波崙菩薩。
220b28|| 復次以善修大悲智慧故具足慧眾。餘人
220b29|| 無是大悲。雖有智慧不得具足大悲。欲
220c01|| 度眾生求種種智慧故。及斷法愛滅六十
220c02|| 二邪見不墮二邊。若受五欲樂若修身苦
220c03|| 道。若斷滅若計常若有若無等。如是諸法邊。
220c04|| 復次佛慧無上徹鑒無比。從甚深禪定中生
220c05|| 故。諸麁細煩惱所不能動故。善修三十七
220c06|| 品四禪四無量心四無色定八背捨九次第定
220c07|| 等諸功德故。有十力四無所畏四無礙智十
220c08|| 八不共法。得無礙不可思議解脫故。佛慧眾
220c09|| 具足。復次能降伏外道大論議師。所謂[9]憂
220c10|| 樓頻[10]蠡迦葉摩訶迦葉舍利弗

简体字

以是故，知佛禅定具足。

复次，佛慧众具足。从初发心，于阿僧祇劫中，无法不行，世世集诸功德，一心专精，不惜身命以求智慧，如萨陀波仑菩萨。

复次，以善修大悲智慧故，具足慧众；余人无是大悲，虽有智慧不得具足。大悲欲度众生，求种种智慧故，及断法爱，灭六十二邪见，不堕二边：若受五欲乐，若修身苦道；若断灭，若计常；若有、若无等，如是诸法边。

复次，佛慧无上，彻鉴无比，从甚深禅定中生故，诸粗细烦恼所不能动故，善修三十七品、四禅、四无量心、四无色定、八背舍、九次第定等诸功德故，有十力、四无所畏、四无碍智、十八不共法，得无碍不可思议解脱故，佛慧众具足。

复次，能降伏外道大论议师，所谓优楼频螺迦葉、摩诃迦葉、舍利弗、

We can know from this that the Buddha has completely perfected the *dhyāna* absorptions.

H. The Buddha's Accumulation of Wisdom

Furthermore, the Buddha's accumulation of wisdom has also been completely perfected. From the time he first brought forth the resolve [to attain bodhi], over the course of *asaṃkhyeya* kalpas, there is no dharma that he has not cultivated. In lifetime after lifetime, he has accumulated all manner of meritorious qualities. He has single-mindedly focused his energies in the pursuit of wisdom, not sparing even his own bodies and lives, doing so in just the same ways as did Sadāprarudita Bodhisattva.[6]

Additionally, it is on account of having well cultivated the great compassion together with wisdom that he has completely perfected the accumulation of wisdom. Others lack such great compassion. Although they may possess wisdom, they are unable to completely perfect it. [That the Buddha was able to accomplish this] is because, in seeking the many different types of wisdom, he relied on the great compassion as he strove to liberate beings. It is also because he cut off the affection for dharmas, extinguished the sixty-two types of erroneous views, and refrained from falling into the two extremes, whether through indulgence in the pleasures of the five types of desires, whether through cultivating the path of physical asceticism, or whether through [clinging to views positing the ultimacy of] annihilationism, eternalism, existence, or non-existence, or other such extreme views with respect to dharmas.

Moreover, the wisdom of the Buddha is unsurpassed. It is incomparable in its qualities of penetration and discernment. This is because it is born from within extremely deep *dhyāna* absorptions. It is also because it is unshaken by any gross or subtle afflictions. It is also because he has well cultivated all of the meritorious qualities inherent in the thirty-seven wings of enlightenment, in the four *dhyānas,* in the four immeasurable minds, in the four formless absorptions, in the eight liberations, in the nine sequential absorptions, and in other related practices.

It is also because he has achieved unobstructed, inconceivable and ineffable liberation by virtue of possessing the ten powers, the four fearlessnesses, the four unimpeded knowledges,[7] and the eighteen dharmas exclusive to the Buddhas. So it is that the Buddha's accumulation of wisdom has become entirely perfected.

Furthermore, he was able to defeat the great non-Buddhist dialectical masters, including Urubilvākāśyapa, Mahākāśyapa, Śāriputra,

正體字

目揵連薩遮
220c11‖ 尼揵子婆蹉首羅長爪等。大論議師輩皆降
220c12‖ 伏。是故知佛慧眾具足。復次佛三藏十二部
220c13‖ 經。八萬四千法聚。見是語言多故。知智慧
220c14‖ 亦大。譬如[11]一居士清朝見大雨處語眾
220c15‖ 人言。昨夜雨龍其力甚大。眾人言。汝何以知
220c16‖ 之。答言。我見地濕泥多山崩樹折殺諸鳥
220c17‖ 獸。以此故知龍力為大。佛亦如是。甚深智
220c18‖ 慧雖非眼見。雨大法雨諸大論[12]議師及釋
220c19‖ 梵天王皆以降伏。以是可知佛智慧多。復次
220c20‖ 諸佛得無礙解脫故。於一切法中智慧無
220c21‖ 礙。復次佛此智慧皆清淨出諸觀上。不觀
220c22‖ 諸法常相無常相有邊相無邊相有去相無去
220c23‖ 相有相無相有漏相無漏相有為相無為相生
220c24‖ 滅相不生滅相空相不空相。常清淨無量如
220c25‖ 虛空。以是故無礙。若觀生滅者。不得觀
220c26‖ 不生滅。觀不生滅者。不得觀生滅。

简体字

目揵连、萨遮尼揵子、婆蹉、首罗、长爪等。大论议师辈皆降伏，是故知佛慧众具足。

复次，佛三藏、十二部经、八万四千法聚，见是语言多故，知智慧亦大。譬如居士，清朝见大雨处，语众人言：“昨夜雨龙，其力甚大！”众人言：“汝何以知之？”答言：“我见地湿、泥多，山崩、树折，杀诸鸟兽，以此故知龙力为大。”佛亦如是，甚深智慧，虽非眼见，雨大法雨，诸大论师及释梵天王皆以降伏，以是可知佛智慧多。

复次，诸佛得无碍解脱故，于一切法中智慧无碍。

复次，佛此智慧皆清净，出诸观上，不观诸法常相、无常相，有边相、无边相，有去相、无去相，有相、无相，有漏相、无漏相，有为相、无为相，生灭相、不生灭相，空相、不空相，常清净无量如虚空，以是故无碍。若观生灭者，不得观不生灭；观不生灭者，不得观生灭。

Maudgalyāyana, Satyaka Nirgranthīputra, *Śreṇika Vatsagotra,[8] Dīrghanakha, and the others. Because the great dialectical masters were all defeated by him, one can therefore know that the wisdom of the Buddha is perfectly complete.

Additionally, as for the Buddha's three-fold treasury [of Dharma] with its twelve categories of scriptural text and its accumulation of eighty-four thousand dharmas, because one observes the sheer volume of discourse contained within it, one may deduce that the wisdom therein must also be vast. This is analogous to the account told of a layman who, in the early morning, observed the site of a great torrential rain and then exclaimed to others, "The strength of the rain dragon who manifest last night is extremely great."

The others said, "How can you know this?"

He replied, "I observed that the earth is wet, that there is much mud, that the mountains have broken apart, that trees have been broken off, and that every variety of bird and beast has been killed. It is on this basis that I have deduced that the power of that dragon is great."

The case of the Buddha is also just like this. Although one may not be able to observe his extremely profound wisdom with one's own eyes, still, when the Buddha let fall the great rain of Dharma, all of the great dialectical masters as well the heavenly kings, Śakra, and Brahmā, were defeated by it. One may realize on this basis that the wisdom of the Buddha is indeed abundant.

Moreover, because the Buddhas have gained unobstructed liberation, their wisdom is unobstructed in its fathoming of all dharmas.

Also, this wisdom of the Buddha is entirely pure and transcends all contemplations. It does not rely upon the contemplation of any dharma as marked by permanence, as marked by impermanence, as marked by limits, as marked by being limitless, as marked by disappearance, as marked by not disappearing, as marked by existence, as marked by nonexistence, as marked by the existence of contaminants, as marked by the nonexistence of contaminants, as marked by being composite, as marked by not being composite, as marked by being produced and destroyed, as marked by being neither produced nor destroyed, as marked by emptiness, or as marked by non-emptiness. It is eternally pure, immeasurable, and like empty space. Because of this, [one may conclude that] it is unobstructed.

[As for those contemplations which are transcended], one who is involved in the contemplation of "production and extinction" is not simultaneously able to contemplate "neither production nor extinction." One who is engaged in contemplation of "neither production nor extinction" is not simultaneously able to contemplate "production

正體字

若不生
220c27|| 滅實生滅不實。若生滅實不生滅不實。如是
220c28|| 等諸觀皆爾。得無礙智故。知佛慧眾具足。
220c29|| 復次念佛解脫眾具足。佛解脫諸煩惱及習。
221a01|| 根本拔故。解脫真不可壞。一切智慧成就故。
221a02|| [1]名為無礙解脫。成就八解脫。甚深遍得故。
221a03|| 名為具足解脫。復次離時解脫及慧解脫
221a04|| 故。便具足成就共解脫。成就如是等解脫
221a05|| 故。名具足解脫眾。復次破魔軍故得解脫。
221a06|| 離煩惱故得解脫。離遮諸禪法故得解
221a07|| 脫。於諸禪定入出自在無礙故。復次菩薩
221a08|| 於見諦道中。得深十六解脫。一苦法智相應
221a09|| 有為解脫。二苦諦斷十結盡得無為解脫。
221a10|| 如是乃至道比智。思惟道中得十八解脫。
221a11|| 一或比智或法智相應有為解脫。

简体字

若不生灭实，生灭不实；若生灭实，不生灭不实。如是等诸观皆尔，得无碍智故，知佛慧众具足。

复次，念佛解脱众具足。佛解脱诸烦恼及习，根本拔故，解脱真不可坏，一切智慧成就故，名为无碍解脱。成就八解脱，甚深遍得故，名为具足解脱。

复次，离时解脱及慧解脱故，便具足成就共解脱。成就如是等解脱故，名具足解脱众。

复次，破魔军故得解脱，离烦恼故得解脱，离遮诸禅法故得解脱，于诸禅定入出自在无碍故。

复次，菩萨于见谛道中，得深十六解脱：一、苦法智相应有为解脱；二、苦谛断十结尽，得无为解脱。如是乃至道比智思惟道中，得十八解脱：一、或比智或法智相应有为解脱；

and extinction." If "neither production nor extinction" is held to be a reflection of reality, then "production and extinction" is not held to be a genuine reflection of reality. If "production and extinction" is held to be a reflection of reality, then "neither production nor extinction" is not held to be a genuine reflection of reality. All such contemplations as these are all of just such a sort. Because he has gained unimpeded wisdom [not subject to any such limitations], one may therefore realize that the Buddha's accumulation of wisdom is perfectly complete.

I. The Buddha's Accumulation of Liberations

Furthermore, [in one's recollection of the Buddha], one also bears in mind the fact that the Buddha's accumulation of liberations is perfectly complete. The Buddha has become liberated from all afflictions and habitual propensities. Because they have been extricated at the very root, his liberation is genuine and indestructible. Because he has perfectly realized all types of wisdom, his is referred to as "unobstructed liberation." Because the Buddha has realized the perfection of the eight liberations to the most extremely profound and universal degree, his liberation is referred to as perfectly complete liberation.

Moreover, because he has left behind "occasion-dependent liberation" (*samaya-vimukta*) as well as "liberation by resort to wisdom (*prajñā-vimukta*)," he has then completely perfected the "double liberation (*ubhayato-bhāga-vimukti*)." It is on account of perfecting liberations such as these that he is said to be perfectly complete in the collection of liberations (*saṃpanna-vimukti-skandha*).

Furthermore, it is on account of destroying Māra's armies that he has obtained liberation. It is because he has left behind the afflictions that he has gained liberation. It is on account of having left behind all dharmas that obstruct the acquisition of the *dhyānas* that he has gained liberation. It is also because he is possessed of unimpeded sovereign mastery in entering and emerging from all of the *dhyāna* absorptions.

Additionally, [when the Buddha was still] the Bodhisattva, he gained sixteen profound liberations on the path of seeing the truths (*satya-darśana-mārga*). The first was the conditioned liberation associated with the Dharma knowledge in regard to suffering (*duḥke-dharma-jñāna*). The second was the unconditioned liberation gained through the complete severance of the ten fetters (*saṃyojana*) related to the truth of suffering. And so it was on through to the comparative knowledge associated with the Path (*marge'nvayajñāna*).

On the path of meditation (*bhāvanā-mārga*), he gained eighteen liberations. The first was the conditioned liberation associated with either comparative knowledge (*anvaya-jñāna*) or with dharma knowledge

正體字

二斷無色
221a12‖ 界三思惟結故得無為解脫。如是乃至第
221a13‖ 十八。盡智相應有為解脫及一切結使盡得
221a14‖ 無為解脫。如是諸解脫和合。名為解脫眾具
221a15‖ 足。復次念佛解脫知見眾具足。解脫知見眾
221a16‖ 有二種。一者佛於解脫諸煩惱中。用盡智
221a17‖ 自證知。知苦已斷集已[2]盡證已修道已。是
221a18‖ 為盡智解脫知見眾。知苦已不復更知。乃
221a19‖ 至修道已不復更修。是為無生智解脫知見
221a20‖ 眾。二者佛知是人入空門得解脫。是人無
221a21‖ 相門得解脫。是人無作門得解脫。是人無
221a22‖ 方便可令解脫。是人久久可得解脫。是人
221a23‖ 不久可得解脫。是人即時得解脫。

简体字

二、断无色界三思惟结故，得无为解脱；如是乃至第十八尽智相应有为解脱；及一切结使尽，得无为解脱。如是诸解脱和合，名为解脱众具足。

复次，念佛解脱知见众具足。解脱知见众有二种：一者、佛于解脱诸烦恼中，用尽智自证知，知苦已，断集已，证尽已，修道已，是为尽智解脱知见众；知苦已不复更知，乃至修道已不复更修，是为无生智解脱知见众。二者、佛知是人入空门得解脱，是人无相门得解脱，是人无作门得解脱；是人无方便可令解脱，是人久久可得解脱，是人不久可得解脱，是人即时得解脱；

(*dharma-jñāna*). The second was the attainment of the unconditioned liberation through the severance of the three fetters related to meditation (*bhavāna-saṃyojana*) within the formless realm. And so it was on through to the eighteenth, wherein he gained a conditioned liberation associated with knowledge of the cessation of the contaminants (*āsrava-kṣaya-jñāna*) and an unconditioned liberation associated with the destruction of all fetters. All of the liberations such as these are collectively referred to as constituting complete perfection of the collection of liberations.

J. The Buddha's Accumulation of the Knowledge and Vision of Liberation

Moreover, one also bears in mind the Buddha's complete perfection of the collection of the knowledge and vision associated with the liberations. There are two categories within the collection of knowledge and vision of liberation.

The first category refers to the fact that, in achieving liberation from all afflictions, the Buddha employed the knowledge of the cessation of the contaminants in his personally-attested awareness that he already knew the existence of suffering, had already cut off accumulation, had already realized cessation, and had already cultivated the path. This constitutes the collection of knowledge and vision of liberation achieved through the knowledge of the cessation of the contaminants.

"Having already known suffering, he had no need to pursue knowledge of it" and so forth until we come to "having already cultivated the Path, he had no need to engage in further cultivation of it" constitutes the collection of knowledge and vision associated with the liberations achieved through the knowledge of the non-arising of the contaminants (*āsrava-anutpāda-jñāna*).

The second category refers to [the knowledge and vision associated with liberation implicit in] the fact that the Buddha knows:

That this person will be able to gain liberation through entering the gateway of emptiness;

That this other person will be able to gain liberation through the gateway of signlessness;

That this other person will be able to gain liberation through the gateway of wishlessness;

That for this other person, there is no expedient means by which they may be influenced to gain liberation;

That this other person will be able to gain liberation after a long, long time;

That this other person will be able to gain liberation before long;

That this other person will be able to gain liberation immediately;

正體字

是人軟
221a24‖ 語得解脫。是人苦教得解脫。是人雜語得
221a25‖ 解脫。是人見神通力得解脫。是人說法得
221a26‖ 解脫。是人婬欲多。為增婬欲得解脫。是人
221a27‖ 瞋恚多。為增瞋恚得解脫。如難陀[3]漚樓
221a28‖ 頻[4]螺龍是。如是等種種因緣得解脫。如法
221a29‖ 眼中說。於是諸解脫中了了知見。是名解
221b01‖ 脫知見眾具足。復次念佛一切智一切[5]知見
221b02‖ 大慈大悲十力四無所畏四無礙智十八不共
221b03‖ 法等。念如佛所知無量不可思議諸功德。
221b04‖ 是名念佛。是念在七地中。或有漏或無漏。
221b05‖ 有漏者有報。無漏者無報。三根相應樂喜捨
221b06‖ 根。行[6]得亦果報得。行[7]得者如此間國中學
221b07‖ 念佛三昧。

简体字

是人软语得解脱，是人苦教得解脱，是人杂语得解脱；是人见神通力得解脱，是人说法得解脱；是人淫欲多，为增淫欲得解脱；是人瞋恚多，为增瞋恚得解脱；如难陀、优楼频骡龙是。如是等种种因缘得解脱，如法眼中说。于是诸解脱中了了知见，是名解脱知见众具足。

复次，念佛一切智、一切见，大慈、大悲，十力、四无所畏，四无碍智、十八不共法等；念如佛所知无量不可思议诸功德，是名念佛。是念在七地中，或有漏、或无漏；有漏者有报，无漏者无报。三根相应：乐、喜、舍根。行得，亦果报得：得者，如此间国中，学念佛三昧；

That this other person will be able to gain liberation through the use of gentle words, that this other person will be able to gain liberation through the use of instruction involving intense criticism;
That this other person will be able to gain liberation through the use of mixed forms of discourse;
That this other person will gain liberation through observing the spiritual superknowledges;
That this other person will gain liberation through the explanation of Dharma;
That this other person who is burdened by much lust will be able to gain liberation through the increase of his lust; and
That this other person who is burdened by much hatred will be able to gain liberation through the increase of his hatred. Instances of this sort are illustrated by the case of the dragons known as Nanda and Urubilva.

As illustrated here, there are many different kinds of causes and conditions conducing to the achievement of liberation. This is as discussed in [this work's discussion of] the Dharma eye.

It is the utterly complete knowledge and vision associated with all of these liberations that is referred to as the complete perfection of the collection of knowledge and vision of liberation.

K. Concluding Statement on Mindfulness of the Buddha Practice

Moreover, [in recollection of the Buddha], one is also mindful that the Buddha possesses omniscience, that he possesses all types of knowledge and vision, the great loving-kindness, the great compassion, the ten powers, the four fearlessnesses, the four unimpeded knowledges, the eighteen dharmas unique to the Buddhas, and so forth. One carries on one's recollection in a manner which corresponds to the actual realizations possessed by the Buddha, appreciating thereby his incalculable, inconceivable, and ineffable meritorious qualities. This is what is meant by "recollection of the Buddha."

This recollection may take place on seven grounds. It may be either "accompanied by contaminants" or "devoid of contaminants." In the case of those who are still subject to contaminants, there is a retributional reward. In the case of those who are beyond contaminants, there may be no retributional reward which occurs. It is associated with three faculties of bliss, joy, and equanimity.

It may be gained through practice or it may be gained as a resultant retributional reward. As for that which is gained through practice, it is such as occurs among those in this country who train in the mindfulness-of-the-Buddha samādhi. As for that which is gained as a

正體字

果報得者如無量壽佛國。人生便
221b08|| 自然能念佛。如是等如阿毘曇中廣分別
221b09|| 大智度論卷第二十一

简体字

果报得者，如无量寿佛国人，生便自然能念佛。如是等，如阿毗昙中广分别。

resultant retributional reward, it is such as occurs with the inhabitants of the land of the Buddha of Limitless Life. People who are born there are naturally able to engage in recollection of the Buddha.

Considerations of this sort are extensively distinguished in the Abhidharma.

The End of "Nāgārjuna on Recollection of the Buddha."

Part Three Endnotes

1 As presented here, this discussion is found at T25.1509.218c28–219a02, 219b02–221b08.

2 KJ preserved the Sanskrit for "forest hermitage": *araṇya*.

3 This is a reference to the ten most standard names for the Buddha, which, when translated into English are: Thus Come One (*tathāgata*); Worthy of Offerings (*arhat*); the One of Right and Universal Awakening (*samyak-saṃbuddha*); the One Perfect in the Practice of the Clarities (*vidyā-caraṇa-saṃpanna*); the Well Gone One (*sugata*); the Knower of the Worlds (*lokavid*); the Unsurpassed Guide of Tamable Men (*anuttaraḥ-puruṣa-damya-sārathiḥ*); Teacher of Gods and Men (*śāstā-devamanuṣyāṇām*); Buddha (*buddha*); World Honored One (*bhagavat*).

4 This short introductory statement occurs somewhat earlier than the rest of the text which explores in greater detail the topic of "recollection of the Buddha" (T25.1509.218c27 - 219a02).

5 "*Vidyā-caraṇa-saṃpanna*" ("Perfect in Practice of Cognition") refers to the three types of cognition, namely: a) the heavenly eye; b) the cognition of past lives; and c) the extinguishing of all contaminants.

6 The story of the Bodhisattva Sadāprarudita ("Ever Weeping" Bodhisattva) is recounted in the *prajñāpāramitā* sutras. He is renowned for selfless pursuit of Dharma and for limitless compassion for beings.

7 The four unimpeded knowledges consist of unimpeded knowledge of meanings, dharmas, language, and eloquence.

8 The Sanskrit reconstruction for this name is slightly conjectural as it is a "one-off" rendering on the part of the Sanskrit-to-Chinese translation team. That said, the only other place this transliteration is mentioned in the entire *Taisho* canon is in a reference dedicated to reconstruction of the meanings of transliterations (翻梵語). This reconstruction is only ambiguously supported there (T54.2130.993c21).

Part Three Variant Readings

[0219006] 〔為〕－【宋】【元】【明】【宮】
[0219007] 〔中〕－【宋】【元】【明】【宮】
[0219008] 無緣＝天【宋】【元】【明】【宮】
[0219009] 〔已〕－【宋】【元】【明】【宮】【石】
[0219010] 羅＋（三[卄/狠]三）【石】
[0219011] 舍＋（喃）【宋】【元】【明】
[0219012] 〔為〕－【宋】【元】【明】【宮】
[0219013] 磨＝摩【明】
[0219014] 性＝姓【元】【明】【石】
[0219015] 〔照〕－【宋】【元】【明】【宮】【石】
[0219016] 我是＝是我【石】
[0219017] 〔陀〕－【宋】【元】【明】【宮】
[0219018] 頗梨＝玻瓈【明】
[0219019] 軟＝濡【石】
[0219020] 好妙＝妙好【宋】【元】【明】【宮】
[0219021] 大＝丈【石】
[0219022] （以）＋如【宋】【元】【明】【宮】
[0220001] 但＝俱【石】
[0220002] 〔生〕－【宋】【元】【明】【宮】【石】
[0220003] 蘇＝酥【元】【明】
[0220004] 〔問〕－【宋】【元】【明】【宮】【石】
[0220005] 尚＝當【宮】【石】
[0220006] 震＝振【宋】【元】
[0220007] 佛＋（言）【宋】【元】【明】【宮】
[0220008] 是＝此【宋】【元】【明】【宮】
[0220009] 憂＝漚【宮】
[0220010] 蠡＝騾【宮】
[0220011] 〔一〕－【宋】【元】【明】【宮】
[0220012] 〔議〕－【宋】【元】【明】【宮】【石】
[0221001] 〔名〕－【宮】
[0221002] 盡證＝證盡【宋】【元】【明】【宮】
[0221003] 漚＝優【宋】【元】【明】【宮】
[0221004] 螺＝騾【宋】【元】【明】【宮】
[0221005] 〔知〕－【宋】【元】【明】【宮】
[0221006] 〔得〕－【石】
[0221007] 〔得〕－【宋】【元】【明】【宮】

Bibliography

Bodhi. (2000). *The Connected Discourses of the Buddha: A New Translation of the Saṃyutta Nikāya* ; translated from the Pāli ; original translation by Bhikkhu Bodhi. (Teachings of the Buddha). Somerville, MA: Wisdom Publications.

Bodhi. (2012). The Numerical Discourses of the Buddha: A Translation of the Aṅguttara Nikāya (Teachings of the Buddha). Boston: Wisdom Publications.

Burlingame, E., Buddhaghosa, & Lanman, Charles Rockwell. (1921). Buddhist legends (Harvard oriental series ; v. 28-30). Cambridge, Mass.: Harvard Univ. Press.

Conze, E., & Suzuki Gakujutsu Zaidan. (1967). Materials for a Dictionary of the Prajñāpāramitā Literature. Tokyo: Suzuki Research Foundation.

Dharmamitra. (2009) Nāgārjuna on the Six Perfections: An Ārya Bodhisattva Explains the Heart of the Bodhisattva Path. A translation of chapters 17-30 of Ārya Nāgārjuna's Exegesis on the Great Perfection of Wisdom Sutra. Seattle: Kalavinka Press.

Dharmamitra. (2009) Nāgārjuna's Guide to the Bodhisattva Path: Treatise on the Provisions for Enlightenment. A translation of the Bodhisaṃbhāra Śāstra by Ārya Nāgārjuna. Seattle: Kalavinka Press.

Edgerton, F. (1953). Buddhist Hybrid Sanskrit grammar and dictionary. (William Dwight Whitney linguistic series). New Haven: Yale University Press.

Hirakawa, A. (1997). Buddhist Chinese-Sanskrit Dictionary / Bukkyō Kan-Bon daijiten. Tokyo]; [Tokyo] :: Reiyūkai : Hatsubaimoto Innātorippusha; 霊友会 : 発売元いんなあとりっぷ社.

Kumārajīva (c. 405). Dazhidulun, *Mahāprājnāpāramitopedeśa (大智度論). T25, no. 1509).

Kumārajīva and Buddhayaśas (c. 408). Shizhu piposha lun, * Daśabhūmika-vibhāṣā (十住毘婆沙論). T26, no. 1521).

Malalasekera, G. (1937). Dictionary of Pāli proper names (Indian texts series). London: J. Murray.

Ñāṇamoli, & Bodhi. (1995). The Middle Length Discourses of the Buddha: A New Translation of the Majjhima Nikāya (Teachings of the Buddha). Boston: Wisdom Publications in association with the Barre Center for Buddhist Studies.

Nattier, J. (2003). A Few Good Men: The Bodhisattva Path According to the Inquiry of Ugra (Ugraparipṛcchā) (Studies in the Buddhist traditions). Honolulu: University of Hawai'i Press.

Powers, J. (2016). The Buddhist World (Routledge worlds). London ; New York: Routledge, Taylor & Francis Group.

Rahder, J. (1928). Glossary of the Sanskrit, Tibetan, Mongolian, and Chinese Versions of the Daśabhūmika-Sūtra. Compiled by J. Rahder. (Buddhica, Documents et Travaux pour l'Étude du Bouddhisme publiés sous la direction de J. Przyluski; Deuxième Série; Documents—Tome I). Paris: Librarie Orientaliste Paul Geuthner, 1928.

Rahder, J., & Vasubandhu. (1926). Daśabhumikasutra. Leuven: J.B. Istas.

Ruegg, D. (1981). The Literature of the Madhyamaka school of Philosophy in India (History of Indian literature ; v. 7, fasc. 1). Wiesbaden: Harrassowitz.

Stefania Travagnin (2013) Yinshun's Recovery of ShizhuPiposha Lun 十住毗婆沙論: a Madhyamaka-based Pure Land Practice In Twentieth-Century Taiwan, Contemporary Buddhism, 14:2, 320-343, DOI: 10.1080/14639947.2013.832497 To link to this article: https://doi.org/10.1080/14639947.2013.832497

Takakusu, J., & Watanabe, Kaigyoku. (1924). Taishō shinshū Daizōkyō. Tōkyō; 東京 :: Taishō Issaikyō Kankōkai; 大正一切經刊行會.

Vaidya, P. L., ed. Daśabhūmikasūtram. Darbhanga: The Mithila Institute of Post-Graduate Studies and Research in Sanskrit Learning, 1969.

Williams, M. Monier, Sir. (n.d.). A Sanskrit-English Dictionary. Delhi: Sri Satguru.

Zhonghua dian zi fo dian xie hui. (2004). CBETA dian zi fo dian ji cheng = CBETA Chinese electronic Tripitaka collection (Version 2004. ed.). Taibei; 台北 :: Zhonghua dian zi fo dian xie hui; 中華電子佛典協會.

Glossary

A

Abhidharma: A category of Buddhist texts devoted to detailed scholastic analyses of the teachings contained in the sutras.

afflictions: Otherwise known as "the three poisons" (*triviṣa*) these are: 1) greed (including lust and desire in general); 2) hatred (including all of the permutations of aversion such as irritation, anger, and rage); and 3) delusion or ignorance. There are many subcategories of afflictions (*kleśa*) listed in the various dharma schemas. For example, in the Sarvāstivāda school, there are six root afflictions and ten subsidiary afflictions.

aggregates: See "five aggregates."

anāgamin: The *anāgamin* or "nonreturner" is one who has gained the third of the four fruits of the individual-liberation path of the śrāvaka disciple.

anuttarasamyaksaṃbodhi: "Anuttarasamyaksaṃbodhi" refers to "the utmost, right, and perfect enlightenment" of a buddha.

arhat: An arhat is one who, having put an end to all of the afflictions, fetters, and contaminants and having put an end to rebirth, has gained the fourth and final fruit on the individual-liberation path of the śrāvaka disciple.

ārya: One who has realized one of the fruits of the path from which they can never fall away. This includes any one of the eight fruits of the arhat path, or any of the irreversible stations on the bodhisattva path to Buddhahood.

asaṃkhya, asaṃkhyeya: In Sanskrit, this is an incalculably and infinitely large number.

asura: As one of the paths of rebirth, this refers to a demi-god or titan. More loosely, this refers to beings much characterized by anger, hatred, jealousy, and contentiousness who may also appear as humans, animals, hungry ghosts (*pretas*), or hell-dwellers.

avadāna stories: Stories of the previous lives of a buddha.

avaivartika: one who has become irreversible on either the individual liberation path of the arhats or on the universal-liberation path of the bodhisattvas and buddhas. Throughout this text, "stage of certainty" (必定, 必定地) is most likely a translation of *avaivartika*.

B

bases of psychic powers: The four bases of psychic power (*catvāra ṛddhi-pāda*) are: zeal (*chanda*); vigor (*vīrya*); [concentration of] mind/

thought (*citta*); and reflective or investigative consideration, examination, or imagination (*mīmāṃsā*).

Bhagavat: "Bhagavat" is one of the titles of a Buddha. It may be translated as "Blessed One," "Lord," or, as rendered in Chinese Buddhist texts, "World Honored One," *shizun* (世尊).

bhikshu: A fully ordained celibate Buddhist monk within one of the traditional schools of Buddhism.

bhikshuni: A fully ordained celibate Buddhist nun within one of the traditional schools of Buddhism.

bhūta ghost: According to MW, one of the many meanings of *bhūta* is: "a spirit (good or evil), the ghost of a deceased person, a demon, imp, goblin." PDB: "A class of harm-inflicting and formless obstructing spirits (i.e. 'elemental spirits')..."; "...sometimes equivalent to *preta* (hungry ghosts)...."; "Because they obstruct rainfall, the *bhūta* are propitiated by rituals to cause precipitation."

bodhi: "Enlightenment" or "awakening." In its most exalted form this refers exclusively to the utmost, right, and perfect enlightenment (*anuttarasamyaksaṃbodhi*) of a buddha.

bodhimaṇḍa: A *bodhimaṇḍa* is the "site of enlightenment" wherein enlightenment is cultivated and fully realized. It may be used as a general reference to Buddhist temples, though it often refers specifically to the site beneath the bodhi tree where a buddha gains complete realization of the utmost, right, and perfect enlightenment.

bodhisattva: A bodhisattva is a being who, in his pursuit of the utmost, right, and perfect enlightenment of buddhahood, is equally dedicated to achieving buddhahood for himself while also facilitating all other beings' achievement of buddhahood. His primary practice is classically described as focusing on the six (or ten) "perfections" (*pāramitā*): giving, moral virtue, patience, vigor, meditative skill (*dhyāna*), and world-transcending wisdom (*prajñā*).

bodhi tree: The tree in Bodhgaya in the Indian state of Bihar under which the Buddha reached enlightenment approximately 2600 years ago.

Brahmā: Per PDB: "An Indian divinity who was adopted into the Buddhist pantheon as a protector of the teachings and king of the Brahmaloka ["Brahma world"] (in the narrow sense of that term)." "Brahmaloka" here refers to the first three heavens of the form realm.

brahmacārin: Per MW, "A young Brahman who is a student of the veda (under a preceptor) or who practises chastity, a young Brahman before marriage (in the first period of his life)."

brahmacarya: Celibacy.

brahmin: Someone who belongs to the highest caste in Hinduism; a member of the Hindu priestly caste.

buddha: Anyone who has achieved the utmost, right, and perfect enlightenment (*anuttarasamyaksaṃbodhi*), whether we speak of the Buddha of the present era in this world, Shakyamuni Buddha, any of the seven buddhas of antiquity, or, in Mahāyāna cosmology, any of the countless buddhas of the ten directions and three periods of time.

C

clear knowledges: "Clear knowledges" refers to the "three knowledges" (*trividyā*): 1) The remembrance of previous lives (*pūrvavanivāsānusmṛti*); 2) Knowledge of beings' rebirth destinies (*cyutyupapattijñāna*); and 3) Knowledge of the destruction of the defiling contaminants or "taints" (*āsravakṣaya*).

contaminants: "Contaminants" (āsrava) are usually defined as either threefold or fourfold: 1) sensual desire (*kāma*); 2) [craving for] becoming (*bhāva*), i.e. the craving for continued existence; 3) ignorance (*avidyā*), i.e. delusion; 4) views (*dṛṣṭi*) This fourth types is not included in some listings. Often-encountered alternate translations include "taints" and "outflows" and, less commonly "influxes" and "fluxes."

D

dāna pāramitā: The perfection of giving

deva: Devas are divinities residing in the heavens that collectively constitute the highest of the six rebirth destinies within the realm of *saṃsāra*. There are 27 categories of devas and their heavens in the desire realm, form realm, and formless realm. Although the lifespans of the devas in these various heavens may be immensely long, when their karmic merit runs out, they are all still destined to eventually fall back into the other five paths of rebirth wherein they are reborn in accordance with their residual karma from previous lifetimes.

dhāraṇī: *Dhāraṇīs* are of many types, but the two main types are mantra-like spells that serve the purpose of protection from negative spiritual forces such as ghosts and demons and formulae that aid the retention even for countless lifetimes of the Dharma teachings one has acquired in this and previous lives.

Dharma: The teachings of the Buddha

dharmas: 1) Fundamental constituent aspects, elements, or factors of mental and physical existence, as for instance, "the 100 dharmas" with which Vasubandhu analytically catalogued all that exists. In this sense, dharmas are somewhat analogous to the elements of the periodic table in chemistry; 2) Any individual teaching, as for instance in "the dharma of conditioned origination."

Dharma realm: As a Buddhist technical term, "Dharma realm" or "dharma realm," *dharma-dhātu*, has at least several levels of meaning:

1) At the most granular level, "dharma realm" refers to one of the eighteen sense realms, dharmas as "objects of mind" (*dharma-*āyatana);

2) In the most cosmically and metaphysically vast sense, "Dharma realm" refers in aggregate to all conventionally-existent phenomena and the universally pervasive noumenal "true suchness" (*tathatā*) that underlies and characterizes all of those phenomena. In this sense, it is identical with the "Dharma body" (*dharma-kāya*);

3) As a classifying term, "dharma realm" is used to distinguish realms of existence (as in the ten dharma realms consisting of the realms of buddhas, bodhisattvas, śrāvaka disciples, *pratyekabuddhas*, devas, *asuras*, humans, animals, hungry ghosts, hell-dwellers) or metaphysical modes of existence (as in the "four dharma realms" of the Huayan hermeneutic tradition that speaks of: a] the dharma realm of the "noumenal" [synonymous with emptiness or śūnyatā]; b] the dharma realm of the "phenomenal"; c] the dharma realm of the unimpeded interpenetration of the phenomenal and the noumenal; and d] the dharma realm of the unimpeded interpenetration of all phenomena with all other phenomena in a manner that resonates somewhat with quantum entanglement and non-locality).

Dharma wheel: The "wheel of Dharma" or "Dharma wheel" (*dharma-cakra*) refers to the eight-spoked wheel emblematic of the Buddha's teaching of the eight-fold path of the Āryas or "Noble Ones" consisting of right views, right volition or intentional thought, right speech, right physical action, right livelihood, right effort, right mindfulness, and right meditative concentration. This term is also synonymous with the three turnings of the four truths as initially taught by the Buddha to his original five disciples.

dhūta, dhūtaṅga, or *dhūtaguṇa* austerities: In contrast to the non-beneficial ascetic practices of non-Buddhists (lying on a bed of nails, etc.), these are austerities beneficial to progress on the path such as wearing only patchwork robes sewn from discarded cloth, eating only food obtained on the alms round, eating only a single meal each day, always sitting and never lying down, dwelling at the base of a tree, residing in a charnel field where one observes the stages of the body's decomposition.

dhyāna: "*Dhyāna*" is a general term broadly corresponding to all forms of Buddhist meditative skill. The Chinese "*ch'an*" or "*chan*" (禪) and the Japanese term "*zen*" are transliterations of the same Sanskrit word "*dhyāna*." All forms of Buddhist "calming" and "insight" meditation are subcategories of "*dhyāna*."

dhyāna pāramitā: The perfection of meditative skill.

E

eight difficulties: Birth in the hells, birth as a hungry ghost, birth as an animal, birth as a long-lived deva, birth in a border region (where there is no Buddha Dharma), birth as someone who is blind, deaf, mute, or otherwise possessed of impaired physical or mental faculties, birth as someone who is possessed of merely worldly knowledge and intelligence (and hence who uses his cleverness to deny the truth of the Dharma); and birth at a time before or long after a buddha appears in the world.

eight precepts: Eight vows involving abstaining from: 1) killing; 2) taking what is not given; 3) sexual misconduct; 4) false speech; 5) intoxicants; 6) use of perfumes, jewelry, other personal adornments, dancing, singing, or watching such performances; 7) sleeping on high or wide beds; and 8) eating after midday.

eighteen sense realms: These consist of the six sense faculties (eye, ear, nose, tongue, body, and mind), the six sense objects (visual forms, sounds, smells, tastes, touchables, and ideas, etc. as objects of mind), and the six sense consciousnesses (visual, auditory, olfactory, gustatory, tactile, and mental).

F

fetters: The fetters (*saṃyojana*) are ten mental characteristics of unenlightened existence that bind beings to uncontrolled rebirths in the six destinies of rebirth. They are: 1) "Truly existent self view," the wrong view that believes in the existence of an eternally existent self in association with the five aggregates; 2) "Skeptical doubt" about the truth of the Dharma and the path to enlightenment; 3) "Clinging to [the observance of] rules and rituals" in and of themselves as constituting the path to spiritual liberation; 4) Sensual desire; 5) Ill will; 6) Desire for rebirth in the form realm [heavens]; 7) Desire for rebirth in the formless realm [heavens]; 8) "Conceit," i.e. the belief that "I" exist; 9) "Agitation" or "restlessness" that prevents deep concentration; and 10) "Ignorance."

five aggregates: 1) form; 2) feelings (i.e. sensations as received through eye, ear, nose, tongue, body, or mind); 3) perceptions; 4) karmic formative factors (such as volitions); and 5) consciousness (visual, auditory, olfactory, gustatory, tactile, and mental).

five desires: Wealth, sex, fame, flavors, and leisure or, alternatively, the objects of the five basic sense faculties (visual forms, sounds, smells, tastes, and touchables).

five faculties: faith; vigor; mindfulness; concentration; wisdom.

five powers: faith; vigor; mindfulness; concentration; wisdom.

five precepts: Five vows involving abstaining from killing, stealing, sexual misconduct, false speech, and intoxicants.

four bases of meritorious qualities: truth, relinquishment, quiescence, and wisdom. (Per VB, the Sanskrit correlates of the Pali *saccādhitthāna, cāgādhitthāna, upasamādhitthāna* (= base of peace), and *paññādhitthāna* would be *satyādhiṣṭhāna, tyāgādhiṣṭhāna, upaśamādhiṣṭhāna,* and *prajñādhiṣṭhāna.*)

four bases of supernatural power: Zeal; vigor; mind; investigation.

four great elements: earth, water, fire, wind.

four right efforts: Causing already arisen evil to cease; causing not yet arisen evil to not arise; causing already arisen goodness to increase; causing not yet arisen goodness to arise.

four requisites: Food obtained on the alms round; robes; residences; medicines.

four stations of mindfulness: Mindfulness of the body; mindfulness of feelings or sensations (experienced via the eye, ear, nose, tongue, body, and mind consciousnesses); mindfulness of thoughts or mind states; mindfulness of dharmas.

four truths / four truths of the Āryas: Suffering; its origination; its cessation; the path to its cessation.

G

gandharva: *Gandharvas* are a type of celestial music spirit that is said to rely on fragrances as their means of survival.

garuḍa: *Garuḍas* are a type of spirit that manifests as an immense golden-winged bird that feeds on young dragons.

ground, grounds: These are levels or planes of spiritual development through which a practitioner proceeds on the way to complete enlightenment.

H

hindrances: "Hindrances" usually refers to "the five hindrances" which are desire, ill will, lethargy-and-sleepiness, excitedness-and-regretfulness, and afflicted doubtfulness. These five hindrances must be overcome in order to successfully enter deep states of meditation.

I

inverted views: The four inverted views (*viparyāsa-catuṣka*) consist of imputing permanence to the impermanent, pleasure to what cannot deliver it, self to what is devoid of any inherently existent self, and purity to what does not actually possess that quality. Standard objects of such upside-down perception are: thought, or mind states, the six categories of "feeling" manifesting in association with the six sense faculties, dharmas (as components of the falsely imputed "self"), and the body.

K

kalaviṅka bird: The Himalayan cuckoo bird that sings with an incomparably beautiful sound even before it breaks out of its shell.

kalpa: The Sanskrit "*kalpa*" roughly corresponds to the English term "eon" with the primary distinction being that, in Buddhist and Hindu cosmology, kalpas occur in various relatively precisely designated immensely long durations.

kāṣāya robe: The robes of an fully ordained bhikshu or bhikshuni.

kinnara: *Kinnaras* (skt. *kiṃnara*) are a type of celestial music spirit with the body of a human and the head of a horse.

kumbhāṇḍa: According to MW: "Having testicles shaped like a *kumbha* [a winter melon]," a class of demons (at whose head stands Rudra). PDB: "In Sanskrit, a type of evil spirit, and typically listed along with especially *rākṣasa,* but also *piśāca, yakṣa,* and *bhūta* spirits. Virūḍhaka, one of the four world-guardians, who protects the southern cardinal direction, is usually said to be their overlord, although some texts give Rudra this role instead. The *kumbhāṇḍa* are also sometimes listed among the minions of Māra, evil personified.

koṭī: A *koṭī* is a number that is defined in the Flower Adornment Sutra Chapter Thirty as the product of multiplying a *lakṣa* (100,000) by a *lakṣa*. Hence it equals 10,000,000, i.e. ten million.

kṣaṇa: A *kṣaṇa,* corresponds to a micro-moment. This is variously defined, one traditional definition being "a ninetieth of a finger-snap." Elsewhere in the text, this may be referred to as "a single thought," "a mind-moment," or "a thought-moment" as approximate translations of the term.

kṣānti pāramitā: The perfection of patience.

kṣatriya: The second of the four castes of traditional Indian culture consisting primarily of the warrior and royalty class.

kṣetra: The Sanskrit word *kṣetra* refers to a land or realm or field and in Buddhist texts it may refer specifically to a "buddha land."

M

mahāsattva: A *mahāsattva* is a great bodhisattva, one who has cultivated the bodhisattva path for countless kalpas.

mātṛkā: *Mātṛkās* are "matrices" consisting of lists of dharmas, technical terms, and concepts discussed in the sutras. They served as the basis for the Abhidharma.

Māra, *māras*: In Buddhism, Māra is generally regarded as the personification of evil and death who is also a particular deity dwelling in one of the desire realm heavens who delights in interfering with spiritual liberation from perpetual rebirths in *saṃsāra*. More specifically, there are said to be four kinds of *māras*: 1) the *māra* of the five mental and physical aggregates in association with which all beings wander endlessly in *saṃsāra*; 2) the *māra* of the afflictions consisting of the three poisons of greed, hatred, and delusion and all of their subcategories; 3) the *māra* of death; and, as mentioned above, 3) the deity known as Māra as well as all of his *devaputra* minions. Additionally, there are also "ghost and spirit" *māras* who may manifest in countless ways to interfere with a practitioner's cultivation of the path.

mind-moment: See *kṣaṇa*.

mahorāga: *Mahorāgas* are a type of serpent spirit often portrayed as having the upper body of a human and the lower body of a snake.

N

nayuta: A very large number, usually defined as a one hundred billion.

nirvāṇa: Nirvāṇa is the ultimate goal of the path of Buddhist spiritual cultivation that corresponds to the elimination of the three poisons (covetousness, aversion, delusion) and the ending of compulsory and random rebirth in *saṃsāra*, the cycle of existences in the deva realm, the demigod realm, the human realm, the animal realm, the hungry ghost realm, and the hell realms.

In the case of the individual liberation path practitioner exemplified by arhats and *pratyekabuddhas*, all future existence ends for them with the acquisition of nirvāṇa.

In the case of the universal liberation practitioners exemplified by bodhisattvas and buddhas, they achieve the direct cognition of the emptiness of all beings and phenomena and realize an ongoing realization of a nirvana-like state even as, by force of vow, they continue to take on intentional rebirths within *saṃsāra* in order to facilitate the spiritual liberation of all beings.

nirvāṇa without residue: The final nirvāṇa realized at death by fully awakened beings whether they be arhats, *pratyekabuddhas,* or buddhas.

nivāsana robe: The *nivāsana* is the monastic's skirt-like inner robe.

O

once-returner: See *sākṛdāgāmin.*

P

pāramitā: One of the six (or ten) "perfections" cultivated and perfected by the bodhisattva on the path to buddhahood.

Paranirmita Vaśavartin Heaven: The Paranirmita Vaśavartin Heaven is the sixth of the six desire realm heavens. PDB: "The heaven of the gods who have power over the creations of others, or the gods who partake of the pleasures created in other heavens."

piśāca: PDB: "In Sanskrit, "flesh-eater," a class of ogres or goblins, similar to rākṣasa and yakṣa, who eat human flesh." The female is called *piśācī.*

prajñā: *Prajnā* is the world-transcending wisdom that cognizes and understands all phenomena associated with "self," others, and the world as they truly are and in accordance with ultimate reality.

prajñā pāramitā: The perfection of wisdom.

pratyekabuddha: One who, in the absence of a buddha or his Dharma, achieves a level of enlightenment comparable to that of an arhat, doing so on his own through the contemplation of the cycle of dependent origination (*pratītyasamutpāda*). Mahāyāna literature attributes this ability to awaken in the absence of a buddha or his Dharma to direct exposure to the Dharma in previous lives, the seeds of which enable enlightenment in the present life.

pratyutpanna samādhi: The *pratyutpanna* samādhi is a samādhi wherein one becomes able to see the buddhas of the present and listen to them teach the Dharma.

provisions (for enlightenment): The provisions for enlightenment (*bodhisaṃbhāra*) are the spiritual prerequisites for enlightenment that must be accumulated in order to fully realize the path to buddhahood. These are usually considered to be merit (*puṇya*) and knowledge (*jñāna*).

pūtana: Per PDB: "Stinking hungry demons."

R

rākṣasa: A swift flying malignant flesh-eating demon which changes its form to seduce humans and eat them.

S

sakṛdāgāmin: The *sakṛdāgāmin* or "once-returner" is one who has gained the third of the four fruits of the individual-liberation path of the śrāvaka disciple.

samādhi: Samādhi refers both to any single instance of one-pointed concentration and also, more usually, to enduring states of persistently maintained one-pointed concentration.

saṃghāṭī robe: The *saṃghāṭī* is the monastic's outer robe.

saṃkakṣikā robe: The *saṃkakṣikā* is the monastic's robe that is worn over the left shoulder and under the right arm.

saṃsāra: *Saṃsāra,* for which the usual Sino-Buddhist rendering is "births-and-deaths," *shengsi* (生死), refers to the endless cycle of rebirths in the six realms of rebirth: devas (gods), *asuras* ("demi-gods" or "titans"), humans, animals, hungry ghosts (*preta*), and hell-dwellers.

Sangha: A community of at least ten fully ordained bhikshus in Buddhist countries or at least five fully ordained bhikshus in countries where Buddhism is only just being established for the first time. As the third object of refuge in "the Three Refuges" or "the Three Jewels," this refers exclusively to those persons who have already acquired one of the fruits of the path from which they can never fall away, whether on the individual-liberation paths of the arhats or *pratyekabuddhas,* or on the bodhisattva path.

śarīra: *Śarīra* are the remains or "relics" of eminent monks, bodhisattvas, or buddhas that are contained in their cremation ashes.

seven enlightenment factors: assessment or skillful selection of dharmas; vigor; joy; mental pliancy; concentration; equanimity with respect to the saṃskāra (karmic formative factors) aggregate.

śīla pāramitā: The perfection of moral virtue.

six rebirth destinies: gods (*deva*), demi-gods or titans (*asura*), humans, hungry ghosts (*pretas*), animals, and hell-dwellers.

skandha: See "aggregates."

skillful means: "Skillful means" (*upāya*) are individually tailored skillful techniques adopted by the bodhisattva in teaching the various kinds of beings. These various techniques are adopted precisely because all beings are possessed of different capacities, karmic obstacles and predilections due to which they respond best to individually tailored teachings.

spiritual superknowledges: The usual Sanskrit antecedent for "spiritual superknowledges" is *abhijñā* ("superknowledges") or *ṛddhi* ("supernatural powers"). This includes such abilities as "the six superknowledges" (the spiritual powers, the heavenly eye, the heavenly ear, the cognition of others' thoughts, past life recall for both self and others, and complete elimination of all "defiling contaminants" or "taints" [*āsrava*]).

śramaṇa: More generally, a *śramaṇa* is a mendicant, one who has left the home life and relies on alms for sustenance. In the Buddhist context, this refers specifically to a bhikshu, i.e. a Buddhist monk.

śrāvaka, śrāvaka disciple: A follower of the individual-liberation path to arhatship.

stream enterer: The stream enterer (*srota-āpanna*) is one who has gained the first of the four fruits of the path to arhatship.

śūdra: A member of the fourth and lowest caste of traditional Indian culture consisting primarily of servants and such.

sutra: A scripture attributed to the Buddha.

T

tathatā: "Suchness," i.e. the true nature of the ultimate reality of any and all things as it really is.

Tathāgata: "*Tathāgata*" ("Thus Come One") is one of the ten primary titles by which all buddhas are known.

Ten directions: North, south, east, west, the four midpoints, the zenith, and the nadir.

Thirty-seven wings of enlightenment / thirty-seven enlightenment factors: These consist of: the four stations of mindfulness; the four right efforts; the four bases of supernatural powers; the five faculties; the five powers; the seven enlightenment factors; and the eightfold path of the Āryas.

Three Jewels: The Buddha, the Dharma, and the Ārya Sangha.

Three periods of time: Past, present, and future.

Three Refuges: The Buddha, the Dharma, and the Ārya Sangha, the Three Jewels in which one "takes the refuges" to become a Buddhist disciple and upon which one must rely to advance on the Buddhist path.

Three Vehicles: The Śrāvaka-disciple Vehicle, the Pratyekabuddha Vehicle, and the Great Vehicle (Mahāyāna) the endpoints of which are arhatship, pratyekabuddhahood, and Buddhahood.

three wretched destinies: The three wretched destinies are rebirth as either an animal, a hungry ghost (*preta*), or a hell dweller.

trichiliocosm: A world system consisting of countless worlds.

tripiṭaka: The three divisions of the three-fold Buddhist canon, otherwise known as "the Tripiṭaka": the sutras (scriptures attributed to the Buddha or disciples authorized by the Buddha), the commentarial treatises (śāstra), and the moral codes (*vinaya*).

tripiṭaka master: A "*tripiṭaka* master" is someone who has completely mastered the three divisions of the three-fold Buddhist canon.

twelve sense bases: the six sense faculties (eye, ear, nose, tongue, body, and mind) and their respective sense objects (visual forms, sounds, smells, tastes, touchables, and ideas, etc. as objects of mind).

Two Vehicles: The two individual liberation vehicles taught by the Buddha, the Śrāvaka-disciple Vehicle leading to arhatship and the Pratyekabuddha Vehicle leading to pratyekabuddhahood.

V

vaiśya: A member of the third caste in traditional Indian culture comprised primarily of the merchant and agricultural classes.

vajra: An indestructible substance equated with the diamond. A symbol of indestructibility. Also, a pestle shaped sceptre or "thunderbolt" weapon held by Dharma protectors and deities.

vibhāṣā: A *vibhāṣā* is an extensively detailed explanatory treatise.

vinaya: The Buddhist moral codes.

vīrya pāramitā: The perfection of vigor.

W

wheel-turning king: In Buddhism, a "wheel-turning king" (*cakravartin*) is a universal monarch.

worthy: In Mahāyāna literature, a "worthy" (*bhadra*) is a bodhisattva practitioner who has brought forth the bodhisattva vow but who is still cultivating the preparatory stages and thus has not yet reached the ten bodhisattva grounds and has not yet become an ārya.

Y

yakṣa: *Yakṣas* are a kind of either good or evil spirit possessed of supernatural powers that may either serve as a guardian or a demon.

yojana: A measure of distance in ancient India usually defined as being the distance that an ox cart would travel in a day without unharnessing (somewhat less than ten miles).

About the Translator

Bhikshu Dharmamitra (ordination name "Heng Shou" – 釋恆授) is a Chinese-tradition translator-monk and one of the earliest American disciples (since 1968) of the late Guiyang Ch'an patriarch, Dharma teacher, and pioneer of Buddhism in the West, the Venerable Master Hsuan Hua (宣化上人). He has a total of 34 years in robes during two periods as a monastic (1969–1975 & 1991 to the present).

Dharmamitra's principal educational foundations as a translator of Sino-Buddhist Classical Chinese lie in four years of intensive monastic training and Chinese-language study of classic Mahāyāna texts in a small-group setting under Master Hsuan Hua (1968–1972), undergraduate Chinese language study at Portland State University, a year of intensive one-on-one Classical Chinese study at the Fu Jen University Language Center near Taipei, two years of course work at the University of Washington's Department of Asian Languages and Literature (1988–90), and an additional three years of auditing graduate courses and seminars in Classical Chinese readings, again at UW's Department of Asian Languages and Literature.

Since taking robes again under Master Hua in 1991, Dharmamitra has devoted his energies primarily to study and translation of classic Mahāyāna texts with a special interest in works by Ārya Nāgārjuna and related authors. To date, he has translated more than fifteen important texts comprising approximately 150 fascicles, including most recently the 80-fascicle *Avataṃsaka Sūtra* (the "Flower Adornment Sutra"), Nāgārjuna's 17-fascicle *Daśabhūmika Vibhāśa* ("Treatise on the Ten Grounds"), and the *Daśabhūmika Sūtra* (the "Ten Grounds Sutra"), all of which are current or upcoming Kalavinka Press publications.

Kalavinka Buddhist Classics

(http: www.kalavinka.org)

Fall, 2019 Title List

Meditation Instruction Texts

The Essentials of Buddhist Meditation

A marvelously complete classic *śamathā-vipaśyanā* (calming-and-insight) meditation manual. By Tiantai Śramaṇa Zhiyi (538–597).

Six Gates to the Sublime

The early Indian Buddhist meditation method involving six practices used in calming-and-insight meditation. By Śramaṇa Zhiyi

Bodhisattva Path Texts

On Generating the Resolve to Become a Buddha

On the Resolve to Become a Buddha by Ārya Nāgārjuna

Exhortation to Resolve on Buddhahood by Patriarch Sheng'an Shixian

Exhortation to Resolve on Buddhahood by the Tang Literatus, Peixiu

Letter from a Friend - The Three Earliest Editions

The earliest extant editions of Ārya Nāgārjuna's *Suhṛlekkha*:

Translated by Tripiṭaka Master Guṇavarman (*ca* 425 CE)

Translated by Tripiṭaka Master Saṇghavarman (*ca* 450 CE)

Translated by Tripiṭaka Master Yijing (*ca* 675 CE).

Marvelous Stories from the Perfection of Wisdom

130 Stories from Ārya Nāgārjuna's *Mahāprājñāpāramitā Upadeśa.*

Nāgārjuna's Guide to the Bodhisattva Path

The *Bodhisaṃbhāra Treatise* with abridged Vaśitva commentary.

The Bodhisaṃbhāra Treatise Commentary

The complete exegesis by the Indian Bhikshu Vaśitva (*ca* 300–500).

Nāgārjuna on Mindfulness of the Buddha

Ch. 9 and Chs. 20–25 of Nāgārjuna's *Daśabhūmika Vibhāṣā*

Ch. 1, Subchapter 36a of Nāgārjuna's *Mahāprājñāpāramitā Upadeśa.*

Nāgārjuna on the Six Perfections

Chapters 17–30 of Ārya Nāgārjuna's *Mahāprājñāpāramitā Upadeśa.*

A Strand of Dharma Jewels (Ārya Nāgārjuna's *Ratnāvalī*)

The earliest extant edition, translated by Paramārtha: *ca* 550 CE

The Ten Bodhisattva Grounds

Śikṣānanda's translation of The Flower Adornment Sutra, Ch. 26

The Ten Grounds Treatise
Nāgārjuna's 35-chapter *Daśabhūmika Vibhāṣā*

The Ten Grounds Sutra
Kumārajīva's translation of the *Daśabhūmika Sūtra*

Vasubandhu's Treatise on the Bodhisattva Vow
By Vasubandhu Bodhisattva (*ca* 300 CE)

www.ingramcontent.com/pod-product-compliance
Lightning Source LLC
Chambersburg PA
CBHW031232090426
42742CB00007B/162
* 9 7 8 1 9 3 5 4 1 3 1 5 8 *